Salesforce Platform Developer I Certification Guide

Expert tips, techniques, and mock tests for the Platform Developer I (DEV501) certification exam

Jan Vandevelde
Gunther Roskams

Packt>

BIRMINGHAM - MUMBAI

Salesforce Platform Developer I Certification Guide

Commissioning Editor: Kunal Chaudhari
Acquisition Editor: Chaitanya Nair
Content Development Editor: Ruvika Rao
Technical Editor: Gaurav Gala
Copy Editor: Safis Editing
Project Coordinator: Vaidehi Sawant
Proofreader: Safis Editing
Indexer: Rekha Nair
Graphics: Alishon Mendonsa
Production Coordinator: Jayalaxmi Raja

First published: May 2019

Production reference: 1220519

Published by Packt Publishing Ltd.
Livery Place
35 Livery Street
Birmingham
B3 2PB, UK.

ISBN 978-1-78980-207-8

www.packtpub.com

Mapt

Mapt is an online digital library that gives you full access to over 5,000 books and videos, as well as industry leading tools to help you plan your personal development and advance your career. For more information, please visit our website.

Why subscribe?

- Spend less time learning and more time coding with practical eBooks and Videos from over 4,000 industry professionals

- Improve your learning with Skill Plans built especially for you

- Get a free eBook or video every month

- Mapt is fully searchable

- Copy and paste, print, and bookmark content

Packt.com

Did you know that Packt offers eBook versions of every book published, with PDF and ePub files available? You can upgrade to the eBook version at www.packt.com and as a print book customer, you are entitled to a discount on the eBook copy. Get in touch with us at customercare@packtpub.com for more details.

At www.packt.com, you can also read a collection of free technical articles, sign up for a range of free newsletters, and receive exclusive discounts and offers on Packt books and eBooks.

Contributors

About the authors

Jan Vandevelde is a Salesforce MVP, speaker, trainer, and blogger, and a Senior Salesforce Consultant at Salesforce Platinum Partner 4C. He is based in Belgium. He has been working on the Force.com platform since 2009. Currently, he is working as a Salesforce Consultant and is a regular contributor to the Trailblazer Community.

He has 15 certifications in Salesforce. He works on all aspects of Salesforce and is an expert in data migration, configuration, customization, and development, with his main expertise being in Sales Cloud, Service Cloud, Community Cloud, and Salesforce Quote-to-Cash. He is the leader of the Belgium User Group of Salesforce. He is one of the board members of Europe's community-led event, YeurDreamin.

I would like to thank my parents, wife, son, and colleagues at 4C for supporting me in every step of my life and career. I would like to thank Packt Publishing for giving me this opportunity to share my knowledge via this book.

Gunther Roskams is a 7x certified Salesforce Application Architect, integration specialist, and Senior Salesforce Developer at Salesforce Platinum Partner 4C. He designs many (integration) solutions and gives advice about how to integrate Salesforce with other platforms or ERPs. Besides that, he still likes to develop nice Salesforce applications with the newest standards and technologies, together with the Salesforce best practices.

You can follow Gunther on Twitter via *@guntherRoskams*, or on LinkedIn as *Gunther Roskams*.

About the reviewers

Maarten Devos is a Salesforce Developer at 4C, with over 5 years' experience in Salesforce. He is Salesforce Certified Developer I, Admin & Integration Architecture Designer. You can find him on LinkedIn as *Maarten Devos*.

Marie-Anne Wouters is a Business Analyst at 4C. She is a Certified Administrator, Salesforce CPQ Specialist and App Builder. Marie-Anne has reviewed this book as a test subject, being a consultant with no prior programming knowledge, making sure all concepts were explained clearly.

Packt is searching for authors like you

If you're interested in becoming an author for Packt, please visit `authors.packtpub.com` and apply today. We have worked with thousands of developers and tech professionals, just like you, to help them share their insight with the global tech community. You can make a general application, apply for a specific hot topic that we are recruiting an author for, or submit your own idea.

Table of Contents

Preface

First of all, now is a great time to become a Salesforce developer. Salesforce and the Lightning Platform are booming all over the world. There is a huge demand for Salesforce professionals such as admins, business analysts, consultants, architects, and especially developers. The demand for developers has never been higher than now (not only in the Salesforce ecosphere)!

So, if you combine the high demand for Salesforce professionals and the huge demand for developers, the potential for job security increases and there should always be a place for you to work at.

This book will help you become a certified Salesforce developer, even if you have no prior programming knowledge!

Who this book is for

Do you want to pass Salesforce Platform Developer I certification? Then this book is for you! This book is for anyone who wants to know all about the powerful Salesforce Platform, ranging from the declarative tools and features at your disposal to the coding side, to extend the standard capabilities and go beyond the limits. This book will prepare you for the actual exam and assumes you have no prior programming knowledge whatsoever. Having Java knowledge is a plus, but is not necessary, as I will be explaining Apex from the ground up. Platform Developer I is one of the pre-requisites of the architect track; for both Application Architect and Systems Architect, you are required to pass this exam. This is also one of the most dreaded exams for Salesforce admins and functional consultants, as they think they won't be able to learn how to code. I'm living proof that this is perfectly possible. Coming from no programming background, I've learned to code in Apex over the years and now hold 15 certifications, including Application and Systems Architect. Something that, a couple of years ago, I would never have imagined, due to my lack of coding knowledge. With this in mind, I wrote this book. I have been there, so I have tried to explain the core concepts in the most simple ways possible, so anyone would be able to understand them.

What this book covers

Chapter 1, *Salesforce Fundamentals*, teaches you about Salesforce Platform in general, and how Salesforce can be used by companies to support their day-to-day business processes for sales, services, marketing, field services, finance, IT, HR, and in other departments.

Chapter 2, *Understanding Data Modeling and Management*, teaches you how to start customizing Salesforce Platform to fit your business needs; how to use the standard objects, create custom objects, and add fields to capture data specific to your business and create relationships between those objects to create a 360° view.

Chapter 3, *Declarative Automation*, shows you the different tools that are available within the platform, such as workflow rules, Process Builder, and Flow, to automate processes such as updating the values of fields, creating automated tasks, sending out emails internally and externally, and even creating and updating records based upon specific user actions.

Chapter 4, *Apex Basics*, explains the Apex programming language. What is it? When is it used? You will learn the basic syntax so you can read and understand how logic is executed on the platform. On top of that, you'll learn how to write it yourself and create your own custom logic from scratch.

Chapter 5, *Apex - Beyond the Basics*, goes over some more advanced concepts of Apex, such as web service callouts and trigger frameworks.

Chapter 6, *The Salesforce User Interface*, teaches you how you can create your own visual interfaces on the platform by using Visualforce pages, Visualforce components, and Lightning components. Salesforce gives you lots of declarative features to modify the look and feel of your user interface, but you never know when you'll come across a requirement for which those are just not enough.

Chapter 7, *Testing in Salesforce*, is a very important chapter because you may have created the most beautiful Visualforce pages with excellent custom logic in your sandbox, but you won't be able to deploy them to your production environment unless you have tested whether all your customizations behave as you would expect. This chapter teaches you the principles of testing your code, making sure you get the expected results, and making your custom logic ready for deployment to another environment.

Chapter 8, *Debugging and Deployment Tools*, focuses on the different development tools available to you as a developer. While creating your custom logic, you will most probably encounter errors. This chapter teaches you how to debug those errors and how to solve them so your code runs smoothly. In this final chapter, we also cover different methods for deploying your custom application to another unrelated environment.

`Chapter 9`, *Mock Tests*, gives you the chance to test yourself. This exam is a representation of what the real Salesforce Platform I certification exam is like. It does not contain the actual questions, but very similar ones. This is meant to give you a feel of what type of questions will be asked, and how many per topic. Score above 80% on this mock exam and you will most likely pass the real exam.

To get the most out of this book

We advise you to not only read the book but actually practice all the exercises in the book. By creating a developer environment and following the steps in every chapter, you will be able to better remember the content, as you will be able to see it right before your eyes. It has been proven that you learn far better by doing rather than just reading.

Every chapter also ends with some quiz questions to check whether you have grasped the content explained in each chapter.

In the *Appendix*, you'll find all the solutions to the quiz questions from every chapter and also the answers for the mock exam.

All the necessary instructions are provided in the respective chapters.

This book will comprise of over five hours of video tutorials.

Download the example code files

You can download the example code files for this book from your account at `www.packt.com`. If you purchased this book elsewhere, you can visit `www.packt.com/support` and register to have the files emailed directly to you.

You can download the code files by following these steps:

1. Log in or register at `www.packt.com`.
2. Select the **SUPPORT** tab.
3. Click on **Code Downloads & Errata**.
4. Enter the name of the book in the **Search** box and follow the onscreen instructions.

Once the file is downloaded, please make sure that you unzip or extract the folder using the latest version of:

- WinRAR/7-Zip for Windows
- Zipeg/iZip/UnRarX for Mac
- 7-Zip/PeaZip for Linux

The code bundle for the book is also hosted on GitHub at `https://github.com/PacktPublishing/Salesforce-Platform-Developer-I-Certification-Guide`. In case there's an update to the code, it will be updated on the existing GitHub repository.

We also have other code bundles from our rich catalog of books and videos available at `https://github.com/PacktPublishing/`. Check them out!

Download the color images

We also provide a PDF file that has color images of the screenshots/diagrams used in this book. You can download it here: `https://www.packtpub.com/sites/default/files/downloads/9781789802078_ColorImages.pdf`.

Code in Action

Visit the following link to check out videos of the code being run: `http://bit.ly/30Fg4LY`.

Conventions used

There are a number of text conventions used throughout this book.

`CodeInText`: Indicates code words in text, database table names, folder names, filenames, file extensions, pathnames, dummy URLs, user input, and Twitter handles. Here is an example: "The Lightning Component framework can only call methods that have the `@AuraEnabled` annotation."

A block of code is set as follows:

```
public Movie__c getMovie() {
        if(this.movie == null){
```

When we wish to draw your attention to a particular part of a code block, the relevant lines or items are set in bold:

```
closeModal: function(component, event, helper){
        var navToMovieTab = $A.get("e.force:navigateToObjectHome");
```

Bold: Indicates a new term, an important word, or words that you see onscreen. For example, words in menus or dialog boxes appear in the text like this. Here is an example: "Click on the **Controller** link to write this part of your controller."

Warnings or important notes appear like this.

Tips and tricks appear like this.

Get in touch

Feedback from our readers is always welcome.

General feedback: If you have questions about any aspect of this book, mention the book title in the subject of your message and email us at customercare@packtpub.com.

Errata: Although we have taken every care to ensure the accuracy of our content, mistakes do happen. If you have found a mistake in this book, we would be grateful if you would report this to us. Please visit www.packt.com/submit-errata, selecting your book, clicking on the Errata Submission Form link, and entering the details.

Piracy: If you come across any illegal copies of our works in any form on the Internet, we would be grateful if you would provide us with the location address or website name. Please contact us at copyright@packt.com with a link to the material.

If you are interested in becoming an author: If there is a topic that you have expertise in and you are interested in either writing or contributing to a book, please visit authors.packtpub.com.

Reviews

Please leave a review. Once you have read and used this book, why not leave a review on the site that you purchased it from? Potential readers can then see and use your unbiased opinion to make purchase decisions, we at Packt can understand what you think about our products, and our authors can see your feedback on their book. Thank you!

For more information about Packt, please visit packt.com.

Section 1: Fundamentals, Data Modeling, and Management

Before we learn how to develop on Salesforce Platform, we need to understand what the platform actually encompasses. We'll learn what the Salesforce Lightning Platform is, how businesses can leverage the multitude of features that come with it, and how it can support business processes. Once we have covered that, we'll learn about the core objects and relationships between objects that form the data model within the platform. We'll also learn how to create our own objects to tailor the platform to every business need.

The following chapters are included in this section:

- Chapter 1, *Salesforce Fundamentals*
- Chapter 2, *Understanding Data Modeling and Management*

Salesforce Fundamentals

1

Salesforce is a company, founded by Marc Benioff and Parker Harris in 1999, that specializes in **software as a service** (**SaaS**). Salesforce started by selling a cloud-based **Customer Relationship Management** (**CRM**) application, which laid the foundation for many of its future services and was built on the Salesforce Platform. Following this, the company began packaging other applications that were closely intertwined on the same platform and divided them into clouds. These cloud-based applications are now popularly known as Sales Cloud, Service Cloud, Marketing Cloud, IoT Cloud, Integration Cloud, Community Cloud, Health Cloud, and Financial Services Cloud, among others.

In this chapter, you will learn about the basic concepts of working on the Salesforce Platform. The material covered in this chapter represents 10% of the exam questions.

We'll learn about the following topics in this chapter:

- What you need to consider when developing in a multi-tenant environment
- The **Model-View-Controller** (**MVC**) paradigm
- The core objects of the Salesforce Platform
- How you can extend an application's capabilities
- How you can solve some common use cases with declarative features

We'll end the chapter with a summary and a quiz so that you can check whether you understand everything that you need to for the exam.

Considerations when developing in a multi-tenant environment

We've briefly mentioned what Salesforce is in the introduction, but it's also important to know what the Lightning Platform is before we start talking about multi-tenancy. The Lightning Platform is the infrastructure in which companies can enable one or more of the aforementioned cloud products, install apps from the *AppExchange* (the Salesforce store), or build their own custom apps.

Using the platform alone—that is, without one of the core cloud products such as Sales Cloud or Service Cloud—is also possible through Salesforce's **platform as a service** (**PaaS**) option. In a similar way to their CRM application, customers can pay a monthly fee to access the shared resources and build custom apps through PaaS.

The biggest benefits of using or buying a cloud service product is that everything is taken care of by the provider – that is, the servers, storage space, the infrastructure, networks, security, backups, and upgrades.

Some characteristics of using cloud-based services are as follows:

- They are subscription-based models
- They have low startup fees
- They have fixed and predictable costs (that is, you pay as you use the service)
- They are scalable
- They include regular, automated upgrades
- They are multi-tenancy platforms; this means that multiple customers use (or share) the same instance

These are important features to bear in mind when talking about multi-tenancy!

What is multi-tenancy?

When I try to explain multi-tenancy to my customers, I always compare it to an apartment block.

For example, consider a scenario, where you – as a company or a customer – rent an apartment in a block that is owned by Salesforce, who is your landlord:

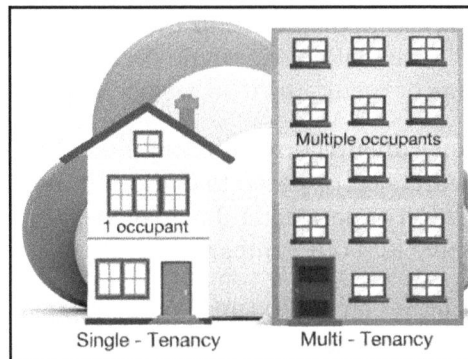

Here, your apartment has specific layouts and resources – that is, it has a number of rooms divided by walls. In addition to this, it has central heating, electricity, water, and more. To access and use this apartment, you pay a monthly rent, and everything else is taken care of for you and the other occupants in the building by your landlord.

Apart from your apartment (which is your private space), all the other resources are shared by the occupants of the building. This means that if Salesforce decides to upgrade the central heating to underfloor heating, then you will automatically benefit from this. You can see this as three releases (that is, upgrades containing new features and enhancements) a year, which Salesforce implements.

The preceding diagram represents the difference between buying a single house, which is yours (**Single-Tenancy**), and renting an apartment in a block with multiple apartments (**Multi-Tenancy**).

Within your apartment, you can design your interior just the way that you want, and adjust it to your needs and personal preference! For instance, you can choose what room to have as your bedroom or your kitchen; or, alternatively, you can use the whole apartment as an office space. You can even paint the walls blue or flashy green if you want to. This is similar to using a Salesforce Platform, where once you have access to your space, you can then create new custom objects, add fields, and automate features to suit your business needs.

The only thing that you can't do is break down the walls – otherwise, the whole building will collapse, right? Even though you have full flexibility in rearranging your apartment, you are still limited when it comes to certain things! For example, you can't put in a 5-meter sofa if the size of the room is smaller than this; additionally, you can't put in a Christmas tree that is higher than the height of your room, or you would need to break the ceiling, and your neighbor would start a lawsuit against you. Alternatively, you can't just install multiple high-voltage accessories or machines in your apartment without the electricity box exploding and leaving the whole building without power!

I use this analogy in order to explain the **governor limits** that Salesforce enforces. Salesforce enforces these limits to make sure that no one single occupant will consume resources that could impact the other tenants or occupants who are using the Salesforce infrastructure.

Salesforce uses a **multi-tenancy architecture**, meaning that a number of **organizations** (**orgs**) share the same IT resources, as opposed to dedicated resources. This results in a standard environment that is fully operated and managed by Salesforce, which is much more efficient and cost-effective for your company.

The self-contained unit that allows an org to run is called an **instance**; it contains everything that is needed to run an org:

- An application and database server
- A file server
- A server, storage, and network infrastructure

An org is an independent configuration (or metadata) and data that is dedicated to a customer. It is represented by a unique ID that you can find in the **Company Profile** section in **Setup**. You must provide this ID each time you contact Salesforce support for **Cases**, **Feature Request**, and more. Each org only runs on one instance, which serves thousands of other orgs.

The org's unique ID is stored in every table in the shared database to allow the filtering of data, and to ensure that a client's data is only accessed by that client alone.

Some advantages of multi-tenancy are as follows:

- All Salesforce customers, from small businesses to enterprise companies, are on the same code base and they all benefit from the same features and new functionality.
- Salesforce upgrades are easy, automatic, and seamless. There are three automatic upgrades a year, which are called the **Spring**, **Summer**, and **Winter** releases.
- With upgrades, a version is associated with every Apex trigger and Apex class. Here, backward compatibility is assured.
- Each class has a version associated with it called the **API version**. When you move to the next release, the Apex class always uses the older version of the compiler to guarantee this backward compatibility. Otherwise, you can modify the code to work on the newest version.

So, if all resources are shared by multiple customers, how does Salesforce ensure that one customer doesn't eat up all resources or break things that could impact all other customers on the same instance?

Salesforce controls this by enforcing two things, which can be considered as the side effects of multi-tenancy:

- **Governor limits**: These are the limits enforced by Salesforce that cannot be changed, and they are the same for anyone using the platform. For example, you can only use 100 queries in one execution context or perform 150 **DML** (short for **Data Manipulation Language**) statements in one execution context. Don't worry if you don't understand this yet, as we'll come back to this later. You can find the list of all the governor limits in the Salesforce documentation at `https://developer.salesforce.com/docs/atlas.en-us.apexcode.meta/apexcode/apex_gov_limits.htm`.

- **Mandatory testing**: Salesforce forces you to test your code before you are allowed to deploy it to production or upload a package to the AppExchange. At least 75% of all code must be covered by tests and they should all pass. Every trigger within your deployment package needs at least some coverage. It's best practice to test all possible scenarios, including positive and negative tests, in addition to testing for bulk updates or creation.

The MVC paradigm

MVC is an architectural design pattern in modern software development that promotes the separation of an application into three components:

- An application's data storage (**model**)
- An application's user interface (**view**)
- An application's logic (**controller**)

The following diagram maps Salesforce's components to this architectural design:

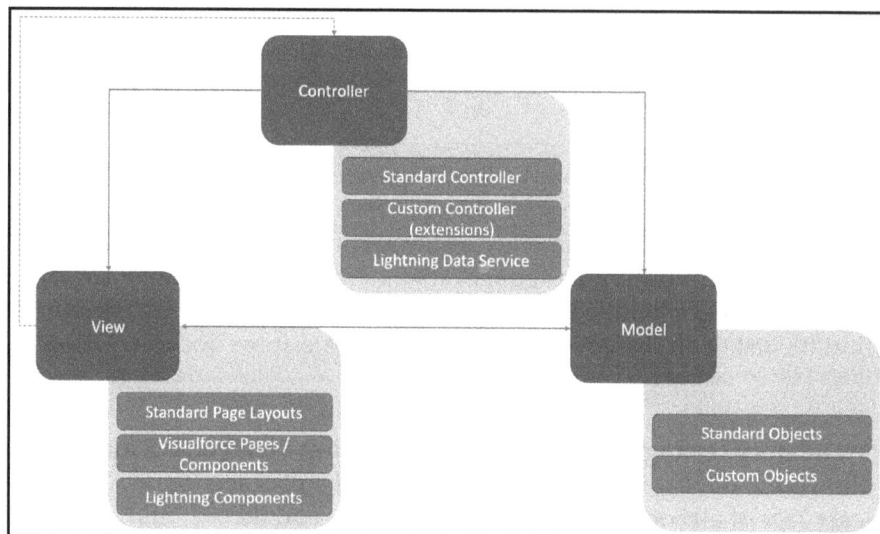

This architecture is used a lot in software development because the isolation of data (that is, the model), user interface (that is, the view), and logic (that is, the controller) allows each component to be developed, tested, and maintained independently.

- **Model**: This is actually where your data is stored and can be used. To store data, you need objects or fields, and these are considered to be part of the model.
- **View**: This is whatever end users see and interact with; that is, what displays data to the clients or customers. This allows you to control how (and what) data is shown on the user interface. So, standard pages, page layouts, Visualforce pages, Lightning components, console layouts, and mini page layouts are all considered part of the view.
- **Controller**: This refers to the actual logic and actions that are executed when someone interacts with Visualforce pages, standard pages, or Lightning components. The controller is the link that binds the client side and the server side. It will mostly consist of Apex; this means that even when building Lightning components, you'll probably need Apex to get the data from the database on the server and pass it to the JavaScript controller. The new Lightning Data Service from Salesforce acts like a standard controller—it connects to objects and fields in the database without writing any Apex.

You could describe MVC like this—when you see a registration form (such as the Visualforce page developed on Salesforce), enter some information into the form, and then hit submit, the details are sent to a database and are saved into tables, columns, and rows (these are Salesforce objects and fields). Which data goes to what object and field in Salesforce is controlled by the logic defined in the standard and custom controllers.

The core CRM objects

I expect that this will be a recap for you; however, just to be sure, I would like to summarize the functionalities paired with some of the most popular core CRM objects. This is important, as a lot of questions in the exam will give you business scenarios around these objects, and before thinking about programmatic solutions, you should consider whether there is any declarative solution that comes out of the box that could be used to meet the requirement.

Leads

The lead object is mostly used for individuals and/or companies that have been identified as potential customers but have not been qualified yet. Leads can be created in several ways; you can create them manually one by one, by clicking on **New** in the **Lead** tab. They are usually imported from `.csv` files (and quite possibly bought by your marketing and/or sales department). Alternatively, they can be created automatically when using the out-of-the-box web-to-lead functionality that generates the HTML form that you put on specific pages of your website(s).

Some of the functionalities that are offered by Salesforce for leads are as follows:

- **Web-to-lead functionality**: This generates an HTML form that you can use on any web page. Here, you select the lead fields you would like the user to fill in on your website and it automatically creates a lead in Salesforce on submission of the form. Be aware that validation rules and duplicate management rules configured on the lead object will also be applied. Web-to-lead functionality works well when combined with auto-response rules and assignment rules. It has a limit of 500 created leads within a 24 hour period. If this limit is reached, Salesforce stores the overflow in a queue and will treat them when the limit is refreshed. Be aware that this queue is limited to 50,000 leads and cases. It is possible to increase the daily limit by submitting a case at Salesforce Support.

- **Lead auto-response rules**: When new leads get created, you can specify whether an email needs to be sent to the lead automatically, and which email template should be sent out.
- **Lead assignment rules**: Upon lead creation, you could set up the automatic assignment of these leads to specific users or queues based on specific criteria, such as by language, segment, or sector. You can only have one active assignment rule per object, but this assignment rule can contain multiple criteria and logic entries.
- **Lead queue**: Custom objects and some standard objects (including leads) can be assigned to a queue. Queues are similar to lists of records, where these records are waiting to be picked up and treated by members assigned to the queue. Queue members can then pick records from the queue and go on to contact the lead, disqualify them, and then start the conversion process. A queue can contain public groups, roles, subordinates, and users as queue members.
- **Lead conversion**: Within a standard sales process, leads usually require some sort of disqualification. This means that someone will try to contact the lead and will try to determine whether they could potentially do business together. A common means of qualification is to determine the **Budget**, **Authority**, **Need**, and **Time** (**BANT**). If the lead does not qualify, then the status is changed to **disqualified**. If the lead does qualify, then the lead will be converted into an account, a contact, and, optionally, an opportunity. This conversion process will map lead fields to corresponding fields on the account, contact, and opportunity, which can be defined by a system administrator:

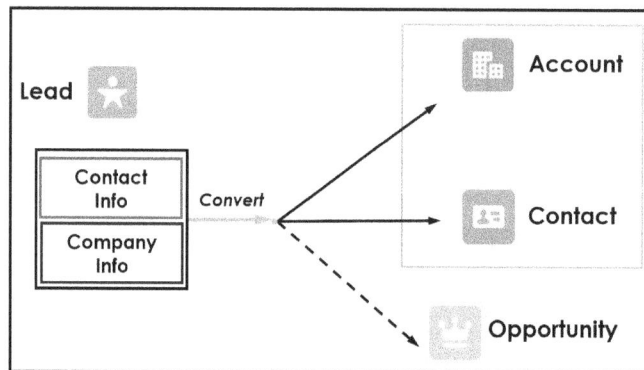

A lead will always convert into a contact, and depending on whether you have **Person Accounts** enabled in your org, an account will also be mandatory (either a new or existing account). If **Person Account** is enabled, then the conversion process will convert your lead to a **Person Account** if the **Company** field is left empty. After the conversion process is successfully executed, the lead will be flagged as *converted* and will no longer be visible in the search results (unless your profile has the **View and Edit Converted Leads App** permission).

Accounts

Accounts are orgs or individuals (when **Person Accounts** is enabled) that are involved with your business in some way (such as the customer, competitor, partner, or supplier).

There are two types of accounts, as follows:

- **Business accounts** (**B2B**): This is the default account type. An account usually contains the general information about a company, such as the name, billing address, shipping address, sector, segment, and VAT number. They also contain several related lists of records, such as the people who work there, the cases that are logged, the opportunities that are sent, the documents that are uploaded, and more.
- **Person accounts** (**B2C**): If your company also deals with individuals, not companies, you can ask Salesforce to enable **Person Accounts** in your org. However, be aware that once this feature has been enabled, it cannot be disabled (but you can still choose not to use the record type). **Person Accounts** are a combination of the account object and the contact object. They mostly contain user information, such as first name, last name, date of birth, gender, hobbies, interests, and more.

Of course, if your company deals in both B2B and B2C, then you can use both business accounts and **Person Accounts** in your org.

The account object also comes with some specific features, as follows:

- **Account hierarchies**: The account object has a standard lookup field called the **parent account**. When this is filled in, it creates a hierarchical relationship between the accounts. When clicking on **View Account Hierarchy** from an account, you can see the whole account relationship from the point of view of the current record. You can easily navigate from one account to the other within the hierarchy. An admin can also modify or adjust up to 15 columns, shown on the **Hierarchy** overview page, through **Setup** | **Object Manager** | **Account** | **Hierarchy Columns**. The following screenshot shows how **Account Hierarchy** is presented to the user on the Salesforce interface:

The **Account Hierarchy** is most commonly used in the following way:

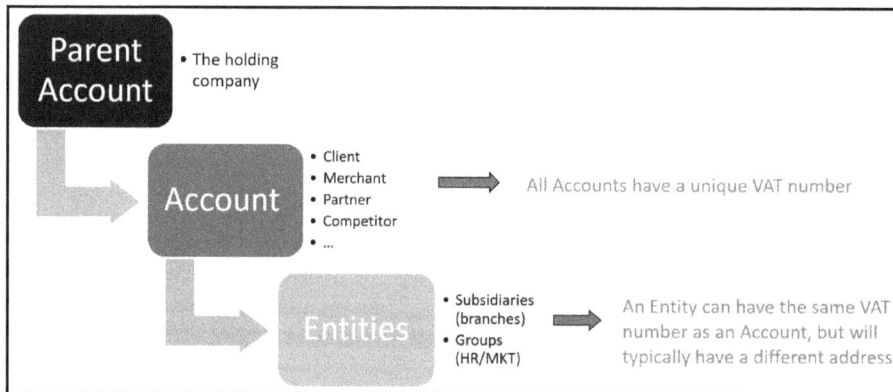

- **Account teams**: These are another way in which to grant access to a specific account record, next to **Organisation-Wide Defaults** (**OWD**), sharing rules, and manual sharing. Here, the owner of an account can specify other users (called **Account Team Members**) working on that same account with a specific business role (such as inside sales, support representatives, and project managers) and specific privileges (read-only or read-write). The user is also able to specify a default account team for each user, which will automatically be added onto the account where that user is the owner of the account. The account teams feature is disabled by default; you can enable it by going to **Setup** | **Feature Settings** | **Sales** | **Account Teams**.

Contacts

This refers to the individuals working on your accounts with whom you have contact. It mostly contains more personal details such as date of birth, gender, and language. Additionally, it can also contain company details, such as title, department, and, optionally, their relationship to another contact to whom they report. This **ReportsToId** lookup field is similar to the **Parent Account** field, and allows you to present a hierarchy between your contacts.

Under normal circumstances, a contact is always directly related to an account. It is possible to mark the account lookup as non-required, but when a contact is not associated with an account, then it becomes a private contact instead. Private contacts are only visible to the record owner and system administrators, and cannot be shared with others.

For marketing purposes, it is important to avoid duplicates between contacts; however, what if the same contact plays a role on multiple accounts?

For this specific reason, Salesforce introduced a new feature called **Contacts to Multiple Accounts**. This feature is disabled by default, but you can enable it through **Setup** | **Feature Settings** | **Sales** | **Account Settings**:

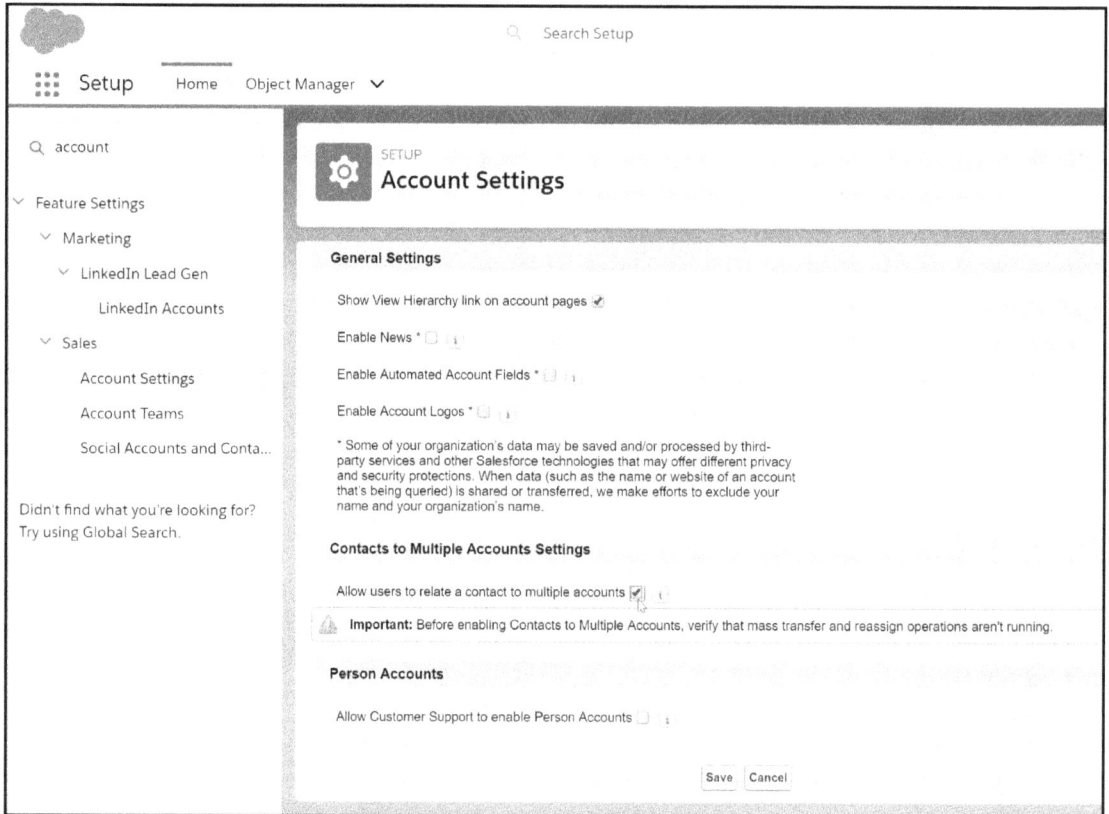

Once enabled, the related list, related account, and related contact details will need to be added to your respective contact's and account's page layouts. You can remove the standard contact's related list from the account page layout because the new related list contains both the direct and indirect contacts or accounts.

Each contact will still have one direct account through account lookup, but you will be able to create extra relationships with other accounts by adding a new **Account Contact Relationship**. These will automatically be marked as indirect. However, because these relationships are with another specific object in the Salesforce database, the individual will only exist once in the contact table, which is fantastic news for your marketing department.

Opportunities

This represents the potential revenue that sales representatives can track through different stages of the sales process until the deal is either won or lost. Opportunities come with multiple sales-related features, as follows:

- Building your company's pipeline
- Forecasting the revenue and determining the next steps to move forward in the sales cycle

In combination with products, price books, and price book entries (prices), opportunities can add a great level of detail to what you are selling to your customers.

The opportunity object comes with some specific features, as follows:

- **Opportunity teams**: This is very similar to account teams; they allow you to add other users to work on the same opportunity with a specific role and access right. In the user record list, it's also possible to add a default opportunity team.
- **Opportunity splits**: If opportunity teams are enabled, then you also enable opportunity splits. These are used to share the revenue of an opportunity between multiple users. In this way, they all contribute to win the deal. This means that the opportunity team members, who are collaborating to win an opportunity, will individually get credit in the pipeline reports, and this will contribute to them achieving their quota. Note that this is not really something that you must know for the exam, so if you want to learn more about this topic, then you can read more at `https://help.salesforce.com/articleView?id= teamselling_opp_splits_overview.htmtype=5`.
- **Collaborative forecasting**: This feature will help you predict the pipeline. A forecast represents the expected revenue based on the sum of the total set of opportunities. They can be adjusted by managers in order to get a more accurate forecast without effectively changing the underlying opportunity's amounts. They are split up by the forecast category, time period, and, optionally, by product.

Extending an application's capabilities using AppExchange

AppExchange is the official Salesforce marketplace for business applications and is available at `https://appexchange.salesforce.com/`.

An app is a bundling of custom objects, fields, programmatic and/or declarative logic, and automations. They solve a specific business requirement or support a specific business process in a better way. You can install an app from AppExchange by simply clicking on the **Get It Now** button and decide on whether to install a production or a sandbox environment.

When you get a new requirement, it's good practice to check on AppExchange first, in order to see whether there is a solution already – either free or paid.

So, what can you find on AppExchange? Well, let's take a look, as follows:

- **Apps**: These are groups of tabs, objects, components, and business logic that work together to provide standalone functionality.
- **Lightning components**: These are the building blocks of functionality that you can drag and drop into a Lightning app, on Lightning pages, or community pages through the Lightning App Builder interface.
- **Flow solutions**: If you want to automate your business process with flow actions, then Lightning flow is considered one of the most powerful, and more advanced, declarative automation tools. The chances are that somebody has already built some flow processes that meet your needs.
- **Lightning bolt solutions**: These are industry template solutions, which are mainly built by partners to help you market faster. Lightning bolts contain process flows, apps, Lightning components, and even whole communities.
- **Lightning Data**: These are pre-integrated, approved, and scalable data solutions. If you want to connect to a data source supplier, such as D&B, then first check whether there is a Lightning Data solution for it.
- **Consulting partners**: If you are looking for help implementing or expanding your Salesforce solution, then AppExchange contains a listing of all consulting partners worldwide, including reviews.

AppExchange is extremely easy to search—you just type in a keyword and it will start giving you suggestions. You can easily filter the search options according to industry to see what apps are popular in your industry. Additionally, you can filter by solution type, price, compatibility with your Salesforce edition, ratings, and language. It will even suggest you learning modules on Trailhead, the free online Salesforce learning platform!

Here are the things that you need to consider when choosing an AppExchange solution:

- Is it free or paid? Does it fit within your budget?
- Is it compatible with your Salesforce edition?
- Does it require you to turn on some features that are not yet enabled in your org?

- Is it Lightning-compatible or does it only work in Classic?
- What do the reviews say? Are any of your requirements not met?
- Always test in a sandbox environment first!

When talking about AppExchange, it's important that we talk about packages, because that's what you will be installing—a package.

> You can expect one or more questions about packages in the exam—just saying!

Packages are bundles of metadata components that make up an app or solution. A typical package will contain objects, fields, **Workflow Rules** (**WFRs**), validation rules, processes, approval processes, flows, Apex classes, Visualforce pages, and Lightning components. There could be hundreds of them in one package.

Packages are used for distribution across unrelated orgs—it's like deploying a change set.

In fact, anybody can create a package for distribution, and then share the link to someone else to install the solution in their org. These packages are private and the receiver must know the exact URL of the package to be able to install it.

If you want your package to be publicly available, searchable, and/or listed, then it must be uploaded on AppExchange.

Packages that are published on AppExchange also come in two variants, as follows:

- **Unmanaged packages**:
    - They are used for distribution across orgs.
    - By installing an unmanaged package, you copy all its contents into your org and, after installation, you can modify everything. You can change the Apex code, the Visualforce code, mark fields as required or not, change their data types, and more.
    - The contents of the package become yours.
    - This also means that the creator or provider loses all control and, in most cases, they cannot offer any support on the package.
    - They don't need to have a namespace.
    - The packaged components will count toward your org limits.

- **Managed packages**:
  - The source code of managed packages is hidden from you
  - You can't see or modify any of the code
  - Managed packages can only be created in a developer environment
  - This also means that the creator or provider has control over the installed version and can offer upgrades
  - The provider will mostly provide support on the package
  - You can grant the provider access to your org to support you, in the same way that you would grant access to the Salesforce support
  - The packaged components do not count towards your orgs limits
  - The use of a namespace is required
  - Managed packages are typically for sale on the AppExchange

Common use cases for declarative customization

It's important to understand one of the biggest differentiators of Salesforce in comparison to other CRMs. Salesforce provides a lot of tools and features to maximize declarative customization (through point-and-click tools). In fact, while configuring Salesforce to suit your business needs, in 80% of cases, you will be able to solve your requirement with declarative functionality. For the remaining 20% of the use cases, you'll need some kind of programmatic development.

Becoming a certified platform developer does not mean that you solve everything with code. Customers, consultancy agencies, and Salesforce all expect a Salesforce developer to be able to use the easiest tool to achieve a solution and, therefore, most of the exam will assess whether you are able to distinguish what can be achieved through declarative configuration and what cannot be, hence, reverting to a more programmatic approach.

In `Chapter 3`, *Declarative Automation,* we'll dive deeper into ways to automate your business through declarative tools and programmatic options. For now, let's just recap the most commonly used declarative features that Salesforce offers an admin out of the box.

Objects and fields

Salesforce comes with a lot of standard objects, all of which have standard fields. Objects and fields allow you to capture data in the database.

Consider the following screenshot; here, you can compare objects and fields by having an Excel file, where you have a sheet for every object, such as accounts, contacts, quotes, and so on. In this case, you will need to keep track of multiple records and specific data:

You will also need a row for each account record, along with columns for the data that you would like to track of for the account. In Salesforce, these are represented by fields. Just like in Excel, a field can have a certain data type depending on what type of data you are tracking—that is, text, phone numbers, URLs, dates, and more.

Each object can be, but doesn't have to be, represented by a tab in Salesforce, just like creating a sheet per object in Excel. Having a tab for the object gives you the benefit of creating filtered list views of records for that type of object.

Additionally, you can extend your database to your needs; this is done by creating new custom objects yourself and creating extra custom fields on the existing standard objects and/or on your newly created custom objects to track whatever data you deem necessary. While creating a field just like in Excel, you have the choice between several data types such as **Text**, **Text Area**, **Rich Text Area**, **Lookup relationship**, **Master-Detail relationship Checkbox**, **Picklist**, **Multi-Select Picklist**, **Phone**, **Email**, **Date**, **DateTime**, **Time**, **Currency**, **Geolocation**, **Formula** fields, and **Roll-up Summary** fields.

Formula fields

A formula field is like a real-time calculation that is calculated when it is loaded or requested. It's like a formula in an Excel spreadsheet. We refer to it as loaded or requested, because it's not a calculation that appears while viewing a record in the user interface. When you request the record data, it is calculated (or recalculated) using the following methods:

- By viewing it in the UI or in a report
- By exporting the data through a data loader
- By reading the data through an API call
- By querying the data in a SOQL query

A formula field is always read-only. This means that it's not a field in which you can type or change it's value manually – it is always calculated. As a result of this, the calculation does not perform an update on the record and this can never trigger any automations. What I mean here is that you can't have something like a WFR that updates a field when that field changes without performing a manual update or other automation update of the record. You can, however, use the value of a formula field in your automation processes as a criterion or to use as a value.

I know this is somewhat confusing, so let's try to explain it using an example. Let's say that we create a formula field returning a date that is calculated, based on the creation date of a record plus 30 days, and we would like to create a task for the owner when we reach that date automatically. You could be tempted to create a Process Builder that evaluates whether TODAY() equals the date field. If it does, then create the task and, as long as that date is not equal, it's still either in the future or already past.

Now, if the record does not get updated by someone manually, or by some other automation, then nobody will touch this record and this Process Builder won't fire—this is because all automations only fire on the creation or updating of records.

Additionally, a formula field is calculated in real time when it gets requested and does not perform an update of the record. You can use your own logic in order to build the calculation that it needs to perform, and Salesforce offers a lot of functions for you to use within your formulas.

For instance, I really like the **Formula Cheatsheet Salesforce** that contains the most used functions. You can find it at https://resources.docs.salesforce.com/rel1/doc/en-us/static/pdf/SF_Formulas_Developer_cheatsheet_web.pdf.

A formula field can return the following things:

- Checkbox
- Currency
- Date
- Datetime
- Time
- Number
- Percent
- Text

Formulas usually perform calculations with other values in the record that it resides on, but it can also use the values of parent records, or grandparent records, up to 10 levels up. However, it cannot use the values of child records. So, a common use case for a formula field is to display data from its parent. For example, let's say that we have a custom **Picklist** field, `Region__c`, on the account page and we would like to show this value on our opportunities page. Because an opportunity is directly linked to an account, we could create a formula field that renders the text using the formula `TEXT` (`Account.Region__c`).

Because a formula is always calculated in real time, this value will always represent the actual value from the `Region__c` field of the account on our opportunity, without manually updating all opportunities of this account whenever the `Region__c` field changes on the account.

A formula field that uses data from its parent, or higher up the hierarchy, is called a **cross-object formula**. Formulas do have some limitations that you need to be aware of; for example, you will get an error message if your formula does not comply with the following limits:

- The maximum number of characters is 3,900.
- The maximum formula size on saved is 4,000 bytes.

When your formula exceeds either of the aforementioned characters or byte limits, then you will receive an error message mentioning this.

> **TIP**
>
> Spaces, comments, and carriage returns are also included while calculating the character count.

Rollup summary fields

A **rollup summary field** (**RUS**) field is very much like a formula field in that it also performs a calculation. However, this is based on child records, and only when these child records are part of a Master-Detail relationship!

It's used to summarize a numeric value based on (filtered) child records and can perform COUNT, SUM, MIN, and MAX.

It is recalculated whenever a transaction on these child records occurs in the following ways:

- When a new child is created
- When one of the children gets updated
- When a child gets deleted

You can use filters to only pull values from specific child records. For example, let's say that we have a custom Invoice__c object that is related to the account as a Master-Detail relationship. In our Invoice__c object, we have an **Amount** field and a **Status** field. We could create a RUS field in the account that represents the total amount that is overdue, which is a calculation of the SUM operation of the **Amount** field on all related invoices, with a filter on the **Status** field that is equal to **Overdue**.

> RUS performs an update of the record they reside in and can, therefore, be used to fire off other automation tools, such as WFRs, Process Builders, and more.

Validation rules

Validation rules are used to make sure that the data entered in fields adheres to the standards you have specified for your business.; for example, making sure that phone numbers always have the same format, or that a field cannot be left blank based on the input or value of another field. If a value does not meet your validation rules, then the user will not be able to save the record. A validation rule is made of a formula or expression to check the criteria and an error message, which will be shown to the user if the values do not meet your specified criteria. The formula evaluates the data in one or more fields, and then returns either true or false. Validation rules ensure data quality in your org.

If the formula returns true, then the defined error message is displayed and the record cannot be saved. The formula can be referenced with more than one field and can also be a cross-object formula. While setting the error message, you can decide to show it next to a certain field or on top of the page.

Validation rules will run while performing operations through an API (through Data Loader, for example), on web-to-lead creations, and on web-to-case submissions. So, make sure that you design your validation rules so that they will not interfere unintentionally with these functionalities. In some scenarios, you may need to disable the validation rules while you import or update data, and then reactivate the rules afterward. Alternatively, you may exclude a specific user or profile in the validation formula so that it doesn't execute when the operation is run, as that specific user or as a user with that profile; this means that they can perform data loads without validation rules firing.

WFR

A WFR tool is one of the oldest and highest-performing automation tools. They help end users save time in their day-to-day activities. A WFR is a set of actions that need to be executed when a record is created or updated to meet specified criteria.

WFRs can be split into two main components:

- **Criteria**: What must be the true record for the WFR to fire and have its associated actions to be executed
- **Actions**: What to do when the record meets the criteria that was defined and which actions need to be executed

WFRs can execute the following actions (either immediately or time-based):

- Sending an email alert
- Performing one or more field updates
- Sending an outbound message
- Creating a task
- Triggering a Lightning flow process

Consider the following screenshot:

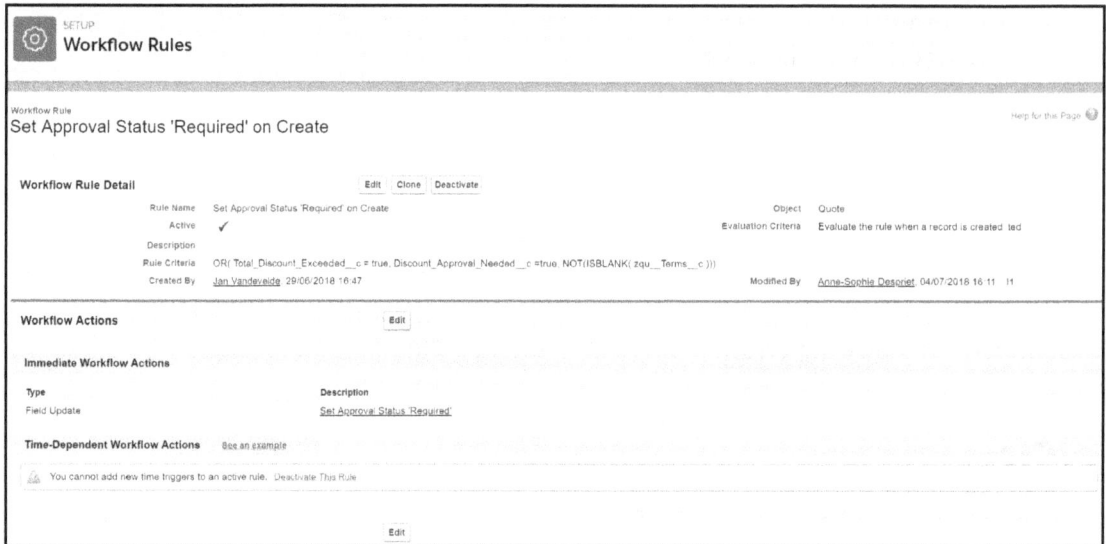

> **TIP**
>
> Only orgs that were in the pilot can have **calling a flow** from a WFR enabled; it's not possible to enable this feature anymore, because it has now been replaced by a Process Builder action that calls a flow.

Approval processes

Sometimes, you may want to create some kind of an approval process in which records need to be approved by one or multiple other users before moving further within your business process.

A very common use case is to submit an opportunity for approval to a sales manager if a specific discount percentage or amount is exceeded.

Well, approval processes are the tools that create these types of processes. They allow you to specify an object, the criteria (or record values) that need to be evaluated before a record must be submitted for approval or not, and who needs to give their approval. After an approval or rejection, you can perform a number of automated actions, such as field updates or sending notifications. In approval processes, after submitting the record, the record is then locked. In this way, nothing can be changed until the data has been approved or rejected.

The user who is submitting the data for approval can also have the option to recall the record, which takes the record back out of the approval process.

Upon final approval or final rejection, the same actions as in WFRs can be executed, such as updating a field, sending an email, and more:

The Process Builder

In the day-to-day life of end users, a lot of repetitive work is done manually. You can minimize these manual actions (such as sending email notifications, assigning records to other users or queues, and performing record updates to certain stages and statuses) by creating automated actions through the Process Builder. The Process Builder is one of the most powerful tools that you can use to automate your business using a nice graphical interface.

The Process Builder can be kicked off in the following three ways:

- When a record is created or updated in Salesforce
- When a platform event occurs on the Salesforce Platform
- When another process invokes it

Each process consists of nodes and actions, as follows:

- In the nodes, you'll define the criteria on which a set of actions need to be executed.
- The actions (immediate or scheduled, that is, time-based actions) need to be executed when a certain criteria node is being entered and evaluated (being true). Pay attention to the fact that only record-change processes support scheduled actions.

> You can perform almost the same actions as WFR with the Process Builder, even more.

With the Process Builder, you can perform the following actions:

- Create records of any object type.
- Update any related record; this is not limited to the record itself or its parent.
- Use quick actions to create or update records or log calls.
- Invoke a process from another process.
- Launch a flow.
- Send an email.
- Post to Chatter.
- Submit a record for approval.
- Call an Apex class.

The Process Builder also comes with an easy-to-read and easy-to-edit drag and drop graphical interface; this is why most people call it *WFR on steroids*:

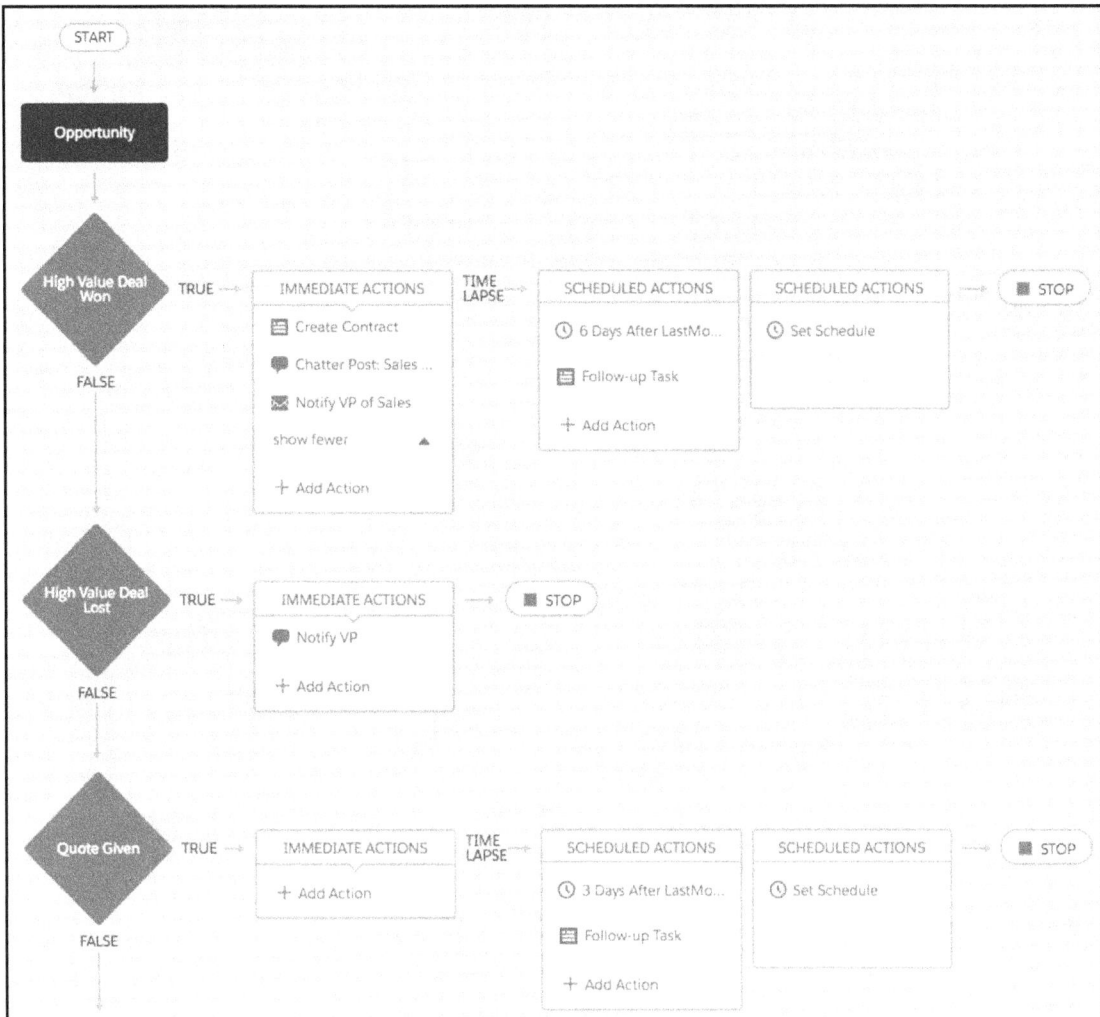

Lightning flow

When it comes to flows, you might have heard of several different definitions or types. To clear up any confusion, the official terms are as follows:

- **Lightning flow**: This is the native platform feature that allows you to build, manage, and run processes
- **Cloud Flow Designer**: This is the graphical interface that is used to design and build your flows; this is done through clicks and dragging and dropping
- **Flow**: This is an actual chain of events, input captures, queries, and actions that will be executed to automate your specific business process when an event takes place in your Salesforce org or on an external system

In short, the Cloud Flow Designer is the tool that helps you create flows:

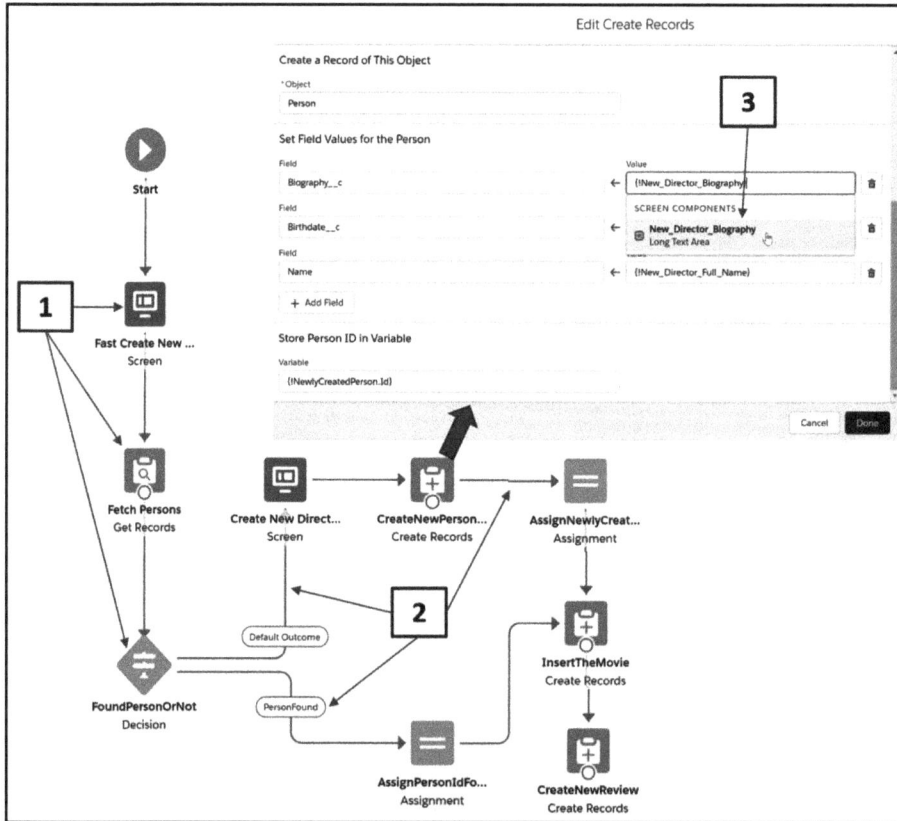

The flowscreen example

Every flow consists of three blocks, as follows:

- **Elements** (**1**): These are dragged onto the canvas; an element can represent a screen input, a query or some kind of action (such as `create record`), a post to Chatter, and more.
- **Connectors** (**2**): These are used to define the order in which elements are executed. They form the path that elements must follow, and they tell the flow what elements must be executed next.
- **Resources** (**3**): These are pieces of storage in the memory of the flow that contain a specific value, such as values from fields or formulas. You can refer to and use these resources throughout your flow; for example, to look for an account's ID, store that ID in a variable resource with a name of your choice, and then later use that ID to update the account or to relate records to that account ID.

Additionally, Lightning flow is the only automation tool that can accept user input without the need to create a Visualforce page or Lightning component for it.

So, Lightning flow is an ideal tool for building—such as for call scripts, in which you guide users through a set of questions to ask a customer and, then, depending on the response, it performs a set of actions at the end of the flow. Additionally, Lightning flow is the only automation tool that is able to delete records.

Salesforce has a very nice comparison chart of the different automation tools, which you should know by heart for the exam. You can keep checking for any updates to this chart at `https://help.salesforce.com/articleView?id=process_which_tool.htmtype=5`.

Consider the following screenshot:

	PROCESS BUILDER	CLOUD FLOW DESIGNER	WORKFLOW	APPROVALS
Complexity	Multiple if/then statements	Complex	A single if/then statement	A single if/then statement
Visual designer	✓	✓		
Browser support	All (Chrome recommended)	All (Safari not recommended)	All	All
Starts when	• Record is changed • Invoked by another process • Platform event occurs	• User clicks button or link • User accesses Lightning page, Community page, Visualforce page, or custom tab • User accesses item in a utility bar • Process starts • Apex is called	Record is Created or changed	• User clicks button or link • Process or flow starts that includes a Submit for Approval action • Apex is called
Supports time-based actions	✓	✓	✓	
Supports user interaction		✓		
Supported Actions				
Call Apex code	✓	✓		
Create records	✓	✓	Tasks only	Tasks only
Invoke processes	✓			
Delete records		✓		
Launch a flow	✓	✓	✓ (Pilot)[1]	
Post to Chatter	✓	✓		
Send email	✓ (Email alerts only)	✓	✓ (Email alerts only)	✓ (Email alerts only)
Send outbound messages without code			✓	✓
Submit for approval	✓	✓		
Update fields	Any related record	Any record	The record or its parent	The record or its parent

[1]The Process Builder has superseded flow trigger workflow actions, previously available in a pilot program. Orgs that are using flow trigger workflow actions can continue to create and edit them, but they aren't available for new orgs.

Summary

So far, we have learned how working on a multi-tenant platform requires your attention while developing your own custom applications. Additionally, we have learned what the MVC paradigm is, how Salesforce comes with some core standard objects, how you can create your own custom objects, and how you can leverage declarative tools to customize and automate your environment to support your business processes.

In `Chapter 2`, *Understanding Data Modeling and Management*, we'll learn more about the Salesforce data model and how you can extend it. Additionally, we'll explore how to relate different objects to each other, how to visualize these different relationships, how you can import data into the platform, and how to export it. We'll be building our own basic international movie database in order to explore all of these concepts.

But, first, let's check whether you are on the right track to becoming a certified Salesforce developer—I definitely hope so!

Quiz

You'll find all the answers to each chapter summary quiz at the end of this book (in the *Appendix*). Try to answer the questions first without looking at the answers:

1. Your manager wants you to build a solution that deletes all open tasks related to an opportunity when the **Opportunity** stage is set to **Closed Won**. In what ways could you build out this solution? Select two answers:

    a. Write an Apex trigger that fires when the **Opportunity Stage** updates to **Closed Won**, queries all the related **Tasks** that have an **Open** status for that opportunity and then deletes them.

    b. Create a Process Builder that performs a delete action on all the related **Children** of the **Task** type with **Status Open**, when the **Opportunity Stage** is set to **Closed Won**.

    c. Create a Process Builder that calls a Lightning flow whenever an **Opportunity Stage** reaches **Closed Won**. The flow then queries all **Tasks** related to the opportunity that kicked off the Process Builder with a status of **Open**, and deletes them.

    d. Create a Process Builder that calls an Apex trigger whenever an **Opportunity Stage** reaches **Closed Won**. The trigger then queries all related **Tasks** with a status of **Open** for that opportunity and deletes them.

2. Object *B* has a master-detail relationship to object *A*, so A is the parent of *B*. You want to display the value of the **Status** field from object *A* on the record of object B. How could you do this?
    a. You create a formula field on object *B* and, in the formula, you reference the **Status** field from its related object *A*.
    b. You create an Apex trigger on object *B* to copy over the value of the `Status` field from its related object *A* record.
    c. You create a RUS field on object *B*, pulling in the **Status** from object *A*.
    d. You use the Process Builder to fire off on object *B* to copy over the value of the **Status** field from its related object A record.

3. A business user would like you to send a notification whenever a case is put in the *Closed* status to the case owner's manager, and to post this on Chatter. What's the best tool to use?
    a. WFRs
    b. Apex trigger
    c. The Process Builder
    d. Lightning flow

4. A cross-object formula field can be one of the following:
    a. Reference fields from parent objects that have a Master-Detail relationship
    b. Reference fields from parent objects related through a lookup relationship only
    c. Reference fields from parent objects related through either a Master-Detail or a lookup relationship
    d. Reference fields from the same record only

5. Your company is in need of a recruitment application for its HR department including jobs, job postings, applicants, and more. How would you go about this?
    a. You start by drawing the data model, create the objects, test them, validate them, and perform a RUS calculation
    b. You start by searching the AppExchange
    c. You advise HR management that this is not something that should reside in Salesforce
    d. You scratch your head because you have no clue how to start providing a solution for this requirement

6. What are some implications of a multi-tenant environment when it comes to Salesforce?

    a. Resources are added to the instance whenever needed, so you should not worry about resource consumption

    b. Multi-tenant means that your org gets its own instance with all its resources dedicated to your org

    c. You should avoid using Salesforce at peak time as it is slower than usual, because everybody is using it at that time

    d. There are governor limits imposed by Salesforce on each org to prevent them consuming all of the instance resources

7. In a multi-tenant environment, which of these statements is true?

    a. Your org shares a Salesforce instance with thousands of other orgs

    b. Your org shares a Salesforce instance with no more than 100 other orgs

    c. Your org has its own Salesforce instance

    d. All Salesforce orgs use the same Salesforce instance

8. What's special about a formula field?

    a. It is calculated once every 24 hours

    b. It is calculated once every hour

    c. It is calculated only when you write the record into the database

    d. It is calculated every time when you read the record in question

9. How is a managed package built?

    a. Through your Salesforce org's sandbox

    b. Through the enterprise edition of the Salesforce org

    c. Through the developer edition of the Salesforce org

    d. Through a Salesforce developer edition's sandbox

10. Your company asks you to create a process that automates holiday requests. There should be two levels of acceptance before the holiday request is granted—first, by the direct manager of the requestor, and then by the HR manager. How would you do this?

    a. Build a flow using the Lightning flow

    b. Build rules by using WFRs to streamline the process

    c. Build a process by using the Process Builder

    d. Build this process by using the approval process

Understanding Data Modeling and Management

2

In Chapter 1, *Salesforce Fundamentals*, we briefly touched about objects, fields, and apps. Let's dive deeper and get our hands dirty to learn some core concepts of building our own apps. Throughout the book, we'll be creating a **basic version of an international movie database** (**BIM DB**) to explain those concepts, because IMDb is an official company. I would advise you to build it too to get a hands-on experience.

You could just keep reading, but you'll grasp the concepts in much more detail if you go into your Developer Org (yes, we set that up for something) and practice what you've learned. It will also help if you take the exam to visualize the requirements and solutions in a Salesforce **Setup**.

In this chapter, we'll be covering the following topics:

- Data modeling
- Relationship types
- Schema design and modification impact on Apex development
- Visualizing and creating entity relationships
- Importing and exporting data into development environments

Data modeling

Lightning speed is the future, so we will be doing everything in the Lightning Experience interface version of Salesforce. Don't worry if you have only just created your Developer Org, this should be the default setting.

So, we know that we will mostly use Salesforce as a database. Data modeling helps us structure our data using custom objects and fields. Let's have a recap, as we already know what those are:

- **Object**: This is used to store specific data, such as our Excel sheet called **Accounts**. We will need to create several objects to store specific data for our BIM DB app, such as **Movie**, **Person** (actor, actress, director), **Review**, and **Company**.
- **Field**: This is used to capture specific data for a specific record of a specific object type; for example. each movie has a name, a release date, and a duration.
- **Tab**: This is a representation of records for a specific object. You can choose whether you wish to create a tab for an object or not. The benefit is that you can create list views from the tab, which will show a list of filtered records of that object, for example, all movies with a release date in 2000.
- **App**: This is a bundle of commonly and frequently used tabs, objects, fields, and permissions to support a specific business process; in our case, we'll create a BIM DB app.

Each standard or custom object automatically consists of a set of fields. There are several different types of fields:

- **ID**: Each standard and custom object automatically gets an ID field, which acts as a unique identifier for records within the Salesforce database table. This is automatically populated by Salesforce and consists of 15 (unique case-sensitive) or 18 (unique case-insensitive) characters. Every record in Salesforce has a unique ID.
- **System Fields**: Every object (standard or custom) in Salesforce has some read-only database fields that you can't delete or modify, and they are as follows:
  - **CreatedDate**: This is the date and time when the record was created in Salesforce, either manually or through an import
  - **CreatedById**: A relationship to the user who created the record, either manually or through an import

- **LastModifiedById**: A relationship to the user who last updated (made any modification to it) the record
- **LastModifiedDate**: This is the date and time when the last modification (update) was made to the record
- **Name field**: This is a required field and is used as a more user-friendly identifier. It can be either **Text** or an **Autonumber**.

Of course, you can then create extra fields as per your business needs. One special type of field that you can create is a relational field, which is used to link one or more records together. We will go into more detail in the next section when we talk about relationship types, but, for now, just remember there are two specific field types to build relationships:

- **Lookup**
- **Master-Detail**

Creating an app

So, let's create our BIM DB app with the following core objects:

- `Movie`
- `Person` (yes, we could use the **Contact** object for this, but let's not use it for the sake of this exercise)
- `Review`
- `Company` (yes, we could use the **Account** object for this, but let's create our own custom object)

To create an app, we will have to follow these steps:

1. Log in into your Developer Org and navigate to **Setup**. In the quick search (in the left sidebar), enter `App` and select **App Manager**.
2. Click the button in the top right called **New Lightning App**.

3. Follow the wizard by filling in `BIM DB` as the **App Name**; **Developer name** fields will be filled automatically when you click out of the **Name** field. It should now have `BIM_DB` as the **Developer name.** Upload a logo if you wish:

4. Click **Next** and leave the defaults for **App options**.
5. Click **Next** and leave the default for **Utility items** (none selected).
6. Click **Next**, select **Home**, and add it to the **Selected Items** on the right pane.
7. Click **Next** and assign all profiles to the selected profiles.
8. Lastly, click **Save**.

You have now created your first app, called `BIM DB`, which should be available for you in the **App Menu**. Go check it out by clicking on the nine little bullets in the top left of your navigation menu, right next to **Setup**. You should see your app as the last tile, as shown in the following screenshot:

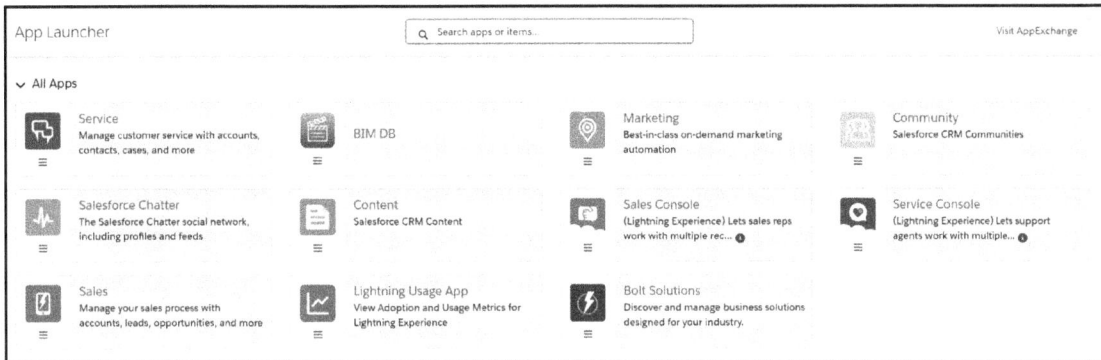

For the moment, our app is quite empty, as it only contains the standard **Home** tab. Let's do something about that by creating and assigning our custom objects.

Creating custom objects and custom fields

As explained before, we need objects to store data, such as a sheet in Excel. In our case, we would like to store movies, actors, actresses, directors, production companies, and maybe more later on. We will need objects for those. For each record of a particular type, you also want to capture some specifics/attributes. For example, if we create a movie record, we don't only want to save the title, but maybe also the release date, the budget, the director, a cover image, and so on. Just like in Excel, the columns you define to capture data in Salesforce correspond to fields for saving data about a particular record. So, let's create some of those and give our app some body (build our app out a bit more).

Let's first create the `Movie` object:

1. Navigate to **Setup** and click the **Object Manager** tab.
2. On the right-hand, side click **Create ǀ Custom Object**.

3. Then, enter the following details:

   - **Label**: `Movie`
   - **Plural Label**: `Movies`
   - **Object Name**: This should be filled automatically with **Movie**
   - **Record Name**: This should be the movie title with a data type of **Text**

4. Check the following checkboxes:

   - **Allow Reports**
   - **Track Field History**
   - **Allow In Chatter Groups**
   - **Allow Sharing**
   - **Allow Bulk API Access**
   - **Allow Streaming API Access**
   - **Deployed**
   - **Allow Search**
   - **Launch New Custom Tab Wizard after saving this custom object** and hit **Save**

5. This will open the **Tab Creation Wizard**. Now, select **TV Widescreen** as the **Tab Style** and hit **Next**.
6. Leave the default for the **Profile** selection, which should be **Default On**, for all profiles and then hit **Next**.
7. Deselect all custom apps and only select our newly created `BIM DB` app in the **Include Tab** column. Leave the checkbox at bottom of the page, **Append tab to users' existing personal customizations,** checked and hit **Save**.

Great! You've just created a custom object called **Movie** that comes with its own tab and you've added this tab to our custom app, called `BIM DB`. Go and check it out as you did previously through the **App Menu**, click the **BIM DB** app, and you should see it has two tabs—our **Home** and **Movie** tabs:

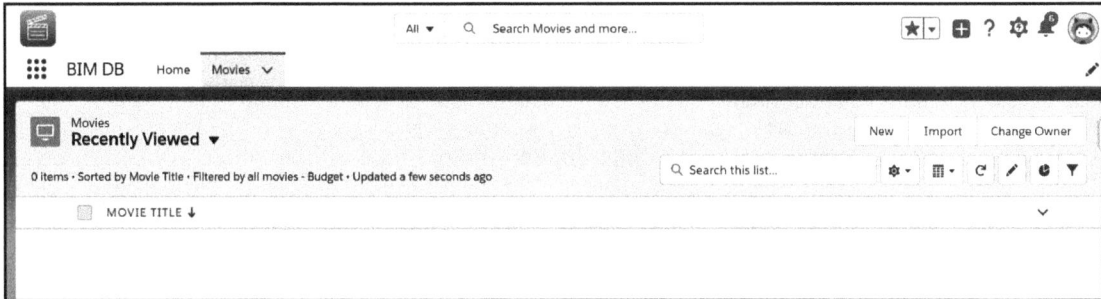

Now, let's add some custom fields to our **Movie** object to capture some relevant information about each movie:

1. Navigate back to **Setup** and click the **Object Manager** tab
2. Use the **Quick Find** search box to easily find our **Movie** object and click the **Movie** object to open it
3. In the **Fields & Relationships** section, click the **New** button to create a new field
4. Chose the **Date** type, click **Next**, and give it a **Field Label** of `Release Date`
5. Make sure that **Field** name is auto-populated with **Release_Date** (watch the underscore), if not, enter it and click **Next**
6. Leave the defaults for field-level security and click **Next**
7. Leave the default **Movie Layout** selected and click **Save**

Congratulations! You have created a new custom field that will capture the date when the movie was released. Now, you need to create the following fields and objects.

Just follow the same steps, but ensure that each field/object is specified from the following table:

Create	On Object	Label	Type	Length	Visible Lines	Profile Security	Layout	Specifics
Field	Movie__c	Description	Text Area (Long)	32.768	10	Visible All Profiles	Movie Layout	
Field	Movie__c	Genre	Picklist (Multi-Select)		5	Visible All Profiles	Movie Layout	Action, Adventure, Animation, Biography, Comedy, Crime, Documentary, Drama, Family, Fantasy, Film Noir, History, Horror, Music, Musical, Mystery, Romance, Sci-Fi, Short, Sport, Superhero, Thriller, War, Western
Field	Movie__c	Cover	Text Area (Rich)	32.768	25	Visible All Profiles	Movie Layout	
Field	Movie__c	Budget	Currency	18		Visible All Profiles	Movie Layout	0 decimals
Field	Movie__c	Runtime	Number	18		Visible All Profiles	Movie Layout	0 decimals
Object		Person						Allow Reports, Allow Search, Launch Tab Wizard, Tab Icon "People"
Field	Person__c	Biography	Text Area (Long)	32.768	5	Visible All Profiles	Person Layout	
Field	Person__c	Birthdate	Date			Visible All Profiles	Person Layout	
Object		Review						Record Name change to "Review Nbr" with datatype 'Auto number', display format = R-{0000}, starting number = 1, Allow reports
Field	Review__c	Description	Text Area (Long)	131.07	25	Visible All Profiles	Review Layout	
Field	Review__c	Rating	Picklist			Visible All Profiles	Review Layout	1,2,3,4,5
Object		Company						Wizard, Tab icon "Building"
Field	Company__c	Address	Text Area			Visible All Profiles	Company Layout	

As a rule of thumb for these exercises, you can always choose **All Profiles** to have access to the fields and objects you are creating. Of course, we could absolutely create more fields on all of those objects, but let's keep it at a minimum for now. We will be adding some fields later in the book.

Creating records

Before checking things out, let's just create one sample movie record:

1. Go to your **BIM DB** app (through the App Launcher).
2. Click the **Movies** tab.
3. Click **New** and enter the following values:

   - Movie Title: `The Godfather.`
   - Release Date: 24th August 1972 (the format is dependent on your user locale settings).
   - Description: `This movie is about the mafia. The patriarch of an empire of organized crime gives his legacy to his reluctant son.`
   - Genre: `Crime, Drama.`

- Cover: This is a rich-text field that allows us to upload images into it. In the `.zip` file with all assets, you'll find a folder called `BIM DB-app` containing a sub-folder called `Movies`. You will find a cover picture in there for **The Godfather**. So, in the field, just click the little image icon to insert an image and upload the picture from the folder.
- Budget: `6.000.000`.
- Runtime: `175` (this will be in minutes!).

4. Click **Save** and you should have the same screen shown in the following screenshot:

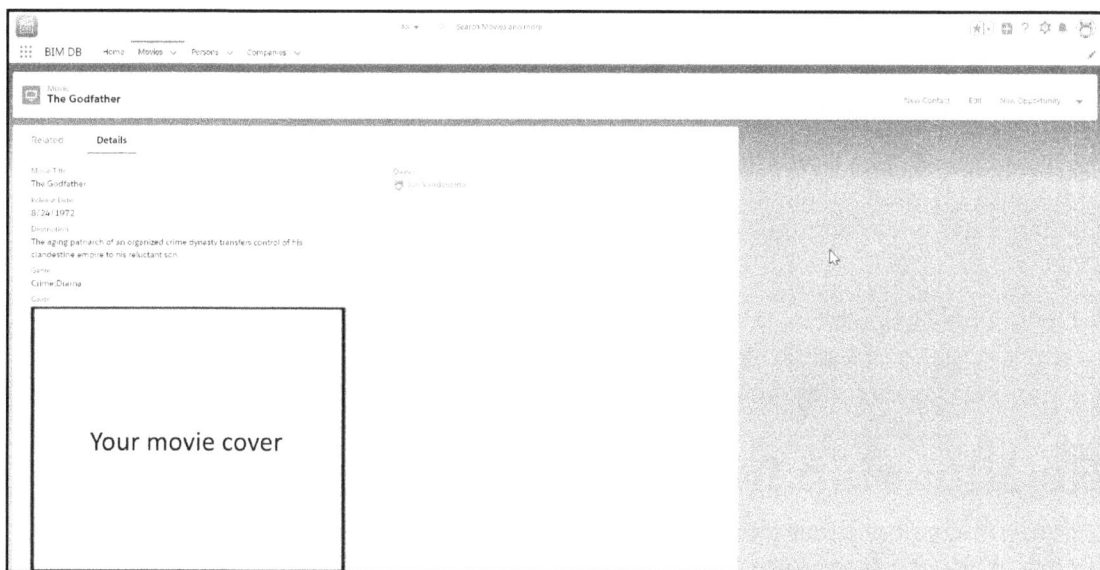

You will see the three tabs (**Movies**, **Persons**, and **Companies**); that's because we **Launched Tab** creation while creating our objects. Following the table, we didn't create a tab for the **Review** object, so it's good if you don't have one. But don't worry if you do, as it won't affect the exercises.

We did not create a tab for reviews because, in the next section when we talk about relationships, we will always want a review to be linked to a certain **Movie**. So, when we wish to see reviews, we should search for the **Movie** and then see all its reviews as a related list on the **Movie**.

Now, let's also create a **Person** record and a **Company** record:

1. Create a new **Person** with the following details:

    - Name: `Al Pacino`
    - Birthdate: April 25th, 1940
    - Biography: `Here comes the biography of Al Pacino, one of the most popular actors in history. Al Pacino became popular in the 1970s and became an iconic figure in the world movies.`

2. Create a **Company** record with the following details:

    - Company Name: `Paramount Pictures`
    - Address: `5555 Melrose Ave, Los Angeles, CA 90038, USA`

I'm pretty sure that you already guessed where we are going with this, right? **Al Pacino** is the main actor in **The Godfather** movie, and **Paramount Pictures** is the production company, but, at the moment, we have absolutely no relationship in our database showing that they have anything to do with each other. We just have three individual records and that is it.

We will solve this problem in the next section, where we will create one or more relationships and add some more data to our database.

Relationship types

So, what is a relationship exactly? A relationship is a bi-directional link between two objects. Without relationships, you could create as many standalone custom objects you would like to, but you would not have a way to link them to each other. By creating links between records, you can expose data about other related records on the page layout of a particular record.

While creating relationships between objects, you have to think in advance on how those objects will relate to each other. Therefore, there are three main relationship types:

- **One-to-one relationship**: This is a direct relation with another object's record and there can only be one at all times. For example, a husband will have only one wife at any given point in time. Historically, he could have been married multiple times, but at any given time, he only has one current wife.

- **One-to-many relationship**: This is a relationship where a certain record can have a relation with multiple records of the other object type. For example, one soccer team has multiple players in the team, but each player belongs only to one soccer team at any given time.
- **Many-to-many relationship**: In this case, each record of object A can have multiple records of object B, and object B can have multiple records of object A. Let's give an example from our movie database—a certain movie can have multiple people playing a role in the movie, and one person can play a role in multiple different movies! I think you can already see the problem here, right? To establish a many-to-many relationship, we will need another object between those two objects that acts as a junction, and such an object is called a **junction object**. So, in our example, we will create a specific object called **Cast** to add relationships between one movie and multiple people with a specific role in the movie, but it will automatically show different movies a person plays a role in.

The following diagram illustrates those relationships types:

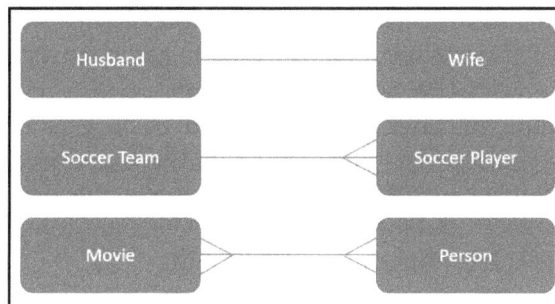

In Salesforce, we create these types of relationships by using one or more relationship fields.

There are two specific types of relationship fields in Salesforce:

- **Lookup**: You use a lookup when there is *no tight relationship*, meaning that a record does not have to have a related record of the other type linked to it
- **Master-detail**: This is used when you define a *tight relationship* between two objects, meaning that the child cannot exist without a related parent

To relate two objects through a one-to-many relationship, you should always first create the relationship field on the child object (the *many* sides). Consider the following table:

Lookup relationship	Master-detail relationship
• Create a relationship that links one object to another object. • The lookup field is created on the child object. • The related list is automatically created on the parent object. • The two objects are loosely related. • Ownership and sharing are set independently. • Record deletion is independent. • Lookup fields can be optionally required for children.	• Create a relationship that links one object to another object. • The master-detail field is created on the child object (Detail) • The related list is automatically created on the parent object • The two objects are tightly related. • The sharing and visibility of the child record are determined by its parent record. (controlled by the parent). • When you delete the master record, all of its detail records are automatically deleted along with it. • Master-detail relationship fields are always required on the child records.

There are other types of relationships in Salesforce too, but these are used less:

- **Hierarchical**: This is a special Lookup relationship that's only available on the **User** object. It lets users use a lookup field to associate a user with another user; for example, to determine someone's manager.
- **External lookup**: This links a child standard, custom, or external object to a parent external object, like when using Lightning Connect (this lets you access external data while using Salesforce) to make a connection to an external database source and making that data visible in Salesforce without storing it in Salesforce (this is less important for the exam).
- **Indirect lookup**: This links a child external object to a parent standard or custom object (this is less important for the exam, but it is good to know that it exists).

The special case here is the many-to-many relationship. A many-to-many relationship allows you to relate each individual record of an object to multiple records of another object and the other way around. To create such a relationship, both objects are linked together through a junction object. A junction object is a custom object that is the *child of both objects* through *two master-detail relationships*!

Creating relationships

In our movie example, we have our **Movie** object and we have our **Person** object. To create a many-to-many relationship between both, we need a junction object. As I mentioned previously, we will be using Cast as a junction object. So, let's create that junction object and see why we did that:

1. Navigate to **Setup | Object Manager**.
2. Create a new custom object with the following details:
   - **Label**: Cast
   - **Plural**: Cast
   - **Record Name**: Role Name
   - **Type**: **Text**
   - **Allow Search**: true
   - Leave the other defaults as is
3. Now, create a new custom field:
   - Type: **Master-Detail Relationship**
   - Related to: **MOVIE**
   - Label: **Movie**
   - Field Name: **Movie**
   - Child Relationship Name: **Cast**
   - Leave all other defaults and click **next**, **next**, **save**
4. Create the second custom field with following details:
   - Type: **Master-Detail Relationship**
   - Related to: **PERSON**
   - Label: **Person**
   - Field Name: **Person**
   - Child Relationship Name: **Cast**
   - Leave all other defaults and click **next**, **next**, **save**

Okay, now that we are able to link people with movies and movies with people, let's create a record in our database. Go to the **The Godfather** movie record that we created earlier. You'll be on the **Details** tab, but for that we have to add a record to the related list, **Cast** (which was added automatically by creating the relationship fields). So, click the **Related** tab and click **New** in the related **Cast** list. Fill in `Michael Corleone` as **Role Name**. Because we are creating a **Cast** record from the **Movie** record, the **Movie** lookup is already pre-populated with **The Godfather**. Now, click the lookup icon next to the **Person** field, select **Al Pacino**, and click **Save** (as illustrated in the following screenshot):

You have successfully added **Al Pacino** (the **Person**), to the **Cast** of **The Godfather** (our **Movie**) in the role of **Michael Corleone**! Now, do yourself a favor and navigate to our `Al Pacino` record and check out the **Related** tab there. You will find the same related **Cast** list and also the record for `Michael Corleone` played by `Al Pacino` in the movie **The Godfather**. I hope this example gives you a clear view on how a many-to-many relationship work.

Understanding the different relationship types and when and how to use them is a very important part of the Platform Developer I exam. So, make sure that you fully understand this. Feel free to create your own custom objects in your Developer Org and create multiple relationships to practice some more.

We will do the same in the next section, because, as you can see, we are not done yet! We'll be adding some extra relationships, but through **Schema Builder** instead of just through the **Object Manager**. Yep, I'm building up towards something here; no joke.

Schema design and modification impact on Apex development

Previously, we have learned how we can define our data model through the user interface (UI), such as creating new objects and new fields and linking them to each other by creating specific relationships.

When you define objects, fields, and relationships, they become instantly available for you to use in declarative automation features and also in Apex code. Everything defined through the UI can be used programmatically with Apex and **Salesforce Object Query Language** (**SOQL**). I'll explain this in more detail in Chapter 4, *Apex Basics*, under the *Working with data in Salesforce* section, but, for now, you need to know when objects and/or fields are used/referenced elsewhere in Salesforce.

You won't be able to delete those fields or objects, as Salesforce won't allow that, and it will come up as a big error message telling you where the field or object you are trying to delete is referenced in your code (like in the following screenshot):

Unable to Complete the Requested Change	
Your changes could not be completed for the following reasons:	
Reason	**Section**
This custom field is referenced elsewhere in salesforce.com.	Custom Formula Field
This custom field is referenced elsewhere in salesforce.com.	Field Set
This custom field is referenced elsewhere in salesforce.com.	Apex Trigger
Can't delete this Custom Field Definition because it's referenced by Yet_Another_Field_Process version 1. Remove the reference from the process.	Open the process in the Process Builder
This custom field is referenced elsewhere in salesforce.com.	Validation Rule
This custom field is referenced elsewhere in salesforce.com.	Field Update
This custom field is referenced elsewhere in salesforce.com.	Workflow Rules
This custom field is referenced elsewhere in salesforce.com.	Field Updates

This is a good thing, because you could easily delete a field and the existing logic that is in your production org would break if you didn't pay attention.

So, if you want to delete or modify a field or object that is used in the code or elsewhere in Salesforce, you need to follow these steps:

1. You need to remove the reference.
2. Then, delete the field or object.
3. Finally, refactor your code or formulas so that everything can continue to work.

Visualizing and creating entity relationships

There is another way though to see, create, and update your data model in Salesforce, and that's through a specific graphical interface called **Schema Builder**.

In the following screenshot, you get a visual representation of the objects created for our BIM DB app in the **Schema Builder**. The **Schema Builder** can be found in **Setup** | **Schema Builder**. You can select/deselect the objects you want to visualize on screen in the sidebar, and drag and drop the screens so that you get a clear overview of all relations between those selected objects:

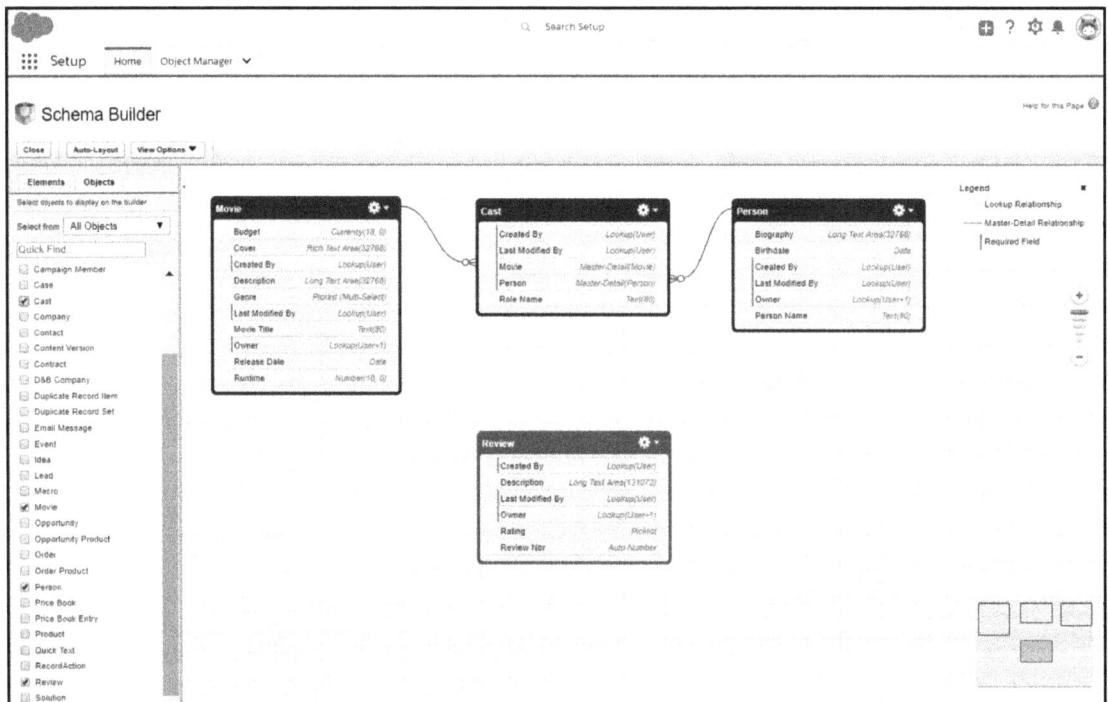

So, **Schema Builder** is a tool to view and modify your Salesforce org data model. It simplifies the task of designing, implementing, and modifying your data model or schema.

As previously mentioned, you are not only able to view your existing schema, but you can also interactively add new custom objects, custom fields, and relationships, by simply clicking, dragging, and dropping elements from the sidebar onto the canvas:

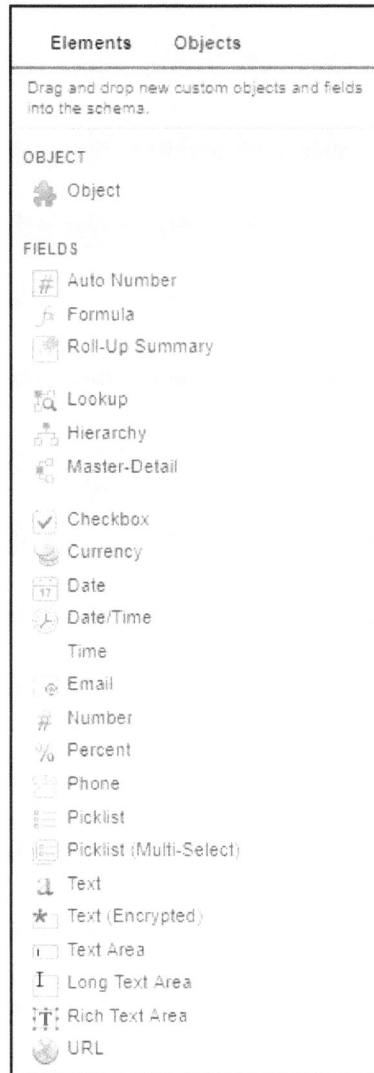

Schema Builder is enabled by default, and it lets you do the following things:

1. Jump directly to the object and layout page that you are used to from **Setup**.
2. Create custom objects.
3. Delete custom objects.
4. Edit custom object properties.
5. Create any custom field with the exception of the **Geolocation** type.
6. Create relationships such as lookup and/or master-detail between objects.
7. Delete custom fields.

The **Schema Builder** has an autosave functionality that will implement your changes immediately and save the layout of your schema when you move an object on the canvas. The biggest benefit is that you don't need to click from page to page in **Setup** to find a relationship or to add a new custom field to an object. The Schema Builder shows details such as the type of fields, which fields are required, and how objects are related to one and other.

Some facts to keep in mind while using **Schema Builder** are as follows:

- While creating new fields through **Schema Builder**, they are not automatically added to your page layouts. You'll need to edit the page layout manually to specify where the new field should be displayed.
- The field-level security for fields created through **Schema Builder** is set to **Visible** and **Editable** for all internal profiles.
- Managing these permissions can be done by clicking on the element name and then selecting **Manage Field Permissions**.

Creating objects and fields with Schema Builder

Now, let's create some extra fields and relationships for our BIM DB app through **Schema Builder**:

1. Go to **Setup**, search for **Schema Builder** and open it.
2. If some objects are already preselected, just click the **Clear All** button under the **Objects** tab in the sidebar and then select our custom objects from our BIM DB app—**Movie**, **Cast**, **Person**, **Review**, and **Company**.
3. Once you have selected them, drag and drop the objects so you can see them all in a clear overview on the page, like so:

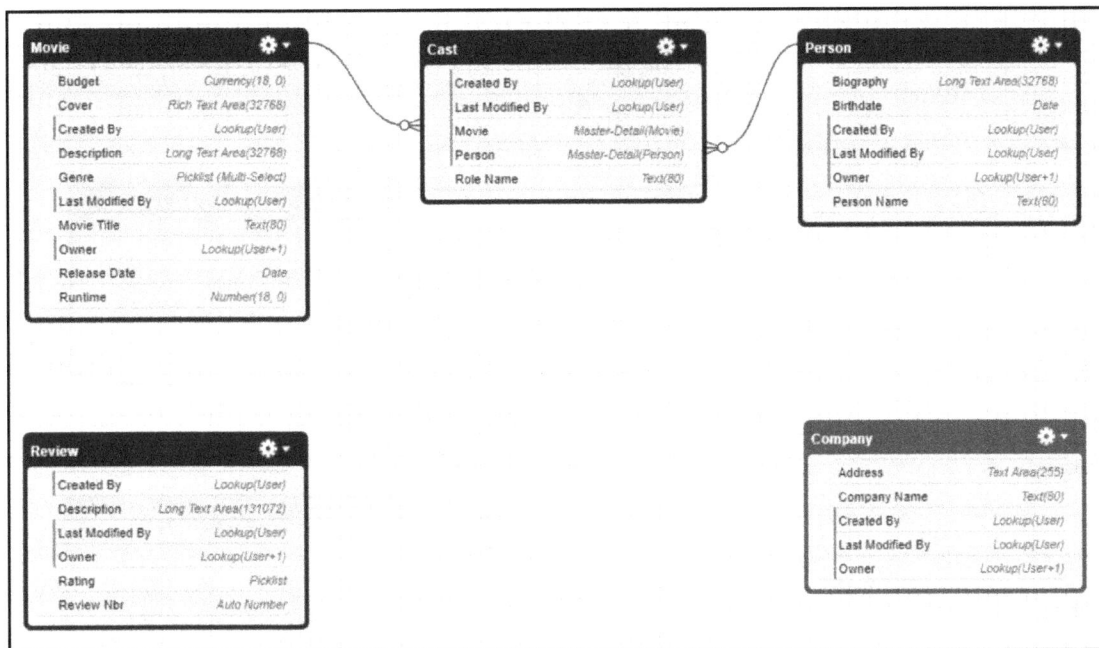

Now, let's create a lookup relationship on our **Movie** object, called `Director` (assuming a movie can only have one director in our app). To do this, we need to follow these steps:

1. Click the **Elements** tab in the sidebar and drag the lookup element onto the **Movie** object on the canvas.

2. In the popup **Create Lookup Field (Object: Movie)**, fill in the following information:
   - **Label**: `Director`.
   - **Field Name** (this will be automatically filled with the same as the **Label** field).
   - **Related To** (select the **Person** object).
   - Leave the **Child Relationship Name and Related List** label as is (it should say `Movies`).
   - Hit **Save**.

3. On the canvas, you should now see a new field called **Director,** in the **Movie** object, that is a direct any-to-one (**Movie** to **Person**) relation to the **Person** on the canvas:

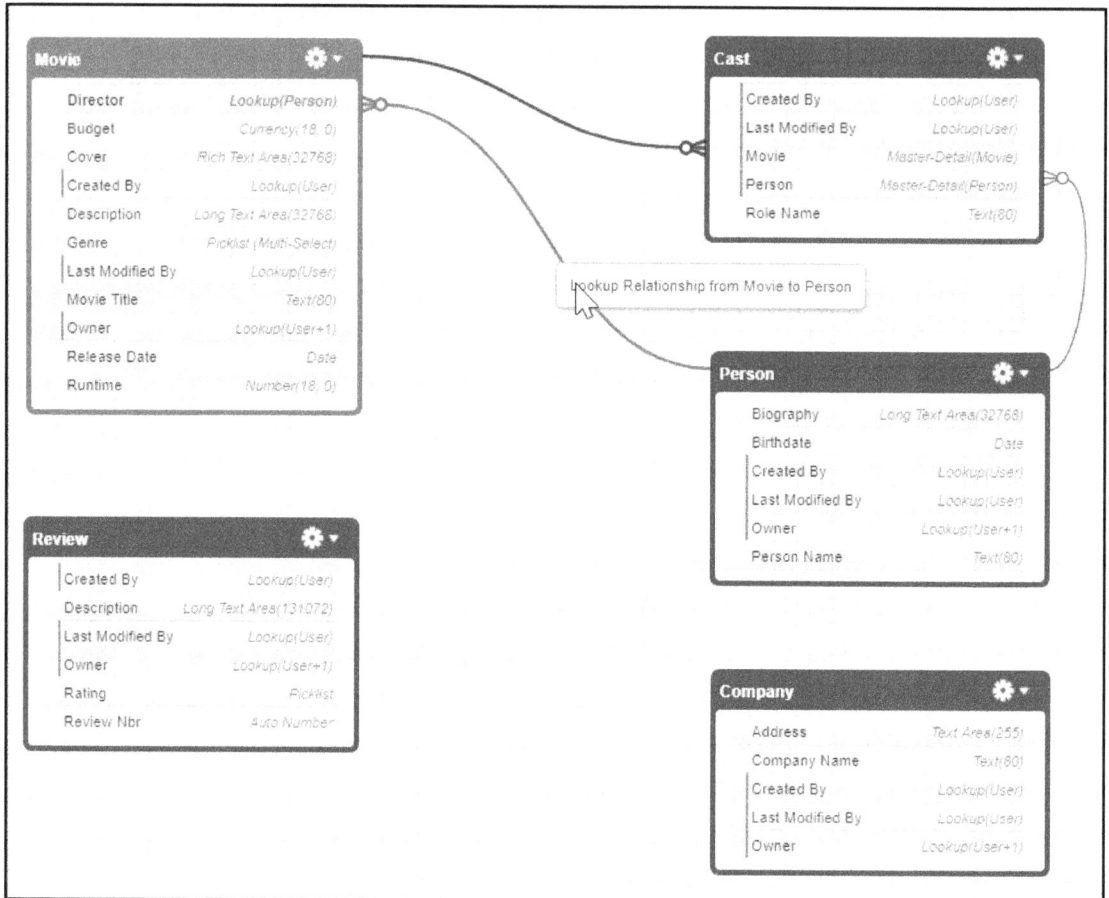

This is exactly what we wanted. A movie has only one director (in our app), so that means that a **Director** (**Person**) can direct multiple movies right? Exactly!

Now, let's create a relationship between **Review** and **Movie**. What kind of relationship would we need here? Think about it for a moment:

- Can a movie have multiple reviews?
- Can one review be about multiple movies at the same time? Would that make any sense?
- Would it make sense to keep reviews about a certain movie if that movie did not exist anymore?

If your conclusion is to create a master-detail field called **Movie Title** on the **Review** object that points to the **Movie** object, you would be correct.

Just to be clear, a movie can have multiple reviews (I certainly hope so, because that will give us a more accurate view of whether people liked it or not). It does not make sense to create only one review for multiple movies. You are reviewing a movie and you should write a review for each movie you are assessing! When you delete a movie from the database, you would have reviews floating around without any reference to the movie the review is about. That would not make any sense either. A master-detail relationship makes sure that you always need a reference to another object on the child and that all reviews would be deleted automatically if we deleted the movie itself.

So, going ahead, just like we did previously, drag a master-detail element onto the **Review** object and call it `Movie Title`. Obviously, it will be related to our **Movie** object, which will automatically generate a child relationship called `Reviews`. In the popup, do not check the **Reparentable Master Detail** checkbox!

I reshuffled the objects a bit on the canvas to see all relationships in a better way, but you should have something like this now:

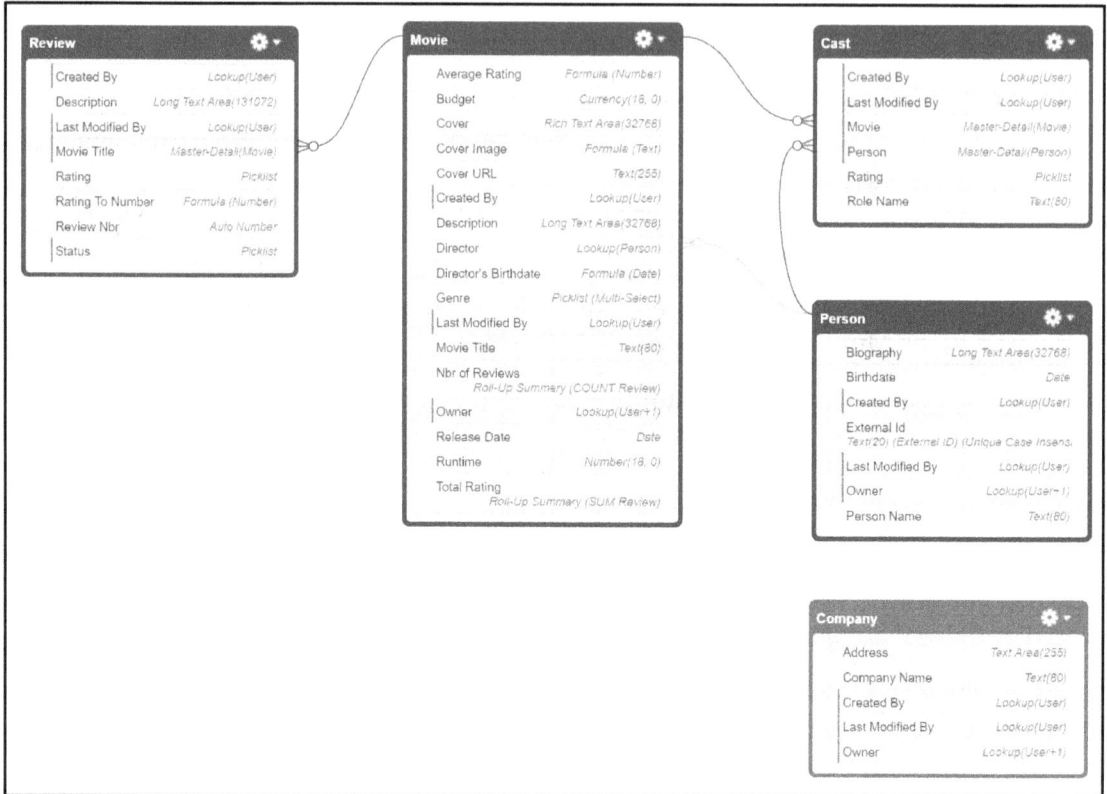

Okay, we still have one unrelated object in our schema—our **Company** object. It's feeling a bit alone without any relatives. Let's do something about that.

What I had in mind is that the **Company** object will contain several entity records such as production houses. I did not call the production house object, because maybe, in the future, we could have companies related to movies or other objects in a different way, for example, investing companies, much like I am anticipating with the **Person** object. We will have actors, actresses, producers, and directors who are all individual people. So, when I lookup *The Godfather* on imdb.com, I can see that it has two production companies related to that movie—**Paramount Pictures** and **Alfran Productions**. So, this means one movie can have multiple production companies and one production company can produce multiple movies! This is a many-to-many relationship, right?

The following is what we have learned about many-to-many relationships:

- You'll need a junction object.
- A junction object consists of two master-detail relationships.
- You always create the master-detail lookup field on the child object, so in our case this means we'll create the two master-detail lookup fields on the junction object.

Go ahead and create a new object called **Production Company,** with a master-detail field (movie title) to **Movie,** and a master-detail field (company name) to **Company** through the **Schema Builder**.

> **TIP**
>
> Give the junction object the **Production Company Nbr** record name, and set the data type to **Auto Number** with **Display format PC-{0000}** and the starting number one.

The result should be like the following screenshot:

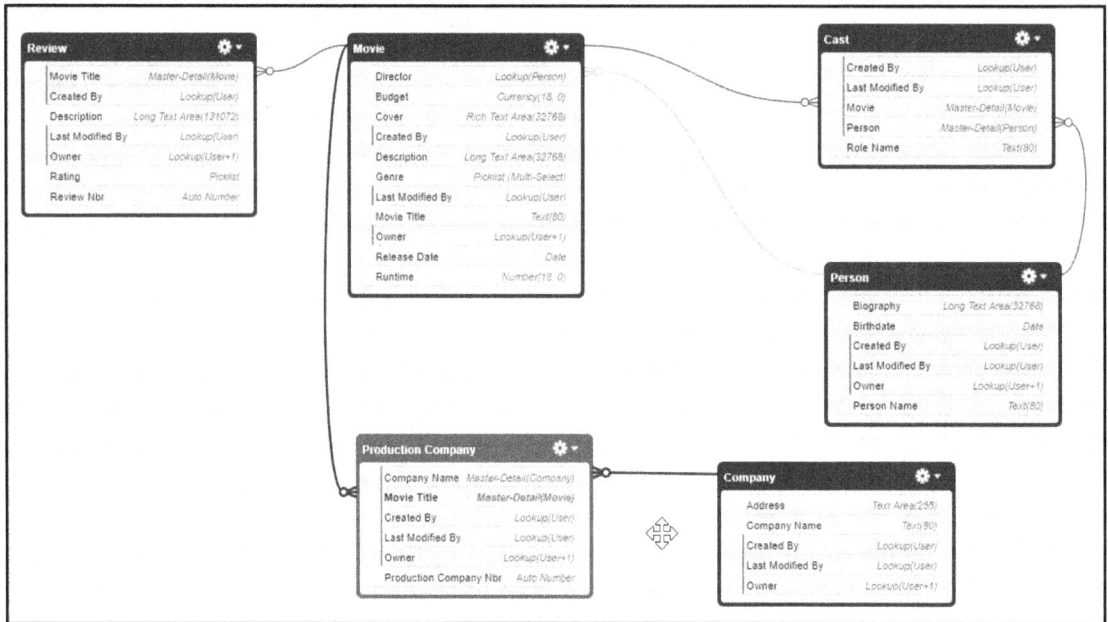

Super duper, dude! You just added fields, objects, and relationships through the **Schema Builder** and added extra value and insights to our BIM DB app. Now, everything will make much more sense, and we will be able to get a clear view on who directed a movie, who was cast in a movie, read movie reviews, and also see what companies produced the movie.

Modifying page layouts through the App Builder

Because we did all this through **Schema Builder**, none of our fields can be filled in through the UI yet and our related lists are not visible yet on the **Movie** and **Company** page layouts. So, we'll need to fix that first:

1. First, navigate to our BIM DB app through the App Launcher and open up our movie, **The Godfather**. Check the page and scroll down. We don't see our **Director** field, right? Also, check out the **Related** tab; we only have our **Cast** related list, which we created through the UI in the previous section. Let's make the necessary changes so that we are able to see and fill in those newly created fields and relationships.

2. From our **Movie** record, click the cog (settings) icon next to your avatar in the upper right corner of Salesforce and select **Edit Page** from the submenu.

3. You will find yourself in the Lightning App Builder interface. This interface lets you change the way the pages appear to your users. You can drag and drop the Lightning components onto specific places on the page to create a better user experience:

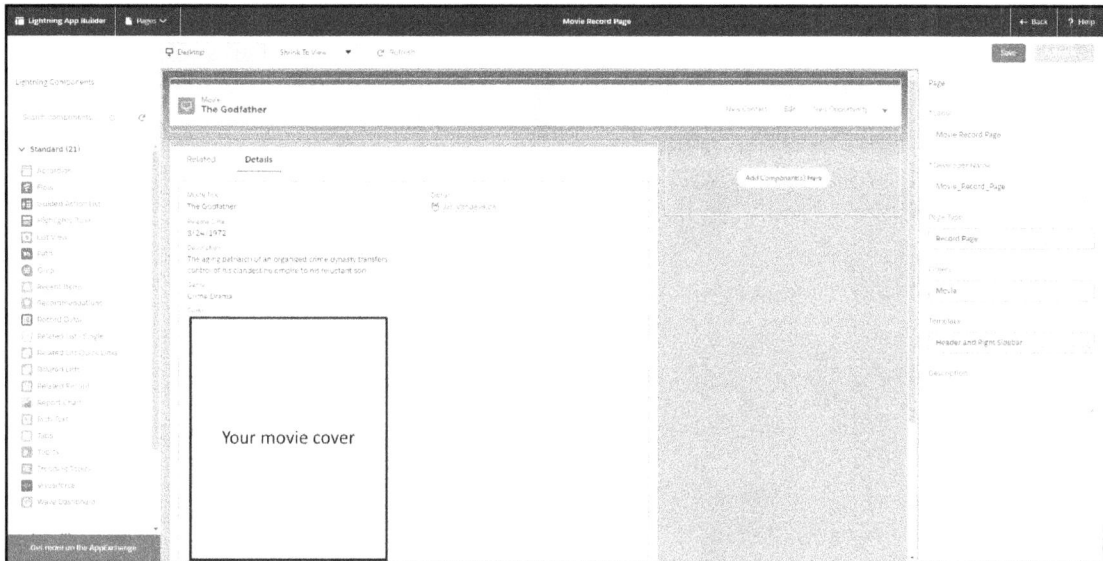

4. Now, click in the **Details** pane of your movie. So now, the **Details** component gets a blue border and you'll see that the sidebar on the right will change and other options will be available to you. Then, click on the **Movie Layout** link in right sidebar, as in the following screenshot:

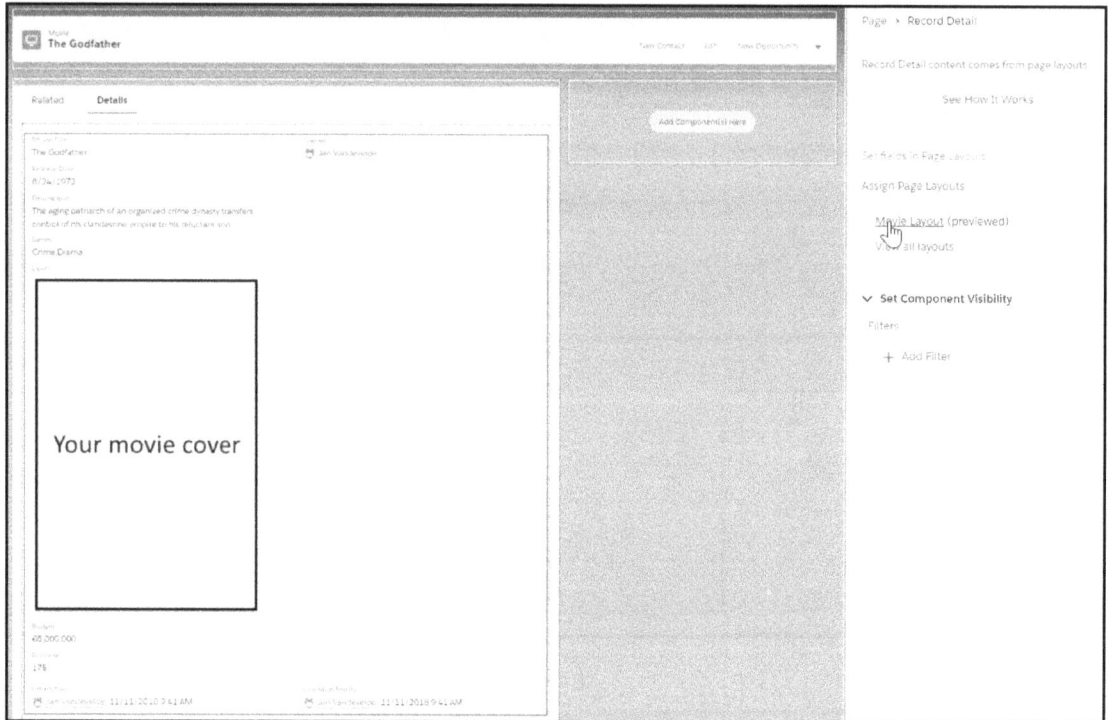

Adding and moving fields on the layout

Consider the following steps:

1. Now you are in the **Page Layouts** section of the **Movie** object. In here, you can add and remove fields to and from the layout, drag them to other places on the layout, and also define which related lists need to be shown. You should see something like the following screenshot:

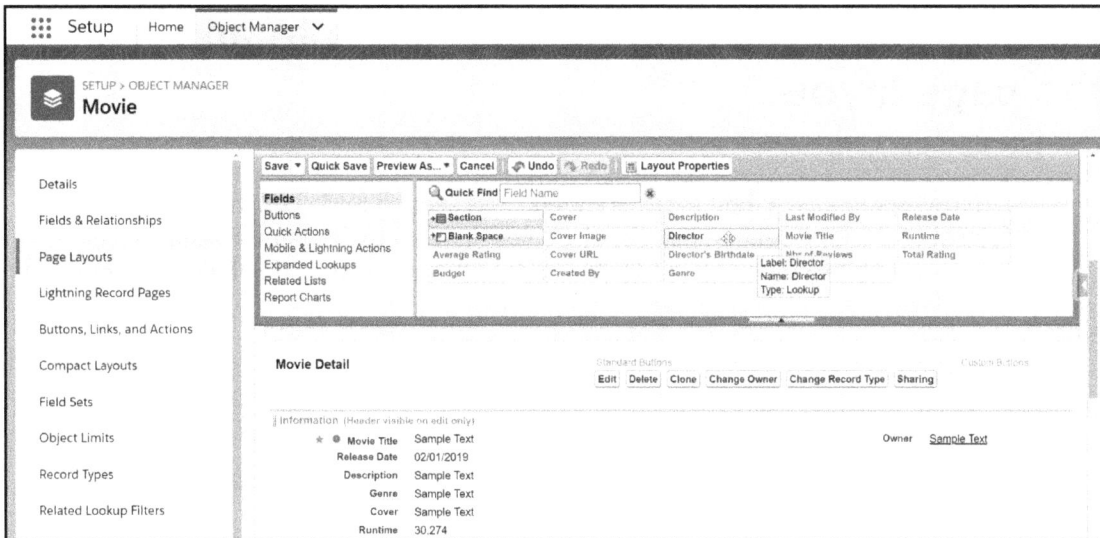

2. In the **Fields** pane on top of the page, you will see that our **Director** field is still selectable. This means that that field is not used on the page layout yet. You can select it and drag it onto the page where you would like it between the other fields that are already present on the page.

3. Add the **Director** field, remove the **Owner** field, and move the fields on the layout to get the following result:

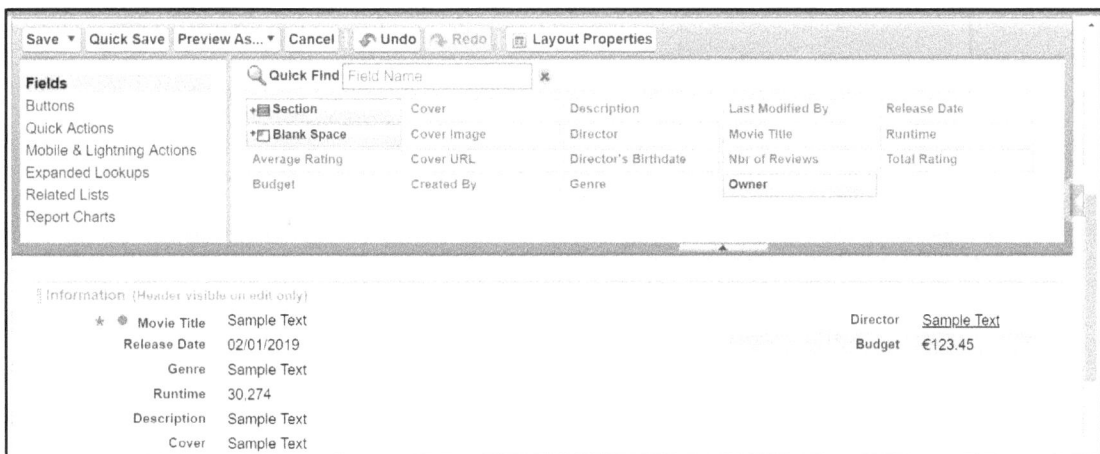

Adding and removing Related Lists to and from the page layout

Consider the following steps:

1. Now, scroll down a bit to the **Related Lists** section and click the little wrench next to the **Cast** related list. For the columns, add the **Person: Person Name** field by adding it to the **Selected Fields** column from the available fields column and hit **OK**, as shown in the following screenshot:

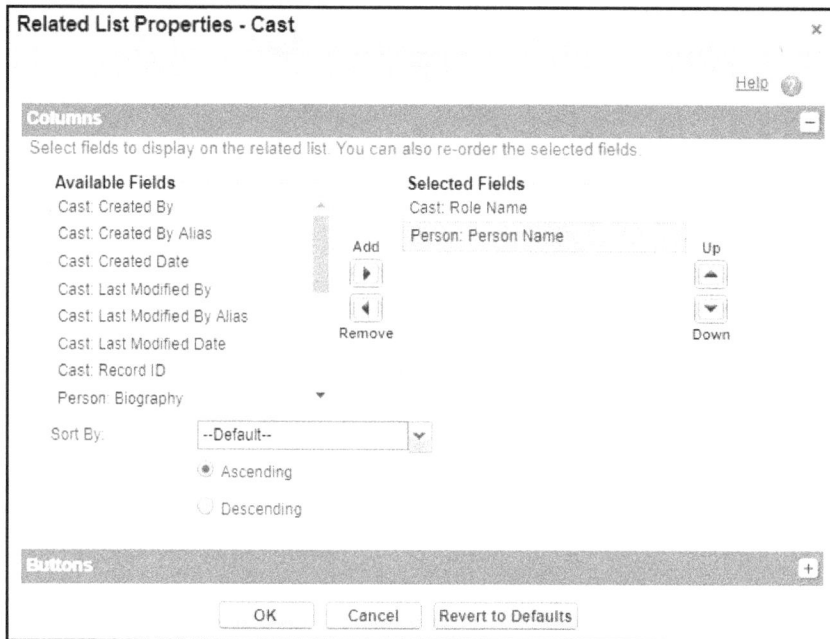

2. This way, we will be able to see the actor name next to his role name for a movie. Let's also add our newly created related lists to the page layout. On top of the page where you will find the fields, you will also see a section called **Related Lists**. Click that, instead of **Fields**; you will now have the ability to see which related lists are available for you to add to the page layout:

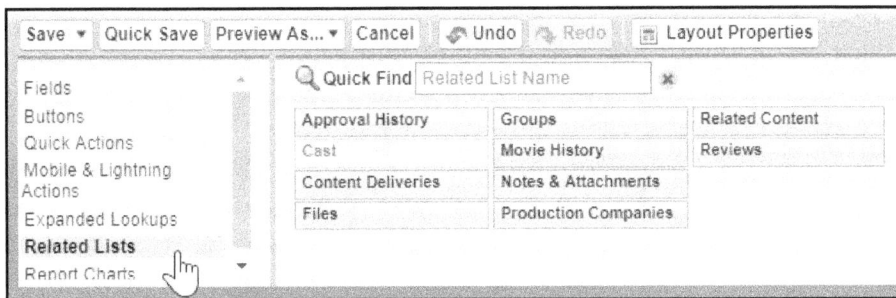

3. Drag the **Production Companies** and **Reviews** related lists to the bottom of the page layout under the **Cast** related list:

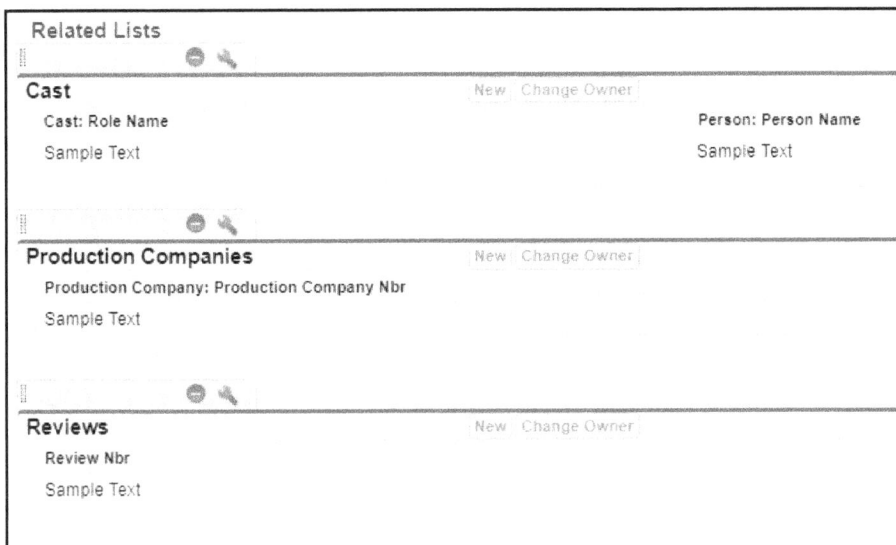

4. Now for each, click the wrench (settings) and select the fields to show as columns (max 10 fields per related list):

   - For **Production Companies,** add **Company Name** and **Address.**
   - For **Reviews,** add **Description** and **Rating.**

5. When finished, click on **Save** on top of the page and confirm that you want to overwrite the users' personal related list customizations by clicking **YES** in the popup.

6. Close this browser tab so that you can come back to your App Builder page and click **Refresh** on the top of the page. You should see your new **Director** field in the preview and any other changes you have made to your fields placements:

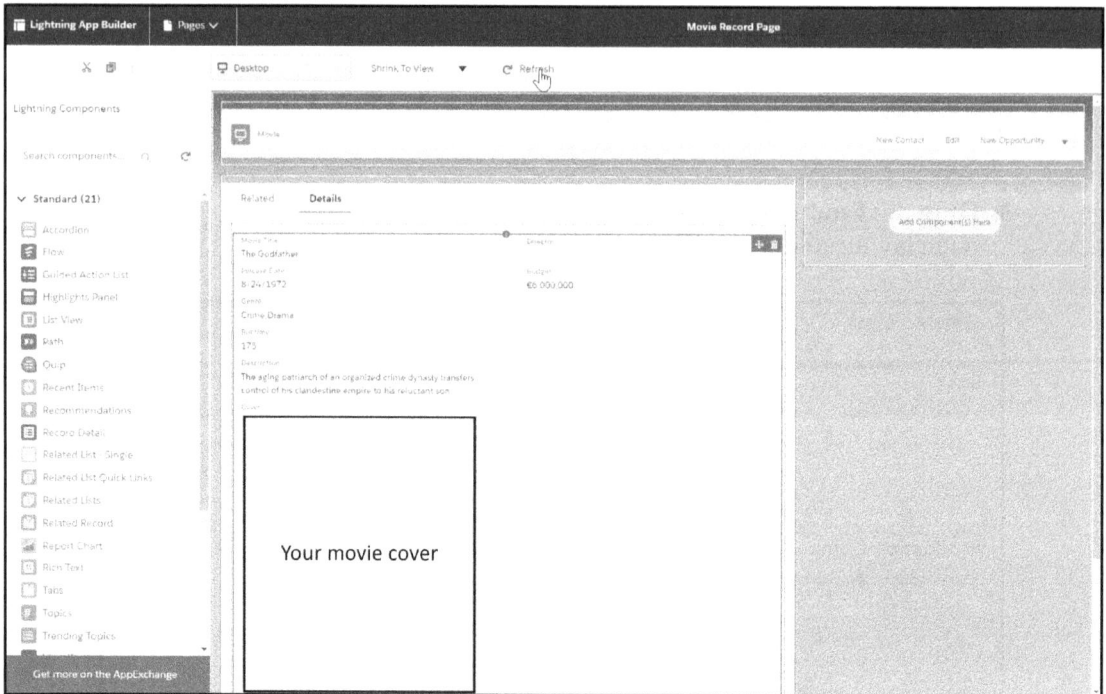

7. Also, click the **Related** inner tab to see whether your related lists have been properly added.
8. You are now done. Save your changes by clicking **Save** in the top-right corner of the App Builder and confirm the activation of the page by clicking **Activate**. In the popup, choose **Assign** as the org default.
9. When that's done, click the back button on the top right of the App Builder to go back to your movie record in our BIM DB app.

Updating records

Now, let's fill in some data in our newly created fields and relationships:

1. Update the **Director** field to `Francis Ford Coppola`; you'll notice that we haven't created a record for Francis Ford Coppola in the **Person** table yet, but you can do that directly while updating the movie record's director lookup. Just click the **New Person** choice and fill in the following details:

   - Person Name: `Francis Ford Coppola`.
   - Biography: `Here comes the biography of Francis Ford Coppola`.
   - Birthdate: April 7th, 1939.

2. Click on **Save**.

3. Now, you should have a clickable link to the `Francis Ford Coppola` person on the movie record of **The Godfather**:

4. Now, if you click on the **Francis Ford Coppola** relation, you'll find yourself on its **Person** record page layout. This seems OK, but check the **Related** tab; here, we see only the **Cast** related list and not the **Movies** related list for which **Francis Ford Coppola** is the director. I'm not going to re-explain how to adapt the page layout, since we just did that, but go ahead and modify the page layout and add the related list **Movies** to the **Person** page layout and make sure that **Movie Title**, **Genre**, **Release date**, and **Runtime** are visible as columns. The result should look like this:

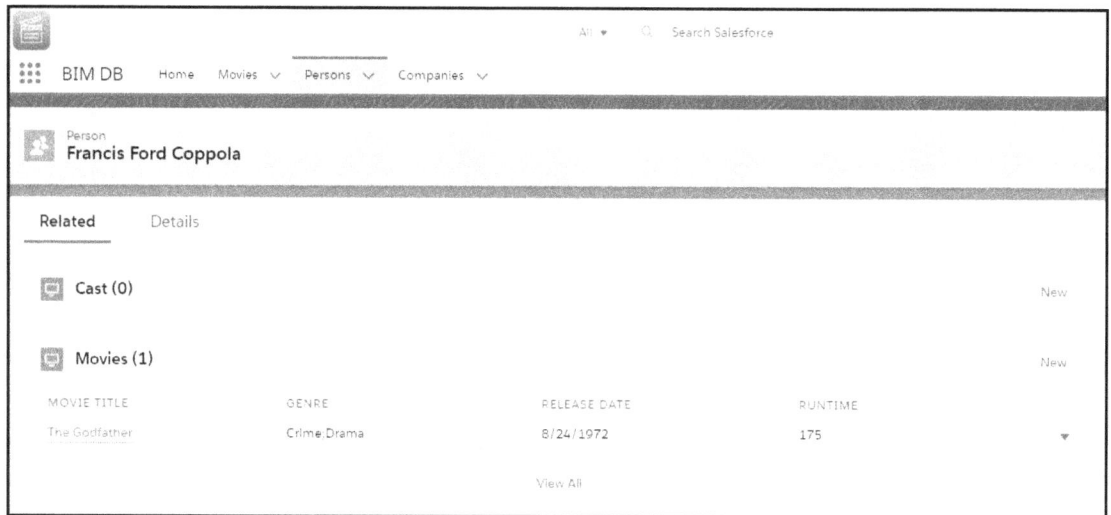

5. OK, great work! Now, let's go back to our movie record, **The Godfather**, and add two production companies in the **Production Companies** related list.

6. Click **New** in the related list and search for **Paramount Pictures** (which we already have as a record in the **Company** table).

7. Add a second production company, but now click the **New** button to create a new company record at once for **Alfran Productions** with the address, **1125 Gayley Ave Los Angeles, CA 90024**. Now, the result should look like the following screenshot:

This is really starting to make sense now. Our BIM DB app is coming to life and we are able to create movies, people, companies, and reviews, linking them and automatically having complete overviews from every angle.

Until now, we have been creating single records manually to test out our app and build it out. It seems that our foundational structure and data model is almost ready to fill our BIM DB with loads of movies, actors and actresses, directors, production companies, and reviews. But, it would be a very tedious work to create those records one by one. Don't worry, we won't be doing that. Luckily for us, in the next section we'll see and learn the different ways we can import data into our Salesforce environment in bulk. So, let's get on with it.

Importing and exporting data into development environments

Often, users will create and update records in your database manually one by one, but you'll often be confronted with the fact that you would like to mass import, export, update, or delete data from your Salesforce database.

Importing data

You can easily import data from external sources into Salesforce as long as the external source can provide you with a comma-separated values format (`.csv`).

Salesforce supports two main methods for importing data:

- **Data Import Wizard**: This is an in-browser wizard that is accessible through the **Setup** menu. It lets you import data in your account, contacts, leads, campaign members, solution-standard objects, and in custom objects. It's a very simple interface that lets you import up to 50,000 records at a time. It can detect and avoid duplicates while importing and it's also possible to deactivate all workflow rules while doing the import. The following screenshot shows the interface of the Data Import Wizard in Salesforce:

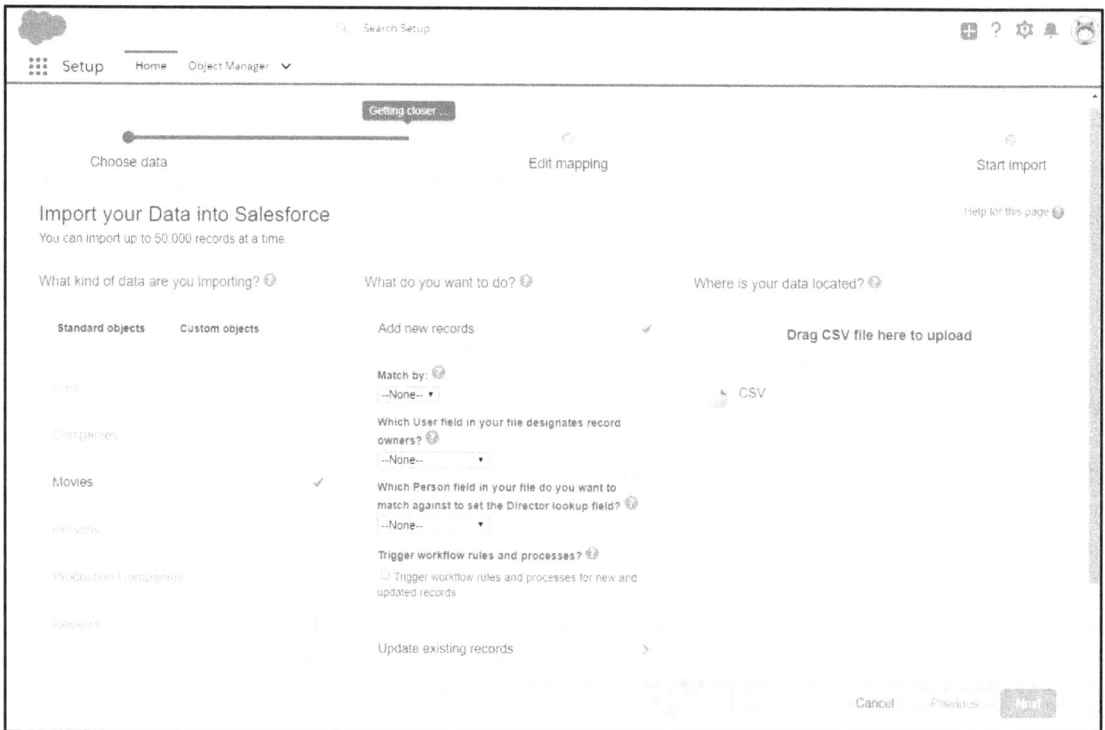

- **Data Loader**: This is a client application that is downloaded onto your local PC and allows access to your org using the Salesforce API. The latest version of Salesforce Data Loader can be downloaded from the **Setup** menu, under **Integrations**. There is a copy for Windows and macOS. Data Loader lets you import data into any object. You can use the Data Loader through its application's UI or through the command line (this makes it possible to automate import and export processes through scripts). It can import up to 5 million records at a time, but cannot detect or avoid duplicates, and there is no setting to deactivate the workflow rules while importing. If necessary, you can first deactivate the workflow rules manually in Salesforce before running the import through Data Loader and, afterwards, the successful import will reactivate them manually:

Data Import Wizard can be used in the following situations:

- When the number of records to load are less than 50,000
- When the data needs to be imported into custom objects or into some of the following standard objects—**Account**, **Contact**, **Lead**, **Campaign Member**, or **Solution**
- When the import process does not have to be automated

Data Loader can be used in the following situations:

- When the number of records to load exceeds 50,000 records, or you need to import up to 5 million records
- When the data needs to be loaded into an object that isn't supported by the Data Import Wizard, such as **Case**, **Task**, **Opportunity**, and **Event**
- If you want to set up an automated import process, such as daily nightly imports

The following table shows the difference between Data Import Wizard and Data Loader:

Data Import Wizard	Data Loader
Embedded in Salesforce **Setup**.	A separate application that requires installation
Up to 50,000 records	For complex imports, up to 5 records
Supports custom objects and only the following standard objects—**Account**, **Contact, Lead, Campaign Member**, and **Solution**	Supports all standard and custom objects
Can not be used to delete records	Can delete records
Can deactivate workflow rules while importing	Can not deactivate workflow rules while importing
Duplicates can be avoided	Can not avoid duplicates
Can not be operated through the command line	Can be operated through the **command-line interface** (**CLI**)
No automatic, scheduled imports available	Can schedule automatic imports using the CLI

Some worthwhile notes on loading data are as follows:

- **Field accessibility**: You can only load data into fields and objects for which you have read and edit access from your profile.
- **New values for picklists and multi-select picklists**: When importing a value that does not exist as picklist value in Salesforce, follow these guidelines:
    - If it's an unrestricted picklist field, the Data Import Wizard and Data Loader will use the value from your import file
    - If it's a restricted picklist field, the Data Import Wizard uses the picklist's default value and the Data Loader will give an error message
- **Multi-select picklists**: To populate a multi-select picklist with multiple values, those values must be in one cell and separated by a semicolon. Only 100 values can be populated in a multi-select picklist field at a time through an import.
- **Checkboxes**: For checkboxes, you can use **TRUE**, **FALSE**, or **1** for checked values and **0** for unchecked values.
- **Default values**: For picklist, multi-select picklist, and checkbox fields, if your import file does not have such fields mapped and in Salesforce, a default value is defined and it will be populated with its default value.

- **Date/time fields**: Make sure the format of any date/time fields you are importing matches the format of your locale setting in Salesforce.
- **Formula fields**: These are read-only and cannot be imported.
- **Field validation rules**: These are evaluated before records are imported. If a record fails a validation, then that record will not be imported. If necessary, you could deactivate validation rules prior to the manual import.
- **Geolocation custom fields**: You must supply two values: a latitude and a longitude, separated by a semicolon.
- **Currency fields**: As with date/time, currency values must be in the same currency format as your local settings in Salesforce.

Exporting data

Data can be exported from Salesforce to `.csv` the files . Salesforce provides two methods for exporting data:

- **Salesforce Data Export**: This is an online tool available through **Setup**. It has a very simple interface, just like the Data Import Wizard. It lets you export data from any object. Exports can be scheduled on a weekly or monthly basis. When a scheduled export is ready for download, you will receive an email notification containing a link that allows you to download your file(s), and you can also access this link from the export page.
- **Data Loader**: Data Loader is a client application that you need to install. The tool accesses your org through the Salesforce API and lets you export any data. It comes with its own UI, but you could also run it through the command line (this makes it possible to automate and schedule exports).

The following table on differences between Data Export and Data Loader in Salesforce:

Data Export	Data Loader
Embedded in Salesforce **Setup**.	Requires installation of an application.
Supports all objects.	Supports all objects.
Can not be operated through the CLI.	Can be operated through the CLI.
Automatic exports are available.	Automatic exports are available through CLI.
Restrictions on schedule intervals (weekly, monthly).	No restrictions on schedule intervals.

So, now that we know which tools exist, let's load some data in our BIM DB app using both tools. Before we start loading any data, I have made some fixes to our database that will make it easier for you to import data and make our cover image rendering better.

I removed the **Cover** rich text area field from the **Movie** object and added a **Cover URL** text field that will contain the full URL to the image hosted from IMDb (`www.imdb.com`) and a formula field that renders the image itself based upon that URL. Although I'll explain formulas in `Chapter 3`, *Declarative Automation*, I would like you to perform those modifications now, so that when we load data, we will all have the same data:

1. Go to **Setup** | **Object Manager** | **Movie** object | **Fields and Relationships**.
2. Then, next to the **Cover** field, click the arrow, select **Delete**, and confirm that you want to delete this field.
3. On this **Movie** object, click **New** to create a new text field called **Cover URL** with a length of 255 characters:

4. Now, create a new field type, **Formula**, with the output **Text** type, and call it **Cover Image**. In the formula editor, enter the following formula:

IMAGE(Cover_Url__c , "Cover", 150, 100)

5. This is an image function that takes a URL (in our case, this references our **Cover_Url__c** field), a text value that is the caption for when you hover over the image, a height for the image (in our case **150** pixels), and a width for the image (in our case **100** pixels). Your screen should look like this once you have saved the field:

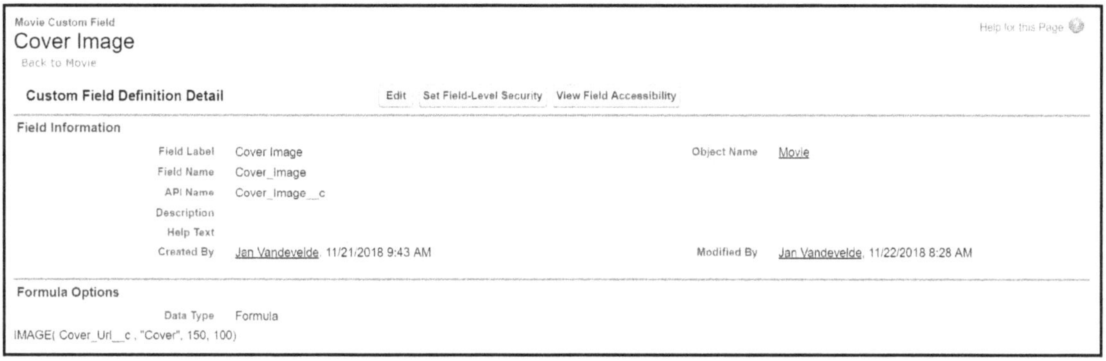

6. Okay, let's check what we did now on our **The Godfather** movie record. Navigate to **The Godfather** record. It should look like the following screenshot:

You see our big cover-image field is gone. Which is good, because we deleted it and at bottom of the page there are now two new fields, **Cover URL** and **Cover Image** (which shows the icon of an irretrievable image). This is perfect, because we haven't entered the URL where the image is hosted. Let's do that.

7. Edit the record and copy/paste `https://m.media-amazon.com/images/M/` `MV5BM2MyNjYxNmUtYTAwNi00MTYxLWJmNWYtYzZlODY3ZTk3OTFlXkEyXkFqcGcGdeQXVyNz` `kwMjQ5NzM@._V1_SY1000_CR0,0,704,1000_AL_.jpg` into the **Cover URL** field and save your changes. The formula now automatically renders the image based upon the URL you entered in the **Cover URL** field. This will make it easier for users to insert covers just by searching them on the internet and entering the URL in that field. It will also make it easier for the next steps when we load the same data.

8. Let's load some data now. I have a couple of `.csv` files for you in the `.zip` folder; one for every object. Just to be safe and make sure we're on the same page here, we'll delete the test data we already created together. Go to the **The Godfather** movie record and hit **Delete** or from the **Movies** tab, click the little arrow on the right next to the movie you want to delete, and delete it.

9. Do the same for **Persons** and for **Companies**. Delete all the data you already created. Remember that **Cast** and **Production Companies** were both master-detail relationships, so, by deleting **Movie**, **Person**, and **Company**, all those child records will also be deleted. I'm telling you this so you won't worry that you have no tab for them and you would not be sure how to delete those. In order to prevent issues on currency and date fields, adapt your user **Locale Settings** to the following:

Locale Settings	
Time Zone	(GMT+02:00) Central European Summer Time (Europe/Paris) ▼
Locale	English (United Kingdom) ▼
Language	English ▼

Now that our database is clean and empty, we can begin. Because we have several objects to load and there are relationships between them, the order in which data is loaded is important. Just like we have built our app together in steps, we'll load data in steps, because, to load the related records, we'll need the generated Salesforce record ID to fill the lookup fields and master-detail fields with their corresponding record IDs.

So, the order we will load data in will be as follows:

1. First, the stand-alone records:
   - **Person**
   - **Company**
2. Then, our movie records, because they have a direct lookup filled to a **Person** for the **Director** field!
3. Finally, all the related records:
   - **Cast**
   - **Production Company**
   - **Review**

This also means that we'll be exporting data once it's created, so we have their corresponding record IDs, and then, in Excel, we'll be attaching those IDs, where needed, with a VLOOKUP function.

Importing data through the Data Import Wizard

Let's load the stand-alone **Person** and **Company** records using the Data Import Wizard:

1. Navigate to **Setup** | **Integrations** | **Data Import Wizard** and click the **Launch Wizard!** button in the middle of the page.
2. Select **Persons** from the **Custom Objects** tab.
3. Select **Add New Records** and leave the **Match by** and **Designated Owner** fields empty (none).

4. Drag and drop the `Person.csv` file that you'll find in the **Data Files** folder from the **Resources Zip** folder into the **Where is your data located** section. Your screen should look like this:

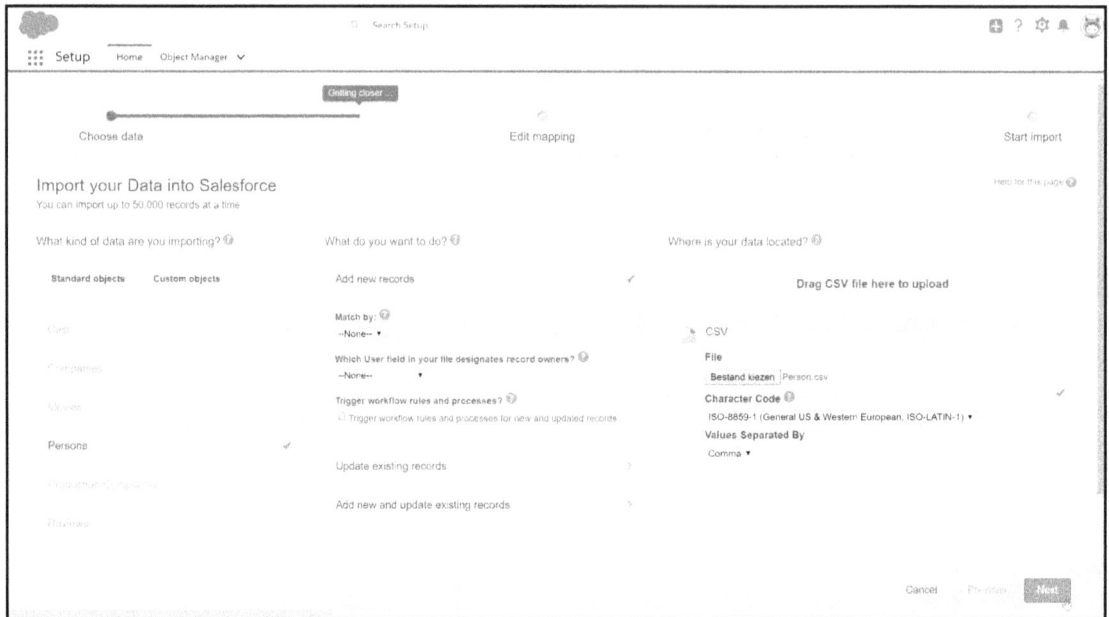

5. Click on **Next** to go to the field mapping wizard:

6. You'll see that **Person Name** has been mapped automatically with the **Name** column from your .csv file, but the biography and birthdate haven't been automatically detected, so we'll need to map those manually.

7. Click the **Map** link to the left of each unmapped field and select the correct column from your `.csv` file that contains the value for that Salesforce field. On the right of the screen, you'll see example data, so you can be sure that you have mapped the correct fields. The end result should look as follows:

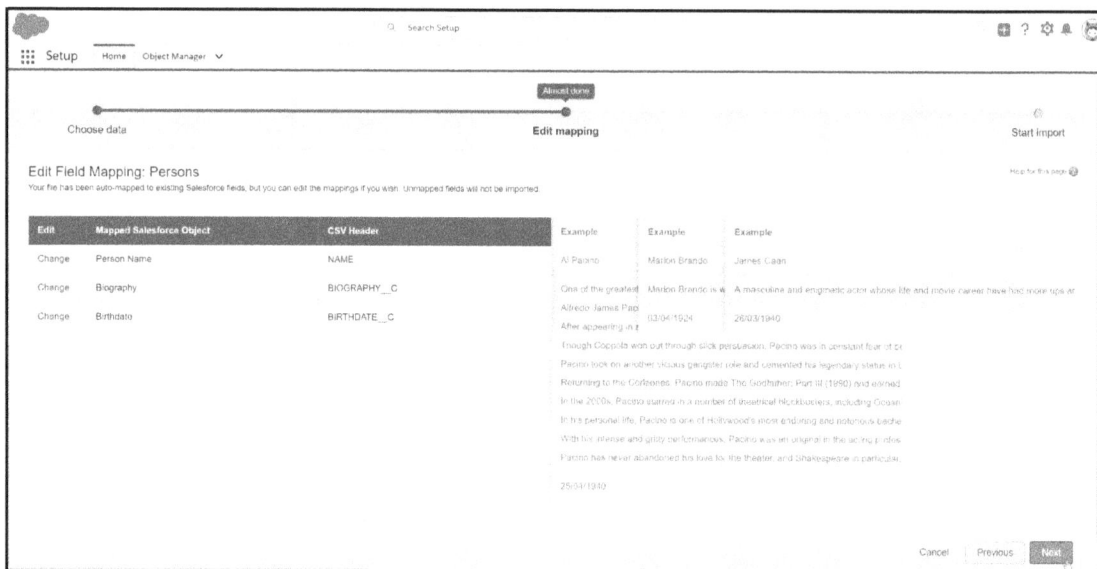

8. Click **Next**. You will get a summary screen showing how many fields have been mapped and how many fields are not mapped before starting the actual import, like this:

9. If everything looks fine to you, hit **Start Import!** You'll get a success screen that the import has started and that you can follow the import from **Setup—Bulk Data Load Jobs Page**, which it will automatically redirect you to:

We can monitor data loads with the Data Import Wizard from this screen. We can see that we processed 22 **Person** records and have no failures. If there where failures, you could click the **View Result** link, which will open a `.csv` file containing the success and errors with an error message, explaining what caused the record not to be create. this could be due to a bad date format or a description that has more characters than a field could contain.

Let's check whether the data is actually in our org by going to our BIM DB app and clicking the **Persons** tab (select **All** from the list view instead of **Recently Viewed**) to see all the loaded records:

	PERSON NAME ↑
1	Al Pacino
2	Ben Kingsley
3	Bob Gunton
4	Christian Bale
5	Christopher Nolan
6	Diane Keaton
7	Francis Ford Coppola
8	Frank Darabont
9	Gary Oldman
10	Heath Ledger
11	James Caan
12	Katie Holmes
13	Liam Neeson
14	Maggie Gyllenhaal
15	Marlon Brando
16	Michael Caine
17	Morgan Freeman
18	Quentin Tarantino
19	Ralph Fiennes
20	Robert Duvall
21	Steven Spielberg
22	Tim Robbins

BIM DB — Home Movies **Persons** Companies

Persons
All ▼

22 items • Sorted by Person Name • Filtered by all persons • Updated a few seconds ago

Now do exactly the same for the `Company.csv` file; six records should have been successfully imported in your **Companies** tab.

Exporting data through Data Export

For the next imports, we will be needing the Salesforce record IDs of the newly created **Person** and **Company** objects. To get those IDs, we'll need to export that data. Let's do that using the built-in Data Export functionality:

1. Navigate to **Setup | Data Export** and click on **Export Now**. Leave the defaults on top of the page, and select our two custom objects, `Person__c` and `Company__c`. The custom objects are at the bottom of the page:

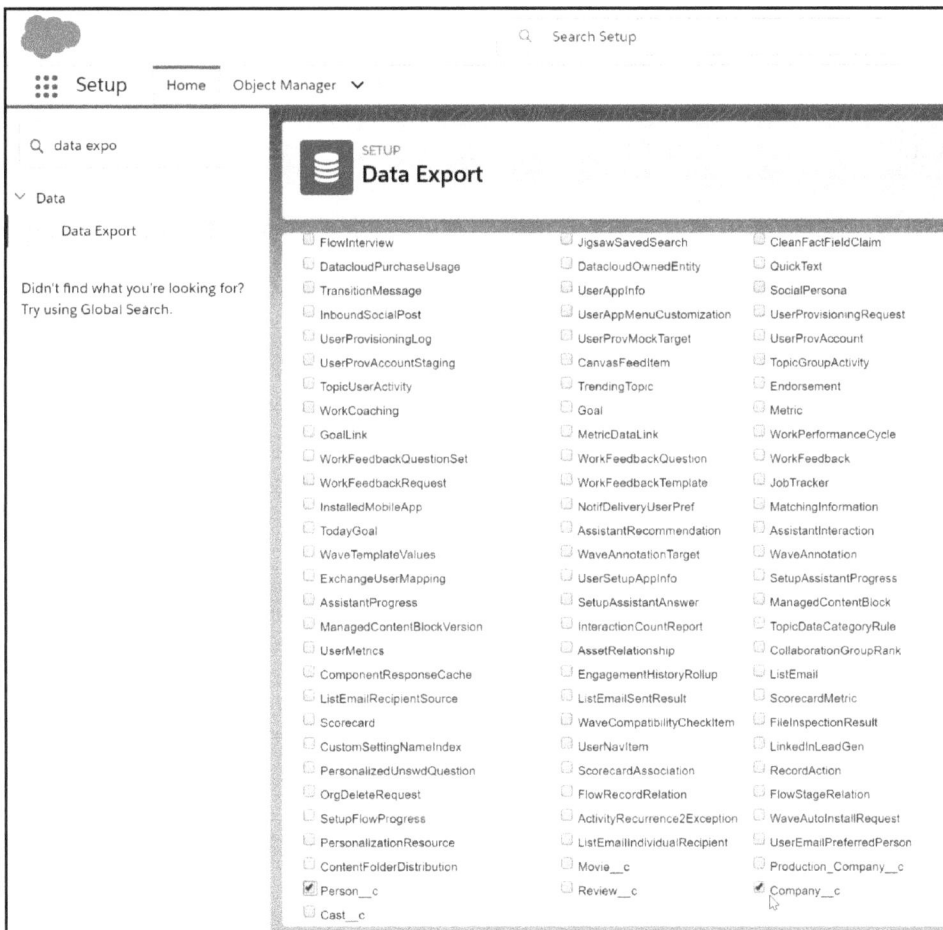

2. After selecting the objects you want to export, hit **Start Export!**. You'll get the following confirmation screen, telling you that the export is now scheduled and that you will be receiving an email when the data is ready:

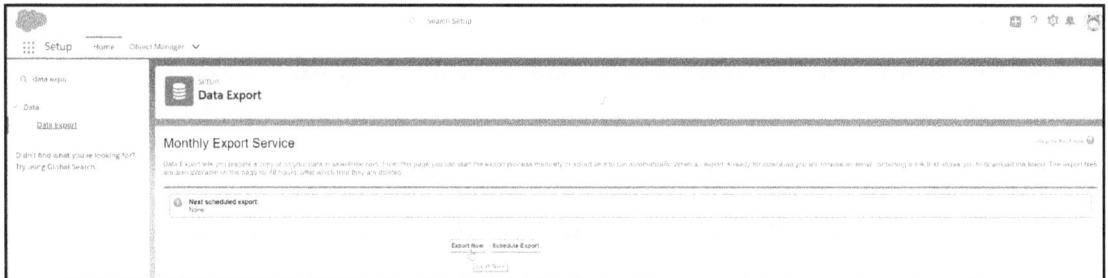

3. The email will look like this, so just click on the link to download the export file(s):

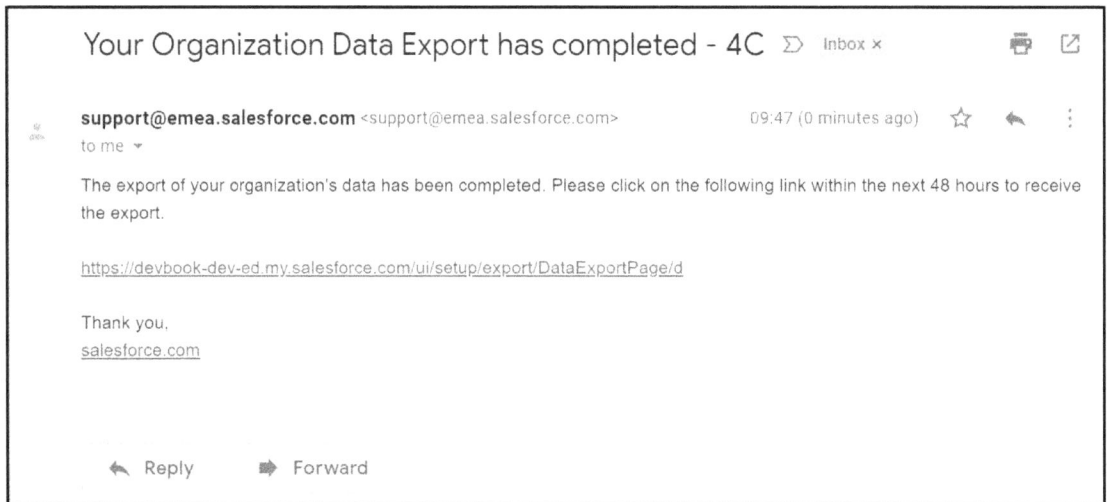

Your Organization Data Export has completed - 4C Inbox ×

support@emea.salesforce.com <support@emea.salesforce.com>   09:47 (0 minutes ago)

to me ▾

The export of your organization's data has been completed. Please click on the following link within the next 48 hours to receive the export.

https://devbook-dev-ed.my.salesforce.com/ui/setup/export/DataExportPage/d

Thank you,
salesforce.com

← Reply   → Forward

4. Click the download link below the **Action** field. This will download a `.zip` file, containing a `.csv` file for each object, containing its records. Save the `.zip` file in any folder you would like or on your desktop. When you open it, it should look like the following:

5. Let's look at the contents of the `Person__c` file. This file contains all fields that currently exist for the `Person__c` object to which you have access, including system fields such as `CreatedDate` and `CreatedBy`. The most important column is the first column, called `Id`. This is the Salesforce record ID for each record, and, in the next sections when we need to create any relationship between records, we will need to fill the lookup fields with the ID of the record we want to associate:

Remember, for example, our **The Godfather** movie, which has a lookup field called **Director**, which is a relationship to a **Person** record that corresponds to that director, right? So, when we load our movies, we will need to populate the `Director` field with the ID of the **Person** record that corresponds to **Francis Ford Coppola**, highlighted in green in the following screenshot:

This means that, for the next imports, we will first have to do some Excel magic by performing `VLOOKUP` functions to populate the lookup columns with their correct corresponding record IDs from those export files. Don't worry, we'll go through it step by step.

So, that's one way to load data into Salesforce by using the Data Import Wizard, and one way to export data from Salesforce by using the Data Export functionality.

Importing data through Data Loader

Now, I'm going to be completely honest; in the 10 years I've worked with Salesforce, this is the method I have used the least. I honestly don't know why, because it's easy to use, but I find myself using Data Loader much more, because it has the most capabilities and I guess I just got used to always using the same tools for importing and exporting.

So, for the next steps, we'll be using Data Loader. As mentioned before, Data Loader is an application that needs to be installed on your computer. So, let's do that first.

1. Navigate to **Setup** | **Integrations** | **Data Loader** to find the download files for Windows or Mac:

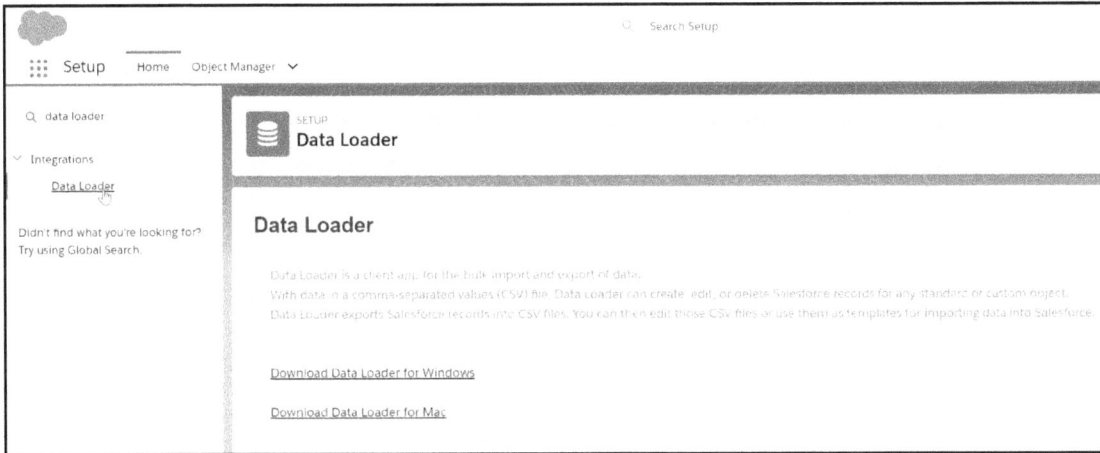

2. Select the one that suits your operating system and install it; you'll need administrator rights on your PC. Accept the license agreements. You can also leave the default install location as it is.

3. Once installed, double-click the cloud icon on your desktop, representing Data Loader, to run the application. Let's first set some settings by clicking **Settings** on the menu. Please make sure that you set your settings exactly the same as mine, as shown in the following screenshot:

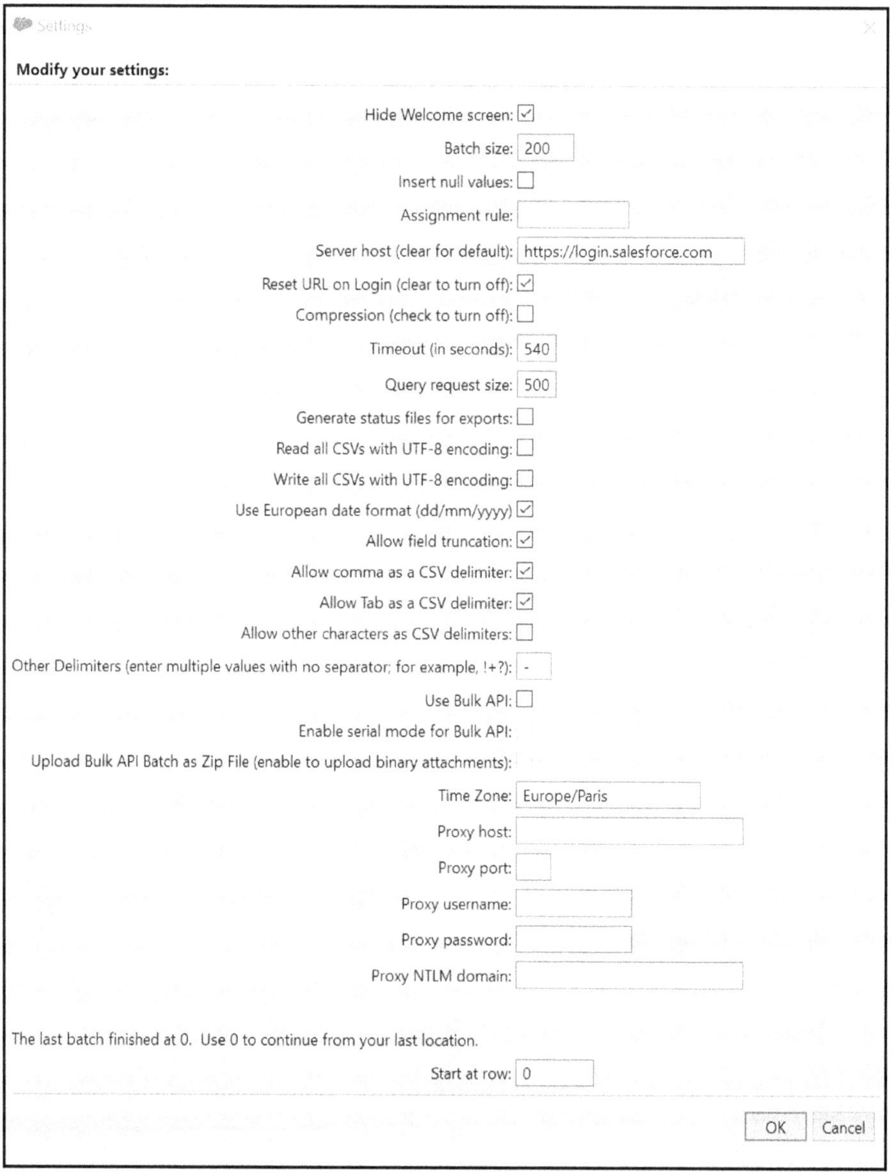

Hide Welcome screen:	☑
Batch size:	200
Insert null values:	☐
Assignment rule:	
Server host (clear for default):	https://login.salesforce.com
Reset URL on Login (clear to turn off):	☑
Compression (check to turn off):	☐
Timeout (in seconds):	540
Query request size:	500
Generate status files for exports:	☐
Read all CSVs with UTF-8 encoding:	☐
Write all CSVs with UTF-8 encoding:	☐
Use European date format (dd/mm/yyyy)	☑
Allow field truncation:	☑
Allow comma as a CSV delimiter:	☑
Allow Tab as a CSV delimiter:	☑
Allow other characters as CSV delimiters:	☐
Other Delimiters (enter multiple values with no separator; for example, !+?):	-
Use Bulk API:	☐
Enable serial mode for Bulk API:	
Upload Bulk API Batch as Zip File (enable to upload binary attachments):	
Time Zone:	Europe/Paris
Proxy host:	
Proxy port:	
Proxy username:	
Proxy password:	
Proxy NTLM domain:	

The last batch finished at 0. Use 0 to continue from your last location.

Start at row: 0

OK Cancel

This is important for the rest of the exercises. If you would like to know what each setting means, I recommend that you read the following page on Salesforce help and training: `https://help.salesforce.com/articleView?id=configuring_the_data_loader.htmtype=5`

4. Okay, let's prepare our **Movie** file for import now! Open up the `Movie.csv` file from the resources zip folder. Ensure that the `Director__c` column is blank and that we have the `Director__R.Name column` next to it. The `Name` column contains the name of the **Person** record. We'll be using this name to do a `VLOOKUP` into the `Person.csv` file we just exported, containing the record IDs, to populate our `Director__c` column:

5. Simultaneously, open up the exported `Person.csv` file. Now, to do a correct `VLOOKUP`, it's important that the value we search for to return the corresponding value from another column is on the right of the result! So, select the whole `Name` column from the person file, right-click, and select **Cut**.

6. Then, select the whole `Id` (first column) column, right-click, and select **Insert Cut cells**. This will result in the `Name` column being before the `Id` column and the rest of the data staying untouched, like so:

	A	B	C	D	E	F	G	H	I	J	K
1	Name	Id	OwnerId	IsDeleted	CreatedDate	CreatedById	LastModifiedDate	LastModifiedById	SystemModstamp	Biography__c	Birthdate__c
2	Al Pacino	a021t000005d7h2AAA	0051t000000jdFwAAI	0	22/11/2018 09:02	0051t000000jdFwAAI	22/11/2018 09:02	0051t000000jdFwAAI	22/11/2018 09:02	One of the greatest act	25/04/1940 00:00
3	Marlon Brando	a021t000005d7h3AAA	0051t000000jdFwAAI	0	22/11/2018 09:02	0051t000000jdFwAAI	22/11/2018 09:02	0051t000000jdFwAAI	22/11/2018 09:02	Marlon Brando is wide	03/04/1924 00:00
4	James Caan	a021t000005d7h4AAA	0051t000000jdFwAAI	0	22/11/2018 09:02	0051t000000jdFwAAI	22/11/2018 09:02	0051t000000jdFwAAI	22/11/2018 09:02	A masculine and enigm	26/03/1940 00:00
5	Robert Duvall	a021t000005d7h5AAA	0051t000000jdFwAAI	0	22/11/2018 09:02	0051t000000jdFwAAI	22/11/2018 09:02	0051t000000jdFwAAI	22/11/2018 09:02	Veteran actor and dire	04/01/1931 00:00
6	Diane Keaton	a021t000005d7h6AAA	0051t000000jdFwAAI	0	22/11/2018 09:02	0051t000000jdFwAAI	22/11/2018 09:02	0051t000000jdFwAAI	22/11/2018 09:02	Diane Keaton was born	05/01/1946 00:00
7	Frank Darabont	a021t000005d7h7AAA	0051t000000jdFwAAI	0	22/11/2018 09:02	0051t000000jdFwAAI	22/11/2018 09:02	0051t000000jdFwAAI	22/11/2018 09:02	Three-time Oscar nom	28/01/1959 00:00
8	Tim Robbins	a021t000005d7h8AAA	0051t000000jdFwAAI	0	22/11/2018 09:02	0051t000000jdFwAAI	22/11/2018 09:02	0051t000000jdFwAAI	22/11/2018 09:02	Born in West Covina, C	16/10/1958 00:00
9	Morgan Freeman	a021t000005d7h9AAA	0051t000000jdFwAAI	0	22/11/2018 09:02	0051t000000jdFwAAI	22/11/2018 09:02	0051t000000jdFwAAI	22/11/2018 09:02	With an authoritative v	01/06/1937 00:00
10	Bob Gunton	a021t000005d7hAAAQ	0051t000000jdFwAAI	0	22/11/2018 09:02	0051t000000jdFwAAI	22/11/2018 09:02	0051t000000jdFwAAI	22/11/2018 09:02	Bob Gunton was born	15/11/1945 00:00
11	Christopher Nolan	a021t000005d7hBAAQ	0051t000000jdFwAAI	0	22/11/2018 09:02	0051t000000jdFwAAI	22/11/2018 09:02	0051t000000jdFwAAI	22/11/2018 09:02	Best known for his cer	30/07/1970 00:00
12	Christian Bale	a021t000005d7hCAAQ	0051t000000jdFwAAI	0	22/11/2018 09:02	0051t000000jdFwAAI	22/11/2018 09:02	0051t000000jdFwAAI	22/11/2018 09:02	Christian Charles Philip	30/01/1974 00:00
13	Heath Ledger	a021t000005d7hDAAQ	0051t000000jdFwAAI	0	22/11/2018 09:02	0051t000000jdFwAAI	22/11/2018 09:02	0051t000000jdFwAAI	22/11/2018 09:02	When hunky, twenty-y	04/04/1979 00:00
14	Maggie Gyllenhaal	a021t000005d7hEAAQ	0051t000000jdFwAAI	0	22/11/2018 09:02	0051t000000jdFwAAI	22/11/2018 09:02	0051t000000jdFwAAI	22/11/2018 09:02	Academy Award-nomi	16/11/1977 00:00
15	Michael Caine	a021t000005d7hFAAQ	0051t000000jdFwAAI	0	22/11/2018 09:02	0051t000000jdFwAAI	22/11/2018 09:02	0051t000000jdFwAAI	22/11/2018 09:02	Michael Caine was bor	13/03/1933 00:00
16	Katie Holmes	a021t000005d7hGAAQ	0051t000000jdFwAAI	0	22/11/2018 09:02	0051t000000jdFwAAI	22/11/2018 09:02	0051t000000jdFwAAI	22/11/2018 09:02	Born two months prem	18/12/1978 00:00
17	Liam Neeson	a021t000005d7hHAAQ	0051t000000jdFwAAI	0	22/11/2018 09:02	0051t000000jdFwAAI	22/11/2018 09:02	0051t000000jdFwAAI	22/11/2018 09:02	Liam Neeson was born	07/06/1952 00:00
18	Gary Oldman	a021t000005d7hIAAQ	0051t000000jdFwAAI	0	22/11/2018 09:02	0051t000000jdFwAAI	22/11/2018 09:02	0051t000000jdFwAAI	22/11/2018 09:02	Gary Oldman is a talen	21/03/1958 00:00
19	Francis Ford Coppola	a021t000005d7hJAAQ	0051t000000jdFwAAI	0	22/11/2018 09:02	0051t000000jdFwAAI	22/11/2018 09:02	0051t000000jdFwAAI	22/11/2018 09:02	Francis Ford Coppola v	06/04/1939 00:00
20	Steven Spielberg	a021t000005d7hKAAQ	0051t000000jdFwAAI	0	22/11/2018 09:02	0051t000000jdFwAAI	22/11/2018 09:02	0051t000000jdFwAAI	22/11/2018 09:02	One of the most influe	18/12/1946 00:00
21	Ben Kingsley	a021t000005d7hJAAQ	0051t000000jdFwAAI	0	22/11/2018 09:02	0051t000000jdFwAAI	22/11/2018 09:02	0051t000000jdFwAAI	22/11/2018 09:02	Ben Kingsley was born	31/12/1943 00:00
22	Ralph Fiennes	a021t000005d7hMAAQ	0051t000000jdFwAAI	0	22/11/2018 09:02	0051t000000jdFwAAI	22/11/2018 09:02	0051t000000jdFwAAI	22/11/2018 09:02	Actor Ralph Nathaniel	22/12/1962 00:00
23	Quentin Tarantino	a021t000005d7hNAAQ	0051t000000jdFwAAI	0	22/11/2018 09:02	0051t000000jdFwAAI	22/11/2018 09:02	0051t000000jdFwAAI	22/11/2018 09:02	Quentin Jerome Taran	27/03/1963 00:00

7. Great, now we'll be performing our `VLOOKUP` in the `Movie` file, in which we want to populate the record ID, found in our `Person` file, corresponding to the `Director_R.Name` value from the `Movie` file for each record in the file!

8. So, navigate to your `Movie` file and click the first empty cell in the `Director__c` column and type the following VLOOKUP formula in that cell:

= VLOOKUP(H2,Person__c.csv!$A:$B,2,FALSE)

What does the formula do?

=VLOOKUP (The value you want to look up (the director name for that row), the range where you want to lookup the value (search for the name in our `Person__c.csv` file in columns A and B, because A contains the values to search in and B contains the record ID we want as result if the name is found!), the column number in the range containing the return value (so the return value of our record ID is in the second column of the selected range columns A and B), exact match or approximate match—indicated as 0/FALSE or 1/TRUE (we set FALSE, so we want an exact matching name found!)).

9. When you hit enter, after having typed the formula, you should see that the first cell gets populated with the corresponding ID from the person file for the director name on the same row:

E	F	G	H
BUDGET_	RUNTIME_	DIRECTOR__C	DIRECTOR__R.NAME
########	142	a021t000005d7h7AAA	Frank Darabont
########	152		Christopher Nolan
########	140		Christopher Nolan
########	195		Steven Spielberg
8,000,000	154		Quentin Tarantino
6,000,000	175		Francis Ford Coppola

But now, we need this formula in every cell of that column, or at least for each record. To copy the formula down for each record, move your mouse to the right-bottom corner of the cell containing your formula until you see the cursor change to a little black cross or plus (+) sign. If your cursor changed to the plus sign, then click (and hold) and drag your mouse down until the last corresponding cell is highlighted. Then, let go of your left mouse-click and your cells will be populated with each corresponding ID:

E	F	G	H
BUDGET_	RUNTIME_	DIRECTOR__C	DIRECTOR__R.NAME
########	142	a021t000005d7h7AAA	Frank Darabont
########	152	a021t000005d7hBAAQ	Christopher Nolan
########	140	a021t000005d7hBAAQ	Christopher Nolan
########	195	a021t000005d7hKAAQ	Steven Spielberg
8,000,000	154	a021t000005d7hNAAQ	Quentin Tarantino
6,000,000	175	a021t000005d7hJAAQ	Francis Ford Coppola

Great, but please note that the values in this column are not ready to be imported yet, because they contain formulas! That's a big no when importing the data, because, at import, they won't contain the actual values! So, we need one more step, and that's replacing those values with the actual data!

10. This is simple—just click the `Director__c` column header so that the whole column is selected, right-click and select **Copy**, then, on the same column, right-click again and select **Paste Special,** and, in the little popup, select **Values** and click **OK**:

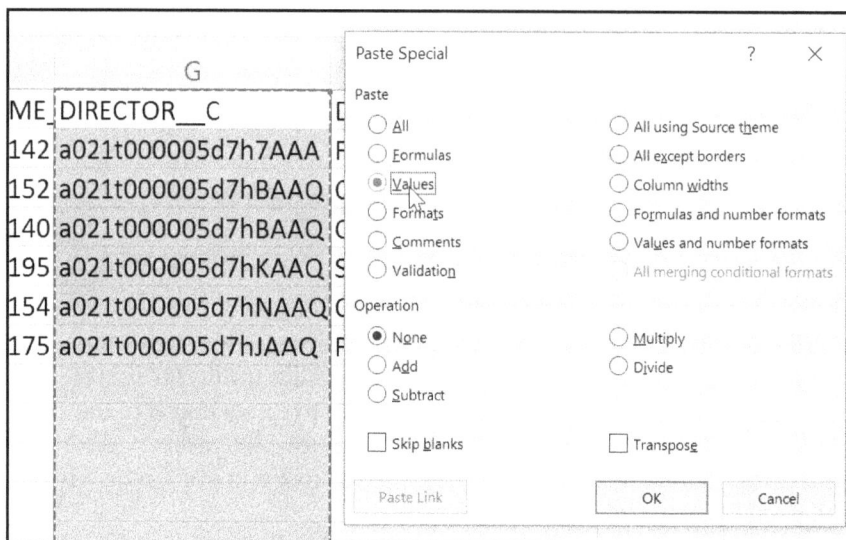

11. To verify that the formula has been replaced by the actual value, click in one of the `Director__c` cells, and in your menu bar you should see the record ID and not the `VLOOKUP` formula anymore!

12. Now, save your `Movie.csv` file so that you have the latest version, including the `Director__c` IDs. You should get used to doing `VLOOKUP` a lot, because, when loading data into Salesforce, this is an action you will need to be performing a lot. Thanks for being patient, I won't be holding off any longer. Let's import this file right now!

13. Start Data Loader. We'll be performing an insert (creating new records into our database), so click the **Insert** button.

14. Data Loader will ask you to connect to your Salesforce org, so choose **Password Authentication**, fill in your login credentials (username and password), and click **Login**. It should display a **Login successful** message, and the next button should get enabled. Hit the **Next** button after successful login.

15. The next step will ask you which object you'd like to insert. In our case, that's the **Movie__c** object. You should also select your import file, so browse your folders and select the `Movie.csv` import file you have just saved, including the director IDs:

16. When you have selected the **Movie** object and selected your import file, hit **Next,** and a pop-up message will tell you how many records you are going to import. Click **OK**.

17. In the next step, it will read the columns from your CSV, and you'll have to map them to their corresponding fields in Salesforce:

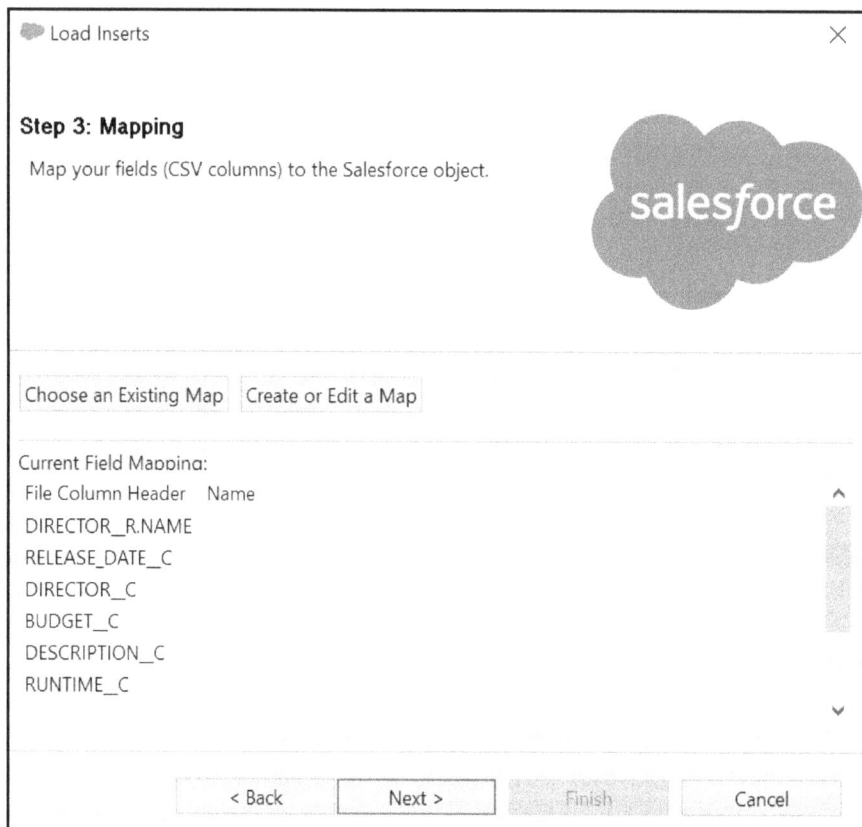

18. Click the **Create or Edit a Map** button. This opens a screen where, on top, you will see the Salesforce fields that have not been mapped yet for the selected object. In the bottom pane, you see the columns from your `.csv` file. Now click the button on top, **Auto-Match Fields to Columns**; this will automatically map fields and columns if the name corresponds:

In our case, it was able to map every field from the **Movie** object to a column, except for Owner ID. If our .csv file would have had an Owner ID, it could have mapped it too, but we didn't have that column. If no Owner ID is provided, the user doing the import will automatically become the owner of the records.

On the other hand, we can see that our `Director_R.Name` column will not be matched to any Salesforce field, and we don't have any left. This is correct because our **Movie** object does not have a director name field; it only has the **Director** lookup. The special thing about lookups is that, to load them, you need to provide the record ID, but, when you look at the field containing a value in Salesforce, a user will see the name of the corresponding record and not the ID. Cool, right? So, if you have mapped exactly like the preceding screenshot, you are ready to import, so click **OK** and then click **Next**.

19. The last step asks you where you would like the success and error files to be saved; the Data Loader will provide this automatically after the import. The success file will contain all the records, including the newly created Salesforce record ID that was successfully inserted. The error file will contain all records that failed with a clear error message stipulating why it failed. So, let's click **Finish** to start the import. You'll get a pop-up message telling you how many successes and errors you had; in our case, six successes and no failures.

20. Now, let's have a look in our BIM DB app on the **Movies** tab to find out whether we can see our six records and whether the director has been correctly related. As you can see in the following screenshot, the records are in:

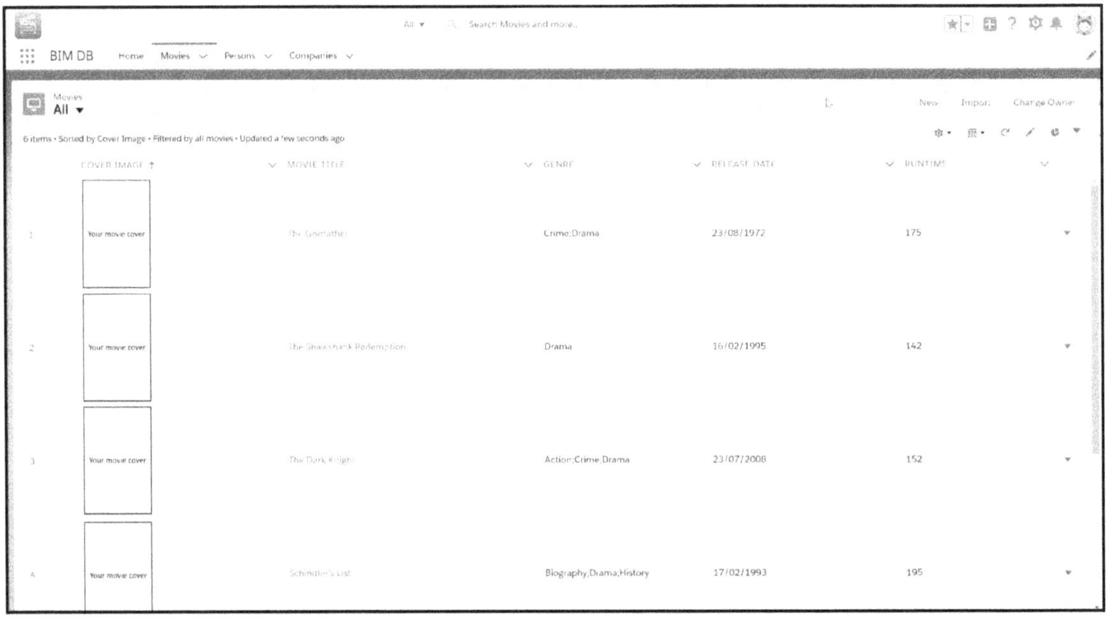

21. You will probably not see the cover images in your list view, but it looks nice anyway. You would like them, too! Now, select the **All** list view, instead of **Recently Viewed,** and then click the wrench icon on the right (right under the **New** button). Then **Select Fields to Display**:

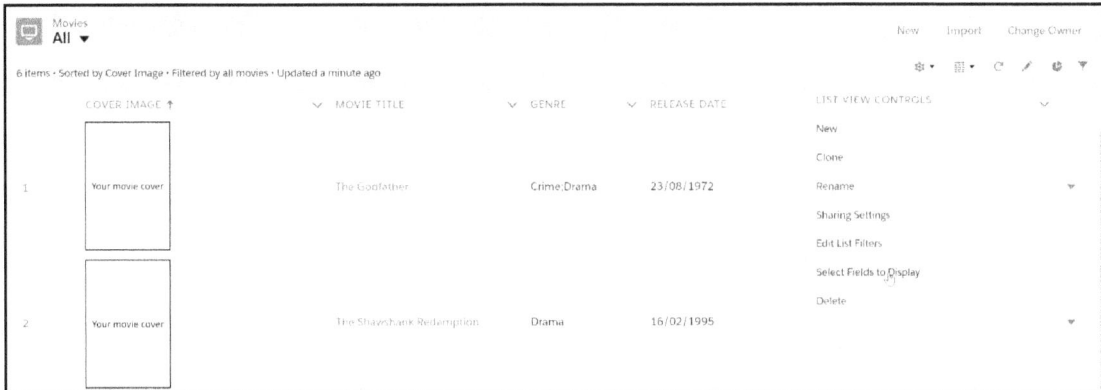

22. Select the columns (up to 10) that you'd like to see in your list view and change the order to your liking. I chose our **Cover Image** formula field as the first column.

23. Click our **The Godfather** record so that we can check whether our director, **Francis Ford Coppola**, has been correctly filled in and related:

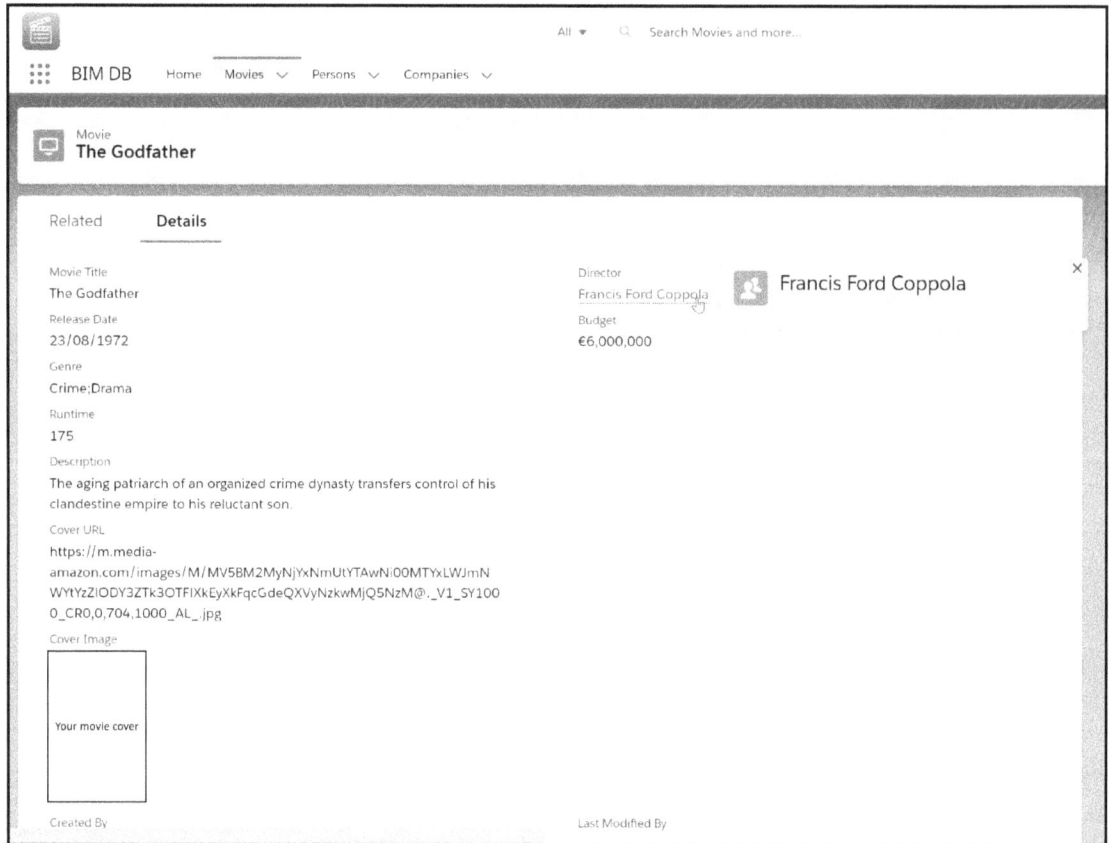

Yep, it has! Perfect, you have done your first import through Data Loader, including a VLOOKUP to relate records from another object!

We aren't done yet! With what you have learned so far, you should be able to import the following files (**Cast**, **Production Companies,** and **Reviews**) in exactly the same manner!

So, next up is **Cast**, but for cast, we will need the IDs of our newly imported **Movie** records, and also the ID's of our **Person** records (we already have this file from our first export).

Exporting data through Data Loader

For our **Movie** records, we could simply use the success file of our previous import, but I also want you to learn how to export through Data Loader, so let's use Data Loader for the export:

1. Open Data Loader (or maybe it's still open) and choose **Export**.
2. Now, select the object from which you would like to export the records; in our case, the **Movie__c** object; and browse to a place on your computer where you want to export file to be saved:

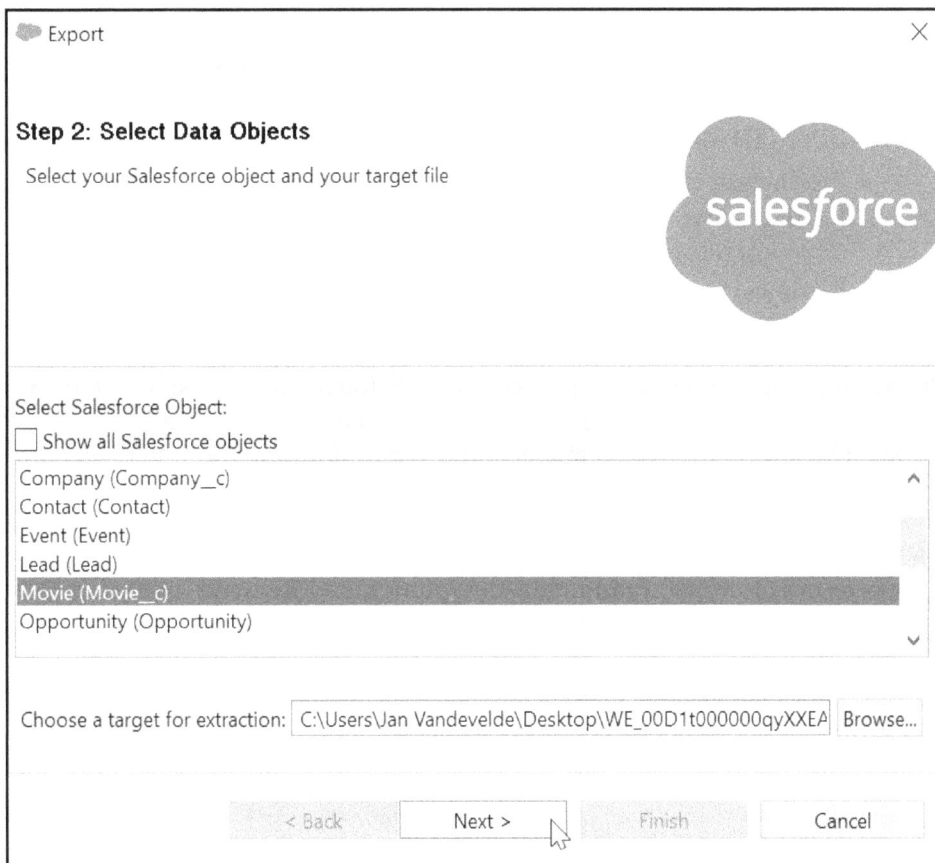

Step 2: Select Data Objects

Select your Salesforce object and your target file

Select Salesforce Object:
☐ Show all Salesforce objects

Company (Company__c)
Contact (Contact)
Event (Event)
Lead (Lead)
Movie (Movie__c)
Opportunity (Opportunity)

Choose a target for extraction: C:\Users\Jan Vandevelde\Desktop\WE_00D1t000000qyXXEA Browse...

< Back   Next >   Finish   Cancel

3. Click **Next** and Data Loader will ask you to select the fields you want to export, just click **Select All**. Pay attention to the fact that, by selecting fields, Data Loader is creating a query at the bottom of the screen. This is actually a SOQL query. Such a query is also used in Apex to query data from Salesforce, and we will learn more about those in `Chapter 3`, *Declarative Automation*.

4. Just click **Finish** now, and your movie records will get exported. A popup will appear telling you how many records have successfully been exported.

5. I actually saved this file in the same folder where my previous exports for person and company resided, so I now have a folder containing three files (person, company, and movie) for which all records also have a Salesforce record ID. So, it's up to you now to import the following files, in this order:

   - **Cast**: The `Cast` file will need to be completed with the record IDs of the corresponding movie for the field `Movie__c` and the corresponding **Person** record ID for the field `Person__c` through `VLOOKUP`

   - **Production companies**: Here, you will need to complete the movie record ID in the `Movie_Title__c` column and a company record ID in the `Company_Name__c` column

   - **Reviews**: In this one, you'll need to complete the movie record ID in the `Movie_Title__c` column

6. If you encounter any errors, check the error file that Data Loader provides after each insert action. You'll find the error reason in the last column from the error file. I haven't encountered any errors while performing these steps to guide you through them, so hopefully you won't either, but never say never. I'm sure everything went fine, so go check in Salesforce on the movie record for **The Godfather** and click the **Related** tab on the detail page to see if our movie now has records for **Cast**, **Production Companies**, and **Reviews**, like so:

Great job! You have learned and practiced the different ways to import and export data to and from Salesforce! I'm so proud of you!

Now, don't waste any time—check whether you have completely grasped everything covered in this chapter by doing the summary quiz!

Summary

In this chapter, we have learned the difference between standard and custom objects, and fields, the possible ways to create them, what different types of relationships can be established between objects, how to create them, and the different ways to import and export data into and from Salesforce.

In `Chapter 3`, *Declarative Automation*, we will learn how to support our business processes by automating actions that users, normally have to perform manually. We'll have a look at the different tools that are provided by Salesforce out of the box and how you can leverage them, and we will explain this further with example exercises.

But first, it's time to check whether you understood everything we learned about in this chapter. So, it is quiz time!

Quiz

Let's see if you are on the right track to becoming a certified Salesforce developer. You'll find all the answers to this chapter summary quiz at the end of this book. Try to answer the questions without looking at the answers:

1. You are cleaning up your org and have do remove a field that is referenced in Apex. You would like to delete this field using the **Schema Builder**. Can you do that? And, if so, how?
    a. Delete it using **Schema Builder;** this will automatically remove any reference to this field from Apex
    b. **Schema Builder** can not be used to delete fields
    c. Remove any reference to this field first from any Apex code, then delete the field using **Schema Builder**
    d. Delete the field using **Schema Builder**. This will keep all references to it in Apex, but your code will not be functional anymore

2. What can not be done using **Schema Builder**?
    a. Creation of a custom object
    b. Creation of a custom field on a standard object
    c. Deletion of a custom object
    d. Deletion of a standard object

3. What type of field can not be created through **Schema Builder**?
    a. An encrypted text field
    b. A geolocation field
    c. A multi-select picklist field
    d. A rich text field

4. You are required to relate two custom objects, Invoice Line Item and Invoice. Invoice Line Items are strongly related to Invoice, and an Invoice Line Item cannot exist without Invoice. What relationship should you use in this scenario?
    a. Use a junction object with two master-detail relationships
    b. Use a master-detail relationship on Invoice to Invoice Line Item
    c. Use a master-detail relationship on Invoice Line Item to Invoice
    d. Use lookup to Invoice on Invoice Line Item

5. You are asked to create a new custom object called Invoice, and it should be related to the Opportunity object. An Invoice should inherit record access from the Opportunity it's related to. What relationship should be created, and on which object?
    a. Create a lookup relationship field on the Invoice object that points to the Opportunity object
    b. Create a lookup relationship field on the Opportunity object that points to the Invoice object
    c. Create a master-detail relationship field on the Invoice object, that points to the Opportunity object
    d. Create a master-detail relationship field on the Opportunity object that points to the Invoice object

6. Two objects in your org (object *A* and object *B*) should be related in a many-to-many relationship. What should you do?
    a. Create a master-detail relationship field on object *A*, pointing to object *B*, and another master-detail relationship field on object *B* pointing to object *A*
    b. Create a junction object, with two master-detail relationship fields, pointing to object *A* and object *B*
    c. Create a many-to-many relationship field on object *A*, pointing to object B, and another many-to-many relationship field on object *B*, pointing to object *A*
    d. Create a junction object, and create a master-detail relationship field on both object *A* and object *B* that each point to the junction object

7. You have received a `.csv` file containing 65,000 movie records and have been asked to load them into Salesforce in one go. How will you do that?

    a. Use Data Import Wizard to load these custom object records into Salesforce in one go

    b. Hire a student to start typing the records in one by one, because none of the tools provided by Salesforce can handle this many custom object records in one go

    c. Use Data Loader to load these custom object records into Salesforce in one go

    d. Both Data Import Wizard and Data Loader can load these custom Object records into Salesforce in one go

8. You have received a `.csv` file containing 10,000 person records, but it is possible that some records from your file already exist in Salesforce. How can you load those into Salesforce without creating duplicates?

    a. Use Data Loader and set the **Match By** field to **Person Full Name**

    b. Use Data Import Wizard and set the **Match By** field to **Person Full Name**

    c. Native Salesforce import tools cannot handle duplicates

    d. You should first remove any duplicate records from the file, then load the file with either Data Import Wizard or Data Loader

9. You would like to export Salesforce account data on a daily basis so that you can import them one way or another into your ERP. How can you do this?

    a. Use the built-in Data Export and schedule it with a daily frequency

    b. Use Data Loader and set the daily schedule from the **Data Loader Settings** menu

    c. Use Data Loader and set up a script that calls the Data Loader to run through the command line on a daily basis

    d. Use the built-in Data Export and set up a script that calls the data export to run through command line on a daily basis

10. You have just loaded more than 25,000 invoice records into Salesforce, but you get complaints from your end users that some of the invoice due dates are wrong. What could be the cause of this?

    a. Your org's company locale is set incorrectly

    b. Your user's locale is set incorrectly

    c. The date format used in your `.csv` file does not match your user's record locale

    d. The date format used in your `.csv` file does not match your org's company locale

2
Section 2: Logic, Process Automation, and the User Interface

This section will focus on extending the native functionalities of Salesforce with our own automation. The platform provides lots of tools to automate actions normally performed manually by users. Eliminating redundant tasks from users' day-to-day activities makes them more productive. In the following chapters, we will dive into different point-and-click features to automate business processes, and will also cover how we can programmatically go above and beyond.

The following chapters are included in this section:

Declarative Automation 3

It's been two chapters only and we have already learned a lot about Salesforce, and this knowledge is actually building a foundation that you need to understand before we dive into detail. The concepts you'll learn from now on (especially the content of `Chapter 3`, *Declarative Automation*, `Chapter 4`, *Apex Basics*, and `Chapter 5`, *Apex - Beyond the Basics*) are largely what the platform developer I exam is all about. Half of the questions you'll see in the exam will be covered in the next three chapters, so pay extra attention.

I have tried to explain all the concepts as clearly as possible, keeping in mind that you would not have any prior knowledge, nor any experience of them. And I have also tried to provide a concrete example, putting the theory into practice, by leveraging our BIM DB app.

In this chapter, we will be covering the following topics:

- Using formula fields and roll-up summary fields
- Automating your business with workflow rules and processes
- Creating approval processes
- More complex automation with flow
- When to use declarative tools versus Apex code

So, let's dive in!

Formula fields

We have already explained what formula fields are in `Chapter 1`, *Salesforce Fundamentals*, but let's recap what we know about formula fields first. We'll learn more about their use in this section:

- A formula is similar to a calculation that is executed or evaluated at the time we access/read the record, through the UI, a Visualforce page, the API, or Apex.
- A formula field is read-only; you cannot edit it! You can edit the formula itself as an administrator from setup, but end users will never be able to edit the value/result from the UI.
- A formula can make use of various data of the record itself or related data and even fixed variables to perform its calculations. Think of them as formulas you would use in an Excel spreadsheet. These formulas can make use of data and operations to calculate a new value for a data type.
- Formula fields can return a value of type, checkbox, date, date/time, currency, number, percent, and text.
- An example of a percent formula would be calculating a margin based on fields containing the cost and the sales price.
- When referencing a parent record field in a formula, we call it a cross-object formula.
- Cross-object formulas are all about getting information from a parent object into the child. Retrieving information pertaining to child records cannot be effected with a formula, but is effected through a roll-up summary field (which we'll explain more about in the next section)!

Let's start off by creating a formula field on our `Movie__c` object called **Director's Birthdate**, which renders the value of the **Birthdate** field of the related director record through our lookup called `Director__c`. This is a typical example of a cross-object formula, fetching data from a related record to show its value on the child record. The greatest benefit of this type of use is that if you modify the related record or reparent the record, the **Director's Birthdate** will always show the correct value of the related director automatically:

1. Go to **Setup** | **Object Manager**, select our `Movie` object, and click the **Fields and Relationships** tab. Click **New** to create a new custom field. Choose the **Formula** and give it the **Director's Birthdate** name and choose **Date** as the data type. The API name should get automatically populated with **Director_s_Birthdate** (if it doesn't, be sure to correct it so that we don't encounter any issues in future exercises):

2. Hit **Next** to go to the formula editor. Click the **Advanced Formula** tab, which is, I find, the easiest to build your formulas with.

3. Now, we could just write our formula like `Director__r.Birthdate__c`, but that's more advanced, and you'll get the hang of this when you have completed the section on *Salesforce Object Query Language (SOQL)* from `Chapter 4`, *Apex Basics*.

4. For now, let's do it the point-and-click way and click on the **Insert Field** button within the formula editor. This will open a popup that will let you select fields from the object level you are creating the formula on; in our case, movie. So, if `Movie` (first column) is our base object, the second column will display all useable fields from that object for you to select.

> When a field is a relationship field, such as an owner, or, in our example, director, the field will be displayed twice.

5. In the second column, there would be a field name with just the word **Director**, and one more with a > after it. The > means you want to traverse the relationship to get to the fields of the related object for use. This is what we will use to get to the **Birthdate** field that is located on the `Person` object. If you select the field name without the >, you would actually want to use the value of that field itself from the base object, which would give you the record ID of the related `Person` record (such as `a021t000005d7hJAAQ`, for example):

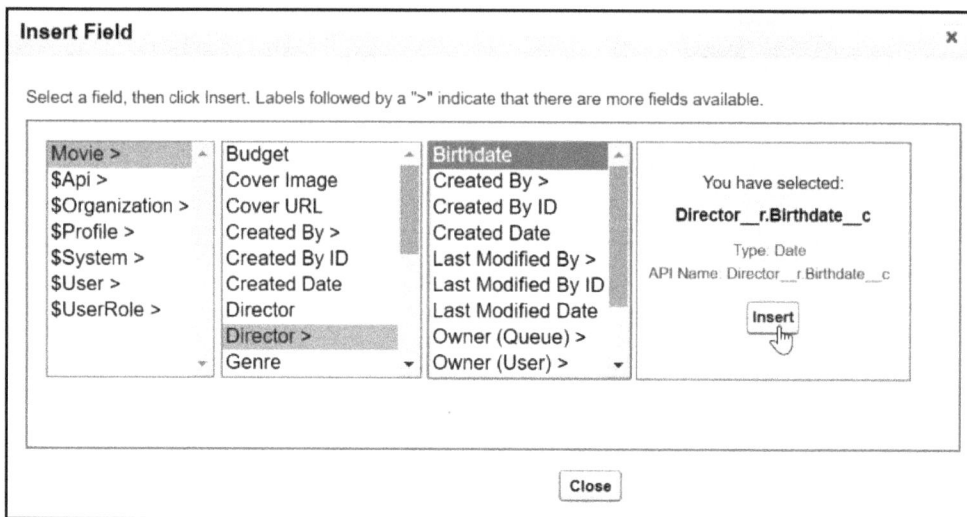

Insert Field			✕
Select a field, then click Insert. Labels followed by a ">" indicate that there are more fields available.			

Movie >	Budget	Birthdate	You have selected:
$Api >	Cover Image	Created By >	**Director__r.Birthdate__c**
$Organization >	Cover URL	Created By ID	
$Profile >	Created By >	Created Date	Type: Date
$System >	Created By ID	Last Modified By >	API Name: Director__r.Birthdate__c
$User >	Created Date	Last Modified By ID	
$UserRole >	Director	Last Modified Date	Insert
	Director >	Owner (Queue) >	
	Genre	Owner (User) >	

Close

6. So, click the **Director >** field from the menu and a third column will appear containing the fields from the relationship object; in our case, the `Person` object. In here, select the **Birthdate** field and click **Insert**.

7. You'll see that it has now put the correct API name of that field in your formula editor, just as I mentioned before: `Director__r.Birthdate__c`.

> **TIP**
>
> It does not say `Director__c.Birthdate__c` though. When you want to traverse the relationship through a custom lookup field, the __c field becomes __r (for relation). If you refer to the **Director** field itself on the `Movie` object, then it would have been the `Director__c` custom field.

8. Hence, it's best practice to click the **Check Syntax** button underneath the formula editor when you think your formula is complete, so that it is checked for any errors, as follows:

| Simple Formula | Advanced Formula | |

Insert Field

Director's Birthdate (Date) =

Director__r.Birthdate__c

Check Syntax No syntax errors in merge fields or functions. (Compiled size: 21 characters)

If your formula contains any errors, the error message would give you a number of clues as to what is exactly wrong with it. It's always good to fill in a description (and optionally some help text). The description is for your own reference, explaining why this field exists, or if any new administrator comes into your org, they can easily ascertain the purpose of this field. The help text is a short message you want to expose to end users in the UI when they hover over the small **?** next to the field itself on the page layout. This is useful for explaining what the value in this field represents to them.

9. At the bottom of the formula editor, there is a section called **Blank Field Handling**. Depending on the data type, your formula returns, in our case, a date. The output of the calculation would be zero or blank, which you would want to show to the user:

Blank Field Handling

If your formula references any number, currency, or percent fields, specify what happens to the formula output when their values are blank.

◯ Treat blank fields as zeroes
◉ Treat blank fields as blanks

10. Hit **Next** and leave all the defaults for the field level security and page layouts.

11. If we go back to our `The Godfather` movie record in our BIM DB app, we'll notice that our new field, **Director's Birthdate,** is put at the bottom of the page layout and contains a value:

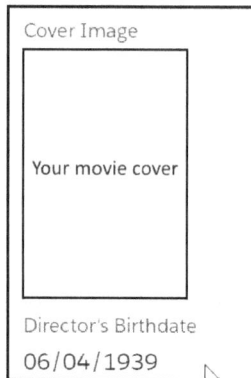

```
Cover Image

┌─────────────┐
│             │
│ Your movie cover │
│             │
└─────────────┘

Director's Birthdate
06/04/1939
```

And that's exactly what we wanted as a result.

We have already seen how to modify the page layout, through the Lightning App Builder, so let's go ahead and place this new field a bit higher on the page layout (maybe right beneath the **Director** field), where it would make more sense to view it.

> You can find some common example formulas on the Salesforce help and training portal here: `https://help.salesforce.com/articleView?id=useful_advanced_formulas.htmtype=5`

Formulas and their logic can be used in other places, such as the following:

- Workflow rules
- Approval processes
- Approval steps
- Assignment rules
- Escalation rules
- Auto-response rules

Some formula rules and limits to be aware of are the following:

- Formulas can reference standard, custom, or other formula fields
- Formulas can reference the object itself, or fields from parent objects, but never from child records!

- Formulas *cannot* reference themselves
- Fields referenced in a formula field cannot be deleted without an administrator first removing the reference from the formula
- Formula fields can contain up to 3,900 characters, including spaces and line breaks
- Cross-object formulas can reference fields from objects that are up to 10 relationships away

Roll-up summary fields

In this section, we'll dive deeper into the use of roll-up summary fields. Let's summarize what we already know about them:

- A roll-up summary field is a type of field only available on a master-detail relationship's parent object.
- It is used to perform a calculation based upon a numeric value of child records.
- A roll-up summary field will grab information from related child object records and perform some calculation with them. Possible calculations are COUNT, SUM, MIN, and MAX.
- It is recalculated whenever you insert, update, or delete one or more of the children, whenever a detailed record is saved to the database.
- You can create up to 25 RUS on a per object basis. This can be increased exceptionally, by submitting a case at Salesforce support, to a maximum of 40. 40 RUS on one object is the *hard* limit at the time of writing!
- While a normal formula field is calculated depending on reading time, a roll-up summary field is recalculated when saving of one or more child records that it is based on. This has as an extra benefit in that the change of the value in a roll-up summary field can trigger automation features, such as workflow rules, Process Builders, or Apex triggers.

Examples of roll-up summary field use include the following:

- To SUM the total number of invoice records in the account
- To COUNT the number of opportunities an account has
- To show the highest opportunity value on the account using the MAX calculation
- To show the lowest review rating a movie has using the MIN calculation

It's important to know that you don't always have to use all child records in your calculation. There is a possibility to filter child records that you want to include (for example, make the SUM of all **Unpaid** invoice records and show it on the account). This way, you can exclude paid invoices from the calculation and show only the total amount still due.

Roll-up summary fields can be created on the following:

- Custom objects that are on the master side of a master-detail relationship.
- Standard objects that are on the master side of a master-detail relationship, and where a detail side is a custom object.
- Opportunities for rolling up values of related opportunity products.
- Accounts rolling up values of related opportunities. (This is a special case, as the relationship from an opportunity to account is a lookup relationship, but it acts as a master-detail relationship. As an administrator, you can't create such a field yourself. These are special fields provided by Salesforce at the core of Salesforce CRM.)
- Campaigns rolling up values of related campaign members.

To get a better grasp of the RUS field concept, we'll be creating two RUS on our Movie object and a formula field that performs a calculation based on those two RUS. We can do that because we created a master-detail relationship between Review__c and Movie__c. To explain further, we consider that we would like a field called Average Rating on our Movie object, but an RUS field has no AVERAGE option:

1. So, first, we'll create a roll-up summary field called Nbr of Reviews, which counts the number of review records. Then, we'll create a second RUS called Total Rating, which will be the SUM of all ratings of all review records. Then our formula field, Average Rating, will divide the Total Rating by the Nbr of Reviews and give us the average rating.
2. So, go to **Setup** | **Object Manager** | **Movie Object** and click the **New** button to create a new custom field. Then, select the **Roll-up Summary** as the data type.
3. Fill in the label with Nbr of Reviews and make sure the API name is Nbr_of_Reviews and hit **Next**. In the object to summarize, select **Reviews, Roll-Up Type** as **COUNT**, and leave filter criteria as **All records should be included in the calculation**. Hit **Next**. See the following screenshot:

Movie

New Custom Field

Step 3. Define the summary calculation

Select Object to Summarize

Master Object	Movie
Summarized Object	Reviews ▾

Select Roll-Up Type

- ◉ COUNT
- ◯ SUM
- ◯ MIN   Field to Aggregate --None-- ▾
- ◯ MAX

Filter Criteria

- ◉ All records should be included in the calculation
- ◯ Only records meeting certain criteria should be included in the calculation

4. Hit **Next**, and then **Save**, leaving all the defaults for page layout and field level security.
5. For our next RUS, we have a small problem. Calculations except **COUNT** can only be performed on fields containing either a number, currency, or percent as a data type and we want to base it on our `Rating__c` picklist. Our picklist only contains numbers as values (1, 2, 3, 4, 5). A picklist is always perceived as **TEXT**.
6. To solve this little situation, we will first create a formula field on our `Review` object, converting the value of our rating picklist into a number.

7. So, from **Setup** | **Object Manager**, select our `Review` object and click the **New** button to create a new custom field. Choose **Formula** as the field type, **Number** as a return value (be sure to set the number of decimal places to **0**), and call your field `Rating To Number`. In the advanced formula editor, we will insert a formula to convert the text from our rating picklist into a number. It's a good thing that Salesforce provides us with a plethora of functions with common calculations to perform. Check out the **VALUE** function in the **Functions** menu on the right-hand side of the formula editor:

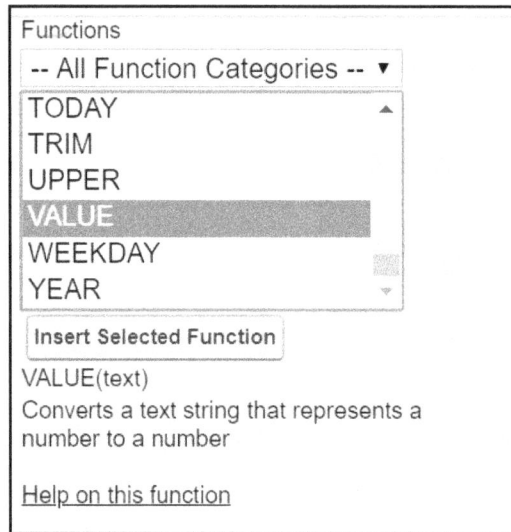

8. The **VALUE** function converts a text string that represents a number to an actual number data type. And that's exactly what we need. So, select the **VALUE** function and click the **Insert Selected Function** button. This will insert the syntax into the formula editor. Now, we need to replace the text placeholder with our picklist field rating. So, remove the text placeholder and make sure your cursor is placed between the parentheses. Click the **Insert Field** button, and you'll find yourself on your base object, which is `Review`, and, in the second column, you've got all fields from the `Review` object. In there, select the rating field and hit **Insert**. Your formula should now look like `VALUE(Rating__c)`. Now, hit the **Check Syntax** button to see whether there are any errors. Whoops:

Formula Options

Formula Return Type	Number ▾
Decimal Places	0 ▾

Enter your formula and click Check Syntax to check for errors. Click the Advanced Formula subtab to use additional fields, operators, and functions.

Example: Fahrenheit = 1.8 * Celsius__c + 32 More Examples ...

| Simple Formula | Advanced Formula |

[Insert Field]   [Insert Operator ▾]

Rating To Number (Number) =

```
VALUE(Rating__c)
```

[Check Syntax] Error: Field Rating__c is a picklist field. Picklist fields are only supported in certain functions. Tell me more

9. You'll encounter this several times in your career. A picklist is a special data type because it comes with some specific functions, such as `ISPICKVAL()`, to compare against one specific value chosen in the picklist. So, therefore, we need to actually specify that we want whatever **TEXT** is chosen from the picklist to be converted. To do this, we wrap the picklist field within a `TEXT()` function, so your formula should end up like `VALUE(TEXT(Rating__c))`. Now, adapt it and check the syntax again. There should no longer be an error, so you can hit **Next** and **Save**, leaving all the defaults.

   Sorry for this little sidetrack, but, hey, that's development on Salesforce for you! Sometimes, you start with building out your solution and hit a little bump on the road that you'll need to solve.

10. Now that we have this actual number on our review, let's continue with our initial requirement and create the second roll-up summary field that will calculate the **SUM** of all ratings. Go back to the `Movie` object (from **Object Manager** in **Setup,** choose the `Movie` object) and click the **New** button to create our second RUS. Select **Roll-Up Summary** as the data type. In the field label, fill in `Total Rating` as the label and the API name should be `Total_Rating`. As we did before, select **Reviews** as an object to summarize, but now set the **Roll-Up Type** to **SUM** and choose our special formula field, `Rating To Number`, as a field to aggregate.

11. Hit **Next** and **Save,** leaving the defaults for page layouts and field-level security:

12. We are almost there now. The last thing we need is the actual average calculation! We stay on the `Movie` object in **Setup | Object Manager**, and click once again on the **New** button to create our last custom field. Select **Formula** as the data type, which will return a **Number** (with **0** decimal places), and call it `Average Rating` with the API name `Average_Rating`. Hit **Next**. In the formula editor, write down the following formula:

Total_Rating__c / Nbr_of_Reviews__c

13. Hit **Next** and **Save,** leaving all the defaults for the page layout and field-level security.

14. Now, let's check out our fields by navigating to our `The Godfather` movie record (you should know how to get there by now!). And there you go:

Because we said **0** decimal places, the **Average Rating** is rounded to the nearest whole number. If you would like to see **4.25**, you could edit the formula field **Average Rating** to show **2** decimal places if you want. I'm going to leave it as it is.

Also, you have already learned how to modify your page layout, so you could clean the page up a bit, by placing those fields somewhere else on the page layout and maybe removing the **Total Rating** field from the page layout, as it is actually used purely for the calculation of the average in the background. Having a **Total Rating** doesn't tell the user much, right? But I'll leave that completely up to you.

Let's move on!

Declarative process automation features – workflow and processes

In this section, we'll dive deeper into workflow rules and Process Builder and its uses, differences, and similarities. Both are used to automate your business processes, without the use of code, and have similar functionality. Process Builder could actually be considered as workflow rules, bigger brother, having a number of extra functionalities and, as such, is more powerful.

Workflow rules

Let's summarize what we already know about workflow rules from `Chapter 1`, *Salesforce Fundamentals*:

- They let you automate standard internal procedures and processes to save your end users time, such as creating a follow-up task in the background instead of having your end user create a task manually each time something specific happens or update a field to another value depending on other values that might have changed
- A workflow rule is the main container for a set of actions/instructions that need to be performed
- It is set on one object at a time
- It is triggered when an event happens (such as when a record is created or when a record changes)
- It automatically performs the actions defined

To create a workflow rule, perform the following steps:

1. Select the object where the rule should apply (the object that will fire the workflow rule).
2. Specify when the rule criteria should be evaluated:
    - On creation: This will make sure the rule can only be executed once per record!
    - On creation and every time the record is edited: The rule will repeatedly be executed every time the record is edited, as long as the criteria meet the rule criteria.
    - On creation and any time it is edited to meet the criteria: The rule can run multiple times per record, but it won't run when the record has already met the rule criteria just before the editing of the record.
3. Specify the rule criteria.
4. Define the actions that need to be performed when the criteria are met. Actions can be immediate or time-dependent. There are only four possible actions:
    - Creating a task
    - Sending an email alert
    - Field update on the record itself, or its parent, in a master-detail relationship
    - Sending an outbound message to external systems

Let's create a simple workflow rule that creates a task for the system administrator to review a newly created movie record:

1. To create a workflow rule, navigate to **Setup | Workflow Rules** and hit the **New Rule** button.
2. Choose **Movie** as the object to which the workflow rule applies, and then hit **Next**. Give `Review Movie Task Administrator` as the rule name.
3. Choose **Evaluate the rule when a record is created**. So, it will only act when new movies are inserted into the database.
4. Choose **criteria are met** instead of **formula evaluates to true.** We have to specify criteria. Since we want it for all new movie records, we'll set **Movie: Movie Title not equal** to empty. We do this by not filling in anything in the **Value** field, as follows:

This way, the rule will fire upon the creation of every new record, as the movie title field is a mandatory field and will never be blank.

5. Click **Save & Next** to enter the actions. Under **Immediate Workflow Actions**, click the **Add Workflow Action** button to create a new action. We want to create a **New Task**, but there is no action to create a new task! How? Why?

    It seems for the moment that we only have an outbound message, field update, send an email alert and choose existing action, but no **Create Task** action. The reason for that is because, when we created the `Movie` object in `Chapter 2, Understanding Data Modeling and Management`, we didn't enable the object to **Allow Activities** related to it. To be able to create tasks (which are activities) for an object, we need to enable this first.

6. So, from the **Object Manager,** navigate to the `Movie` object, click **Edit**, enable the **Allow Activities** checkbox, and then save it like this:

7. Now, go back to edit your workflow rule and click the **Add Workflow Action** button again. You should also have the **Create Task** action. Select it and fill in the following details:

- **Assigned To**: Click the lookup icon next to it to select a user. Choose yourself to get the task assigned to you.
- **Subject**: Set whatever subject you would like that describes the task you need to be performed by that user. I set it to **Please review this newly created Movie record for completeness** (the unique name will automatically be filled depending upon your subject).
- **Due Date**: As tasks have a due date when they should have been completed, we have to set a due date. I chose **Rule Trigger Date** (which would be the same as the movie creation date, which you could also choose from the menu) plus two days. So, I expect the assigned user to have completed a completeness check for each new movie record within two days of creation:

New Task

Configure Task

Save | Save & New | Cancel

Create a task to associate with one or more workflow rules, approval processes, or entitlement processes. When changing a task, any modifications will apply to all rules, approvals, or entitlement processes associated with it.

Edit Task | = Required Information

Object Movie
Assigned To Jan Vandevelde
Subject Please review this new Mov
Unique Name Please_review_this_new_M
Due Date Rule Trigger Date ▼ plus ▼ 2 days
Protected Component

Status Not Started ▼
Priority Normal ▼

Description Information

Comments

8. Click **Save** and **Done**.

> **Now,** and this is **very important**: Don't forget to activate. This is very often forgotten!

This is what we get as a result:

Now comes the time to test our workflow rule. Perform the following steps:

1. Simply navigate to the **Movies** tab in our BIM DB app and create a new movie record yourself.

   > Check www.imdb.com for some movie details if you need inspiration and don't forget a cover image URL.

2. Now, to see your activity, we'll need to adapt the page layout to add the **Activities** component. It's not there by default because we enabled **Allow Activities** at a later stage, so we'll need to add it manually.

3. So, from your newly created Movie record (in my case, the Bumblebee record), click the settings icon in the top-right of the page and select **Edit** page to launch the App Builder.

4. Drag the **Activities** component onto the sidebar on the right of the page and don't forget to click **Save**:

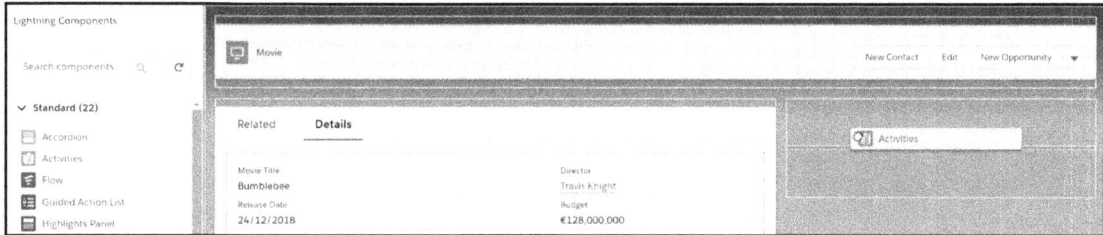

You should be back on your movie record page now and see the created activity in the **Activities** component, as shown in the following screenshot:

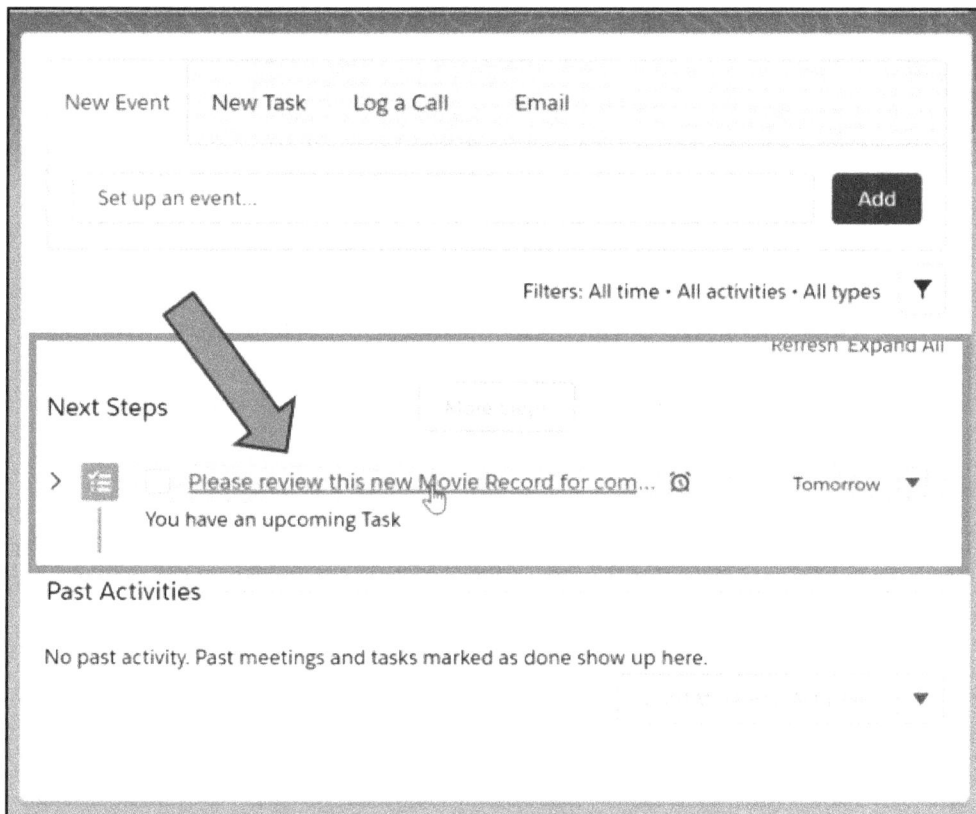

Process Builder

Let's summarize what we already know about Process Builder:

- Process Builder is a Salesforce feature to automate actions that need to happen in your business processes.
- It comes with a nice, graphical overview of your automated process while you are creating or updating it.
- Process Builder can carry out the following:
    - Create processes using a graphical interface through point-and-click configuration
    - Execute a chain of actions, based on criteria in one place instead of creating multiple workflow rules
    - Automate simple tasks that you can't do with workflow rules without using code
- It launches when a specified event happens (such as the creation of a record or the updating of a specific field), just like workflow rules would.
- Process Builder can be built to be launched by another Process Builder as an action, giving you the power to build reusable processes and call them when needed. This way, you wouldn't need to recreate the logic again and again.
- Processes are defined with the following:
    - Criteria that define when a group of actions needs to be executed
    - Actions to execute immediately when criteria are met
    - Actions that need to be executed in the future (scheduled actions) when criteria are met (not supported for processes that are invocable by another process!)
- Process Builder can execute the same, and even more, actions as workflow rules. It can do the following:
    - Update any related record—not just the record itself or its parent
    - Send an email
    - Create any record
    - Call Apex (it can be used as a replacement for an outbound message to external systems, too)
    - Use a quick action to create a record, update a record, or log a call
    - Invoke another process that is created as `Invocable`
    - Launch a flow
    - Post to chatter
    - Submit for approval

- Process Builder *cannot* send outbound messages. This you can only do with workflow rules or Apex.

At this stage, I wanted to create an exercise to showcase the use of Process Builder, and I have a great example in mind, But it requires an approval process first. And we only see that in the next section. So, I'm going to do you a solid. Let's first dive into the next section to learn all about approvals and flows, and, further down the road, we'll create the following:

- A flow with screen elements to easily create a new `Movie` record, including a director, and a first review, all in one go and from our home page.
- Process Builder that kicks off when a new review is added, to be submitted for approval.
- An approval process to approve or decline a review (because in real life, reviews could be submitted through the web and contain spam. The approval process will update a **Status** field on our review record with **Approved** or **Rejected**.
- We'll adjust our roll-up summary fields on the `Movie` object to only count the reviews with a status of **Approved** by adding filters.

Ready to get down to it? Let's continue with the next section then.

Declarative process automation features – approvals and flows

In this section, we'll dive deeper into approval processes, Visual Flows, and their uses. Both are used to automate parts of your business processes, without the use of code. Approvals are used when someone, or a particular department/team, needs to verify something and give their consent to it before the end user can continue with the rest of the business process. Flows are the big brother of Process Builder. They let you automate most, if not all, of your business processes and are much more powerful, but also a bit more complex to set up.

Approval processes

If you require a chain of steps that need to be followed in order to get a specific record approved, then approvals can take this automation a step further. Businesses sometimes need some departments or people to review the data of a specific record for compliance reasons.

For example, you let sales representatives create and negotiate opportunities with products and customer negotiated prices and/or discounts, but you want a sales manager to first review and approve the final prizes before a quote gets sent out to the customer. Or you could have an internal process for employees to submit holidays, leave requests, or expense notes, and have them first approved by their line manager before those are assigned to HR for further treatment.

In an approval process, you can specify each step that needs to be taken to get an approval, including who can request an approval, who needs to approve at each step, and what needs to happen in Salesforce at each point of the process.

The following are the steps to create an approval process:

1. Specify the entry criteria.
2. Specify the approver and editable record properties while the record is within the approval process.
3. Select email notification templates (notify the approver, and notify the submitter of approval or rejection).
4. Select which fields of the record to display on the approval page layout for easy review by the approver.
5. Specifying the initial submitters (which users are allowed to submit a record for approval).

Once the approval process has been created, you can do the following:

- Specify an initial submission action: What needs to happen when a record is submitted for approval, such as locking the record so it can no longer be edited while within the approval process
- Specify one or more approval steps
- Specify final approval actions; for example, unlocking the record and updating a field to **Approved**
- Specify final rejection action; for example, unlocking the record and updating a field to **Rejected**
- Specify a recall action: What needs to happen if a user recalls his approval request, such as unlocking the record and updating a status back to the previous value

You can make use of the same actions to perform, such as in workflow rules:

- Creating a task
- Sending an email alert

- Performing field updates to the record itself or its parent in a master-detail relationship
- Sending an outbound message to external systems
- In addition to those, you have an extra action to lock or unlock the record for editing:

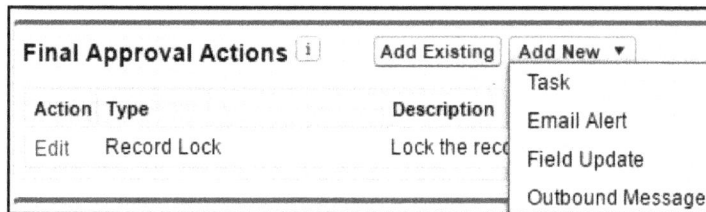

But, actions can only be executed immediately. Hence, no time-dependent actions are possible within an approval process. Of course, with what you have already learned, you can find some workarounds, right? These include creating a hidden checkbox or other field type and having your approval flow update that checkbox, and then having a workflow rule kick off of this field update, performing a time-dependent action. But that's not what we are going to show you in this course. Just keep in mind that you can creatively work around some limitations of the tools provided by the platform.

Let me give you a high-level example of a possible approval process—when sales representatives put an opportunity in the stage proposal/quote, management wants to check whether what was proposed adheres to company pricing rules. The approval needs to automatically assign the opportunity for approval to the correct user in your org based on the amount of the opportunity.

If the amount of the opportunity is 0, then users should not be permitted to submit the opportunity for approval, as this would cause a major overload of approval requests. The opportunity record should be locked for editing while it's pending approval. The criteria for assigning the correct approver are as follows: if the amount is less than 50,000, the request may automatically be approved; if the amount is less than or equal to 500,000, an approval is required by the direct manager of the submitter.

Finally, if the amount is greater than 500,000, secondary approval is needed by the VP of Sales. If all requests are approved, the status of the opportunity can be updated to **Approved** and the record should be unlocked. If any requests are rejected, the status needs to be changed to **Rejected** and the record needs to be unlocked. Of course, approvers need to be notified by email that they have a record to approve and the submitters need to be notified upon approval or rejection of their submission.

This is a typical example of a business process that you would use an approval process for.

For the approval process, the requirements are as follows:

1. First, we'll need a new field called **Status** on our `Review` object with values of **Pending Review**, **Approved**, and **Declined**, and we'll set **Pending Review** as the default value.
2. When a **Review** has the status **Pending Review**, or the status is changed to **Pending Review**, the **Review** needs to be approved by a specific user (you!).
3. When it gets approved, the status should be updated to **Approved**, or, if it gets declined, the status should be updated to **Declined**.
4. We'll also update our roll-up summary fields on the movie record, to not include `Review` records that are not (yet) approved in the `Nbr of Ratings` and `Total Rating` fields.

Creating the approval process

Now, let's create an approval process using our BIM DB app:

1. Navigate to **Setup | Object Manager**, select the `Review` object, and click **Fields & Relationships**. Click the **New** button to create a new custom field.
2. Choose **Picklist** as the type, and set the label name to **Status**. For values, select the second radio button, **Enter values, with each value separated by a new line**, and, in the big editor box, enter the following values each on a new line (don't use commas or anything to separate the values; just hit enter to go to the next line):

   - **Pending Review**
   - **Approved**
   - **Declined**

3. Also, select the **Use first value as default value** checkbox and mark the field as **Required.** Hit **Next** and **Save**, leaving all the defaults for the page layouts and field level security:

Field Label	Status [i]

Values	◌ Use global picklist value set
	◉ Enter values, with each value separated by a new line

```
Pending Review
Approved
Declined
```

☐ Display values alphabetically, not in the order entered
☑ Use first value as default value [i]
☑ Restrict picklist to the values defined in the value set [i]

Field Name	Status [i]
Description	
Help Text	[i]
Required	☑ Always require a value in this field in order to save a record
Default Value	Show Formula Editor
	[i]

Use formula syntax: Enclose text and picklist value API names in double quotes : ("the_text"), include numbers without quotes
: (25), show percentages as decimals: (0.10), and express date calculations in the standard format: (Today() + 7)

Now that we have the field created, we also have some review records in our database present. Let's assume that they are all correct and can be published. We could update all those records with the Data Loader and set the **Status** field to **Approved**, or, because we just created this **Status** field and they are all blank, and we can assume that all current review records are correct and can be approved (because we created them ourselves), we can also use the picklist value replacement tool on this field itself.

4. So from **Setup** | **Object Manager** on our `Review` object in **Fields & Relationships**, click the dropdown on the right-hand side of our **Status** field and select **Replace**:

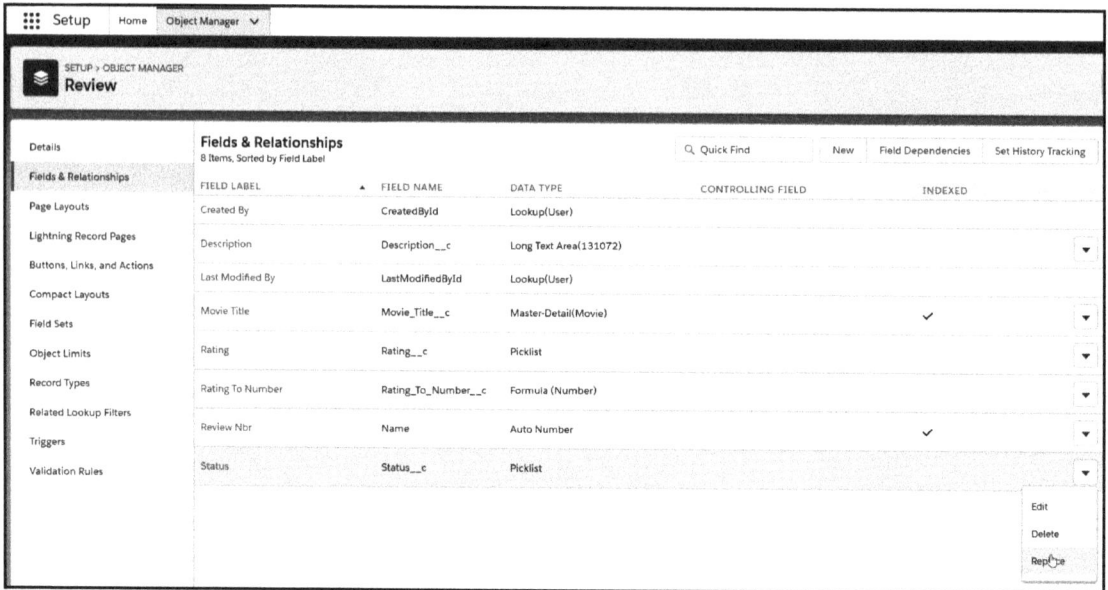

This is a little menu only available for picklist fields that lets you replace old value or blank fields with a new value.

5. You could write a value in **Exact Value Changing From**, but, in our case, there is no value. Since it's the blank values that we now want to populate with **Approved**, select the **Replace all blank values** checkbox and set **Select Value Changing To Approved** and click **Replace**:

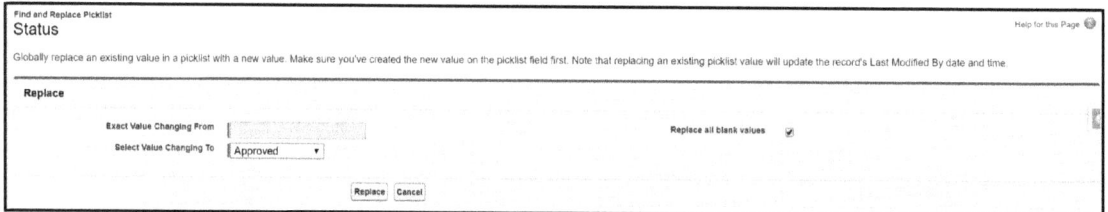

6. Depending on the number of records in your database that need to be updated, you'll be presented with a confirmation message, as shown in the following screenshot:

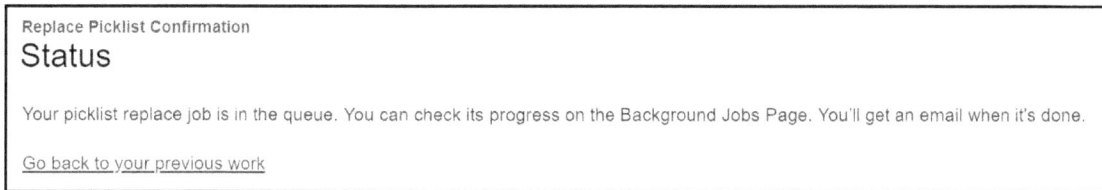

Replace Picklist Confirmation
Status

Your picklist replace job is in the queue. You can check its progress on the Background Jobs Page. You'll get an email when it's done.

Go back to your previous work

7. Wait until you receive the following email confirmation that the job has been successfully executed:

Your Picklist Replace Job Status ∑ Inbox ×

support@salesforce.com <support@salesforce.com>   15:58 (4 minutes ago)

to me ▾

Your picklist replace job is done.

For the picklist "Status" on object "Review", an empty value was replaced with Approved.

↩ Reply   ➡ Forward

8. If you now navigate to our BIM DB app, open up `The Godfather`, and then open up one of its reviews through the related list and you'll see that our new **Status** field is there and filled in with **Approved**, as follows:

Review
R-0023

Related   **Details**

Review Nbr
R-0023

Description
This isn't just a beautifully crafted gangster film. Or an outstanding family portrait, for that matter. An amazing period piece. A character study. A lesson in filmmaking and an inspiration to generations of actors, directors, screenwriters and producers. For me, this is more: this is the definitive film. 10 stars out of 10.

Rating
5

Rating To Number
5

Status
Approved

Movie Title
The Godfather

Created By
Jan Vandevelde, 25/11/2018 10:00

Last Modified By
Jan Vandevelde, 19/12/2018 15:58

---

9. Before we can start on our approval process, we'll need to create an email template for use within our approval process. So, navigate to **Setup** and choose **Classic Email Templates** from the sidebar, under the **Email** category:

10. Click **New Template** and choose **Text** (we are not going to bother creating an HTML template for this exercise; otherwise, we would also need to create an HTML header first, and that's not what this course is about).

Use the following details to create the email template:

- **Folder: Unfiled Public Classic Email Templates**
- **Available for Use**: Checked
- **Email Template Name: Review Approval Notification**
- **Template Unique Name**: Review_Approval_Notification
- **Subject: A Review has been sent for approval**
- **Body**:

```
Dear {!ApprovalRequest.Process_Approver},
{!Approval_Requesting_User.Name} has submitted a new
Review: {!Review__c.Name} for approval.
Please verify this review and approve or reject it by
navigating to: {!ApprovalRequest.Internal_URL}
```

11. Only approved reviews will be published and count toward a movie's rating:

![TIP] Please observe that you can insert merge fields through the picklists on top of the page, which will give you the correct tag to use within your text. **Merge Fields** will be replaced with the actual data of the `Review` record, the submitter, and the approver.

12. Now that we have an email template to use, let's continue with creating our approval process.

13. Navigate back to **Setup** and, in the setup search bar, type `Approval` to find the **Approval Processes** menu, which is located under the **Process Automation** category and click it:

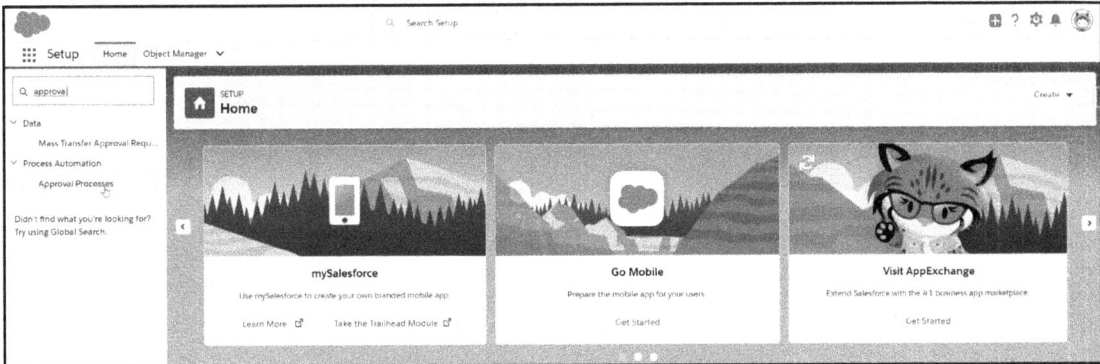

14. Select the `Review` object in the **Manage Approval Processes For** picklist, which will show you all currently active and inactive approval processes that exist in your org for the `Review` object. Currently, there should be none. Click the **Create New Approval Process** button and use the standard setup wizard:

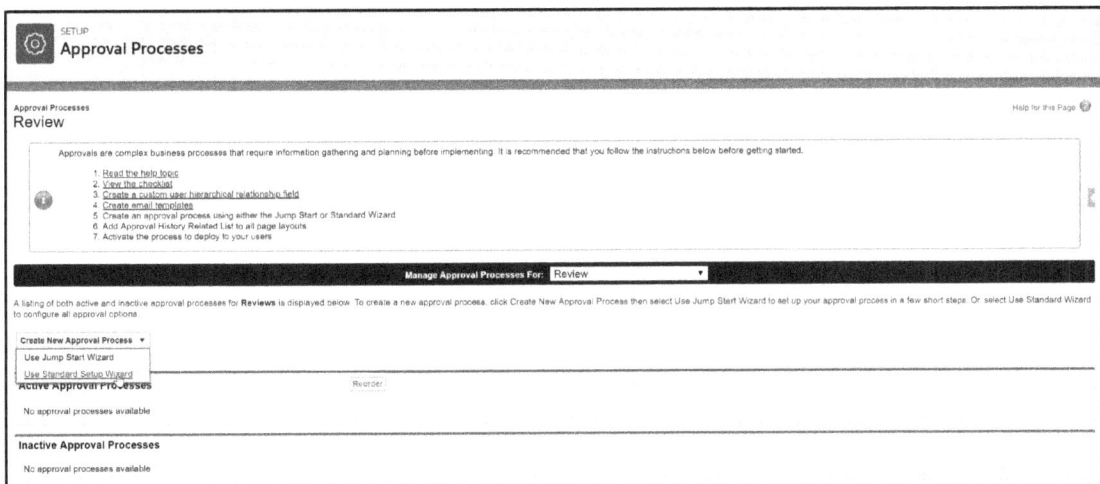

15. Set **Default approval for reviews** as the name and hit **Next**:

16. For the **Entry Criteria**, set it to **Review: Status - equals - Pending Review**, and hit **Next**:

17. On the approver selection page, set the **Next Automated Approver Determined By** field to **Manager**, and also select the second radio button, so that administrators and the current approver may edit the record while it is in the approval process, and hit **Next**:

18. Select our newly created email template called **Review Approval Notification** and hit **Next**:

19. On the next page, you can select a number of fields that you want to show on the approval page so that an approver can have a quick glimpse of what the contents of the record are without having to navigate to the record itself. Select **Review Nbr**, **Movie Title**, **Description**, **Rating**, and **Created By**. Also, check the checkbox to show approval history information on the approval page and the **Allow approvers to access the approval page from within the Salesforce application, or externally from a wireless-enabled mobile device** option, and hit **Next**:

20. Select the people who can submit a review record for approval. I've selected the **Movie Owner** and the **Record Creator** of the review itself. I've also enabled the **Allow submitters to recall approval requests** and hit **Save**:

21. The wizard will ask you whether you want to add a first approval step, or whether you would like to do this later and already save your approval process. Choose to add the first step. As our flow will only contain one step, give it the name, **New Review.** It will have defaulted to **Step Number 1.** Hit **Next**:

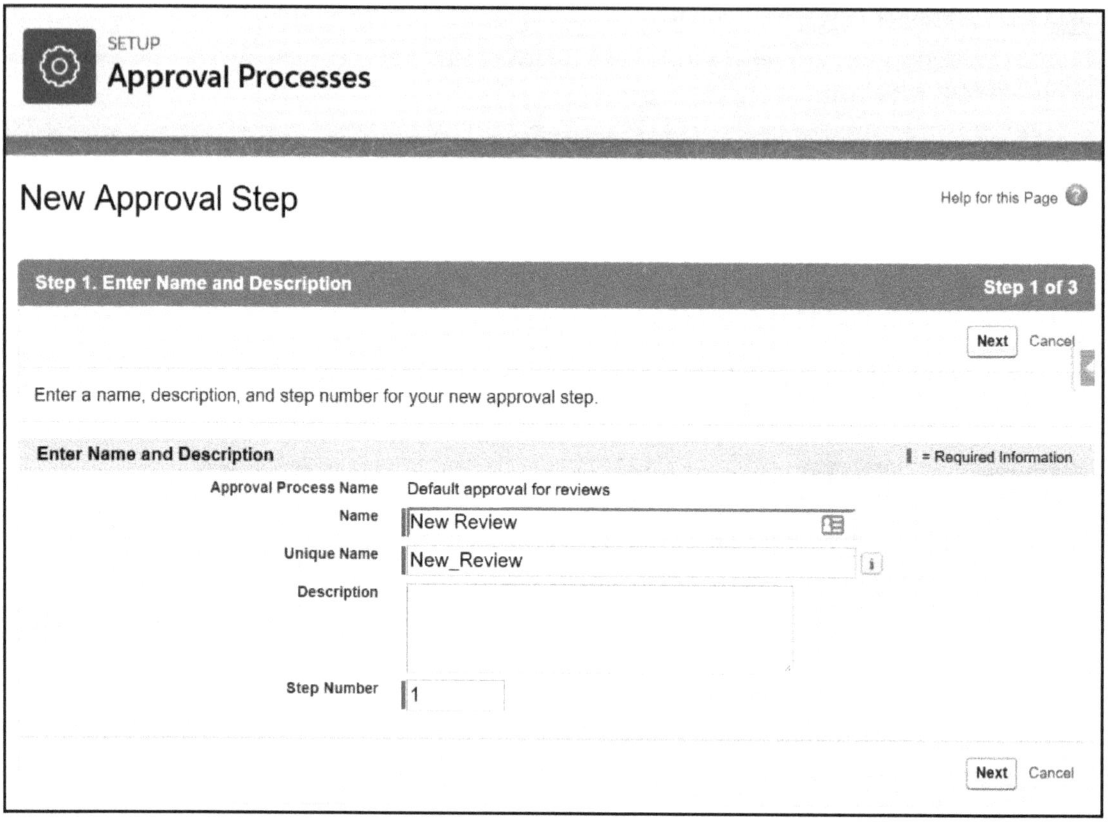

SETUP
Approval Processes

New Approval Step

Help for this Page

Step 1. Enter Name and Description	Step 1 of 3

Next Cancel

Enter a name, description, and step number for your new approval step.

Enter Name and Description ▮ = Required Information

Approval Process Name	Default approval for reviews
Name	New Review
Unique Name	New_Review
Description	
Step Number	1

Next Cancel

---

22. Select **All records should enter this step** and hit **Next**:

New Approval Step

Step 2. Specify Step Criteria   Step 2 of 3

Specify whether a record must meet certain criteria before entering this approval step. If these criteria are not met, the approval process can skip to the next step, if one exists. Learn more

Specify Step Criteria

- All records should enter this step.
- Enter this step if the following [criteria are met ▾] , else [approve record ▾] :

23. Now, you can select who will need to approve the record. Select a fixed approver (third option) and select yourself as **User**. Leave the **Approve or reject based on FIRST response**, as we won't have multiple steps, and also select **The approver's delegate may also approve this request** checkbox. This allows an approver to select a backup user on his user record to approve on his behalf while on holiday or in case of illness. Hit **Save**:

New Approval Step

Step 3. Select Assigned Approver   Step 3 of 3

Specify the user who should approve records that enter this step. Optionally, choose whether the approver's delegate is also allowed to approve these requests.

Select Approver

- Automatically assign using the user field selected earlier. (**Manager**)
- Automatically assign to queue.
- Automatically assign to approver(s).

  [User ▾] [Jan Vandevelde]
  Add Row Remove Row

  When multiple approvers are selected:
  - Approve or reject based on the **FIRST** response.
  - Require **UNANIMOUS** approval from all selected approvers.

☑ The approver's delegate may also approve this request.

24. Now, the wizard will ask you whether you would like to define an approval action for this step, a rejection action, or just save your process and create the actions later. Let's choose to create an approval action already and select **Field Update** and click **Go!**:

SETUP

Approval Processes

What Would You Like To Do Now?

Help for this Page

You have just created an approval step. You can optionally specify workflow actions to occur upon approval or rejection of this step. Would you like to do that now?

- ● Yes, I'd like to create a new approval action for this step now. | Field Update ▼ |
- ○ Yes, I'd like to create a new rejection action for this step now. | Email Alert ▼ |
- ○ No, I'll do this later. Take me to the approval process detail page to review what I've just created.

[Go!]

25. In the name of the **Field Update** action, fill in **Update Review To Approved**, select **Status** as a field to update, and choose **Approved** to set it to a specific value, and then hit **Save**:

SETUP

Approval Processes

Edit Field Update
Update Review to Approved

Help for this Page

Define the field update, including the object associated with the workflow rule, approval process, or entitlement process, the field to update, and the value to apply. Note that the field to update may be on a related object. Fields are shown only for the type that you select.

Field Update Edit		Save Save & New Cancel
Identification		I = Required Information

	Name	Update Review to Approved
	Unique Name	Update_Review_to_Approve :
	Description	
	Object	Review
	Field to Update	Status ▼
	Field Data Type	Picklist
	Re-evaluate Workflow Rules after Field Change	☑

Specify New Field Value

Picklist Options

- ○ The value above the current one
- ○ The value below the current one
- ● A specific value | Approved ▼ |

[Save   Save & New   Cancel]

26. You'll now find yourself on the approval overview page. Find the **Approval Steps** section and click the **Show Actions** link on the left of step **1**:

27. You'll see the **Field Update** action in the **Approval Actions** section you just created, but we don't have **Rejection Actions** for our step yet. So, click **Add New** in the **Rejection Actions** section and select **Field Update**:

28. Now, set the name to **Update review to declined**, select the **Status** field as the field to update, and set the value to **Declined**, and then hit **Save**:

29. Now, you'll be back on the approval overview page and you have defined an approval action and also a rejection action. Our approval process is done, but we still need to activate it.

Activating the approval process

This is something that is often forgotten, so hit the **Activate** button on top of the approval process:

Once we click the **Activate** button your approval process will be activated and ready for use. Let's test if it works:

1. Let's check our approval process out. Go to our `The Godfather` movie, and click the **Related** tab. In the related **Reviews** list, click the **New** button and create a new review to test it out. You'll see that the **Status** field is automatically populated with **Pending Review.** That's because we set it as a default value for new records. Leave it like that and hit **Save**:

2. Now that you have created a new review record, look in the related list of **Reviews**, find your new review record, and click it open to see the details. Notice that we haven't submitted the record for approval yet, but we don't have the button to **Submit For Approval**:

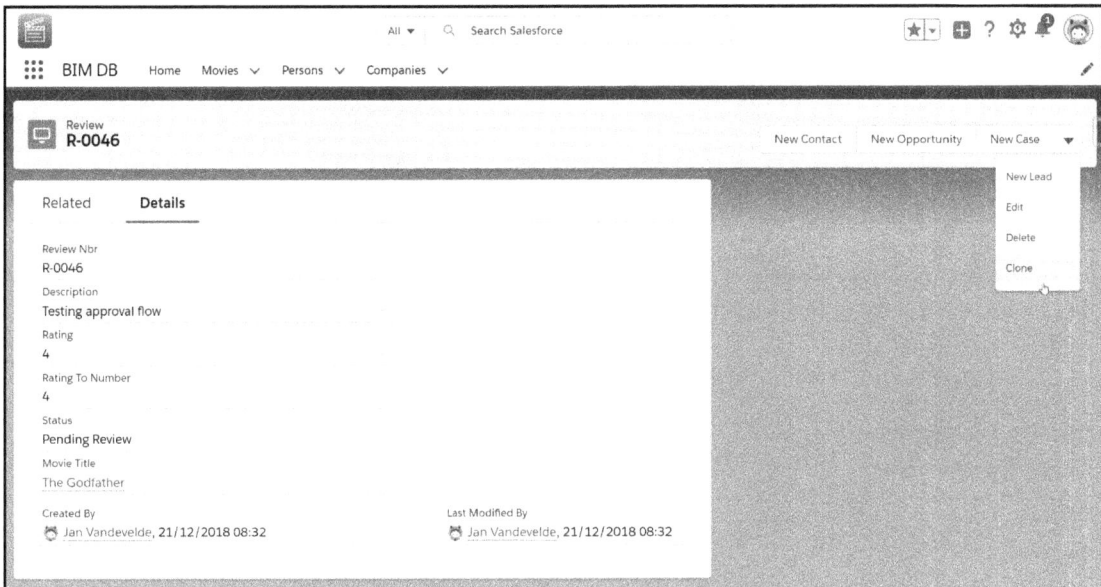

3. Therefore, click the wheel icon and click the **Edit** page to navigate to the Lightning App Builder so we can add this button to our page layout. Click within the details pane so it's marked with a blue border and gives you the page layouts section in the sidebar. Click on the **Review Layout (previewed)**:

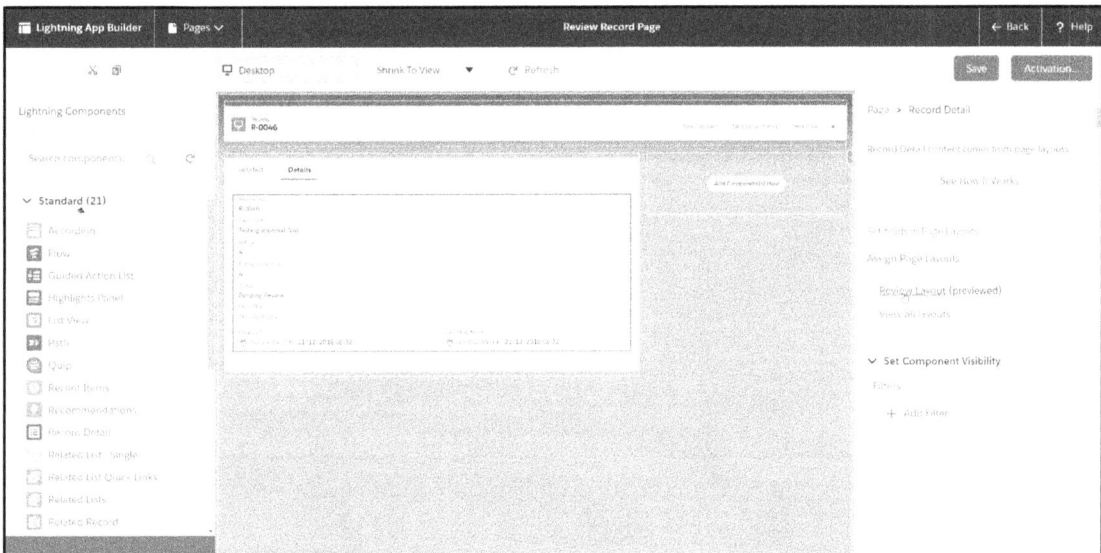

4. Click the **Buttons** section and you should find the **Submit For Approval** button. Drag and drop it into the standard buttons placeholder:

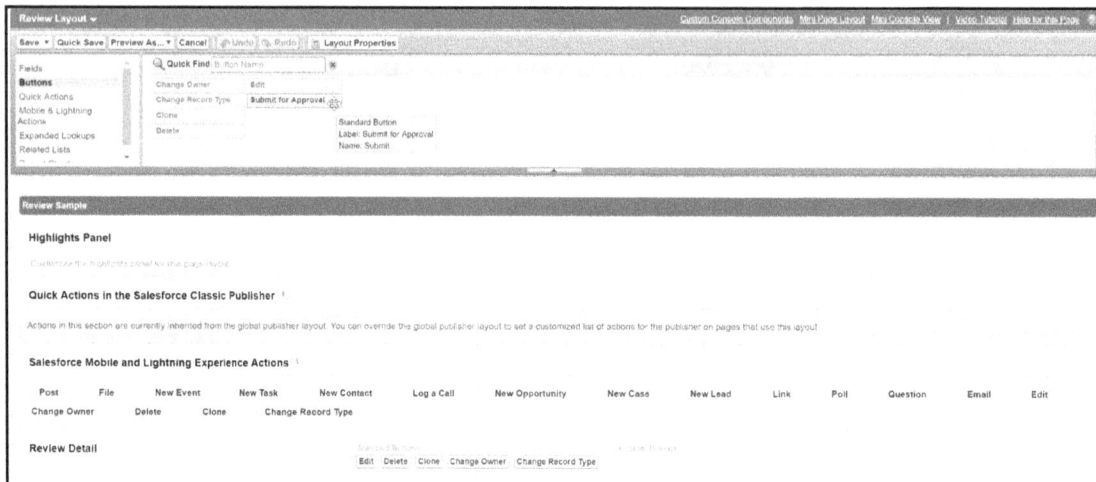

5. Also, click on the **Mobile & Lightning Actions** section and drag and drop the **Submit For Approval** button into the **Salesforce Mobile and Lightning Experience Actions** placeholder:

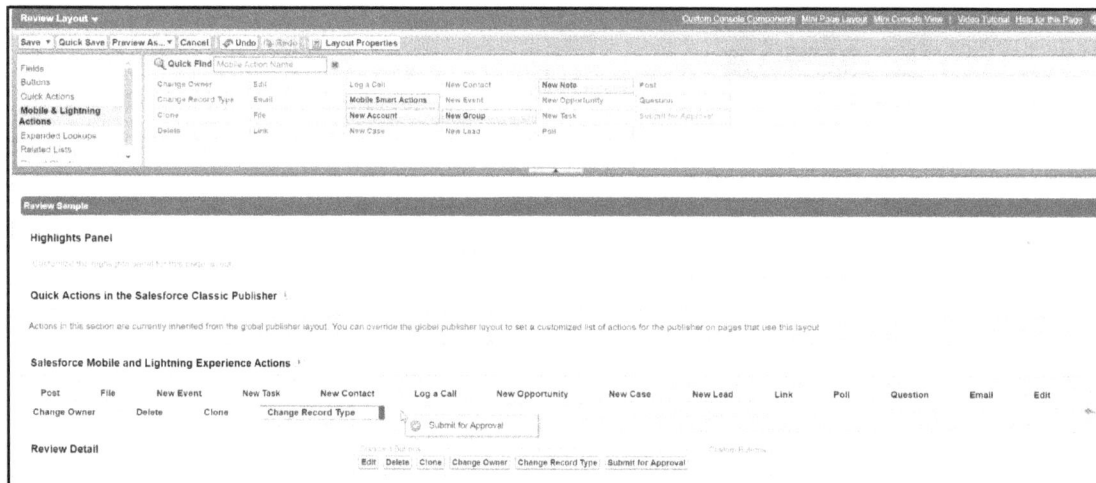

6. Don't forget to save your page layout and also save and activate (as the org-wide default page for the `Review` object) in the Lightning App Builder. When you click **Back**, you'll return to the `Review` record. Check the button menu now and you'll find the **Submit For Approval** button:

7. Submit the record (you can put in a comment or leave the comment field blank; your choice). Then, click the **Related** tab and check the new related **Approval History** list:

8. You can see that it was submitted by **Jan Vandevelde** (or you in your org) and the assignee, in this case, is also **Jan Vandevelde** (or you, in your case). In real life, there would be different names, but this is fine for now. You should also have received the email notification that you have a record to approve, as follows:

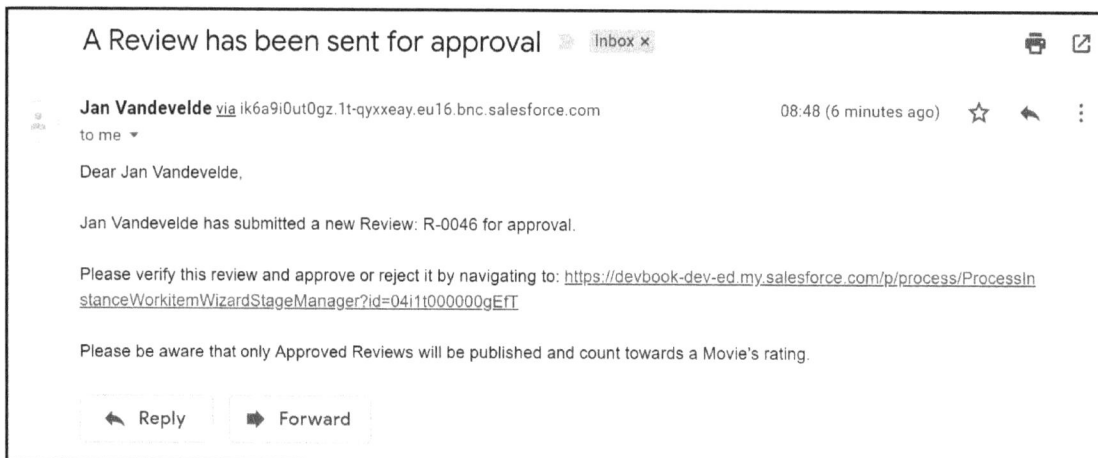

A Review has been sent for approval ▷ Inbox ×

Jan Vandevelde via ik6a9i0ut0gz.1t-qyxxeay.eu16.bnc.salesforce.com   08:48 (6 minutes ago) ☆ ↰ ⋮
to me ▾

Dear Jan Vandevelde,

Jan Vandevelde has submitted a new Review: R-0046 for approval.

Please verify this review and approve or reject it by navigating to: https://devbook-dev-ed.my.salesforce.com/p/process/ProcessInstanceWorkitemWizardStageManager?id=04i1t000000gEfT

Please be aware that only Approved Reviews will be published and count towards a Movie's rating.

↰ Reply   ➡ Forward

9. Clicking the link in the email should open up the approval page for this review record and should have an **Approve** and **Reject** button.
10. Now, click the **Approve** button and enter a comment. The status in the related approval history list should be **Approved**, and if we navigate back to the **Details** tab of this review record, we should see that the **Status** has also been updated to **Approved** by our **Field Update** action from the approval process:

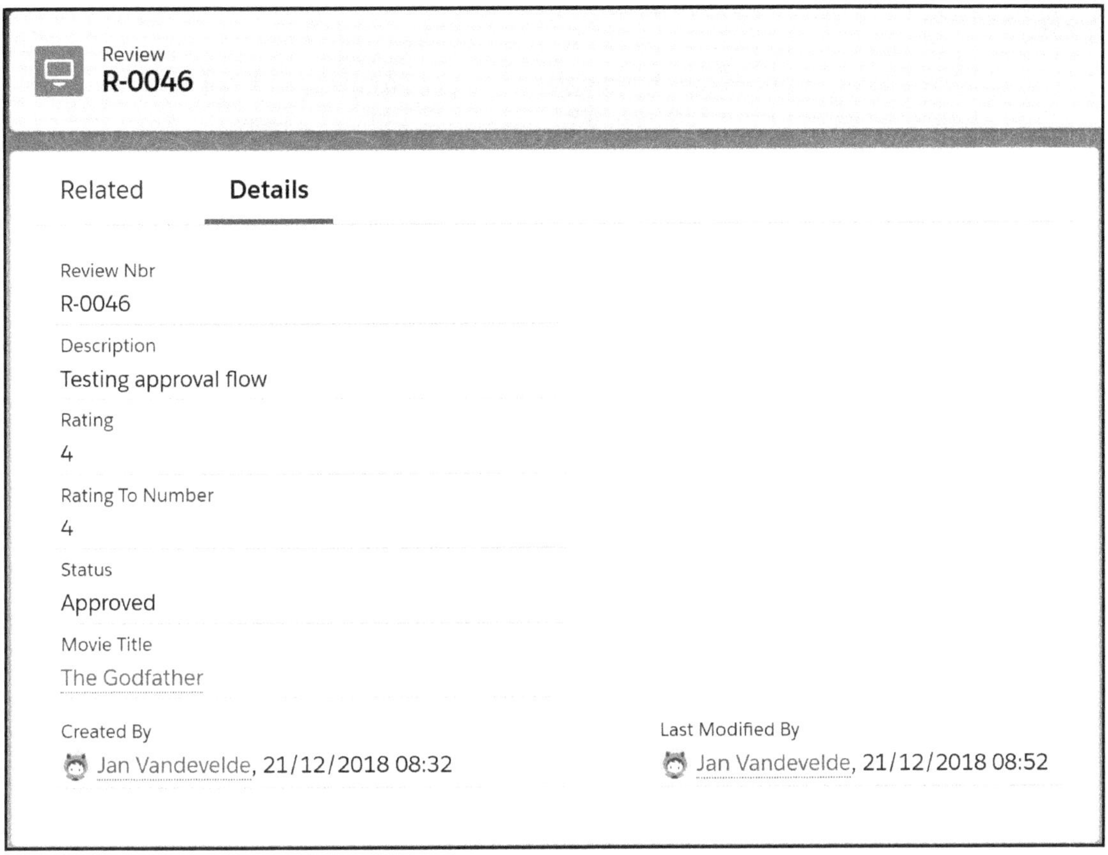

Review
R-0046

| Related | **Details** |

Review Nbr
R-0046

Description
Testing approval flow

Rating
4

Rating To Number
4

Status
Approved

Movie Title
The Godfather

Created By
👤 Jan Vandevelde, 21/12/2018 08:32

Last Modified By
👤 Jan Vandevelde, 21/12/2018 08:52

Perfect! Our approval process seems to be working as expected now.

As explained before, our exercise is not yet complete. We will have to configure two more things:

- We'll need to adapt our roll-up summary fields in order to exclude non-approved reviews from the rating calculations.
- We'll need to automate **Submission for Approval** by building Process Builder that does this for us, instead of the user needing to click the **Submit For Approval** button themselves.

So, let's get to it!

1. Navigate to **Setup** ∣ **Object Manager** and open up the `Movie` object. Then, select the **Fields & Relationships** section. Click the **Edit** button next to the **Nbr Of Reviews** roll-up summary field. At the bottom of that page, you can filter the records that need to be taken into account. Set it to **Only records meeting certain criteria should be included in the calculation** and set the criteria to **Status equals Approved** and hit **Save**:

2. Now, you do the same for the **Total Rating** roll-up summary field. Before we check the filter, let's first build and activate our Process Builder. This is just to buy some time, because if you look at our `The Godfather` movie record now, you wouldn't see any change to our roll-up summary fields, as they are all approved, for the moment. And to test our Process Builder in a minute, we'll need to create a new `Review` record anyway, so let's test and verify both at once in a minute.

3. To create our Process Builder that will submit `Review` records for approval automatically, navigate to **Setup** | **Process Builder** (which is located under the **Process Automation** section). This page will give you an overview of what Process Builder is, as we don't have any processes yet. Click the blue **New** button in the top-right corner of the page to create our first one.

4. As it is best practice not to create multiple Process Builders on the same object, for every little piece of automation you want, you may want to give it a proper name. I usually create a maximum of two Process Builders per object:

   - One with **On Create** actions only
   - And one with **On Create and/or Edit** actions

5. So, let's call this one **Reviews on Create/Edit** because we want to ascertain when a new review is created with the default status of **Pending Review**, but we could possibly also have existing records in the future that get updated and maybe we want those to be submitted for approval again. Give it a nice description, choose the **Process Starts When A Record Changes** option, and then click **Save**:

New Process

Process Name *

Reviews on Create/Edit

API Name * ⓘ

Reviews_on_Create_Edit

Description

Automate stuff when Review records are created and/or edited

The process starts when *

A record changes ▾

Cancel   **Save**

---

6. The first thing we need to do is define which object will be evaluated. In our case, that's the `Review` Object. Click the **+ Add Object** and, in the sidebar, choose **Review** as the object. We will start the process **when a record is created or edited** and don't check the **Recursion** checkbox.

Checking the **Recursion** checkbox is something you only want to do in exceptional circumstances! It allows the record, processes, workflow rules, flows, and Apex triggers to fire and re-evaluate up to five times, over and over. Within the same execution, the `Review` record would get updated through some kind of field update, which could cause you to hit **Governor Limits** if all automation processes are not crafted carefully!

7. The process screen should now look like the following screenshot:

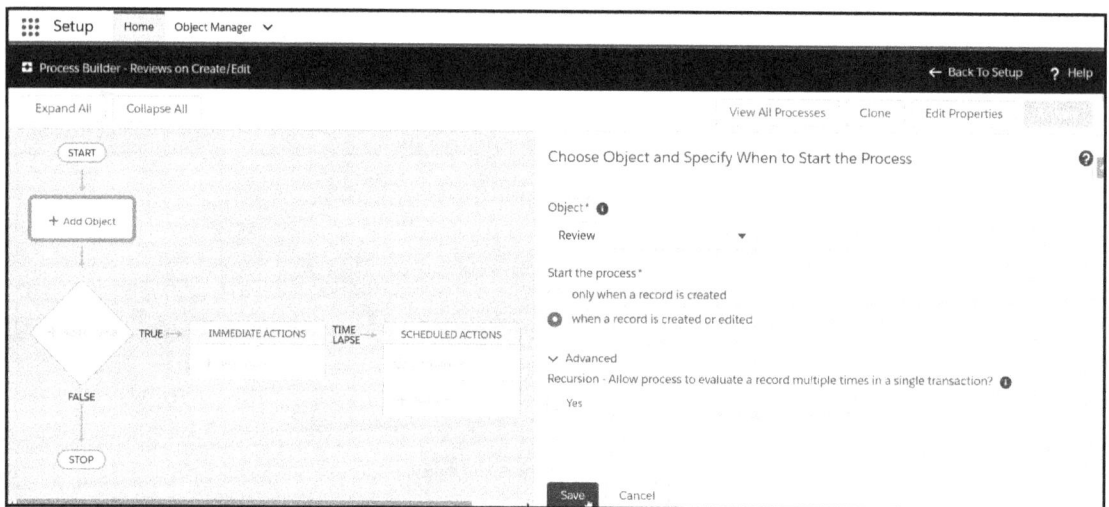

8. Next, we'll add the criteria we want to evaluate. Click the **Add Criteria** first node and fill in **New or Status Changed to Pending Review**, so that the node has a clear title. Because there is no `ISNEW` function in the picklists when you choose **Conditions are met**, we will choose to write our own formula. So, choose **Formula evaluates to true**, copy/paste the next formula in the formula editor, and then click **Save**:

```
(
ISNEW() && ISPICKVAL([Review__c].Status__c, 'Pending Review')
) ||
(
ISCHANGED([Review__c].Status__c) &&
```

```
PRIORVALUE([Review__c].Status__c) != 'Pending Review' &&
ISPICKVAL([Review__c].Status__c, 'Pending Review')
)
```

Let's explain this formula:

The first thing you need to know is that the double pipes (||) mean OR and that two ampersands (&&), mean AND! So, our formula evaluates two things:

- If it's a newly created record (ISNEW()) *and* it has the status **Pending Review**, then perform our actions.
- If it's an existing record (ISCHANGED()) that can only be used on existing records *and* the status field has been changed from a value that was different to **Pending Review** *and* its new value now becomes **Pending Review**, then perform our actions.

Your screen should look similar to the following screenshot:

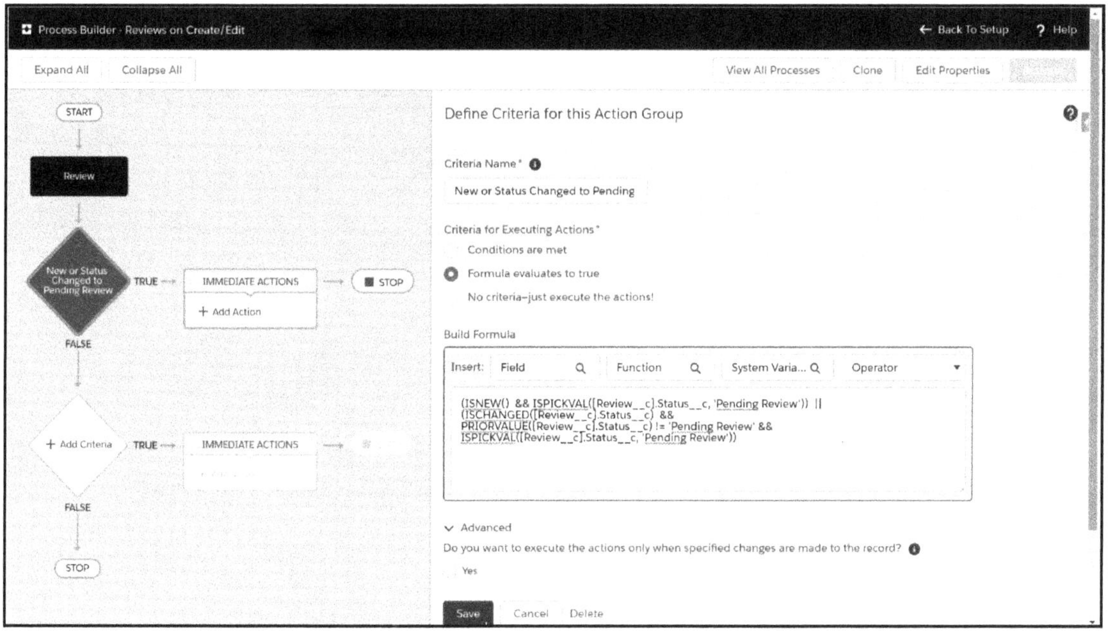

9. The next step is to *add action(s)* to be executed if the previous criteria are met. Click **Add Action** under **Immediate Actions** in that node. Select **Submit for Approval** as **Action Type**, give it a proper name (I chose **Submit Review for Approval)**, and choose a specific approval process, which is our **Default approval for reviews**. Do not check the **Skip the entry criteria for this process** checkbox because we want to adhere to our entry criteria set in the approval flow. And, as a submitter, choose the **Current User** (this will either be the creator of the record or the user changing an existing review's status field back to **Pending Review)**, and the hit **Save**. Your settings should look like this:

10. Now, don't forget to activate your process by clicking the **Activate** button in the top-right corner of your process:

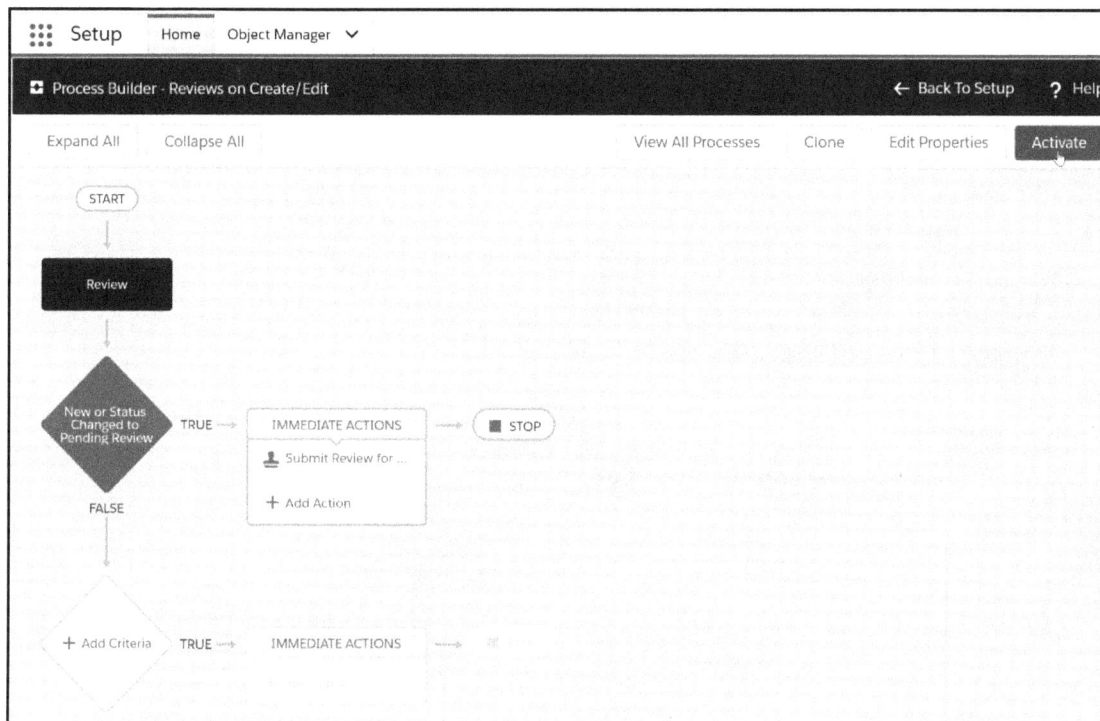

11. That's it! Now, to test everything we've just built, we'll go back to our The Godfather movie record. We'll check out our current **Total Rating** and **Nbr of Reviews** values. Then, we'll create a new review and we would expect that it gets automatically submitted for approval, right? Also, while it is not approved yet, our **Total Rating** and **Nbr of Reviews** values should not have changed yet (as this new review is not approved yet and should not be counted!). Then, we'll approve the review, and, after that, our **Total Rating** and **Nbr of Reviews** values should have been updated to take into account this new review.

12. So, if I go and look at **The Godfather** now in my org, I see that **Nbr of Reviews** is set to **5** and **Total Rating** is set to **21**:

13. Now, I'll create a totally new review:

14. Without hitting the **Submit for Approval** button myself manually, I immediately received the approval notification email and, if I check the related **Approval History** list on this new review, I can see that it has been correctly submitted for approval automatically:

15. Now, before approving or rejecting this submission, I first want to check on my movie record whether the values for **Total Rating** and **Nbr of Reviews** are still the same! And, yes, they are, which is great news:

Cover Image

Your movie cover

Director's Birthdate
06/04/1939

Nbr of Reviews
5

Total Rating
21

Average Rating
4

Created By
🦉 Jan Vandevelde, 24/11/2018 11:18

Last Modified By
🦉 Jan Vandevelde, 21/12/2018 08:32

16. Now, let's approve our new review:

Approve Review

Comments

It's okay, good review

Cancel   Approve

So, now, I expect the **Total Rating** and **Nbr of Reviews** to have changed, and they did! Yeah, how cool is this?! I now have **6** approved reviews (previously **5**) and the **Total Rating** has incremented with a value of two, which was the rating I gave in the last review:

Cover Image

Your movie cover

Director's Birthdate
06/04/1939

Nbr of Reviews
6

Total Rating
23

Average Rating
4

Created By
Jan Vandevelde, 24/11/2018 11:18

Last Modified By
Jan Vandevelde, 21/12/2018 10:23

I know there were a lot of steps to follow, and I really hope it was sufficiently clear for you to follow, but we achieved a lot in this section:

- We have created an approval notification email template
- We have created an approval process that updates the status of review records accordingly to **Approved** or **Declined**
- We have adapted our roll-up summary fields to include a filter so that only approved reviews are counted
- We automated the submission for approval by creating a Process Builder that submits reviews automatically

Now, let's dive into the last automation feature—Visual Workflow!

Visual Workflow

As we already learned in Chapter 1, *Salesforce Fundamentals*, Visual Workflow is the product that lets you design, manage, and run flows. You create and manage your flows through a tool with a graphical interface, previously called the Cloud Flow Designer (now called Flow Builder). Each flow is actually an application that automates a business process by collecting, updating, editing, and creating Salesforce data. Flows can execute actions based upon criteria you set, interact with records in your database, call Apex classes, and they can even guide your users to wizard-like screens to collect and/or update information.

At the time of writing (Spring 2019), the Cloud Flow Designer just got a major revamp and got a new name: Flow Builder! So, I'll be showing you the latest version in our examples.

The following screenshot shows the new Flow Builder in all its glory:

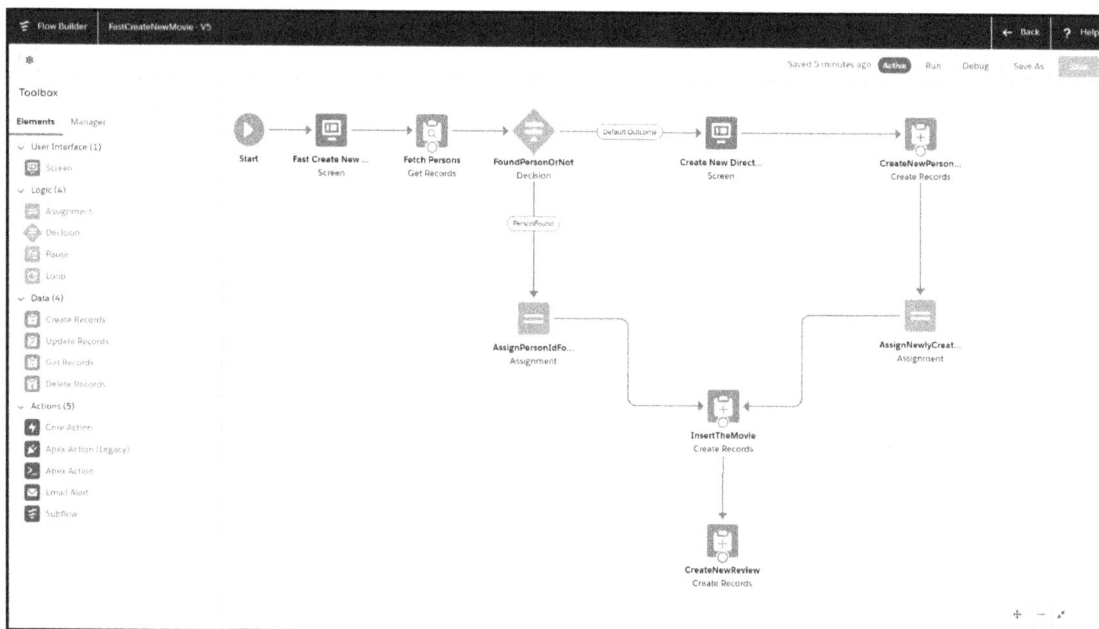

The Flow Builder interface has two parts:

- The **Toolbox**: This is the sidebar, which contains two tabs—**Elements** and **Manager**. Firstly, the **Elements** tab: This contains all elements that you can drag and drop onto the canvas and connect together to build out your flow. Then, the **Manager** tab gives an overview of all elements in use within your flow.
- The canvas: This is your actual flow. You chain elements together and configure each element so that they perform a certain action.

Use the more powerful Visual Flows to perform even more actions than Process Builder or workflow rules! With Visual Flow, you can perform the following tasks:

- Accept user input
- Call Apex (can be used to send outbound messages too)
- Create records
- Delete records
- Post to chatter
- Send emails
- Submit for approval
- Update fields on any record
- Quick actions
- Query records
- Loop through records
- Make multiple decisions

Tips, before you start creating your flows, include the following:

- Draw your business process out before you try to automate it.
- My principle is always that you must be able to do each action sequentially through the user interface before you can start automating it. Automation is all about automating actions that a user would otherwise perform manually and removing the burden.
- Be aware of required fields when creating records from within your flow.
- Give your actions, variables, decisions, and screens meaningful names so that you keep a clear overview of your flow.

In the previous chapter, I promised you that we would create a flow that provides the user with a little wizard to create a new movie, director, and review in one go. We'll do that right now.

1. To create our flow, navigate to **Setup** | **Process Automation** | **Flows** and click the **New Flow** button:

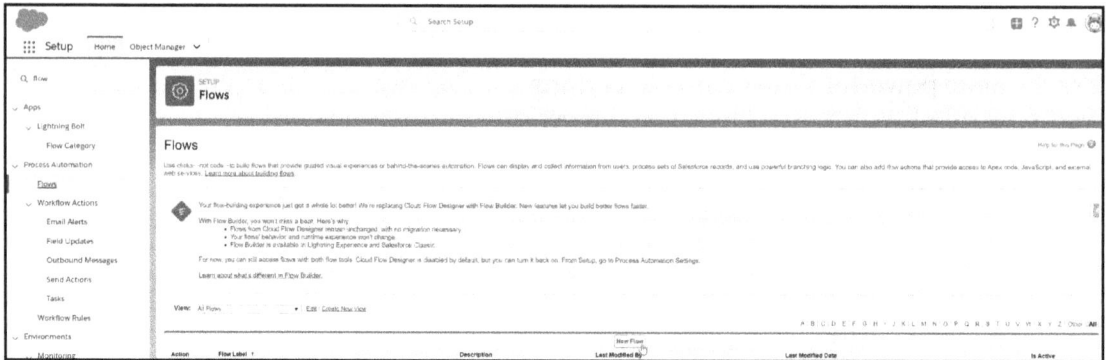

2. You'll see a big blank canvas with only a start element on it. In the sidebar, you'll find your **Toolbox** containing elements you can choose from to build out your flow. The first thing we'll need is an input screen for our users to fill in some details, which we will use to create our movie, (possibly) a person, and a review.

3. So, drag the **Screen** element onto the canvas and it will open the element configurator, as shown in the following screenshot:

New Screen

Screen Components

Search components... 🔍

∨ Input (22)

⚡ Address
☑ Checkbox
📋 Checkbox Group
📷 Currency
📅 Date
📅 Date & Time
⚡ Dependent Picklists
⚡ Display Image
⚡ Email
⚡ File Upload
📋 Long Text Area
📋 Multi-Select Picklist
⚡ Name
🔟 Number
🔡 Password
⚡ Phone
📋 Picklist
🔲 Radio Buttons
⚡ Slider

Get more on the AppExchange

[Flow Label]

Pause   Previous   **Finish**

Screen Properties   ↗

* Label

* API Name

Description

∨ Configure Frame   ⓘ
✓ Show Header
✓ Show Footer

> Control Navigation   ⓘ

> Provide Help

Cancel   **Done**

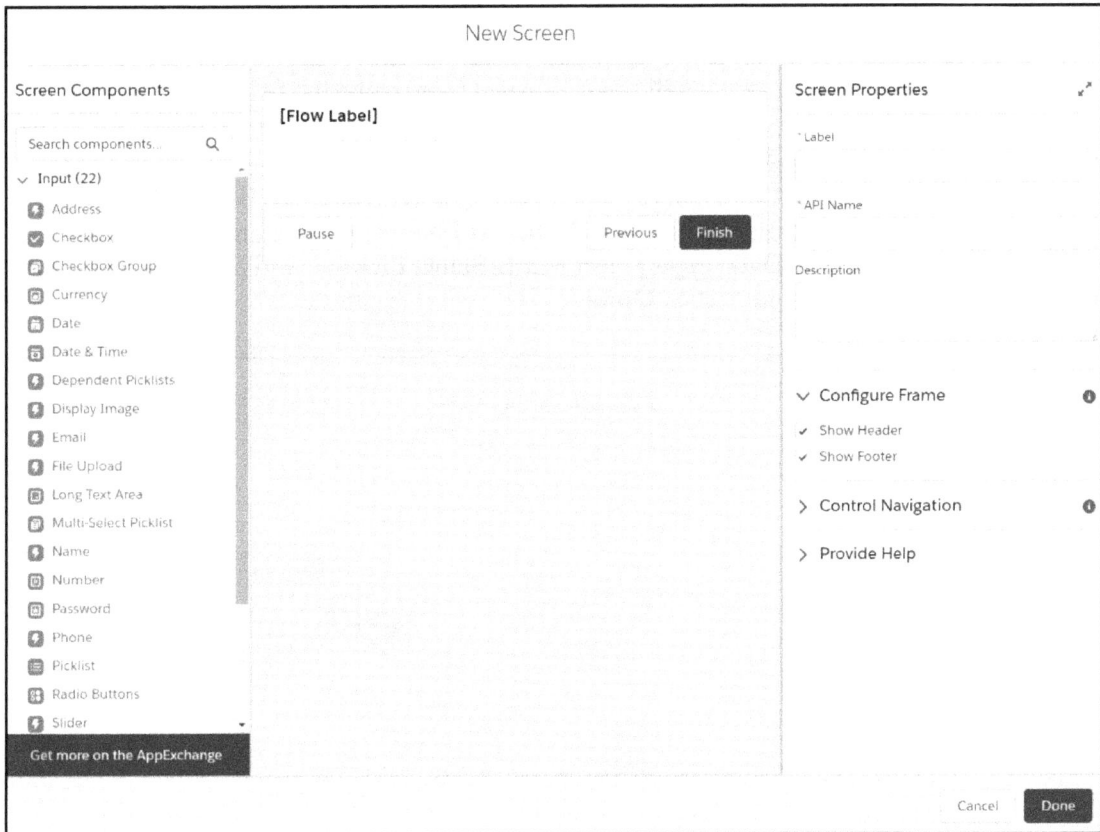

Start by filling in the **Label** with Fast Create New Movie. The API name should get filled in automatically based upon the label. Leave all other settings as default. Perform the following steps very carefully:

1. Drag a **Display Text** component as the next component and fill in DisplayNewMovie as the **API Name**. In the white box underneath the API name, copy/paste the following text: Fill in the necessary fields to create a new movie record.

2. Next, drag a **Text** component into the screen part (not a **Long Text Area**!). As the label, fill in the **Movie Title**. The API name should be **Movie_Title**. Check the **Require** checkbox.

3. Drag a **Date** component onto the screen, and call the label **Release Date**. The API name becomes **Release_Date.** Leave the rest as default.

4. Next, drag a **Multi-Select Picklist** into the screen. As the label, put **Genre.** As the **API Name,** overwrite the default to **GenrePick** (this is because an API name must be unique and we will select our real **Genre** picklist field from the `Movie` object to provide us with values). The data type is **Text.** Don't set a default value.

5. In the **Select Choices** section, put your cursor in the first choice box and click **New Resource**. A new window will pop open with a search box for **Resource Type.** Select **Picklist Choice Set.** As the **API Name,** fill in **Genre,** for **Object,** select **Movie,** as **Data Type,** select **Multi-Select Picklist,** and as **Field,** select our **Genre__c** field. Then, click **Done:**

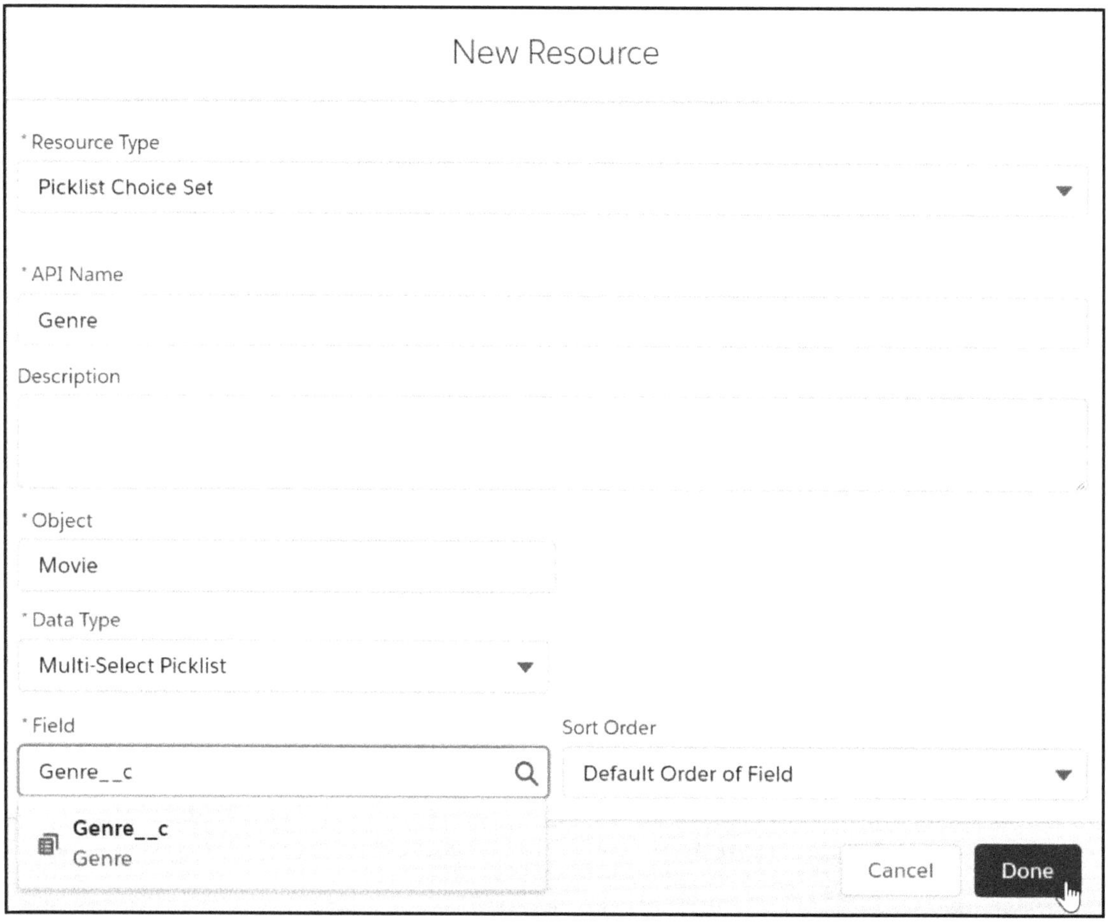

New Resource

* Resource Type

Picklist Choice Set ▾

* API Name

Genre

Description

* Object

Movie

* Data Type

Multi-Select Picklist ▾

* Field	Sort Order
Genre__c 🔍	Default Order of Field ▾

📇 **Genre__c**
Genre

Cancel   **Done**

---

6. After clicking **Done**, you will see that the **Choice** field is still empty, so click in it again. But now, you will be able to select the **Genre** picklist choice set we just created. Select this, as shown in the following screenshot:

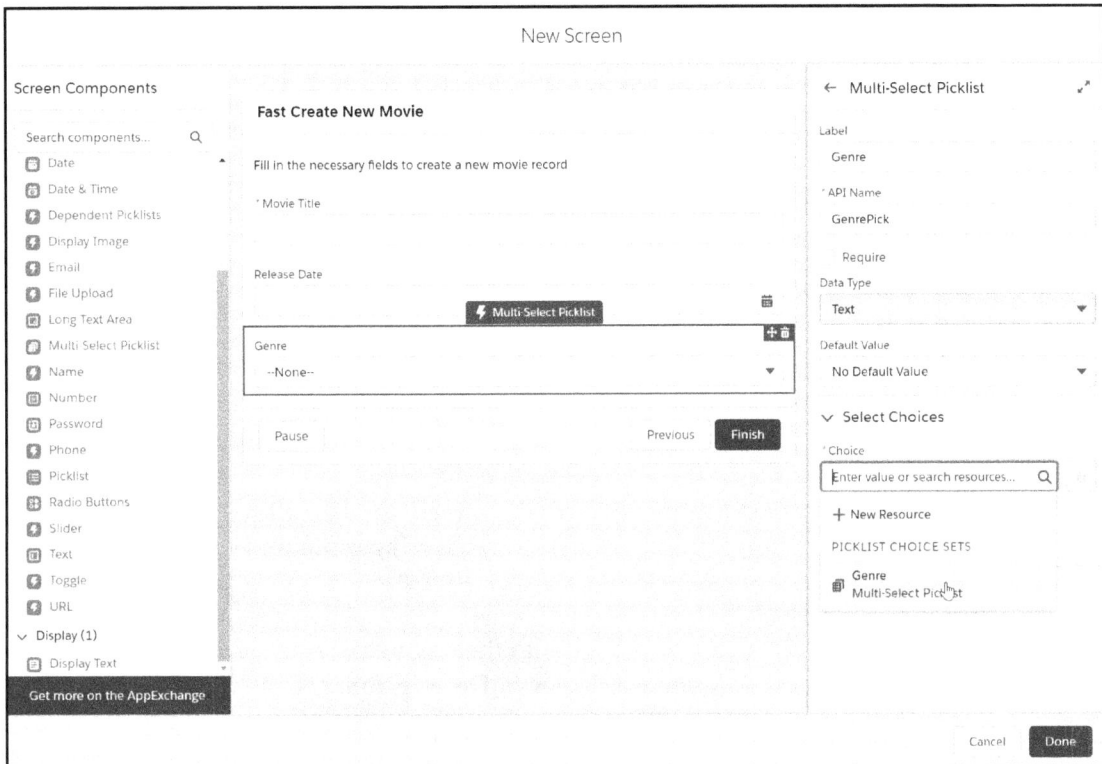

7. Drag a **Number** component into the screen and set **Label** as **Runtime**, the **API Name** as **Runtime,** and decimal places equal to **0**.

8. Drag a **Currency** component into the screen and set **Label** as **Budget**, the **API Name** as **Budget,** and decimal places equal to **0**.

9. Drag a **Text** component into the screen and set **Label** as **Cover URL**, and the **API Name** as **Cover_URL**.

10. Drag a **Long Text Area** component into the screen and set **Label** as **Description** and the **API Name** as **Description**.

11. Drag a **Display Text** component into the screen and set the API name as **DisplayDirector** and copy/paste the following sentence into the big white box: `Fill in First Name and Last Name of the Director. If the Director already exists, it will be linked automatically. If not you'll be asked to enter some more details in the next step.`

12. Drag a **Text** component into the screen, set its **Label** to `Director Full Name` and the **API name** as `Director_Full_Name`, and then check the **Require** checkbox.

13. Drag a **Display Text** component into the screen, set the **API name** as **DisplayNewReview**, and copy/paste the following sentence in the big white box: `Please enter a first review for this movie. It will be automatically sent for approval after successful creation.`

14. Drag a **Long Text Area** component into the screen and set its **Label** to `Review Description`, the API name to **Review_Description**, and check the **Require** checkbox.

15. Drag a **Picklist** component into the screen and set its **Label** to **Review Rating**, and the API name to **Review_Rating.** Check the **Require** checkbox and choose **Data Type** as **Text**. Under the **Select Choices** section, put your cursor in the choice box and click **New Resource**. Select **Picklist Choice Set** as **Resource Type**, set the API name to `ReviewRating`, choose **Review** as **Object**, choose **Picklist** as **Data Type,** and choose **Rating__c** as **Field.** Then, click **Done**:

16. Just as with our previous picklist choice, the **Choice** is again blank. Click on it and you'll find your newly created **ReviewRating** picklist choice set. Select this option.

17. Your screen element is now finished and should appear as follows (I can't get all the fields on one screen, so this is the bottom part):

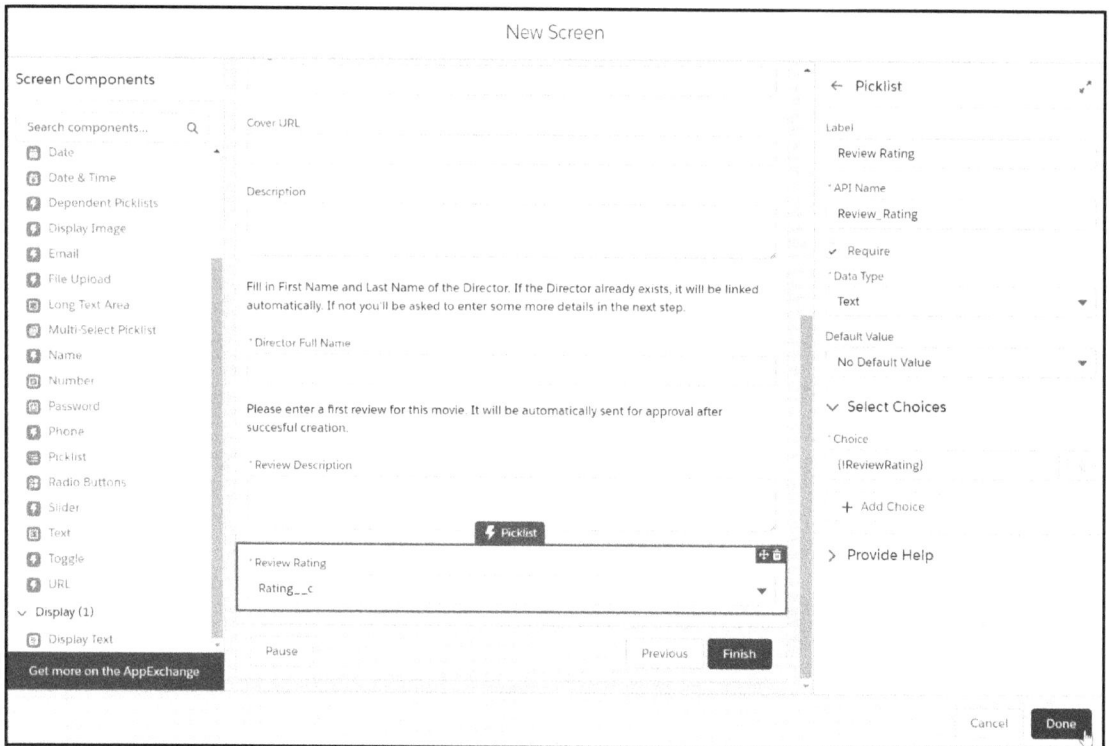

If your screen looks the same and you have paid attention to very carefully create all the components with the exact labels, names, and settings as I've instructed (if you're not sure, go over every step one more time), you can click the **Done** button to save your screen element and go back to the Flow Builder canvas. It should look like this:

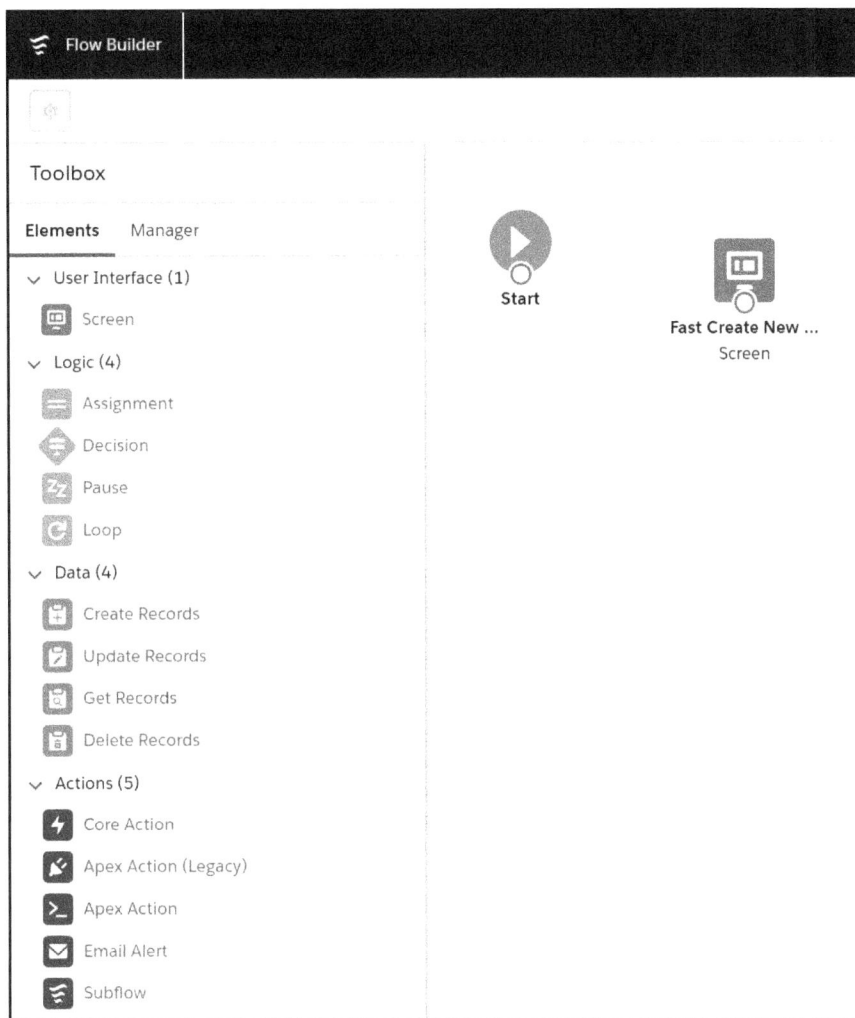

18. Now that we have our first element, we need to connect it with the **Start** element. To do that, click and hold the little white circle of the **Start** element and drag the connecting line onto our **Fast Create New Movie Screen** element. This will connect both elements, as follows:

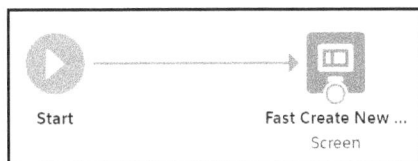

What we've actually created right now is an input screen for our users with fields that are required to create a movie, a person (as director), and a review. By marking some fields as mandatory, we are sure we have a minimum of data required to create a record of each type. But for now, all we would have is that data in memory, in variables within our flow, but not in the database!

And what we also want to do is check, based upon the director's full name, whether this person already exists in our BIM DB. If so, we won't create a second person with the same name, but relate the movie to the existing one. If the person doesn't exist, we'll provide the user with a second screen asking for some more details (a biography and a birthdate).

Let's continue. We've got a lot of steps ahead, so keep paying attention and follow the next steps very carefully:

19. Drag a **Get Records** element onto the canvas. This opens the element configurator screen. Fill in **Fetch Persons** as **Label**, and the **API Name** as **Fetch_Persons**.
20. In the **Get Records of This Object** section, select the **Person** object.
21. In the **Filter Person Records** section, select **Conditions are Met** and choose the **Name** as a field, **Equals** as operator, and select **Director_Full_Name** (under the screen components section) as the value.
22. In the **Sort Person Records** section, choose **Ascending** as **Sort Order** and select the **Name** as **Sort By** value. Now, for **How Many Records to Store**, choose **Only the first record** and for **Where to Store Field Values,** select the **Together in a record variable** radio button, and also check the **When no records are returned, set specified variables to null.** checkbox!
23. In the **Select Variable to Store Person** section, put your cursor in the **Record Variable** search box and click **New Resource**. A new screen opens. Choose **Variable** as the resource type, set the **API name** to **FoundPerson**, select **Record** as the data type, and **Person** as the object. Check the **Available for output** checkbox, and then hit **Done**.
24. Just like before, our **Record Variable** is still empty, but click in it and now you can select our new **FoundPerson** record variable. Lastly, in the **Select Person Fields To Store in Variable**, the ID is already set for you and marked as read-only. Add the **Name** field also. If your screen looks like the following screenshot, you can hit the **Done** button at the bottom:

Edit Get Records

Find Salesforce records and store their field values in flow variables.

* Label

Fetch Persons

* API Name

Fetch_Persons

Description

Get Records of This Object

* Object

Person

Filter Person Records

Condition Requirements

Conditions are Met

Field	Operator	Value
Name	Equals	{!Director_Full_Name}

+ Add Condition

Sort Person Records

Sort Order

Ascending

* Sort By

Name

To use the returned **Person** records in the flow, store their fields in variables.

How Many Records to Store
- Only the first record
- All records

Where to Store Field Values
- Together in a record variable
- In separate variables

✓ When no records are returned, set specified variables to null.

Select Variable to Store Person

* Record Variable

{!FoundPerson}

Select Person Fields to Store in Variable

Field

ID

Field

Name

+ Add Field

Cancel   Done

What we did here was to create a **Get Records** element. This is basically a query we will perform to find person records in the database with the same name as what the user fills in the director full name screen element. We don't care if we find multiple records. We only store the first one found in a record variable called `FoundPerson`, so our `FoundPerson` variable will contain the record ID and the name of that record.

If no match is found, our `FoundPerson` variable will be null and, as a result, **not set**. We will use this query to make a decision if we need to create a new `Person` record and ask for more details, or if we can relate an existing `Person` record as the director for this new movie. That's actually our next step.

25. Drag a **Decision** element onto the canvas. This opens the element configurator screen. Enter `FoundPersonOrNot` as **Label** and the API name.

26. In the **Outcome Details** section, fill in **PersonFound** as **Label** and the API name, select **All Conditions Are Met** for when to execute the outcome, and, from the resource box, select **FoundPerson** under the **Record Variables** section and select its ID field. Then, as the operator, choose **Was Set** and, as the value, select **GlobalConstant.True**. Then, hit **Done**:

New Decision		
*Label		*API Name
FoundPersonOrNot		FoundPersonOrNot
Description		

Outcomes For each path the flow can take, create an outcome. For each outcome, specify the conditions that must be met for the flow to take that path.

OUTCOME ORDER ❶ ＋	OUTCOME DETAILS	
≡ PersonFound	*Label	*Outcome API Name
	PersonFound	PersonFound
Default Outcome	When to Execute Outcome	
	All Conditions Are Met ▼	

Resource	Operator	Value
{!FoundPerson.Id}	Was Set ▼	{!$GlobalConstant.True}

＋ Add Condition

Cancel   Done

What we did here was create an IF/ELSE decision. Each decision element always has a default outcome, and as we did not set that, it will act as our person not found outcome. We also created a PersonFound outcome that checks whether, in a previous step, our FoundPerson variable has been set (this means that we found at least one person record with the exact same name as the director's full name, filled in by the user).

27. Drag an assignment element onto the canvas. The element configurator will open. Set the **Label** to **AssignPersonIdFound**, and the API name as **AssignPersonIdFound.**

28. In the **Set Variable Values** section, click in the **Variable** box and select **New Resource**. Select **Variable** as the resource type, the API name as **PersonIdToUse**, and the data type as **Text**. Select the **Available for output** checkbox, and then click **Done**.

29. As always, you need to select the newly created variable now as the variable, so select **PersonIdToUse** and set the operator as **Add,** As the value, select our existing **FoundPerson** as its ID field, and hit **Done**. Your assignment element should look like the following screenshot:

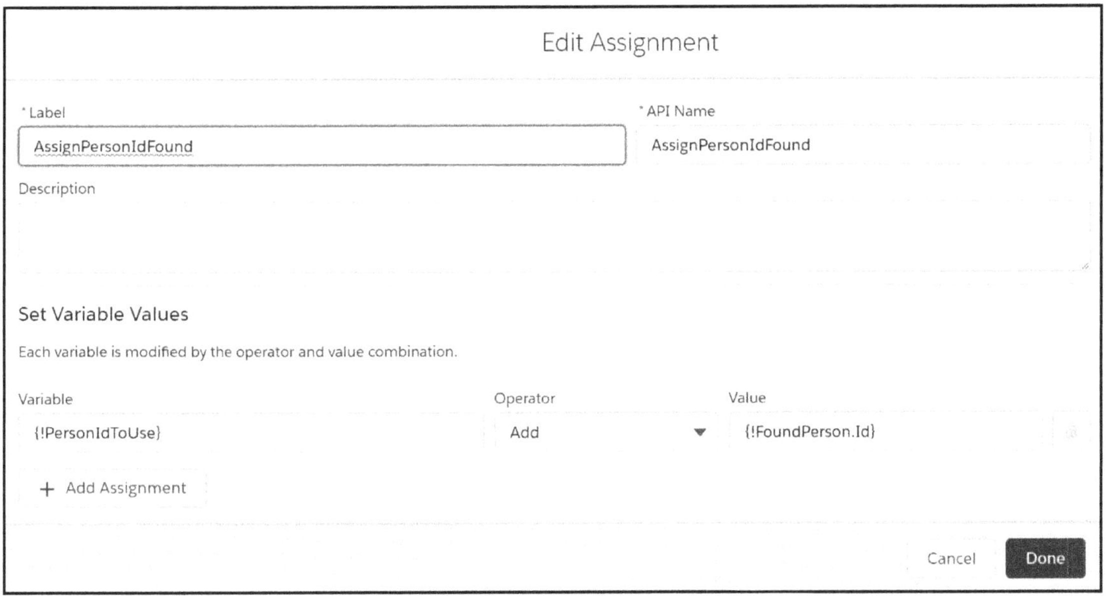

	Edit Assignment	
* Label		* API Name
AssignPersonIdFound		AssignPersonIdFound
Description		

Set Variable Values

Each variable is modified by the operator and value combination.

Variable	Operator	Value
{!PersonIdToUse}	Add ▼	{!FoundPerson.Id}

+ Add Assignment

Cancel   **Done**

What we did here was to create an assignment element that we will use to assign the ID of the `Person` record that we found through our query to a text variable called `PersonIdToUse`. We will connect this assignment element to our decision element for the outcome when a `Person` has been found!

30. So, before we continue creating other elements, let's first connect the elements we already have. Click and hold the white circle of the **Fast Create New Movie** screen element and connect it to the **Fetch Persons Get records** element.

31. Then connect the **Fetch Persons** element to our **Decision** element. Now, connect our **Decision** element to our **Assignment** element.

32. A popup will open in which you need to choose the outcome for which you want this assignment action to be executed. Choose the outcome **PersonFound** and click **Done**:

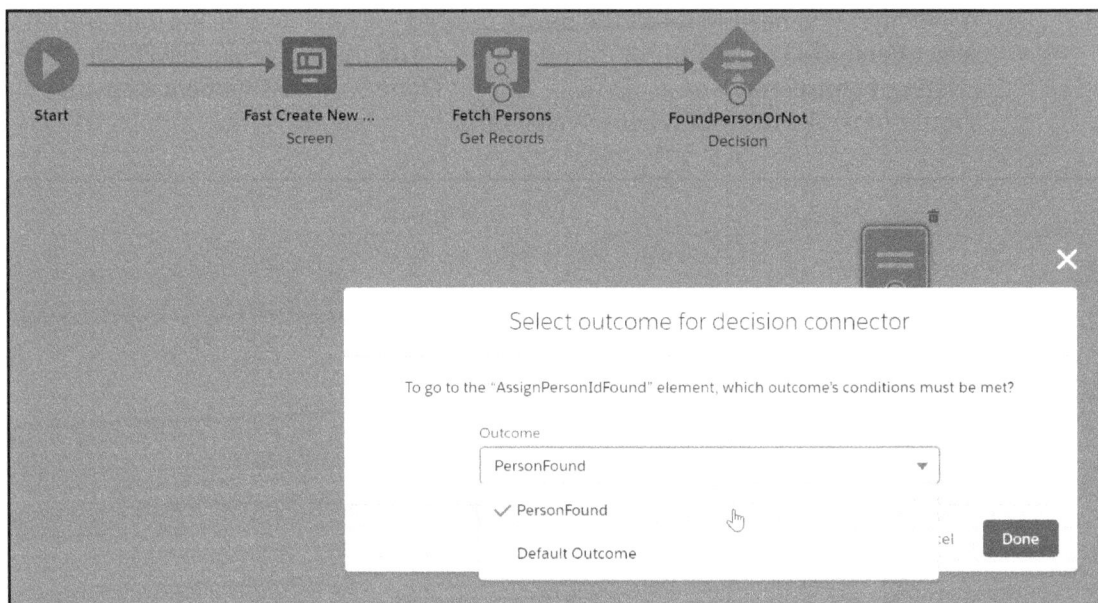

Your flow should now look like the following screenshot:

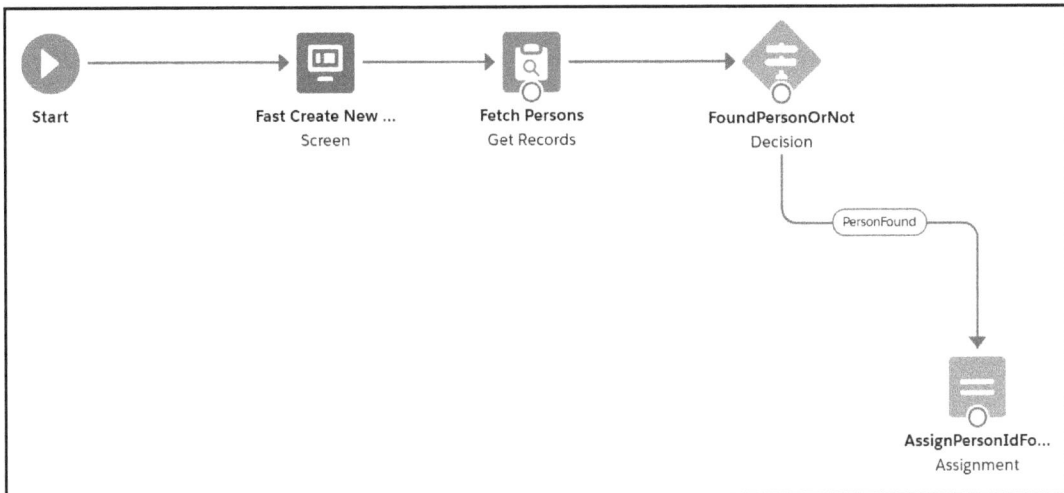

It should become clear to you that we are now following the path (decision) where we found an existing `Person` record that has the exact same full name as the director's full name value that the user would have entered in our wizard, right? So, let's continue first finishing this path; afterward, we will build out the path where the director does not yet exist in our database.

33. Drag a **Create Records** element onto the canvas. The element configurator opens. Fill in the **Label** with **InsertTheMovie** and the API name with **InsertTheMovie**. Choose **One** record to create and **Use separate variables, resources, and literal values** for how to set the record fields. In the object, choose **Movie**, and then map the following fields (of our `Movie` object) to values we have in memory:

    - Field: **Budget__c**; **Value**: Budget (under the screen components section)
    - Field: **Cover_URL__c**; **Value**: Cover URL (under the screen components section)
    - Field: **Description__c**; **Value**: Description (under the screen components section)
    - Field: **Director__c**; **Value**: **PersonIdToUse** (under the variables section)
    - Field: **Genre__c**; **Value**: **GenrePick** (under the screen components section)
    - Field: **Name**; **Value**: Movie title (under the screen components section)
    - Field: **Release_Date__c**; **Value**: Release date (under the screen components section)
    - Field: **Runtime__c**; **Value**: Runtime (under the screen components section)

34. Now, in the **Store Movie ID in Variable** section of the configurator, click **New Resource**. Select **Variable** as the resource type, as the API name, fill in **NewlyCreatedMovieId**, as the data type, choose **Record,** and, as the object, choose **Movie**. Select the **Available for output** checkbox, and then click **Done**:

Edit Create Records

Create Salesforce records using values from the flow.

* Label

InsertTheMovie

* API Name

InsertTheMovie

Description

How Many Records to Create
● One
  Multiple

How to Set the Record Fields
  Use all values from a record variable
● Use separate variables, resources, and literal values

Create a Record of This Object

* Object

Movie

Set Field Values for the Movie

Field	Value
Budget__c	← (!Budget)
Cover_URL__c	← (!Cover_URL)
Description__c	← (!Description)
Director__c	← (!PersonIdToUse)
Genre__c	← (!GenrePick)
Name	← (!Movie_Title)
Release_Date__c	← (!Release_Date)
Runtime__c	← (!Runtime)

+ Add Field

Store Movie ID in Variable

Variable

{!NewlyCreatedMovieId.Id}

Cancel   Done

Don't forget that you have to set the variable now to your **NewlyCreatedMovieId** its ID field and then hit **Done** again to save your element.

Let's first create the last element of this path and then we'll recap what we have done so far. I appreciate that it's a lot!

35. Drag a **Create Records** element onto the canvas. The element configurator pops open. Set the **Label** to **CreateNewReview** and the **API Name** to **CreateNewReview**. Select **One** record to create and **Use separate variables, resources, and literals** for how to set the record fields option. Choose the **Review** object as the record to create and map the following fields and values:

    - **Field**: **Description__c**; **Value**: **Review Description** (under the screen components section)
    - **Field**: **Movie_Title__c**; **Value**: **NewlyCreatedMovieId** (under the **Record** variables section)
    - **Field**: **Rating__c**; **Value**: **Review Rating** (under the screen components section)
    - **Field**: **Status__c**; **Value**: **Pending Review** (under the picklist values section)

36. Now, in the **Store Review ID in Variable** section of the configurator, click **New Resource**. Select **Variable** as the resource type, as the **API Name**, fill in **NewlyCreatedReview**, as the data type, choose **Record,** and, as the object, choose **Review**. Select the **Available for output** checkbox, and then click **Done**. Don't forget that you have to set the variable now to your **NewlyCreatedReview**, its ID field, and then hit **Done** again to save your element.

It should now look like this:

New Create Records

Create Salesforce records using values from the flow.

* Label
CreateNewReview

* API Name
CreateNewReview

Description

How Many Records to Create
● One
  Multiple

How to Set the Record Fields
  Use all values from a record variable
● Use separate variables, resources, and literal values

Create a Record of This Object

* Object
Review

Create a Record of This Object

* Object
Review

Set Field Values for the Review

Field	Value	
Description__c	← {!Review_Description}	🗑
Movie_Title__c	← {!NewlyCreatedMovieId.Id}	🗑
Rating__c	← {!Review_Rating}	🗑
Status__c	← Pending Review	🗑

+ Add Field

Store Review ID in Variable

Variable
{!NewlyCreatedReview.Id}

Cancel   Done

37. To complete our path for when we found an already existing director, connect our **Assignment** element to the **InsertTheMovie** record create element, and then connect the **InsertTheMovie** record create element to our **CreateNewReview** record create element. Our whole flow now looks like this (you may want to move your elements a bit on the canvas, so you get a clear flow):

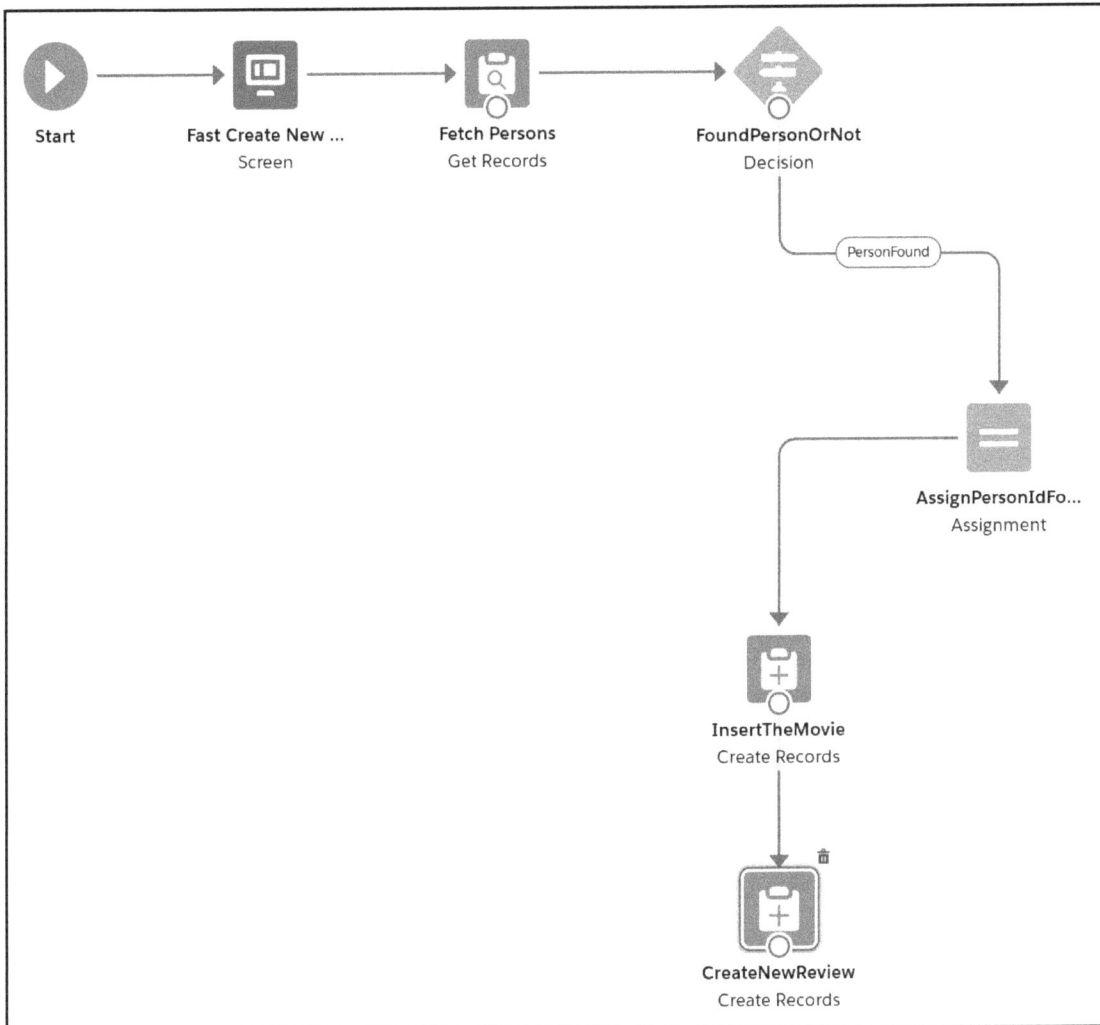

The first part of our flow is done! Let's recap what we have now.

Our goal was to create a wizard-like screen that lets a user create a new movie, related to a director with at least one review, in one go. So when our flow starts, the first thing that happens is a screen that opens up to the user, so that he can input the necessary data to create a movie record, at least a name for the director, and the necessary fields to create a review.

We know about our data model, so we know that the **Director** field on the `Movie` object is a lookup. We will need the ID of a `Person` record and we also know that a review needs to be related to the movie, so we will need the movie record ID before we can create the review record. This proves that you need to draw your flow and the order in which things need to happen beforehand! So, our user fills in all the necessary details in our screen element, which has saved all this data in memory into screen component variables.

The first thing we do, after the user has filled in our form, is to query our database to see whether we can find a person with the exact same name as our director's full name. This can give us two results: either we find at least one, or we don't find any. This is where our decision comes into play because, based on the outcome, we either can use the record ID of the person we found, or we will first need to create this new person (the second part of our flow, which we still need to build).

We now create the next steps that need to happen in case we find an existing person, so we assign the ID of the person found in a variable called **PersonIdToUse**. At this point, we have all the necessary data to create our records. We first create our new movie record, set the fields to the values provided by the user, and then we fill the lookup relation with the ID value stored in our **PersonIdToUse** variable.

Once the movie has been created, Salesforce gives us back the Salesforce record ID of that movie and we store that in a record variable called **NewlyCreatedMovieId**. In the last step, we create our review with the values provided by the user, and fill the relation to the movie with the **NewlyCreatedMovieId** ID value.

Now, let's continue with the second part of our flow. This is the part where we couldn't find any existing `Person` record with the same name as the director, which is the default outcome of our decision element!

38. Drag a **Screen** element onto the canvas. The element configurator will pop open.
39. In the screen properties section, fill in the **Label** with **Create New Director** and the **API name** with **Create_New_Director**. Now, drag a **Text** component onto the page, set the **Label** to **New Director Full Name**, and the **API name** to **New_Director_Full_Name**. Check the **Require** checkbox and, as the default value, select **Director Full Name** (under the screen components).

We don't want our user to have to type the name twice, right? So, we can already prefill the name with the value the user entered when they started the flow.

40. Now, drag a **Long Text Area** onto the page, set its **Label** to **New Director Biography,** and the **API name** to **New_Director_Biography**. And, lastly, drag a **Date** component onto the page and set its **Label** to **New Director Birthdate**, and the **API name** to **New_Director_Birthdate**. Then, click **Done**.
41. Now, connect our decision element to this **Create New Director** screen element and it will automatically map as **Default outcome**. This is because we only had two outcomes, and **PersonFound** has already been used.
42. Drag a **Create Records** element onto the canvas. The element configurator will pop open. Enter **CreateNewPersonAsDirector** as the **Label** and **API name**. Choose to create only **One** record and the **Use separate variables, resources, and literal values** for how to set the record fields section. Choose **Person** as the object and map the following field to the variables:

    - **Field: Biography__c; Value: New Director Biography** (under the screen components section)
    - **Field: Birthdate__c; Value: New Director Birthdate** (under the screen components section)
    - **Field: Name; Value: New Director Full Name** (under the screen components section)

43. Now, in the **Store Person ID in Variable** section of the configurator, click **New Resource**. Select **Variable** as the resource type, as the **API name** fill in **NewlyCreatedPerson**, as the data type, choose **Record,** and, as the object, choose **Person.** Select the **Available for output** checkbox, and then click **Done**. Don't forget that you have to set the variable now to your **NewlyCreatedPerson,** its ID field, and then hit **Done** again to save your element. It should now appear as follows:

New Create Records

Create Salesforce records using values from the flow.

* Label | * API Name
CreateNewPersonAsDirector | CreateNewPersonAsDirector

Description

How Many Records to Create
● One
　Multiple

How to Set the Record Fields
　Use all values from a record variable
● Use separate variables, resources, and literal values

Create a Record of This Object

* Object
Person

Set Field Values for the Person

Field		Value	
Biography__c	←	{!New_Director_Biography}	🗑
Birthdate__c	←	{!New_Director_Birthdate}	🗑
Name	←	{!New_Director_Full_Name}	🗑

+ Add Field

Store Person ID in Variable

Variable
{!NewlyCreatedPerson.Id}

Cancel Done

We are almost there. There is one more element to create and that's an assignment to assign the ID of our **NewlyCreatedPerson** to our **PersonIdToUse** variable.

44. Drag an **Assignment** element onto the canvas. The element configurator pops open. As the **Label,** fill in **AssignNewlyCreatedPersonId** and the **API name**, **AssignNewlyCreatedPersonId.** As the variable, select our **PersonIdToUse** variable, the operator should be **Add,** and, as the value, select our **NewlyCreatedPerson** record variable, its ID field, and then click **Done**. Refer to the following screenshot:

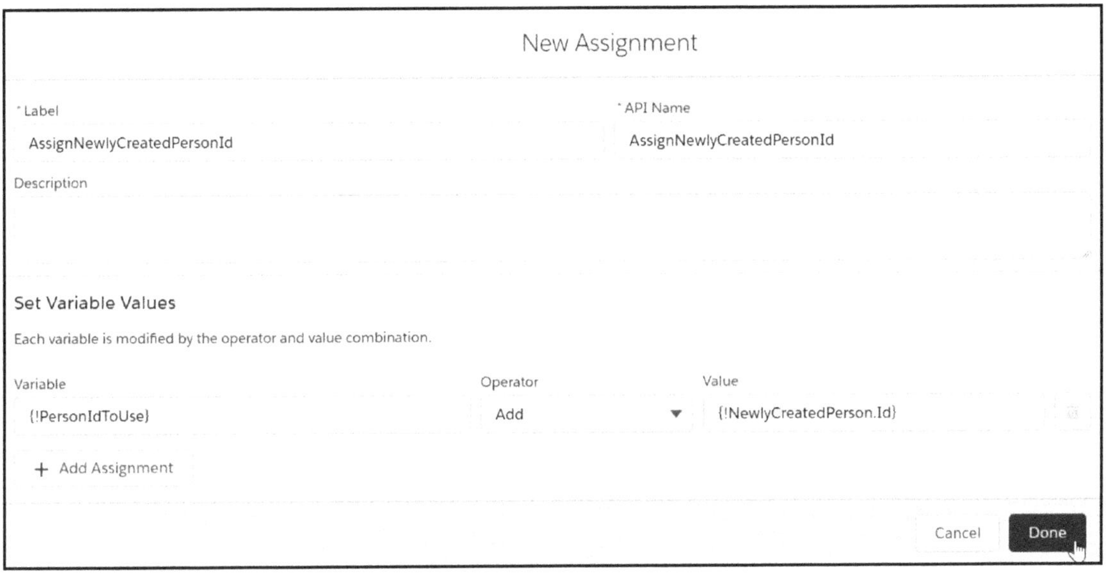

New Assignment

* Label

AssignNewlyCreatedPersonId

* API Name

AssignNewlyCreatedPersonId

Description

Set Variable Values

Each variable is modified by the operator and value combination.

Variable	Operator	Value
{!PersonIdToUse}	Add ▼	{!NewlyCreatedPerson.Id}

+ Add Assignment

Cancel | **Done**

45. To finish everything off, connect our **Create New Director** screen element to the **CreateNewPersonAsDirector** create records element. Afterward, connect this one to the **AssignNewlyCreatedPerson** assignment. Lastly, connect this assignment to our already existing **InsertTheMovie** create records element. Your finished flow should now look like this:

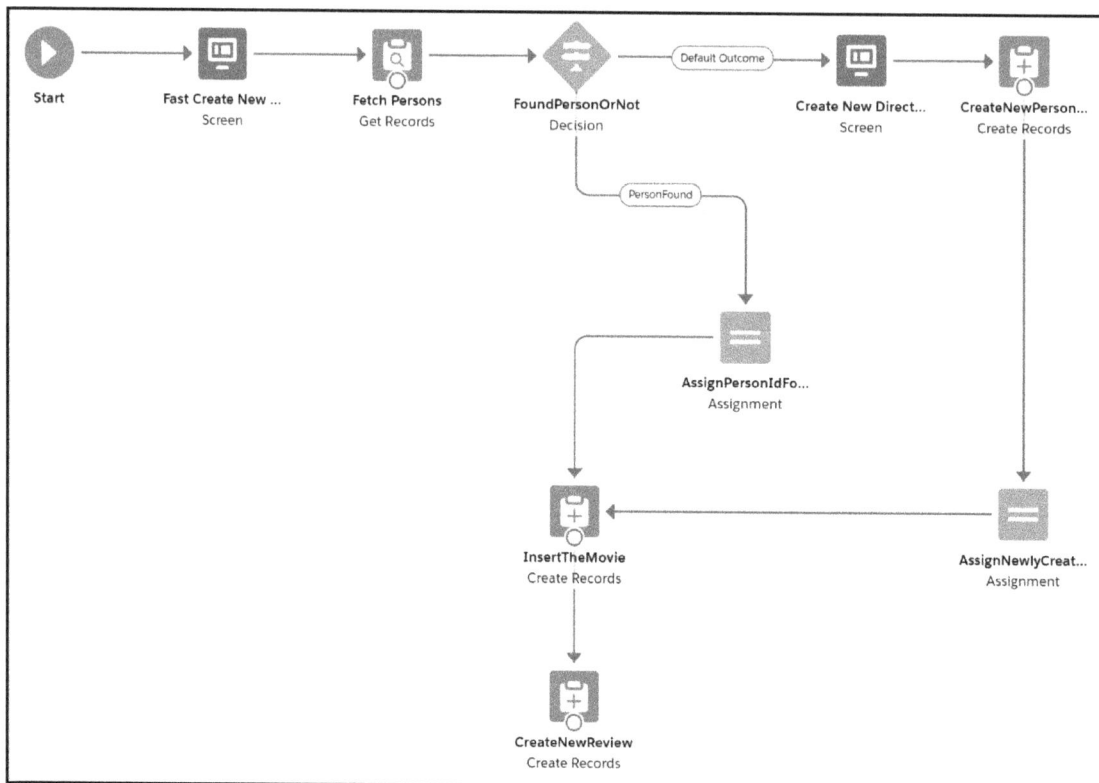

46. Now, save your flow by hitting the **Save** button in the top-right corner of the Flow Builder, give it the name **FastCreateMovieWizard**, and choose **Screen Flow** as the type. Then, hit **Save**, as follows:

However, your flow is still inactive. You'll need to activate it first by clicking the **Activate** link next to your flow in the **Flows** screen:

Now, you're done and you probably, just like me, can't wait to test this out, right?

Testing the workflow

To test our flow, we have a couple of ways to start it (as we learned in `Chapter 1`, *Salesforce Fundamentals*). We'll put a flow component on our home page so that we can quickly create new movie records straight from our home page:

1. Navigate to our BIM DB app, and, on the home page, click the wheel icon and select **Edit Page**. In the App Builder, remove all the components from the page, so you have a clean canvas.

2. Drag a flow component (from the standard components side menu) into the top section of the page. On the right-hand side, a sidebar will appear in which you can set flow attributes.

3. As flow, select our **FastCreateMovieWizard** flow and choose the **One Column** layout (our flow screen elements are not ordered properly to use the two-column layout).

4. Now that we are adjusting our home page, drag two **List View** components in the right section of the page. Set the **Attributes** for the first list view to **Object = Movie, Filter = All, Records To Show = 5,** and check the **Enable Inline Edit** checkbox. For the second list view, set **Object = Person, Filter = All, Records To Show = 5,** and check the **Enable Inline Edit** checkbox.

5. Now, click the **Activate** button in the top-right corner (assign as org default) and then click **Save** and then **Back**. You should now see this as your home page:

6. To test your flow, fill in all the fields with movie details (you can find movie details at `www.imdb.com`) and, as the director's full name, specify a name for which you know there isn't a record in our database yet.

7. After you have clicked the **Next** button, a second screen will appear asking for the director's biography and birthdate. Then, hit **Finish**. Check out the new movie record you just created and it's director lookup (which should correctly be related to a new `Person` record you just created).

8. On the **Related** tab of the movie, you should also see a new review. When you open that review in the related **Approval History** list, you should also see that our Process Builder submitted your review automatically for approval.

9. As a second test, fill in new details of another movie, but from the same director. This time, you shouldn't receive a second step asking for director's details (as this director already exists in the database). Your flow should have immediately created the new movie, linked to the same director, and also have a review that is awaiting approval.

I know there were a lot of steps to follow, but what kind of amazing things will you be able to create to make processes easier for your users?

You did a great job and, as a Salesforce Platform Developer, it's super important to understand and leverage all the declarative tools and features provide by Salesforce.

When to use declarative process automation features versus Apex

With all those tools that Salesforce provides us with, it's sometimes not that easy to decide which tool to use.

As a rule of thumb, if you can solve your business requirement with declarative features, then use declarative features. They are faster to create than coding, easier to manage and maintain by administrators in the future, and don't require a developer to create or modify them.

Apex classes and triggers offer greater flexibility and full control, but they are harder to create and maintain, and will always require a developer. But hey, don't let that stop you, as you will be able to do this yourself after reading this book, right?

For the exam, learn the comparison chart, by heart, that you can find in the *Common use cases for declarative customization* section of `Chapter 1`, *Salesforce Fundamentals*, of this book!

Which automation tool do you use?

By now, you might feel overwhelmed by all the possibilities Salesforce has to offer. Some of the tools provided can perform similar actions. So the question is; *When do you use which tool?* Well, that's exactly the question I'll try to answer in this section.

A record needs approval

For example, when an employee submits expenses because they needed to go abroad for a customer and desire a refund for their travel and maybe accommodation, that expense note has to be approved by the employee's manager before it gets sent to payroll. You need to ensure that when an expense note is submitted for approval, the right person (the employee's manager) receives the request. To automate these kinds of processes, you would create an approval process.

When a record has certain values or meets certain criteria

Three of the Salesforce declarative features can handle this use case:

- Workflow rules
- Process Builder
- Visual Workflow
- Apex triggers

In my opinion, I will always try to solve this requirement with workflow rules first, if it can be done within its limitations. If not, I will evaluate whether it can be done with Process Builder and use that to solve the requirement. If there is some specific requirement that cannot be done with Process Builder, I will look at Visual Workflow to solve the requirement. If none of those tools can solve the whole use case, then I will consider using Apex triggers to solve the problem, as a last resort.

> For the exam, Salesforce will prefer Process Builder before workflow rules (except for sending an outbound message!). Keep that in mind when choosing your answers. Although I don't agree with that principle, since workflow rules don't count against governor limits and Process Builder does (using an SOQL query for each action that needs to be performed), you need to be aware of the fact that Salesforce actively promotes the use of Process Builder above workflow rules and the exam questions will reflect this.

You need to capture input and then do something with that information

If you need to build a wizard of some kind, to collect information pertaining to the user or customer, then Visual Workflow is the tool for you!

For example, you need to create a flow that walks a customer support representative through a call script that asks several questions that need to be answered by the customer and, based on the answers, perhaps other questions need to be asked or something different needs to be done in the database. The flow would use the information entered, such as the caller's name and account number, to create a case that's assigned to the correct person with all the answers to the specific questions asked.

Summary

In this chapter, you've learned to master all of the declarative automation capabilities Salesforce has to offer you. You've learned the following:

- How to visualize data from related records and make custom calculations through formula fields
- How to perform automated field updates, send email notifications, and create tasks through workflow rules
- How to perform more complex updates, create records, and launch approval processes through Process Builder
- How to create screen elements to capture user information, make complex decisions based on that info, and execute actions automatically through Visual Flow
- When to use which tool when you need to automate some of your business processes

Let's see whether you are on the right track to becoming a certified Salesforce developer. You'll find all the answers to this quiz at the end of this book. Try to answer the questions without looking at the answers.

Quiz

1. What are the capabilities of cross-object formula fields? (choose two options)
    a. Formula fields can expose a user to data, to which they do not have access on a record itself
    b. Formula fields can reference fields from a collection of child records
    c. Formula fields can reference fields from objects that are up to 10 relationships away
    d. Formula fields can be used in up to three roll-up summary fields per object

2. Using only standard object relationships, on which standard objects could you create a custom roll-up summary field? (choose three options)
   a. On the `Opportunity` object rolling up `Opportunity Product` records
   b. On the `Account` object rolling up `Case` records
   c. On the `Campaign` object rolling up `Campaign Member` records
   d. On the `Account` object rolling up `Opportunity` records

3. Which of the following scenarios can you *not* achieve with formula fields?
   a. Display a clickable link using the `HYPERLINK` function to a specific record in a legacy system.
   b. Display the previous value for a field using the `PRIORVALUE` function to the user.
   c. Calculate whether the value from a datetime field is in the past using the `NOW` function.
   d. Determine which of three different images to display using the `IF` function.

4. Who can edit a record after it has been submitted for approval and has been locked? (choose two options)
   a. A user who is assigned as a current approver
   b. Any user who approved the record previously
   c. Any user higher in the role hierarchy that the current approver
   d. An administrator

5. How can a developer enforce the fact that a reviewer is required to provide a reason in a specific field only when a review has a rating lower than three?
   a. By creating a formula field
   b. Creating a reason field and marking it as required
   c. Creating a validation rule
   d. This can't be done declaratively

6. A developer needs to create an application that tracks machines and their parts. Individual parts can be related to different machine types. How should the developer set up their data model to keep track of this data and prevent unrelated parts?

    a. Create a lookup relationship to relate `Parts` to their parent `Machine`.

    b. Create a junction object to relate many `Machines` to multiple `Parts` through a master-detail relationship.

    c. Create a master-detail relationship to represent the one-to-many data model of `Parts` to `Machines`.

    d. Create a junction object to relate many `Machines` to many `Parts` through a lookup relationship.

7. A developer needs to update a picklist field on related contact records when a modification to the associated account is detected. How could a developer provide a solution?

    a. Create a workflow rule that performs a field update

    b. Create a Visual Workflow on `Account` that updates the contact records

    c. Create a process with Process Builder on `Account` that updates the contact records

    d. This requirement cannot be solved declaratively

8. Which of the following statements is true?

    a. A roll-up summary field can be created on any object that is on the master side of a master-detail relationship

    b. A roll-up summary field can be created on any object that is on the parent side of a lookup relationship

    c. A roll-up summary field can be created on any object that is on the detail side of a master-detail relationship

    d. A roll-up summary field can be created on any object that is on the child side of a lookup relationship

9. Object X has a lookup to Object Y. Which of the following statements is true? (choose two options)

    a. Fields of object X can be accessed from object Y

    b. Fields of object Y can be accessed from object X

    c. Fields of both X and Y are accessible from object Y

    d. Fields of both Y and X are accessible from object X

10. The business asks a developer to make sure that when a record of object X gets deleted, all records with the same name pertaining to another unrelated object Z also get deleted. How would a developer solve this request?

    a. Create a Process Builder that invokes a Visual Flow when a record of object X gets deleted. The Visual Flow then queries for records of object Z with the same name and deletes them.

    b. Replace the **Delete** button on object X with a custom **Delete** button that calls a Visual Flow. This Visual Flow first queries all records of object Z with the same name as the record where the button was clicked, then deletes that X record, and also deletes all Z records it found.

    c. Create a Process Builder that deletes all records of object Z with the same name when record X gets deleted.

    d. There is no way to meet this requirement declaratively.

4
Apex Basics

Apex is an **object-oriented programming (OOP)** language, similar to Java or other OOP languages, that is executed by the **Lightning** Platform. Like any other OOP language, Apex uses classes, methods, variables, constants, annotations, and so on. However, unusually, Apex is not case-sensitive, while other languages (such as Java) are.

If you don't know what the definition of OOP is, I can recommend the book, *Head First Java, 2nd Edition* (you can buy it from `http://bit.ly/HeadFJava`). If you are familiar with programming in Java, you will see some similarities and some differences. In this book, I will explain how we use OOP within Salesforce by using Apex.

In this chapter, we will cover the following topics:

- What Apex is and how to develop it
- Understanding data types in Apex
- Understanding access to classes in Apex
- Controlling your logic with control flow statements (`if` statements and loops)
- Querying and updating our Salesforce data with various databases
- Define the key features of the Apex language
- Know when to use Apex (and when not to)
- Create a class with methods and call those methods through **Anonymous Apex**
- Use the Developer Console to analyze the execution results

In `Chapter 5`, *Apex - Beyond the Basics*, you'll get a deeper dive into the Apex language. We will learn how to build interfaces, virtual classes and bulk processing records.

A little introduction about class in OOP. If you are already familiar with classes (from Java or other development languages), you can skip these paragraphs.

What is a class and an instance?

To go over what we have just done and to explain the concept of a class and an instance a bit more clearly, let's take a look at the following screenshot and explanation:

A class acts as a blueprint to create objects from. In this example, we created a class called `Car`. This `Car` class acts as a blueprint to build instances of cars from. So, because it's a blueprint, we define what each car has in the class—these are called **member variables** (in our case, that's a model, a brand, and a color). We also define actions that a car can perform and what a car can do, and we call these methods! In our car example, we have defined that a car can start, stop, and also accelerate.

Note that there is one special member variable, the `count` variable, which we declared as `static`, which means that this is a class variable and not a member variable. This means that contrary to member variables (where each instance will have its own values), the class variable (`static`) will not get its own instance and will be the same for all objects (instances) created out of the class! In this example, you'll see that in the constructor, we declare `count++`, which will increment this `count` variable each time a new instance is created in memory.

An instance of a class is what we call an object. Each object, when it's instantiated (created) from the class, gets its own little space in the memory, which we can access by the name we give it at the time of creation. In the example, we create three separate instances/objects from the `Car` class, called `blueCar`, `redCar`, and `yellowCar`. Our constructor requires us to pass parameters to set the brand, the model, and the color when a new instance for each car is created. So, when creating our `redCar` object (instance), we passed `Renault` (as a brand), `Clio` (as a model), and `red` (as the color). We did this for each object.

By doing that, we can now use each object to output their member variables or to call their methods, by using **dot notation**. Dot notation is how you access the fields and/or methods of an object. You use the name (the reference to the object in the memory) followed by a `.` (dot), and then the name of the variable or method you want to call, like `blueCar.model`, which will give you the value of the model variable of the `blueCar` instance from the memory.

This should look familiar to you. Think back to `Chapter 3`, *Declarative Automation*, in the first part about formulas. How do you access the value of the email field of an account in Salesforce? That's right: by using the `Account.Email` method.

Now, everything should start to fall into place. This is why I mentioned in the earlier chapters that each custom object you create (like our `Movie__c` object) is immediately available for you to use in Apex code, as they are classes from which you create objects (instances). In fact, in Salesforce, they are called **sObjects**, which helps them make the distinction between classes that represent real objects from within the Salesforce database, such as `Account`, `Lead`, or `Movie__c`, and classes you've created yourself (that do not represent real database objects, but just act as blueprints to use in your code with custom logic), such as our `MovieSelector` class.

I hope this makes things a bit clearer now. We will go more in-depth on these concepts later on in the book (in `Chapter 5`, *Apex - Beyond the Basics*, in the *Classes and interfaces* section).

Understanding the features of Apex

Since we what Apex is, let's see which editions of Salesforce can support it:

- Performance Edition
- Unlimited Edition
- Enterprise Edition
- Developer Edition
- Database.com

Apex can be used to add business logic to Lightning applications, execute database triggers, and build a customized UI by programming controllers. The language and all its features (such as governor limits, future methods, and so on) run in a multi-tenant environment and can be integrated with the following components:

- The database that includes your standard and custom objects.
- A **Salesforce Object Query Language** (**SOQL**)/**Salesforce Object Search Language** (**SOSL**), which will help you search for or select the records you need.
- Web services support helps you integrate web services, such as Google, Amazon, or the customer's backend systems:

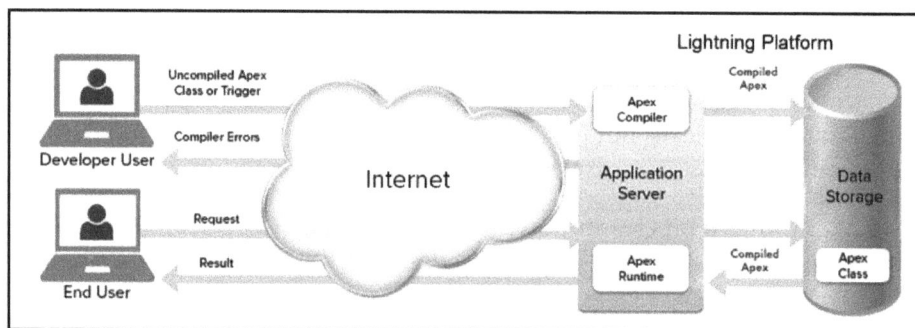

How to develop Apex

To develop Apex, you can use different development tools—some of them are free, and for some, you need to pay. Now, you might be wondering which one of these is the best, or you might be wondering which one you should choose. The answer to this is that it depends on your personal taste and what kind of use you prefer. It can be Salesforce DX, admin plus developer tasks, a more visual interface, or a `less` command line.

The following is an overview of the different tools, which are used by 95% of Salesforce developers:

- **Welkin Suite** (`https://welkinsuite.com`): A Force.com IDE for administrator and developer tasks in Salesforce, which is based on Visual Studio. No additional software is required. A free trial is available.
- **Illuminated Cloud** (`http://www.illuminatedcloud.com`): A Force.com IDE for developers, where you can write the code and manage the full metadata. Installation of **IntelliJ** is required (the community Edition is free and fits the requirements to develop Apex). This plugin is paid.
- **Visual Studio Code** (`https://code.visualstudio.com`): A free IDE based on Visual Studio of Microsoft, where you can add additional plugins for Salesforce (`https://marketplace.visualstudio.com/search?term=Salesforcetarget=VSCodecategory=All%20categoriessortBy=Relevance`). From now, this is the only one that is supported by the Salesforce IDE.
- **Developer Console**: A free tool included in the Salesforce interface, where you can open the **Developer Console** by clicking on the **Setup** gear and clicking **Developer Console**. This is the one that we will be using throughout the book:

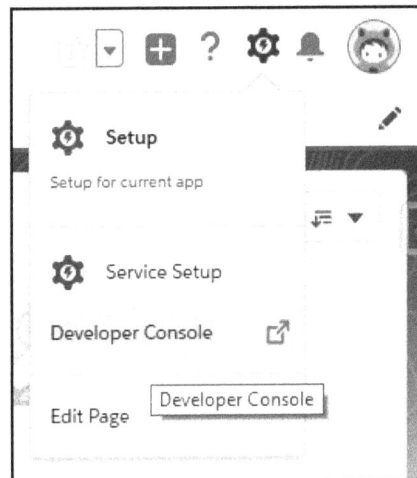

For the code examples in this book, we will use the **Developer Console** of Salesforce, but don't hesitate to use your own tools.

When should you use Apex?

Salesforce pre-builds a lot of tools and has a powerful CRM and development platform. However, customers may have complex business processes or desire branded site applications that are not supported by the existing out-of-the-box functionality. Apex can help you to build more complex logic and applications.

You can use Apex if you want to do the following things:

- Create web services
- Create email services
- Create complex validations over multiple objects
- Create complex business processes that are not supported by workflow, Process Builders, or Visual Flow
- Create custom transactional logic (more than one record or object, for example, overnight batches)
- Custom logic for Visualforce pages
- Server-side controllers for Lightning components

To visualize Apex, you can use Visualforce pages, Visualforce components, Lightning components, or the new Lightning web components.

In all other circumstances, you should first consider a declarative solution for the requirements. The following diagram shows an overview of the standard (declarative) functionalities and custom (programmatic) functionalities that you can modify or build:

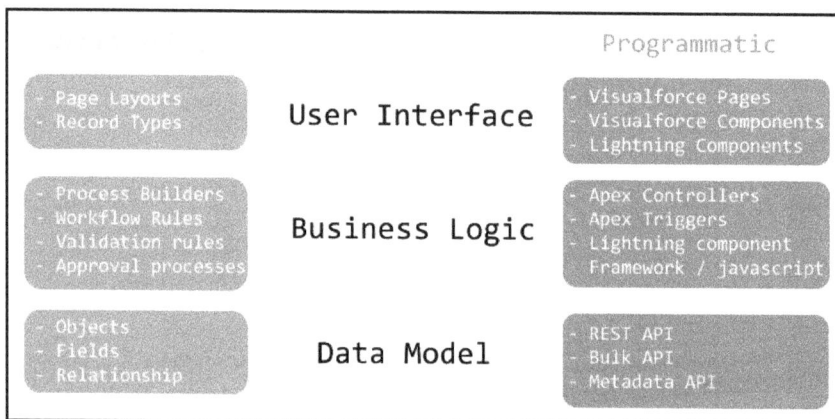

Let's look at the Developer Console now.

The Developer Console

The Developer Console is a browser-based tool where you can write and debug your code, analyze the debug logs, execute queries, and so on. It's embedded into the Salesforce platform. Through the browser, you can easily create and deploy classes and execute them in an anonymous window, which is the next exercise.

Exercise 1 – opening the Developer Console and looking around for possibilities

I assume you already have a developer org from the beginning of this book. If not, make sure you create one right now. You can find out how to create a developer org at the beginning of this book.

In this exercise, we will create and deploy a class in the Developer Console, step by step:

1. Open your Developer Console by clicking on the **Setup** gear at the right corner of the org, and then click **Developer Console**.
2. This opens a new window. If it doesn't, then a pop-up blocker is probably stopping you from opening this window. Allow your browsers to open this pop-up window; otherwise, you know, no programming in Salesforce for you today.

Let's walk around the menus and functionality of this tool. I will only explain the most important functionalities.

The top menu consists of the following:

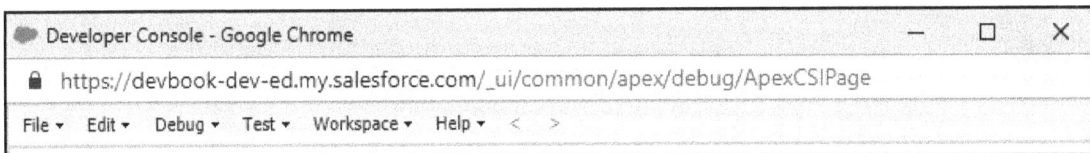

As shown in the preceding screenshot the top menu consists of the following:

- **File**: This helps in creating new components, opening existing components, opening debug logs, downloading debug logs, and saving your changes.
- **Edit**: This helps in finding keywords in the currently opened file or the full org files.
- **Debug**: This helps in opening an anonymous window to execute code and view perspectives.
- **Test**: This helps in creating and running test suites and settings of how for run the tests.

The middle part of the console consists of the following:

- The log of your execution (can be test or anonymous)
- A class, page, component, or trigger

The following screenshot illustrates a log of an execution:

Log executeAnonymous @10-11-2018 16:28:15

Execution Log

Timestamp	Event	Details
16:28:15:001	USER_INFO	[EXTERNAL]|0051t000000lwEm|gunther.roskams@weare4c.com.googledrive|Heure d'Europe centrale|GMT+01:00
16:28:15:001	EXECUTION_ST...	
16:28:15:001	CODE_UNIT_ST...	[EXTERNAL]|01p1t000006UKBg|Account_TriggerHandler_Test.CreateGoogleFolders()
16:28:15:004	SYSTEM_MODE...	false
16:28:15:004	SYSTEM_MODE...	false
16:28:15:004	SYSTEM_MODE...	false
16:28:15:006	SYSTEM_MODE...	false
16:28:15:013	DML_BEGIN	[77]|Op:Insert|Type:Account|Rows:1
16:28:15:035	CODE_UNIT_ST...	[EXTERNAL]|DuplicateDetector
16:28:15:035	DUPLICATE_DE...	
16:28:15:037	DUPLICATE_DE...	DuplicateRuleId:0Bm1t000000yPXx|DuplicateRuleName:Standard Account Duplicate Rule|DmlType:INSERT
16:28:15:059	DUPLICATE_DE...	EntityType:Account|ActionTaken:Allow_[Alert,Report]|DuplicateRecordIds:
16:28:15:059	DUPLICATE_DE...	EntityType:Account|NumRecordsToBeSaved:1|NumRecordsToBeSavedWithDuplicates:0|NumDuplicateRecordsFound:0
16:28:15:059	DUPLICATE_DE...	
16:28:15:059	CODE_UNIT_FI...	DuplicateDetector
16:28:15:098	CODE_UNIT_ST...	[EXTERNAL]|01q1t000000QdgT|Account_Trigger on Account trigger event AfterInsert|__sfdc_trigger/Account_Trigger
16:28:15:100	SYSTEM_MODE...	false

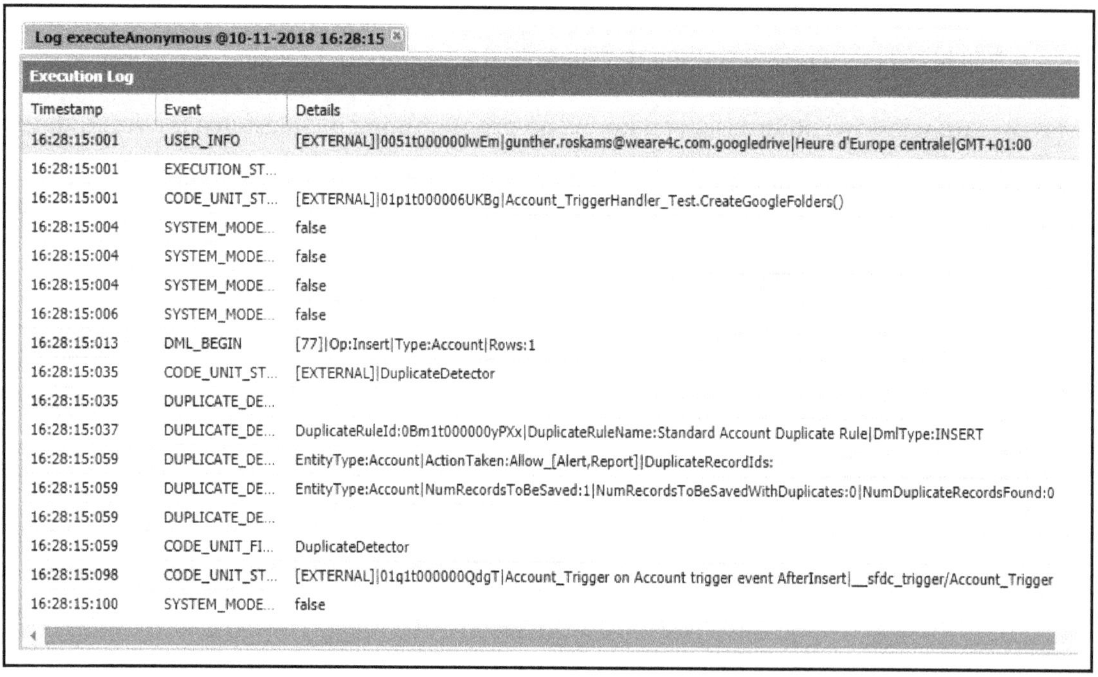

The following screenshot shows a window in which you write your Apex code:

The bottom of the console consists of the following:

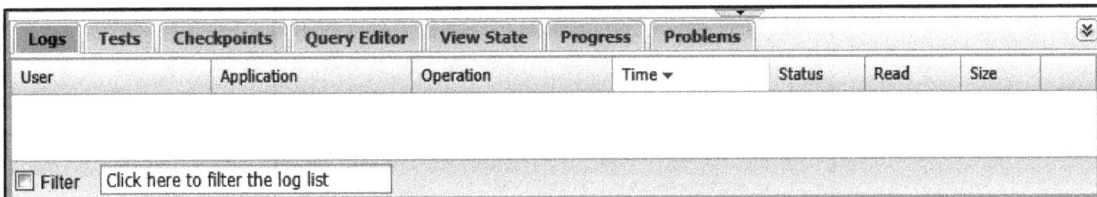

As shown in the preceding screenshot the console consists of the following components:

- **Logs**: The log lines when an action is executed (can be an execution of a test, an anonymous code block, or a user who executes an action (adds a new account or updates an opportunity)).
- **Tests**: The test executions.
- **Checkpoints**: The checkpoints in your code, defined during a debug process.
- **Query Editor**: Executes SOQL or SOSL queries.

- **View State**: The status for a Visualforce page and the values it contains in its memory at a certain point in time.
- **Problems**: If you write any errors in your code, you will see here where you need to check the error, and you won't be able to save your code until there are no more errors.

Let's move on to the next exercise.

Exercise 2 – creating a new class in the Developer Console

During the tour of the **Developer Console**, you must have found a way to create a new class. Let's do this now. We will reuse this class later on in this book:

1. Log in to Salesforce (if you are logged out or if you closed your previous screens).
2. Click on the gear in the top-right corner and click on **Developer Console**.
3. A new window opens in the browser. Click on **File** | **New**.
4. Now, you have a lot of choices. For this exercise, you click on **Apex Class**:

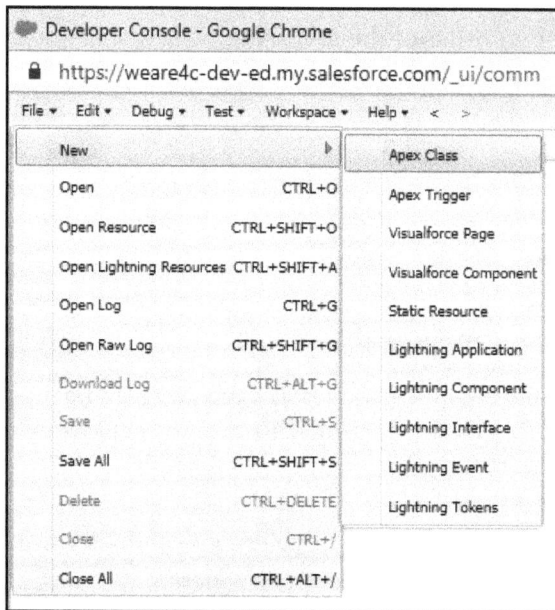

5. A modal window will now ask you the name of your class. The best (and generally accepted) practice is to use camel case to define a class (the first character of each word is in uppercase), such as PlatformDeveloperGuide or ShoppingCart. Names of classes cannot contain spaces or other weird characters. Give the name MovieSelector to your class and click **OK**.

6. Congratulations! You have created your first class in the **Developer Console**.

7. Let's write some stuff in it now. Remove all the code from the screen of the **Developer Console**. Copy the following code, and paste it in the screen (it doesn't matter if you don't know what the code is doing now; I will explain that later):

```
public class MovieSelector {
 public static String sMovieTitle = '';

 public MovieSelector(String aMovieTitle){
   sMovieTitle = aMovieTitle;
 }

 public String getTheMovieTitle(){
   return sMovieTitle;
 }

 public static String getAMovieTitle(String aMovieTitle){
   sMovieTitle = aMovieTitle;
   return sMovieTitle;
 }

 public static List<Movie__c> searchMovies(String aMovieTitle){
   List<List<SObject>> lstSearchResults = new List<List<SObject>>();
   String sQuery = 'FIND \'' +
String.escapeSingleQuotes(aMovieTitle) + '\' IN ALL FIELDS
RETURNING Movie__c(Name)';
   lstSearchResults.addAll(Search.query(sQuery));
   if (lstSearchResults.size() > 0){
    return lstSearchResults[0];
   }

   return new List<Movie__c>();
 }
}
```

8. Save the code (with *cmd* + *S* or *Ctrl* + *S* for Windows users, or through the top menu **File** | **Save**). Your code should have saved successfully; if it has not, then check the **Problems** tab at the bottom.

Great; you have created a class with a class variable, a constructor, and three methods. That doesn't tell you much, does it? Let me explain:

- The sMovieTitle class variable contains the title of your movie.
- The MovieSelector(String aMovieTitle) constructor creates an instance of your MovieSelector class, and while creating that instance, the constructor expects you to provide a movie title. You need to define a string, which contains the title.
- The getTheMovieTitle() method helps you get the title of this instance of the MovieSelector class that you've created.
- The searchMovies(String) method will return a list of Movie records, which contains the titles that you had passed to this method.

Later in this chapter, in the *Understanding code and its execution* section, I will explain what this code means and what the different components are in this class. The previous explanation is just a high-level explanation, for now.

Executing the code

Now, we're going to execute this code in the anonymous window, as follows:

1. In the **Developer Console**, open the anonymous window through the top menu **Debug** | **Open Execute Anonymous Window** (or through the shortcut *cmd + E*, or *Ctrl + E* for Windows users).

2. A little popup opens in your **Developer Console**. Enter the following code in the pop-up window:

```
MovieSelector ms = new MovieSelector('Lethal Weapon');
System.debug(ms.getTheMovieTitle())
```

3. Click the **Execute** button to execute the code. Check the **Open Log** checkbox, if it is not checked:

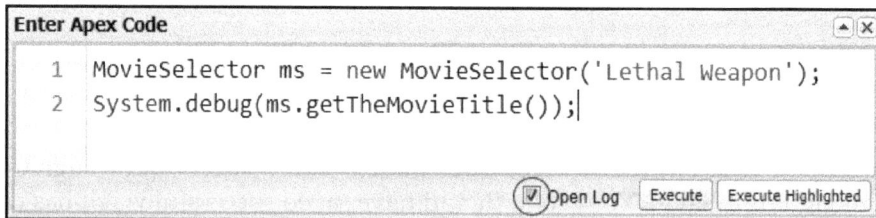

```
Enter Apex Code                                                    ▲ ✕
  1  MovieSelector ms = new MovieSelector('Lethal Weapon');
  2  System.debug(ms.getTheMovieTitle());|

                                    ☑ Open Log   Execute   Execute Highlighted
```

4. At the bottom of the screen, you will find the rule with the logs. If you didn't check the **Open Log** checkbox in the preceding step, double-click on the rule you've just created (the debug logs open in the **Developer Console**). If you did check the **Open Log** checkbox, the log will automatically open in the main window for you to analyze:

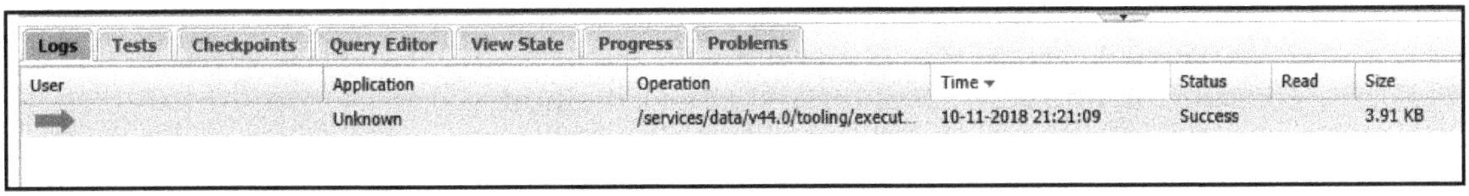

5. You can find the logs in the main window. Each step that the system does is logged in these logs. You can modify the content and the number of the logs through the log levels (through the top menu **Debug** | **Change Log Levels**). There are different levels for each component of the logs (**System**, **Database**, **ApexCode**, **Validation**, **Workflow**, and **Profiling**). What you need to know is on which level you need to configure which log component to see your **Debug** statements (the `System.debug` statement in the Anonymous Apex execution screen, line **2**). I had a question about these levels on my exam. The answer is—component Apex code, minimum level—**DEBUG** (see the following screenshot):

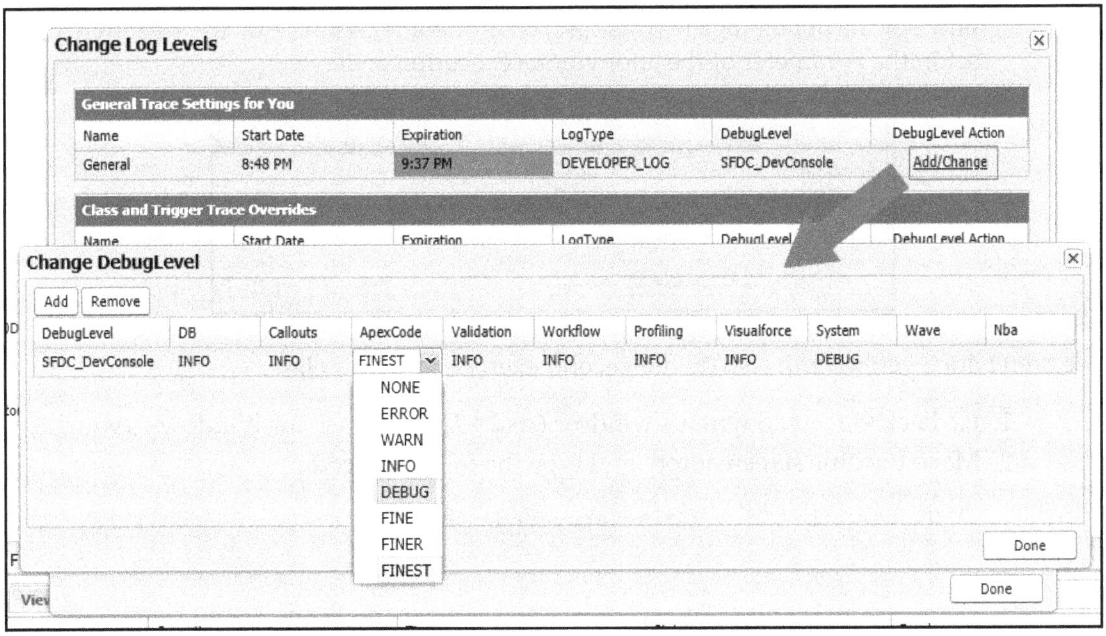

What have we done now? We created a class and executed this code. Let's take a deeper look into that initial code and the execution code.

Understanding code and its execution

Let's start with the basics:

- We created a `MovieSelector` class with the `sMovieTitle` class variable, the constructor, and a `getTheMovieTitle()` method.
- The constructor of the class will be used when you create an instance of the class (with the keyword `new`, in this case, `MovieSelector ms = new MovieSelector('Lethal Weapon';)`.
- During the creation of the class, the constructor executes every single line of code in this constructor only once. In this case, we assign the title **Lethal Weapon**, defined in the string parameter in the constructor, to the `sMovieTitle` class variable. And that's all. It's just as if we created a new movie record, in memory, with the title **Lethal Weapon**.
- The second line of code in the execution gives me an output of the class variable after I create the instance of the class. I do this by calling the `getTheMovieTitle()` method, and then this method returns the `sMovieTitle` class variable.
- If you activate the **Debug Only** checkbox in your Developer Console, you will only see the debug logs (in this case, only one line). That's exactly the movie you set in the parameter of the anonymous execution code:

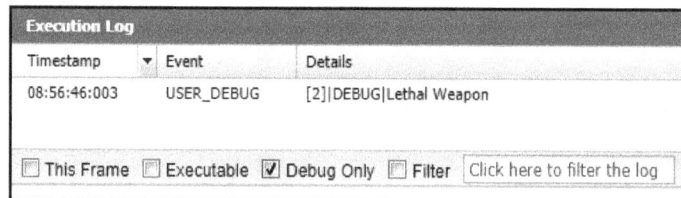

We aren't done yet; we will also do our second exercise with our class:

1. Go back to the anonymous window (*cmd* + *E*, or *Ctrl* + *E* for Windows users).
2. Make the little screen empty and type the following code:

```
System.debug(MovieSelector.getAMovieTitle('Lethal Weapon'));
```

3. Execute it again. What do you see in the debug logs now? Hopefully, the following:

Execution Log		
Timestamp	Event	Details
08:59:51:004	USER_DEBUG	[1]|DEBUG|Lethal Weapon

Indeed, the commands are the same! But do you know what the difference is between the two commands?

In the first anonymous code block, we used the `getTheMovieTitle()` method. However, the method is not defined as a `static` method. Hence, we first created an instance of the `MovieSelector` class to execute this method, with the following snippet:

```
public String getTheMovieTitle(){
    return sMovieTitle;
}
```

In the second anonymous code block, we used the `public static` method (as shown in the following snippet), where we didn't have to create an instance of the class. And that's how OOP works:

```
public static String getAMovieTitle(String aMovieTitle){
    sMovieTitle = aMovieTitle;
    return sMovieTitle;
}
```

We will remove this method later in this book because it's not relevant to use this static method here. But now you know the difference between a static and a non-static method and how you need to call both of these types of methods. Remember this for the exam:

- A static method can be called without creating an instance of a class.
- A non-static method can only be called when you have first created an instance of the class containing the method.

Congratulations! You created your first full class with logic, and executed this logic in an anonymous window.

Now, let's go to the next part, which will cover the different types of variables, the different data types, and expressions.

Apex variables, constants, and expressions

You have different types of variables that you can define in your class. In Chapter 3, *Declarative Automation*, we used a String (the most-used variable type) to define our movie's title, but there are more of these variable types that exist. If you are familiar with Java, you will recognize some of these types.

Besides the type, you can define whether the variable is visible or editable outside your class. Just like a user can view or edit a field in a record, a class can also view or edit a variable in another class.

We'll start by explaining the different data types available to you.

Apex data types

Each variable in Apex has a data type. This can be a primitive data type (such as String, Decimal, and so on), an sObject, an enum, an Apex class, or a collection of these types.

The following table will give you an overview of all the different variable types you can use in Apex:

Blob	Binary data is being stored as a single object. By using the toString() or valueOf() methods, you can convert this data type to a string. Examples of a blob are web service arguments, the content of a document, and attachments.
Boolean	A value that can correspond to a checkbox. The value can only be true, false, or null.
Date	A variable that contains a day as a value. Date values must initiate the system static method (Date.newInstance(Year, month, day)). You can add or subtract an Integer value from a Date value. This returns a date again.
DateTime	A variable that contains a day and time as a value, such as a timestamp. The DateTime values must always initiate with a system static method (DateTime.newInstance(Year, month, day, hour, minutes, seconds, milliseconds)). You can add or subtract an Integer or a Double value from a DateTime value. This returns a Date value (no DateTime value).

Decimal	A 32-bit number that contains a decimal point. Currency fields in your data model are automatically assigned as a decimal value. If you don't set the number of decimal places, the scale of the decimal (the number of decimal places) is the number that you configured in the data model.
Double	In contrast to a decimal, a `Double` is a 64-bit number that contains a decimal point. The minimum value of a double is -2^{63} (-9,223,372,036,854,775,808) and the maximum value is 2^{63}-1 (9,223,372,036,854,775,807).
ID	A Salesforce valid Lightning Platform record identifier. This can be 15 or 18 characters. If you use the 15-character `ID` value, Apex automatically converts the `ID` to its 18-character value.
Integer	A 32-bit number that does not contain a decimal point. The minimum value of an integer is -2^{31} (-2,147,483,648); the maximum value is 2^{31} (2,147,483,646).
Long	A 64-bit number that does not contain a decimal point. The minimum value of a long number is -2^{63} (-9,223,372,036,854,775,808); the maximum value is 2^{63}-1 (9,223,372,036,854,775,807).

Object	Any data type supported in Apex. This is the definition of a generic data type. You can cast an object that represents a more specific data type to its underlying data type:
	`Object theObject = 10;`
	`Integer i = (Integer) theObject;`
	`System.debug(i); // the output is 10`

String	Any set of characters surrounded by single quotes: `String s = 'Hello World';`
Time	A value that indicates time. Time values must always be initiated with the `static` method `Time.newInstance(Hours, minutes, seconds, milliseconds)`.
sObject	Any database Salesforce object type that is supported in Apex. sObject is the definition of a generic sObject type, but you can also use a specific sObject, like `Account`, `Contact`, or your custom objects, such as `Movie__c`.

enum	An enum is a data type consisting of a set of named values called elements, members, enumeral or enumerators of the type. For example, the four seasons in a year may be four enumerators named `Spring`, `Summer`, `Autumn`, and `Winter`, belonging to an enumerated type named `Season`.

`Set<Object>`	An **unordered** collection of **unique** elements that do not contain any duplicates:
	`Set<String> set1 = new Set<String>{'New York', 'Paris', 'New York'};`
	`System.debug(set1); // this would output 'New York' and 'Paris' only!`

`List<Object>`	An **ordered** collection of elements that are distinguished by their indices (starting by 0) and can contain duplicates: `List<String> list1 = new List<String>{'New York','Paris'};` The following table is a visual representation of the list: `Index	Value` ` 0	New York` ` 1	Paris`
`Map<Object,Object>`	A collection of key-value pairs where each unique key maps to a single value: `Map<String, String> countryCurrency = new Map<String,String>{'USA' => 'Dollar', 'Belgium' => 'Euro', 'UK' => 'Pound'}` The following table is a visual representation of the list: `Index	Value` `USA	Dollar` `Belgium	Euro` `UK	Pound` `System.debug(countryCurrency.get('USA')); // this would output 'Dollar'`

Apex class	Every defined Apex class (or subclass), defined in the system or defined in your application:
	`Database.SaveResult theResult = Database.insert(aRecord);`
	`MyClass theClass = new MyClass();`

Constants

Besides the variables, you can define a `static` definition, where the value does not change after the initialization. These `static` definitions are constants. A constant is defined with the keyword `final`. Make it a common practice to define the constant names in all capitals. Let's look at how you write this in an example:

```
private static final Integer MAX_NUMBER_OF_MOVIES = 3;
```

Expressions

An **expression** is a construction or a command, made from variables, operators, and method invocations, that evaluates to one single value. The following is an example to define a movie title in our BIM DB application:

```
String s = 'Lethal Weapon';
Movie__c a = new Movie__c(Name = s);
```

Operators

In the previous chapters, you learned to write formulas for validation criteria, for workflow criteria, and to define some calculated content in a field.

In Apex, we need to have similar operators to calculate or to define what needs to be executed.

In the following table, you will find an overview of operators that we can use in Apex:

=	**Assignment operator**: The data type of the variable x must be of the same type of the variable y: `Integer x = 3`

+=	**Addition and assignment operator**: It adds the value to the original value and reassigns the new value to the initial variable:
	`Integer x = 2;`
	`Integer y = 4;`
	
	`y += x; // y becomes 6`
	`y = y + x; // this would be the same as using '+=' but longer`

`*=`	**Multiplication and assignment**: Multiplies the value with the original value and reassigns the new value to the initial variable:
	```Integer x = 2;```
	```Integer y = 4;```
	
	```y *= x; // y becomes 8```

`-=`	**Subtraction and assignment**: Subtracts the y value from the original value and reassigns the new value to the initial variable:
	```Integer x = 2;```
	```Integer y = 4;```
	
	```y -= x; // y becomes 2```

`/=`	**Division and assignment**: Divides the original value with the y value and reassigns the new value to the initial variable:
	```Integer x = 2;```
	```Integer y = 4;```
	
	```y /= x; // y becomes 2```

`==`	**Equal-to operator**: Compares two variables. If the values are equal, the expressions are true; otherwise, they are false. In Apex, you need to have the same value. To determine whether two sObjects are equal, a deep scan will be done (all field values need to be the same) before evaluation:
	```Integer x = 2;```
	```Integer y = 4;```
	
	```x == y; // returns false```
	
	```Account a = new Account(Name = 'Acme');```
	```Account b = new Account(Name = 'Acme');```
	
	```a == b; // returns true```

`&&`	**AND logical operator**: If at least two Boolean expressions are true, the expression evaluates true; otherwise, it is false:
	
	``
	Integer i = 1;
	String s = 'a';
	
	if (i == 1 && s == 'a'){
	    // this code will be executed. Both expressions are
	    // true
	}
	
	if (i == 1 && s == 'b'){
	    // this code will not be executed. Only one
	    // expression is
	    // true
	}
	``

`||`	**OR logical operator**: At least one Boolean expression needs to be true to evaluate to true. If none of the expressions are true, the expression evaluates to false:
	
	``
	Integer i = 1;
	String s = 'a';
	
	if (i == 1 || s == 'a'){
	    // this code will be executed. Both expressions are true
	}
	
	if (i == 1 || s == 'b'){
	    // this code will be executed. One expression is true
	}
	
	if (i == 0 || s == 'b'){
	    // this code will not be executed. None of the expressions
	    // are true
	}
	``

`===`	**Exact equal**: This indicates whether the two variables reference the exact same location in the memory:
	
	``
	Object a = 5; // this is an integer in a more specific
	              // variable Type
	Object b = '5'; // this is a string in a more specific
	                // type
	if (a === b){
	    // Do some logic
	}
	``

<	**Less than**: If x is less than y, the expression returns true; otherwise, it is false:
	``
	Integer x = 1;
	Integer y = 2;
	If (x < y){
	    // return true
	}
	``

>	**Greater than**: If x is greater than y, the expression returns true; otherwise, it is false:
	``
	Integer x = 2;
	Integer y = 1;
	If (x > y){
	    // return true
	}
	``

<=	**Less than or equal to**: If x is less than or equal to y, the expression returns true; otherwise, it is false:
	``
	Integer x = 1;
	Integer y = 1;
	If (x <= y){
	    // return true
	}
	``

>=	**Greater than or equal to**: If x is greater than or equal to y, the expression returns true; otherwise, it returns false:
	``
	Integer x = 1;
	Integer y = 1;
	If (x >= y){
	    // return true
	}
	``

!=	**Not equal to**: If x is not equal to y, the expression returns true:
	``
	Integer x = 2;
	Integer y = 1;
	If (x != y){
	    // return true
	}
	``

!==	**Exactly not equal**: If x and y do not reference the exact same location in the memory, the expression returns true.

+	**For integers:** Adds the value of x to the value of y (x + y); for example:
	``
	Integer x = 2;
	Integer y = 2;
	System.debug(x + y); // returns 4
	``
	For strings: Concatenates the string together: ('x' + 'y' ⇒ 'xy');
	for example:
	``
	String x = '2';
	String y = '2';
	System.debug(x + y); // returns '22'
	``

–	**Subtract**: Subtracts the value of y from the value of x (x - y).
*	**Multiply**: Multiplies the value of x by y (x * y).
/	**Division**: Divides x by y (x/y).
++	**Increment**: Adds 1 to the current value x (x++).
--	**Decrement**: Subtracts 1 from the current value (x--).
()	**Parentheses**: Evaluates which compound needs to be calculated first; for example, (x + y) * z has another outcome as x + (y * z).

Because you can have a lot of classes, variables, and methods in your application, we might need some way to restrict access to some of those. We can do this by using **access modifiers**, which you will learn about in the next section.

Access modifiers

As the name suggests, access modifiers help to restrict the scope of a class, constructor, variable, or method. Let's take a look at the different access modifiers and see how to impact our logic.

Let's go back to our class and analyze the code a little bit more in depth. The first line in our code is the definition of our class:

```
public class MovieSelector {
}
```

In this line of code, you have three parts:

- public: Our access modifier
- class: Because we define a class
- MovieSelector: The name of the class

The first part is the most important in this chapter.

The access modifier allows you to define the visibility of your classes, variables, or methods. I will give you an overview of the different access modifiers and what they mean for the visibility when you call the class or method in other classes, subclasses, or outside the application.

Let's take a look at all the access modifiers.

Private

This is the default definition. If you don't add an access modifier to your class, variable, or method, then Apex will automatically add the `private` modifier (you don't see it, but it is there, believe me). The variables and methods defined as `private` are only usable in the defining class (not in another class, and not in a subclass, and not even in a Visualforce page, if you write Visualforce controllers or extensions).

Protected

The method or variable is visible to any inner classes in the Apex class itself and to the classes that extend the Apex class, where you define your variable or method. You can only use the `protected` access modifier for methods and variables, not for classes.

Public

This means that the method or variable can be used by any Apex outside the defining class, but inside the namespace of the application. If you define two classes with a `public` method in the same Salesforce org, the methods are visible. If the classes are defined in another Salesforce org (class plus method 1 in org 1 and class plus method 2 in another org), the class and the method are not visible for the first org, and vice versa.

Global

The method or variable with the `global` access modifier can be used by any Apex code that has access to the `global` class. This access modifier should be used for any class or method that needs to be referenced from outside the Salesforce application, like web services, SOAP, or REST services. I rarely recommend this modifier, because this is the most open modifier. Most of the time, this type is used to define web services and integrations with external applications (from the application to Salesforce).

You know the different types of access modifiers. Now, you should know the solution to our previous question: Why did we receive an error in the Developer Console?

If you checked the access modifier on the method, it is defined as `private`. If I call the method outside the class (the anonymous window in the Developer Console is always outside the class), it is not visible. That's why we receive the error.

What do we do if we need to call that function outside the class? Define the method as a `public` method, and the problem is solved:

1. Let's take a look at the following code:

    ```
    public class ActorSelector{
      public static String myString = '';

      public static List<String> getActorsByMovie(String sMovieTitle){
        System.debug(sMovieTitle);
        return null;
      }
    }
    ```

2. Now, enter the same code in the anonymous window:

    ```
    ActorSelector.getActorsByMovie('Lethal Weapon');
    ```

3. Click on the **Execute** button and review the logs. What do you see now? You should see my favorite movie, *Lethal Weapon*:

```
public class ActorSelector{
    public static String myString = '';

    public static List<String> getActorsByMovie(String sMovieTitle){
        System.debug(sMovieTitle);
        return null;
    }
}
```

Enter Apex Code   ▲ X

1   ActorSelector.getActorsByMovie 'Lethal Weapon' |;

☑ Open Log   Execute   Execute Highlighted

In the debug logs, you'll see that the **5** before the line means the line where you requested the `debug` statement. This is the statement on line **5** in the `ActorSelector` class:

Execution Log		
Timestamp	Event	Details
15:49:21:003	USER_DEBUG	[5]|DEBUG|Lethal Weapon

Now, you have a lot of information about how to define a class, which types of variables you can use, and which types of access modifiers you can use to access (or protect) your code.

Exercise – building a new class and defining a private access modifier

Since we know how to define a class, let's see how to create it and a `private` modifier:

1. Build a new class and open the Developer Console.
2. Create a new class, `ActorSelector`, and paste the following code:

```
public class ActorSelector{
 public static String myString = '';

 private static List<String> getActorsByMovie(String sMovieTitle){
  System.debug(sMovieTitle);
  return null;
 }
}
```

3. Don't forget to save your class! Now, in the anonymous window, execute the following line of code:

```
ActorSelector.getActorsByMovie('Lethal Weapon');
```

Let's take a look at the following steps:

1. Open the **Execute Anonymous Window** (*Ctrl* + *E* for Windows users or *cmd* + *E* for macOS).
2. Copy and paste the preceding code.
3. Check the **Open Log** checkbox and click on the **Execute** button.

You should receive an error in the Developer Console. Consider why that might be happening:

Execute Anonymous Error ☒

Line: 1, Column: 28
Method is not visible: List<String> ActorSelector.getActorsByMovie(String)

OK

Now, since you know about the access modifiers, you should find the solution in that overview.

In case you've missed it, if you checked the access modifier on the method, it is defined as `private`. If I call the method outside the class (the anonymous window in the Developer Console is always outside the class), it is not visible. That's why we received the error.

So, you have now learned what classes are, how to create them, what the different data types are, and how to make things publicly accessible or make things private. Now, it's time to add some logic to your methods. In the next section, we'll do just that, in some different ways. Let's take a look.

Apex control flow statements

To write some code, you actually type statements into a file. It can be an Apex class, a trigger, or a Visualforce page. Without any control flow statement, the platform executes the statements in the order they appear, from top to bottom and from left to right.

You can use control flow statements to execute code in certain circumstances (conditions), to repeatedly execute a block of code, or to break up the execution when a certain condition is true. Let's dive into the different control flow statements in Apex. If you are familiar with programming Java, you will recognize some similarities.

Conditional statements

Conditional statements (better known as `if-else` statements) execute code in certain circumstances. You can use these types of statements when you need to execute code when a variable has a certain value. The syntax of a conditional statement is as follows:

```
If (Boolean_Condition){
  // Execute code block
}
```

You can also execute default code in an `if` statement. For instance, if a variable has a certain value, execute `block 1`; in all other circumstances, execute `block 2`:

```
If (Boolean_Condition){
 // Execute code block 1
} else {
 // Execute code block 2
}
```

You can also add several conditions when you need to execute the code:

```
If (Boolean_Condition){
 // Execute code block 1
 } else if (Another_Boolean_Condition){
 // Execute code block 2
 } else {
 // Execute code block 3
 }
```

Otherwise, you can also nest if statements (if a second criterion needs to be validated into a first condition):

```
If (Boolean_Condition1){
 If (Boolean_Condition2){
  //Execute Nested Code block 1
 }
 }
```

Let's take a look at this example:

```
Integer iPlace = 2;
String sMedalColor = '';

If (iPlace == 1){
 sMedalColor = 'Gold';
 } else if (iPlace == 2){
 sMedalColor = 'Silver';
 } else if (iPlace == 3){
 sMedalColor = 'Bronze';
 } else {
 sMedalColor = 'Unfortunately, no medal';
 }
```

In the first two lines, we do an assignment of two variables: an integer and a string.

In the next lines, we check which value is assigned to the iPlace integer. In the second case, when we execute this code and we add a system.debug statement for the sMedalColor (System.debug(sMedalColor); variable on the last line), we should see 'Silver'. If you change the value iPlace to 7, you should see 'Unfortunately, no medal'.

Switch

In the previous piece of code, you saw the nested `if...else` statement. If you always need to compare the same variable in your code block, you can use the `'switch'` statement. You define a certain variable, and, depending on the value of that variable, the platform executes your block of code.

The syntax of a `switch` statement is as follows:

```
switch on expression {
 when value1 {
  // execute code block 1
 }
 when value2 {
  // execute code block 2
 }
 when value3 {
  // execute code block 3
 }
 when else {
  // execute the default code block, this is optional
 }
}
```

I've rewritten the `if-else` structure from `Chapter 3`, *Declarative Automation*, in a `switch` statement. It looks like this:

```
Integer iPlace = 2;
String sMedalColor = '';

switch on iPlace {
 when 1{
  sMedalColor = 'Gold';
 }
 when 2{
  sMedalColor = 'Silver';
 }
 when 3{
  sMedalColor = 'Bronze';
 }
 when else {
   sMedalColor = 'Unfortunately, no medal';
 }
}
```

Do you see the difference? The code does exactly the same thing, but the performance of the `switch` statement is higher than the `if-else` structure.

Loops

The second type of control flow statement is **loops**. With loops, you can repeat the same logic multiple times. So, if you have a loop from 1 to 10, you always add 1, and you repeat this statement 10 times (it's like counting out loud).

There are three types of loops that you can use in Apex:

- The `do...while` loops
- The `while` loops
- The `for` loops

All these types of loops allow the following statements for loop control structures:

- `break`: This statement exits the entire loop (for example, if you need to find a specific item in a loop).
- `continue`: This interrupts the execution of the current code and skips to the next iteration of the loop.

The do-while loop

A `do-while` loop executes a block of code for an indefinite number of times and stops when a Boolean condition remains true. The syntax of a `do-while` loop is as follows:

```
do {
  // Code_block to execute
} while (Boolean_Condition);
```

In the following example, we display the numbers from 1 to 10 through a `do-while` loop:

```
Integer iCount = 1;
do {
  System.debug(iCount);
  iCount++;
} while (iCount < 11);
```

The while loop

The `while` loop executes a block of statements for an indefinite number of times, as long as a Boolean condition remains true. The basic syntax is as follows:

```
while (Boolean_Condition){
  // execute the code block
}
```

The difference from the `do-while` loop is the check of the condition. In the `while` loop, the condition is checked before the execution of the code; in the `do-while` loop, the condition is checked after the execution of the code, which results in the fact that the code will certainly be executed at least once!

The same logic for counting from 1 to 10 in a `while` loop looks like this:

```
Integer iCount = 1;
while (iCount < 11){
  System.debug(iCount);
  iCount++;
}
```

This gives exactly the same output, but with less code!

The for loop

Aside from the `while` and the `do-while` loops, we can also use extended versions of the `for` loop in Apex. Extended? Yes. A normal `for` loop (where you want to count from 1 to 10) is possible in every programming language.

In Apex, you can also use a `for` loop to walk through the records of a list or the results of an SOQL/SOSL query. (Don't panic if you don't know what SOQL or SOSL are. We will cover SOQL and SOSL queries in the next section of this chapter, *Working with data in Salesforce*).

In Apex, you have three types of `for` loops:

- The traditional `for` loop
- An iteration of a list or a set
- An iteration of a collection (maps or results of an SOQL/SOSL query)

First of all, let's discuss the traditional `for` loop. The `for` loop contains three important elements during the initialization of the loop:

- The start statement: This is where the loop needs to start.
- The exit condition: A Boolean condition that is verified before the code in the loop will be executed. If the Boolean is false, the loop exits (stops).
- The increment statement: The steps to increment the initial start statement (without this, you would end up in an infinite loop).

We'll look at the same example as in the `do-while` loops, counting from 1 to 10:

```
for (Integer iCounter = 1; iCounter < 11; iCounter++){
  System.debug(iCounter);
}
```

In this code block, you can see the three different parts:

- The start statement (`iCounter = 1`)
- The exit condition (`iCounter < 11`)
- The increment statement (`iCounter++`) in which we add 1 to the number in the variable of `iCounter` with each iteration

Iterations

Aside from the traditional `for` loop, Apex also supports two other types of `for` loops: an iteration of a list or a set and an iteration of a collection (a map or a collection of records).

Iteration of a set or list

In Chapter 3, *Declarative Automation*, you learned the difference between a set and a list. In a `for` loop, the iteration of the code in your `for` loop will happen for every object (record) in your set or list. Let's see an example to clarify this:

```
for (variable : list_or_set){
  // your code
}
```

The variable will be declared in the loop, and the set or list is declared outside the loop. The code will be executed for each iteration:

```
Set<Integer> setIntegers = new Set<Integer>{1,2,3,4,5,6,7,8,9,10};
for (Integer iInLoop : setIntegers){
  System.debug(iInLoop);
}
```

> Reading code out loud helps you to better understand what is going on, and also shows you that it's not just jibber-jabber.

Read it out loud, as follows:

1. Define the `Set` of the data type, `Integer`, and call this set `setIntegers`.
2. Assign it with a new instance of the `Set` class, which will contain the values of the `Integer` data type, and add the values 1, 2, 3, 4, 5, 6, 7, 8, 9, and 10.
3. Loop through each value in `setIntegers`, and for each value that you encounter, assign it to a temporary variable of the `Integer` data type, called `iInLoop`.
4. Then provide the current value of `iInLoop` to the debug logs.

When you execute this code in your Developer Console and run the code, you will see the numbers from 1 to 10 in the debug logs.

Iteration collections

A collection can be a collection of `Set`, `List`, or `Map` instances. The `for` loop is used to iterate the code in a structure when looping a collection of records.

When looping through a map with records, you always need to define which of the two values you want to iterate. Here is an example:

```
Map<Integer, String> mapNumbers = new Map<Integer, String>{
    1 => 'One',
    2 => 'Two',
    3 => 'Three'
};

// Iteration over the indexes of the map

For (Integer iNumber : mapNumbers.keySet()){
  // the keyset()-function of a map returns a set of the keys from the map.
This is always a set of objects, defined in the map. In this case 1, 2 and
3
  ...
}

// iteration over the values of the map
For (String sString : mapNumbers.values()){
  // the values()-function of a map returns a set of the values from the
map. This is always a set of objects, defined like the map. In this case,
'One','Two' and 'Three'
  ....
}
```

Now, you are ready to write some code that executes in repeat or executes when a criterion is met.

Let's go to one of the most used functionalities of Apex: selecting data from the Salesforce database with SOQL and/or SOSL, understanding the query language of Salesforce, and then manipulating this data.

Working with data in Salesforce

So, your Salesforce database now contains a lot of data to work with. You have created movies, actors, production companies, and reviews. In Apex, you might want to work with and manipulate this data. This also means you need some ways to query the data you want to manipulate, and that's what we are going to discuss in this section.

Selecting data with SOQL and SOSL

Since you are familiar with databases, you have learned about SQL, MySQL, PostgreSQL, or other database languages to select data out of a database. After the selection, we can execute some logic, manipulate the data, or display the data.

In Apex, you will use a similar type of language, named SOQL or SOSL. I can imagine that you are thinking: *Why are there two language types in Salesforce?*

There are some differences between SOQL and SOSL. Let's take a look at them:

SOQL	SOSL
Similar syntax to other database languages (like MSSQL and MySQL).	Salesforce search syntax.
Returns a list or map with records out of one object type (a list view in Salesforce would be a typical SOQL; it returns records of only one object type).	Returns two nested lists with results out of one or more object types (searching for a keyword in the Salesforce global search box uses SOSL. It returns a page with results of different objects in which it found your keyword).

Used when you know exactly which data you want (I want to select the authors from a movie where the title starts with an *A*).	Used when you don't know which table the data is present in or you want to select more than one object with the same search criteria (I want to select the movie titles and actor surnames that start with an *A*).
You can count the number of records that meet specific criteria (aggregate queries).	Searches in different types of fields (name fields, phone fields).
You can sort your data in your query.	In general, SOSL is much faster than SOQL, except when your search is too general (you're only searching for an A in the whole database, with millions of records). Create criteria-specific queries with filtering on indexed fields, so you receive your search results in milliseconds.

You can see the differences between SOQL and SOSL; actually, the languages are not the same. Between the regular SQL language and SOQL, there are a number of differences and limitations. The following is an overview of the limitations of SOQL:

- You cannot select all the fields from an object with the joker element (`Select * from Account`). If you want to do that, you need to select the fields from the object through the database schema and create a dynamic query (but that's too advanced for this book).
- You cannot use calculation expressions (`Select UnitPrice * Quantity from OpportunityLineItem`).
- You cannot use join statements. (Salesforce has another methodology to select data from linked tables. We will discuss that later in this chapter, in the section *SOQL relationships*.)
- For some objects, you need to specify some filters (for instance, for the `Vote` object, you need to specify the filter field `ParentId`, `Parent.Type`, OR `Id`).
- The results returned can be a maximum amount of 50,000 records (synchronous).

SOQL syntax

The SOQL syntax is similar to the regular database SQL language. It also starts with SELECT; you select data FROM a table, and you can ORDER BY field in that table and select data WHERE field values meet specific criteria. The basic syntax of an SOQL query looks like this:

```
SELECT COUNT(Id), ShippingCountry FROM Account WHERE AnnualRevenue > 10000
GROUP BY ShippingCountry
```

Let's split up everything you see in this query and more possible ways to select data out of your database tables.

SELECT fieldList [subquery] [...]

This query specifies a list of one or more fields, separated by commas, that you want to retrieve from the specified object. The bold elements in the following examples are lists of fields:

```
SELECT Id, Name, Genre__c FROM Movie__c
SELECT COUNT() FROM Cast__c
SELECT Movie__r.Name, Name FROM Cast__c
```

You need to specify at least one valid field name, and you must have read-level permissions for each field specified in the query. The list can include a subquery if you want to select child records that are related to a parent record. You can only select one level deep for related records. The following is an example:

```
SELECT Name, (SELECT Name FROM Cast__r) FROM Movie__c
```

In the previous query, we actually say this: Give me the field Account.Name for all records from the Account table, and also give me the Contact.LastName from the related list, Account.Contacts.

The result of this query is a list with accounts, and in this list, a list with the linked contacts to that account. You cannot select a second level into your inner query, such as the following query:

```
SELECT Account.Name, (SELECT Amount, (SELECT UnitPrice FROM
OpportunityLineItems) FROM Opportunities) FROM Account
```

The list of fields can also contain an aggregate function, such as COUNT() and COUNT(fieldName), or they can contain translating results (toLabel()); for example, see the following:

```
SELECT COUNT() FROM ACCOUNT;
// this query will return an integer, the number of all accounts in your
database

SELECT toLabel(picklistfield) FROM ACCOUNT;
// This query will provide you the translated version of a picklist value.
If you translate your picklist values with the translation workbench, with
the toLabel(field), you receive the translated value in the user's
language.
```

FROM objectType[...]

This part of the query specifies the type of object that you want to select. You need to specify a valid object, such as Account, and you must have at least read-level permissions to the object you want to select.

[WHERE conditionExpression]

This part of the query determines the criteria in the specified object to filter against. If the criteria are not specified, the query returns all the rows in the object that are visible to the user:

```
SELECT Id, Name FROM Account WHERE Name LIKE 'A%'
```

The preceding query shows you every Account record ID and Name where the name starts with an 'A'.

[GROUP BY {fieldGroupByList|ROLLUP (fieldSubtotalGroupByList)|CUBE (fieldSubtotalGroupByList)}

This part of the query specifies a list of one or more fields, separated by commas, that are used to group the retrieved results. A GROUP BY clause is used with aggregate functions to summarize data. With this function, you are able to roll up query results, rather than having to process the individual records in your code.

The results will include extra subtotal rows for the grouped data when you group the results with the functions GROUP BY rollup or GROUP BY cube:

```
SELECT ShippingCountry, SUM(AnnualRevenue) totalRevenue FROM Account GROUP
BY ShippingCountry
```

This query gives you the total annual revenues from the accounts, grouped by the shipping country:

ShippingCountry	totalRevenue
UK	4000000
USA	850000000
France	30000000

`GROUP BY Rollup` adds subtotals in query results. This action enables the query to calculate subtotals, which you don't need to implement in your logic:

```
SELECT ShippingCountry, COUNT(Id) numberOfAccounts, Status FROM Account
GROUP BY Rollup(ShippingCountry, Status)
```

This query provides you the results for each combination between the `ShippingCountry` and the `Status` field. The following is a table with the possible results:

Shipping Country	Number of accounts	Status	Comment
UK	36078	Prospect	36,078 account rows in the status prospect in the UK
UK	45039	Customer	45,078 account rows in the status customer in the UK
USA	530945	Customer	530,945 account rows in the status customer in the USA
USA	8765	Prospect	8,765 account rows in the status prospect in the USA
France	4782	Prospect	4,782 account rows in the status prospect in France

Group by cube provides you the subtotals for all combinations of a grouped field in the query results. With this type of query, you can use grouping, and it is very efficient for building and displaying custom matrix reports.

[ORDER BY fieldOrderByList {ASC|DESC} [NULLS {FIRST|LAST}]]

This is a list of one or more fields, separated by commas, that are used to order the retrieved results. For example, you can query for people in the movies and order the results by the movie name, and then by the actor name. You can sort them in ascending order (from low to high, A to Z, dates in the past, to dates in the future) or descending order (the opposite of ascending).

In the following example, we sort the records by the last name, from A to Z, and after that, a sort on the first name, from Z to A:

```
SELECT Id, LastName, FirstName FROM Contact ORDER BY LastName ASC,
FirstName DESC
```

[LIMIT numberOfRowsToReturn]

This specifies the maximum number of records you want to select. If the result in the query has more than this number of records, the LIMIT statement will limit your results list to this number. Sometimes, you can use it in conjunction with ORDER BY to showcase a top 5 or a top 10 list:

```
SELECT Name FROM Account LIMIT 5
```

[OFFSET numberOfRowsToSkip]

This specifies the number of records that need to be skipped in the results of the query. This functionality can be used in paging functionalities, where a limited set of records are selected and displayed on a page or component (for example, show results 6 to 10):

```
SELECT Name FROM Account LIMIT 5 OFFSET 5
```

The query up here will return the respective set of data in different circumstances:

- If the selected record set has less than five records, the result is an empty list.
- If the selected record set has more than five records, but less than 10 records, the result is a list with the records, starting from the sixth record.
- If the selected record set has more than 10 records, the result contains five records (from the sixth record until the tenth).

The result of a query is always a list of objects from the type which you are looking for. If your query selects data from the object Account, the result of your query is a list of accounts:

```
List<Account> lstAccounts = [SELECT Name FROM Account WHERE Revenue > 10000
ORDER BY Revenue DESC];
```

The query contains a list with the Account records (the name of the account), where the field Revenue has a number higher than 10,000. The results are ordered by the revenue field, in descending order (from the highest revenue to the lowest revenue).

Selecting records with dynamic parameters

Custom build applications, or trigger functionality, does not have some of the queries we saw previously. These queries are based on the user's input or on dynamic parameters. In that case, you can create your queries in two ways:

- Dynamic queries: We create a string with the full query and execute the query with the `Database.query(String)` statement:

```
String sAccountName = 'Burlington%';
String sQuery = 'SELECT Id, Name FROM Account WHERE Name Like \'' +
sAccountName + '\'';
List<Account> lstAccounts = (List<Account>) Database.query(sQuery);
// we cast the result of the query (a list with SObjects) to a list
with accounts
```

- A dynamic parameter in your query: This is the recommended way to perform SOQL statements with dynamic parameters. This way, the parameters are protected against SQL injection (when a user enters some malicious SQL code into a form to retrieve all the information from your database). We add the parameters with a colon, as shown in the following example (what we call a **bind variable** in SOQL; we will also use this term later in this book, when we create Visualforce controllers):

```
String sAccountName = 'Burlington%';
List<Account> lstAccounts = [SELECT Id, Name FROM Account WHERE
Name LIKE :sAccountName];
```

Both pieces of code do the same, but one piece is more vulnerable for an SQL injection than the other, and has a different performance (especially when you use this type of query to select a huge amount of data). More details on the vulnerable queries and how to avoid SQL injection can be found later in this book, as you might get a question like this in the exam.

Variable assignment

If you select data from a data table, you assign the results to a variable. This can be one record or a list of records. But what if the result doesn't contain any records? Maybe you have observed that I always use an assignment of a new list, and add the records to that list. When you assign a variable to a simple query (without the definition of a list), you receive `QueryException` (more about that in the exception handling, later in this book).

You can avoid this to assign your query results to a `List<SObject>` variable, instead of an sObject variable. Here is an example to illustrate this. The following is a simple query, assigned to a variable from the `Account` type. If the query doesn't have any results, the execution fails with `QueryException`:

```
Account a = [SELECT Id FROM Account WHERE Name = 'I think this account does
not exists'];
System.debug(a);
```

If you execute the preceding code in your Developer Console (executed anonymously), and you don't have an account with the name from the `WHERE` clause in the query, you will receive a `QueryException`. This is an error you'll encounter lots of times in your developer career, when you are not paying attention:

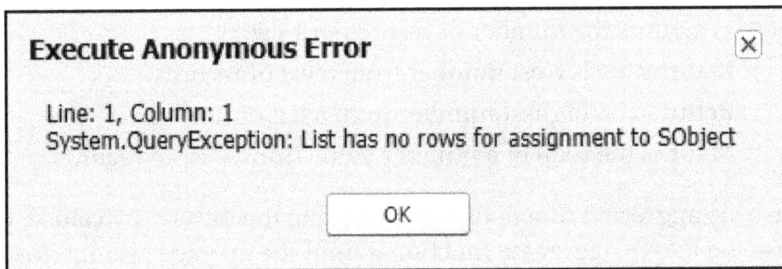

Execute Anonymous Error   ☒

Line: 1, Column: 1
System.QueryException: List has no rows for assignment to SObject

OK

If you assign `List<SObject>` to your query, you will receive an empty list. The following code will execute and receive an empty list, and won't throw an error:

```
List<Account> lstAccounts = [SELECT Id FROM Account WHERE Name = 'I think
this account does not exists'];
System.debug(lstAccounts);
System.debug(lstAccounts.size());
```

This will result in the following debug logs:

Execution Log		
Timestamp	Event	Details
14:45:04:007	USER_DEBUG	[2]|DEBUG|()
14:45:04:007	USER_DEBUG	[3]|DEBUG|0

Let's take a look at the next section now.

SOQL aggregate, optional clauses, and return

In query languages, you can also select aggregate results from data in your database. A simple customer requirement might be, how many accounts do I have in my database that had no opportunity in the last year? We will probably, we need to set these accounts as inactive.

You are able to use some aggregate functions in a GROUP BY clause in SOQL queries to generate analytical reports. Aggregate functions are functions for performing small calculations of a list of records, such as calculating the average of the amount of a list of opportunities or counting the maximum value in a list of records (what was the hottest day in March, 2019?). The most used aggregate functions are as follows:

- AVG(): The average of a list of records.
- COUNT(): Counts the number of records in a list.
- MIN(): Returns the lowest number from a list of records.
- MAX(): Returns the highest number from a list of records.
- SUM(): Returns the total of a number value from a list of records.

You can also use the aggregate functions without using the GROUP BY clause. In the next example, we use the AVG() aggregate function to find the average Amount for all your opportunities from a certain Account:

```
SELECT AVG(Amount) FROM Opportunity WHERE Account.Name = 'Acme'
```

The following query will return one result, with the number of accounts whose names start with 'A':

```
SELECT COUNT() FROM Account WHERE Name LIKE 'A%'
```

The following query will return the results with the average of the amount of all opportunities, and will group by the campaign linked to the opportunity:

```
SELECT CampaignId, SUM(Amount) totalAmount FROM Opportunity GROUP BY
CampaignId
```

This query will return a list with AggregateResult records, which contains the campaign ID and the sum of the amount of all opportunities with that CampaignId. Pay attention to *the alias* I use to name the sum of the amounts of the different opportunities. You can see the same alias in the table with aggregateResults (the second following table).

We have an original table with opportunities, with their respective amount and `CampaignId`:

CampaignId	Amount
X1	300000
X2	20000
X3	80000
X2	600000
X1	40000

The result of the query would be a table with `AggregateResults`:

CampaignId	totalAmount (this is the alias)
X1	340000
X2	620000
X3	80000

SOQL relationships

In each database, you need to link one record to a record from another table. And, as I mentioned in the introduction to this section, SOQL has the limitation that you cannot use `JOIN` statements in your query. So, the next question is this: How can you select related records (or related fields) from another type of object that is linked to the initial record you want to select?

Before we go into the practice to write the relationship queries, we need to understand the relationship names of each object. Two objects always have two relationships:

- **Parent-to-child relationship**: One movie can have multiple cast records.
- **Child-to-parent relationship**: Each cast record always has only one linked movie, and that movie record has a title, budget, and description.

In the parent-to-child relationship, you will create an inner query to select the child records from the parent record (we select the actors from the movie). The name of the relationship is different than the **API Name** of the object, and you can find the relationship name in the database schema (available through the workbench) or in the **Object Manager** (from Salesforce Lightning Experience, in the setup menu).

In the following example, we are going to query for all related `Cast` records of movies:

1. We will look in the **Cast__c** object for the **Movie__c** field. In the field definition, you will find **Child Relationship Name**. Complete this name with the __r extension, because it's a custom built relationship:

Cast Custom Field
Movie
Back to Cast

Help for this Page

Validation Rules [0]

Custom Field Definition Detail [Edit] [Set Field-Level Security] [View Field Accessibility]

Field Information

Field Label	Movie	Object Name	Cast
Field Name	Movie	Data Type	Master-Detail
API Name	Movie__c		
Description			
Help Text			
Created By	Jan Vandevelde, 12/11/2018 04:37	Modified By	Jan Vandevelde, 12/11/2018 04:37

Master-Detail Options

Related To	Movie	Child Relationship Name	Cast
Related List Label	Cast		
Sharing Setting	Read/Write: Allows users with at least Read/Write access to the Master record to create, edit, or delete related Detail records.		

---

2. In the workbench, we will go to our parent object and look for the **Child Relationships**, and we'll find **relationshipName**:

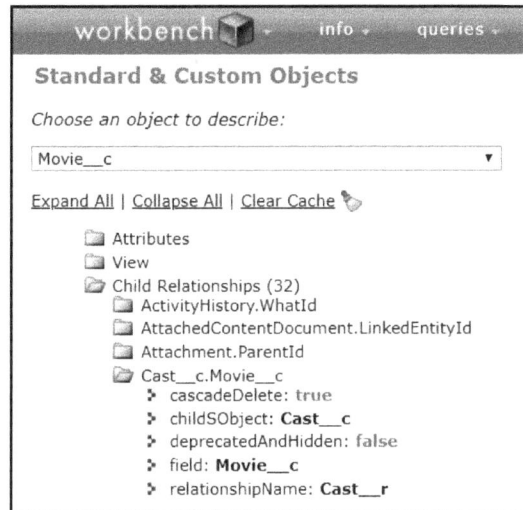

The following diagram presents our database design. Notice the two types of related fields in the Cast object. The Movie__r object will have all the information of the related movie record, while Movie__c only the has Id. This will be similar for both the Person__c and Person__r relationships:

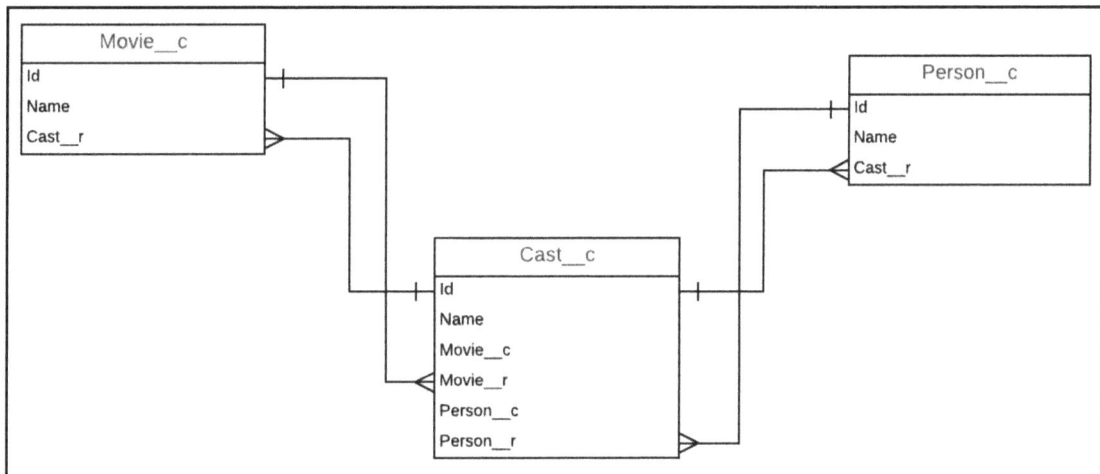

In both single objects (Movie__c and Person__c), you'll see the relationship with the Cast object in the relationship Cast__r. This is not a field, but the child relationship name notation for the relationship between the movie and the cast on one side, and between the person and the cast on the other side.

We go back to the definition of our query and want to select our movies with the list of actors. You can try the following examples along with me in the query editor of the Developer Console. To select all the actor names from all the movies in our database, we need to select data from these three tables. Let's build the query using these steps.

The requirement is to select all the actors from the movies, so the parent object is the movie. The first step of our query is as follows:

```
SELECT Name FROM Movie__c
```

This would result in the following output:

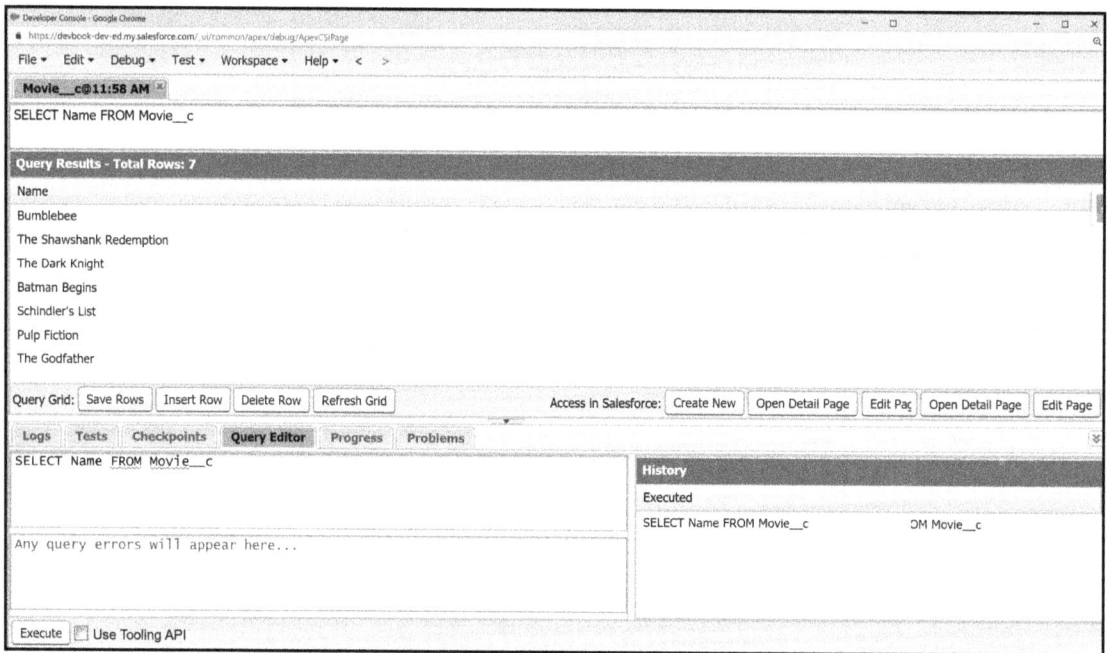

This is easy, isn't it? We select all the movies from our database. So far, so good. Now, we need to select the actors from these movies, their real names, and the names of the characters they play in the movies. How can we do that in our query?

First, we need to select the cast records from the movie. If we need to select these records in a single query, we should enter the following query:

```
SELECT Name, Movie__r.Name FROM Cast__c
```

This results in the following output:

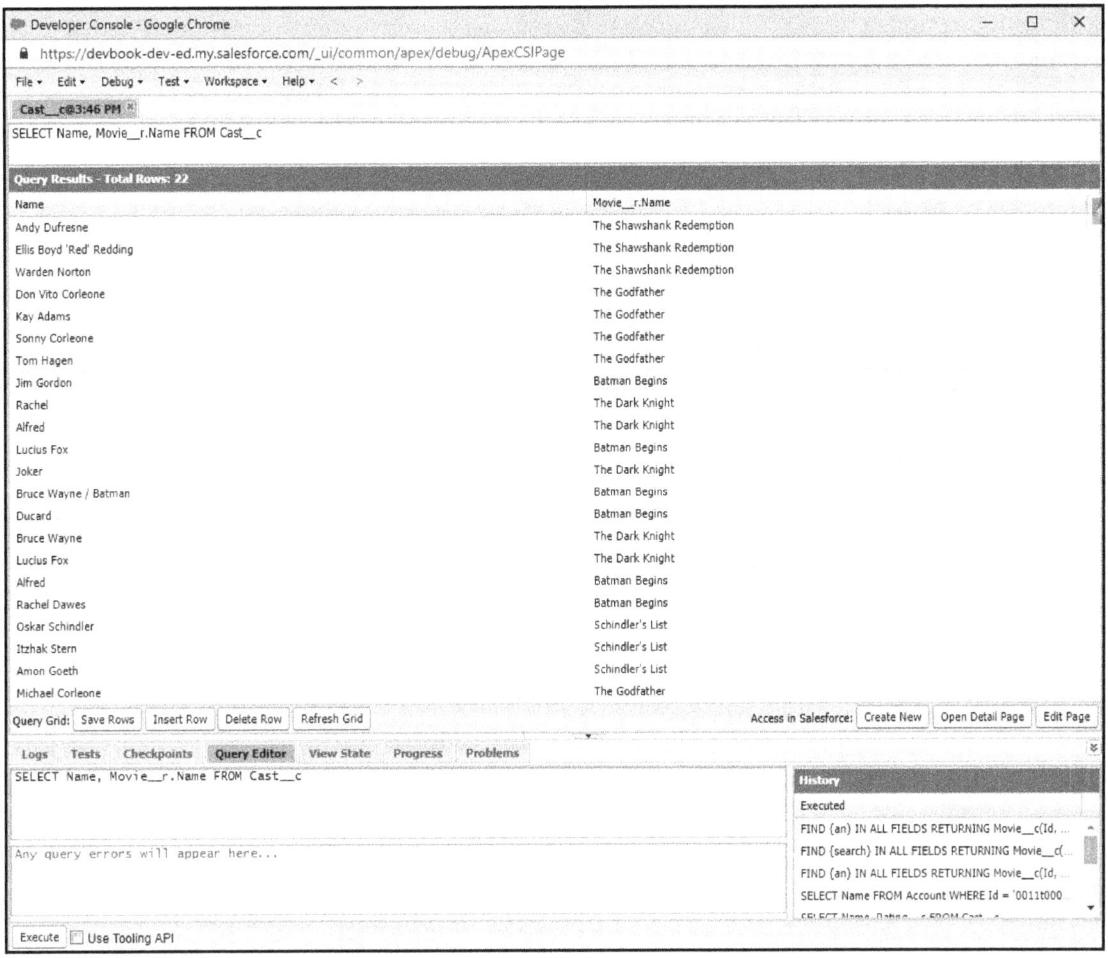

We would receive a list with the names of the actors in the movie, and the same movie multiple times (if more actors play in the same movie). This is just a part of the result that we want.

We want each movie one time, and in the record of the movie, the list with the actor names and the names of the characters they play in those specific movies. So, we need to create an inner query in our main query with the child relationship name. It looks like the following query:

```
SELECT Name, (SELECT Name FROM Cast__r) FROM Movie__c
```

This would result in the following output:

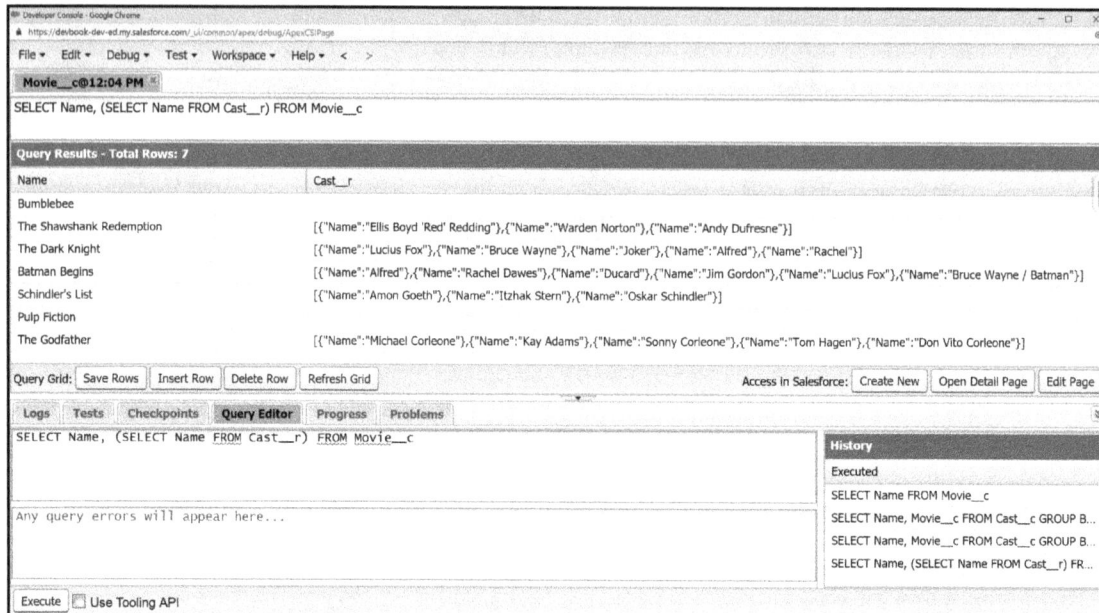

Great! Now, we have all the movies with the actors and the roles they play, but still no actor names. So, we should use the second type of relationship to display the name of each actor.

The name of the actor is defined in the `Person` object and is linked in the `Cast` object. When we use a standalone query, we use the child-to-parent relationship, and we create the following query:

```
SELECT Person__r.Name FROM Cast__c
```

This would result in the following output:

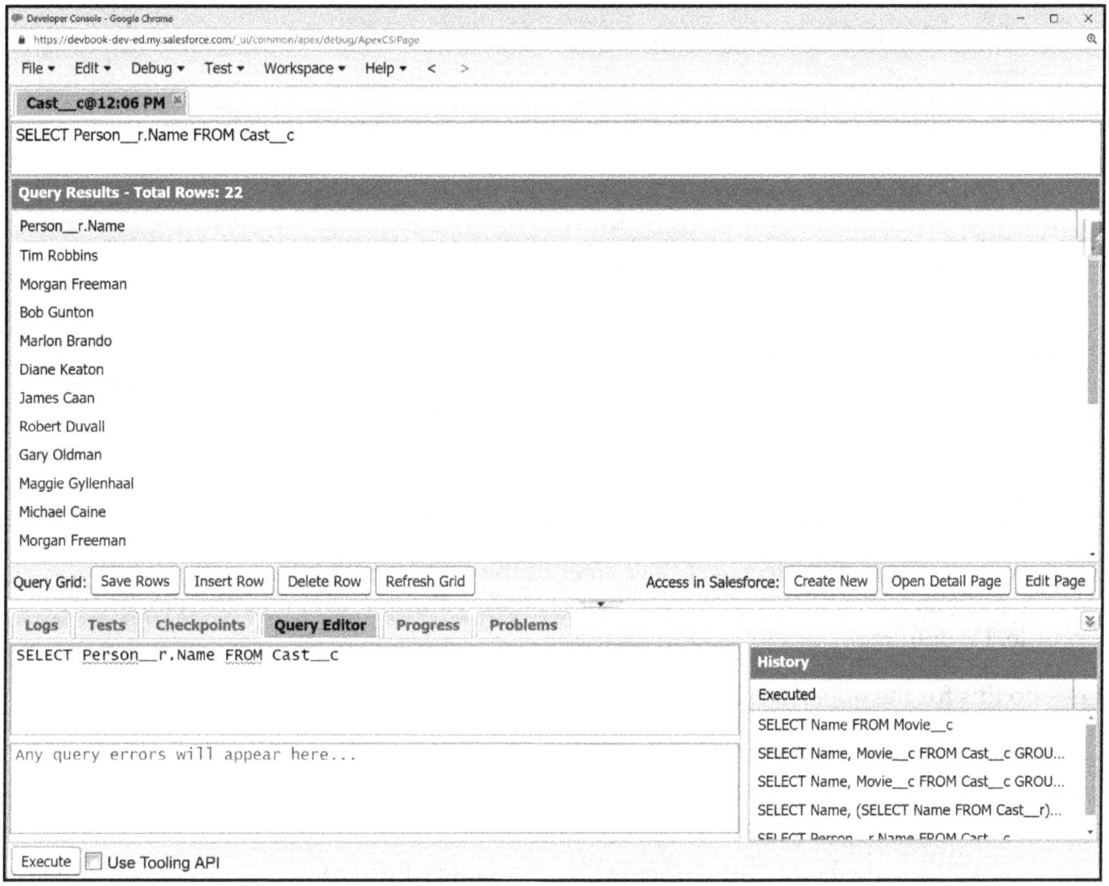

This query gives the result with the name of the person, linked to the cast record. In the query, we will add the person's name into the inner query, because we select the details from the person, which is linked to the cast record:

```
SELECT Name, (SELECT Name, Person__r.Name FROM Cast__r) FROM Movie__c
```

This would result in the following output:

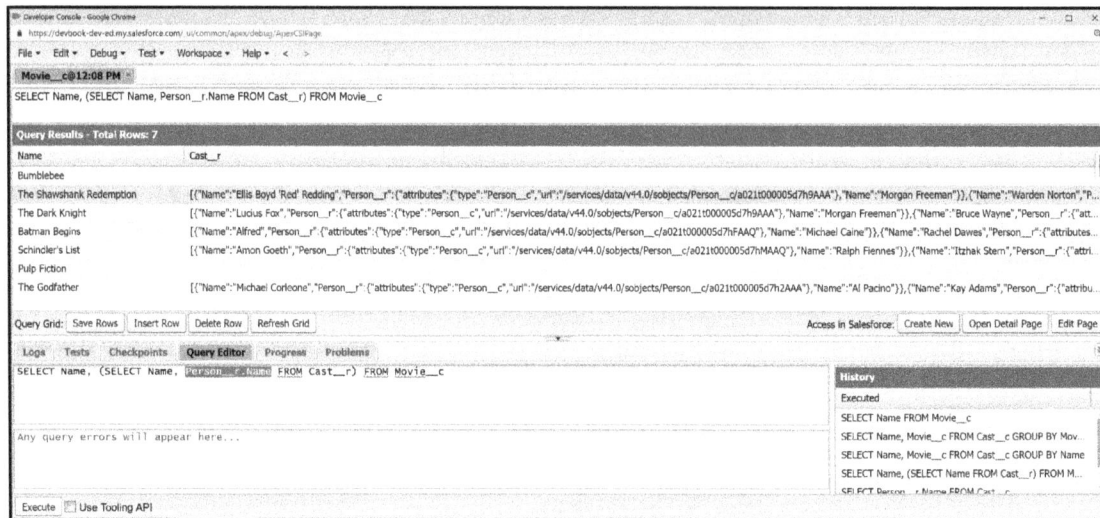

This is the complete query to select the names of the actors in all the movies of our database. If you haven't already, you can always test your queries in the Developer Console. I would really advise you to do this.

Let's do this for the query we just created, as follows:

1. Open the Developer Console:
   - Go to the upper-right corner and click on the **Setup** gear.
   - Click on the **Developer Console.**
2. Click at the bottom of the screen, on the **Query Editor** tab.
3. Type your query into the screen and click **Execute**.
4. Look at the results.

Did you check the names of the actors? The following example is from the movie The Shawshank Redemption. We have three records, with the role name in the movie and some attributes of the linked Person record. The type and url fields are always inserted with this type of relationship (you can see the ID in the URL, and you can create a link to the respective record with this URL), and of course the selected fields in your inner query (in our case, only the Name of the person):

```
[
{"Name":"Ellis Boyd 'Red'
Redding","Person__r":{"attributes":{"type":"Person__c","url":"/services/dat
```

```
a/v44.0/sobjects/Person__c/a021t000005d7h9AAA"},"Name":"Morgan Freeman"}},

{"Name":"Warden
Norton","Person__r":{"attributes":{"type":"Person__c","url":"/services/data
/v44.0/sobjects/Person__c/a021t000005d7hAAAQ"},"Name":"Bob Gunton"}},

{"Name":"Andy
Dufresne","Person__r":{"attributes":{"type":"Person__c","url":"/services/da
ta/v44.0/sobjects/Person__c/a021t000005d7h8AAA"},"Name":"Tim Robbins"}}
]
```

Great; you created your first queries to select data from a single object, and with the two types of relationships.

As I've mentioned, Salesforce has a second type of query language, named SOSL. Let's take a look at that specific language.

SOSL

You have probably found the global search functionality of Salesforce. Search for a criteria in every object and in each field. That's the greatest use case to use SOSL instead of SOQL. You can use this powerful search functionality in your application, as well.

The definition of SOSL is slightly different from the SOQL definition.

FIND {SearchQuery}

This specifies the text (words or phrases) to search for. Enclose these words with curly braces. Look out for the following remarks:

- No result is returned when the text between the braces is longer than 10,000 characters.
- The logical operators are removed if the text is longer than 4,000 characters. For instance, the AND operator in a statement with a query of 4,001 characters will have defaulted to the OR operator, which will have more results than you expected.

Be careful here, as when you define a search query in Apex, you need to enclose your criteria between single quotes (FIND 'my Criteria' ...). When you test your query in the Developer Console, you need to use curly braces to enclose your criteria (FIND {my criteria}).

[IN SearchGroup]

This is the scope of fields to search. It be one of following values:

- ALL FIELDS
- NAME FIELDS
- EMAIL FIELDS
- PHONE FIELDS
- SIDEBAR FIELDS

If it's not specified, the default is ALL FIELDS.

[RETURNING FieldSpec [[toLabel(fields)] [convertCurrency(Amount)] [FORMAT()]]]

This is your search result data. The result is a list of one or more objects. Within each object, you will find the records in a list with these specified fields, with optional values to filter against. If unspecified, the search results will contain the IDs of all objects found. The field in the function toLabel will translate the results in the user's language.

Use FORMAT with the FIND clause to apply localized formatting to standard and custom number, date, time, and currency fields. The FORMAT function supports aliasing. In addition, aliasing is required when the query includes the same field multiple times.

[LIMIT n]

You are able to specify the number of rows you would like to return, with a maximum of 2,000 (see the Salesforce limits). If you don't specify this parameter, the default will be 2,000. Let's find some stuff in our database. You can also test these queries in your Developer Console.

In this case, the criteria are not important; you can play with them. The definition and the return of the results are more important. If we want to find some criteria in the name field, we define the SOSL query like this:

```
FIND {search} IN NAME FIELDS
```

This would result in the following output:

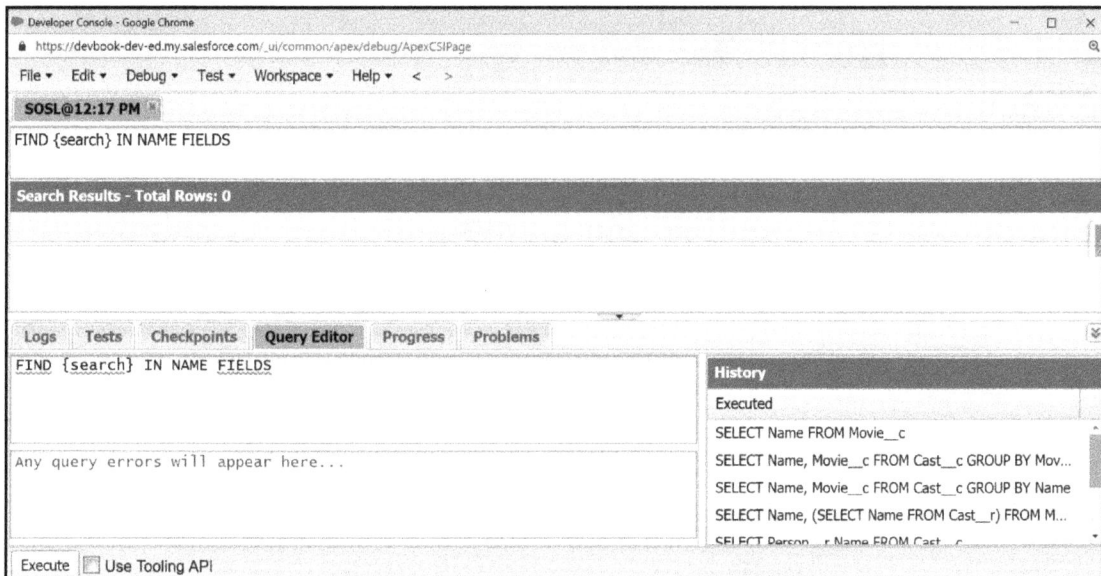

The query results in a list with all the records from all the database objects, where one of the name fields contains the word `search`. In our case, it returns no results whatsoever.

The next query will look for the word `an` in any of the fields of the objects `Movie` or `Person`:

```
FIND {an} IN ALL FIELDS RETURNING Movie__c(Id, Name), Person__c(Name)
```

This would result in the following output:

This query results in a list with the records from the `Movie__c` and `Person__c` types (see the two tabs), where a field contains the word `'an'`. I received one movie and 14 people, where one of the fields contains the word `'an'`. From the movies, we select `Id` and `Name`; from the people, we select only the name.

> **TIP**
> You could have different results, depending on the number of test records you created in your environment.

Please don't hesitate to play with all the other advanced options of these queries. During the Developer 1 certification exam, you will receive some questions about queries; all of them are regarding the basic scenarios we discussed in this book.

Now that you know how to select data, you are ready to manipulate this data with **Data Manipulation Language**, or **DML**, for short.

DML statements

We use these statements if a company wants to control the inserts and updates of accounts through a complex process, and also wants to compare the data to an external data source. Plenty of companies have this (at first sight) simple requirement. During this process, we will insert and/or update records with new field information, received from the external data source.

What about the deletion of old data? Does it happen through an automated process, or do we need to archive the data and delete it afterward? For all these requirements, we need to use a language that can modify our data. You need to insert, update, delete, and/or merge data to display this data to your users and keep the data up to date.

As a developer, you need to decide which user can execute which DML statement. The developer of an application (this can be a simple trigger) needs to configure the profile of the users that determines whether a certain object may be deleted and specifies the ability to update a field (and which fields). You can configure this level of access and permissions in the profiles of users, but in some circumstances, you can use Apex to avoid/bypass these rules, such as updating fields in records where the user doesn't have access to but needs to be updated for data integrity. How do you solve that kind of problem?

We will discuss the security in Apex (especially in combination with the selection of data and DML) later in this book (in `Chapter 5`, *Apex - Beyond the Basics*, in the *DML security* section). For now, we will discuss the DML statement that is possible in Apex.

Salesforce DML provides a way to manage records by executing simple statements, such as `insert`, `update`, `merge`, `delete`, and `undelete`. Because Apex is a data-focused language and operates on the Lightning Platform, you have direct access to your data in Salesforce. Other programming languages (such as PHP or Java) require additional setup to connect to data sources. With DML statements in Apex, you can easily manage your records. By calling a DML statement, you can quickly perform these operations on your Salesforce records.

Different types of DML statements

In the previous paragraph, you learned what DML in Apex means, and how it works. In Salesforce, we can use two types of DML:

- The short version of DML (`insert`, `update`, `upsert`, `delete`, `undelete`, and `merge`)
- The database version of DML

Both have pros and cons. Most of the time, it will depend on how you want to manipulate your data. The following is an overview of the pros and cons of the two types of DML:

Short DML	Database class
Short means short—with the statement `insert new Movie__c(Name = 'Independence Day')`, you just inserted a new movie with the title `Independence Day`.	This is a longer piece of code. You call the database class and the action you want to do: `Database.insert(new Movie__c(...))`.
DML with a list of records—if one of the records fails, none of the records are processed.	DML with a list of records— it is possible to catch the erroneous records and process the partial successes (`AllorNone`). The erroneous records can be recovered and retired to process.
It is not possible to detect which record fails in a list.	With the database and result classes, it is possible to detect which records failed during the operation.

Let's see how to choose a DML type.

Which type of DML should I use?

Use the short DML statements—to get any error that occurs during bulk DML processing that immediately interrupts the control flow (by using a `try...catch` construction). This behavior is similar to how exceptions are handled in most database languages.

Use the `Database` class methods—if you want to allow partial successes of a bulk DML operation. The DML statement can inspect the rejected records. When using this flow, you can write code that never throws a DML exception error. Instead, your code can use the database results list to judge success or failure.

> **TIP**
>
> Database methods also support a syntax to throw exceptions, similar to DML statements.

Methods of DML

When you want to use DML in other programming languages, you need to connect to the database, and, depending on the language, you create your statements to manipulate the data you need. For example, in PHP, you need to connect to your database and write a query to update your data.

In Salesforce (Apex), we use some predefined statements that insert, update, delete, and recover data in the database. Because Apex is a data-focused language, we have direct access to the database. Let me give you an overview of all the DML statements in Apex, with the short version and the database version, including the result, as follows:

Action	DML statement	Database DML statement
Insert records	`(void) insert records;`	`(List<Database.SaveResult>) Database.insert(records,AllorNone);`
Update records	`(void) update records;`	`(List<Database.SaveResult>) Database.update(records,AllorNone);`
Upsert records	`(void) upsert records;`	`(List<Database.UpsertResult>) Database.upsert(records,AllorNone);`
Delete records	`(void) delete records;`	`(List<Database.DeleteResult>) Database.delete(records,AllorNone);`
Recover deleted records (from the recycle bin)	`(void) undelete records;`	`(List<Database.UndeleteResult>) Database.undelete(records,AllorNone);`
Combine data from records	`(void) merge records;`	`(List<Database.MergeResult>) Database.merge(records,AllorNone);`

You can immediately see the difference between both functionalities. The simple DML statements execute your statement and return (if one record failed) a DML exception. The database DML statements will return a list with the results of your operation. If you specify the Boolean parameter `AllorNone` to false, you will perform a partial success. In the list with results, you can find the successful records and the failed records.

By default (the parameter is not set), the parameter is true, and an exception is thrown when one of the records has failed to process. Let's do some exercises with the DML statements and add, modify, and delete some records.

Inserting records

To insert records into the database, the user needs the create permissions for that object. If we want to insert records, we use the DML statement `insert`, or `Database.insert(Object)`. I'll explain the two methods to insert records into the database.

When you want to insert records, you can insert only one record or a list of records. Pay attention; it's only a list of records (not a `Set` or `Map` with records). Most of the time, you prepare the records in a variable and insert that variable (that corresponds with your record or list of records) into the database; an example is as follows:

```
Movie__c newMovie = new Movie__c(Name = 'Grease', Genre__c = 'Family');
Insert newMovie;
```

With this code, you prepare a movie object with the properties of this movie. You probably remember the paragraph about OOP in Apex. This is a beautiful example of it: the `Movie__c` object with the properties `Name` and `Genre`. Some other properties are defined in your data model. When the data is prepared, you can insert the data. The second line will insert the movie into your database.

With this code, the insert of the record can succeed or fail. If the insert succeeds, nothing's wrong, but if you configured a validation rule or a required field that's not defined in your record, a DML exception will be thrown. That's what we always want to avoid in good, working software! If you use this type of DML statement (the short version), I recommend to always use the `try...catch` block, which we will discuss later in detail in exception handling in Apex. Do you want a little sneak preview? Here you are:

```
Account newAccount = new Account();
try {
  insert newAccount;
} catch (DMLException ex){
  system.debug(ex.getMessage());
}
```

The preceding code will `try` to insert your movie, but it will fail. The name in the movie is a required field, so we cannot add this record into the database. If one of the rules of code between the curly brackets in the `try` block fails, you `catch` the exception. We log the exception message in the debug logs here (which will display the error message about why the record cannot be inserted).

If you use the `Database.insert` statement and you want to insert partial successes, you don't need the `try...catch` construction. If one record fails, the logic proceeds with the next record. The record is not inserted, and with the `SaveResult` class, you can get the error about why the record is not inserted. Here is an example:

```
// Prepare the records to insert into the database
Account newAccount1 = new Account();
Account newAccount2 = new Account(Name = 'My new Account');
List<Account> lstAccounts = new List<Account>{newAccount1,newAccount2};

// execute the DML statement
List<Database.SaveResult> insertedAccounts = Database.insert(lstAccounts,
false);

// loop through the results and check if the records are inserted
For (Database.SaveResult savedAccount : insertedAccounts){
  If (!savedAccount.isSuccess()){
    // the record is not inserted, we display the error message in the
debug log
    System.debug(savedAccount.getErrors()[0].getMessage());
  } else {
    // the record is inserted. We can grab the Id from the inserted record
    System.debug('Account Successfully inserted. Id: ' +
savedAccount.getId());
  }
}
```

The preceding code will produce your complete list of records. The first record will not be inserted (because of the missing name), but the second will be inserted. After the DML statement, we will go through the errors and see which error is thrown.

Copy the preceding code and execute it in your Developer Console (`executeAnonymous`). You will see that one account is inserted; the other fails, because the account name is missing:

Log executeAnonymous @12/28/2018, 11:50:38 AM ⊠	Log executeAnonymous @12/28/2018, 11:58:12 AM ⊠	
Execution Log		
Timestamp	Event	Details
11:58:12:097	USER_DEBUG	[13]|DEBUG|Required fields are missing: [Name]
11:58:12:097	USER_DEBUG	[16]|DEBUG|Account Successfully inserted. Id: 0011t00000CiQOkAAN

You can see the difference in the number of lines of code. The database statement uses more lines of code to handle the processing of your statement and returns the failed records (which is not possible with the short statements). When you use the short version of the DML statements with the `try...catch` block, you will get the error from the first failed record, and the processing of the next records will not executed anymore. This is a huge difference in the way you want to process your records. The following are some scenarios, and their respective solutions:

- Insert a list of records of the same object. The list needs to be completely inserted, or no record should be inserted. Use the short statements with the `try...catch` block.
- Insert a list of records of the same object. The list doesn't need to be completely inserted, but we need the failed records. Use the database statement with partial successes: `(Database.insert(ListRecords, false))`.
- Insert a list of records of the same object. The list does not to be inserted completely, but you need every record that failed. You only need to execute the statement one time. Use the database statements. While you are not able to grab all the failed records with the short version of the DML statements, you need to use the database DML statements. Use the transaction control to roll back to the previous status of the database.
- Insert a list of records with a retry mechanism. You want to insert a list of records. If there is no validation error, you want to retry the insert of the failed records. Use the database statements. The collection of the failed records and the processing of the success records is crucial in this decision.

I touched on one of these scenarios: transaction control. What is this?

Transaction control

Each DML operation is a transaction. Like a record, which has a previous and a next version (you will learn about that during the explanation of triggers later on), a database operation also has a previous version (called a **savepoint**) and a next version (the version after the insertion of records).

When you need to insert two types of records, such as a list of accounts and contacts, you want to know whether your account is correctly inserted before you insert the contacts. Because DML statements only support only one type of object in one transaction, we need to perform two DML statements: one for the account, and a second statement for the contacts.

However, what if you entered an account, and one of the contacts failed during the insertion of the contacts? If you don't want partial insertion of the contacts in the account, you need to remove all the inserted contacts and the inserted account.

With Apex, you can control these transactions as you wish. In this scenario, we need to define a savepoint before the insertion of the account. If one of the contacts fails, we perform a rollback until the savepoint. Let's look at an example:

```
// we set the current status of the database with the setSavepoint
statement
System.Savepoint currentDatabase = Database.setSavepoint();

// prepare the account to insert
Account a = new Account(Name = 'TestAccount');

try {
  // we insert the account
  insert a;

  // prepare the list with contacts
Contact c1 = new Contact(LastName = 'test Contact 1', AccountId = a.Id);
Contact c2 = new Contact(LastName = 'test Contact 2', AccountId = a.Id);
Contact c3 = new Contact(LastName = 'test Contact 3', AccountId = a.Id);
Contact c4 = new Contact(AccountId = a.Id);
List<Contact> lstContacts = new List<Contact>{c1,c2,c3,c4};

insert lstContacts;
System.debug('Records successfully inserted');
} catch (DMLException ex){
  // if the insert of 1 of the records fails, we go to the initial state of
the database, our savepoint
  Database.rollback(currentDatabase);
  System.debug('Records not inserted: ' + ex.getMessage());
}
```

Copy this code into your Developer Console (`executeAnonymous`) and execute it. What do you see in the logs? Indeed, the records are not inserted, due to an error in the last contact (we didn't provide a `LastName` for `c4`):

Execution Log		
Timestamp	**Event**	**Details**
14:05:12:200	USER_DEBUG	[22]|DEBUG|Records not inserted: Insert failed. First exception on row 3; first error: REQUIRED_FIELD_MISSING, Required fields are missing: [LastName]: [LastName]

But what happened now? I ran two DML statements: the first, in which I insert the account, and the second, in which I tried to insert a list with contact. The first statement succeeded, so in normal circumstances, the account is inserted.

The second statement failed, due to a missing name in the last contact. I used the short version of the DML statements, so no contact is inserted (remember the difference between the two types of DML statements). But what about the inserted account? Consider the following screenshot:

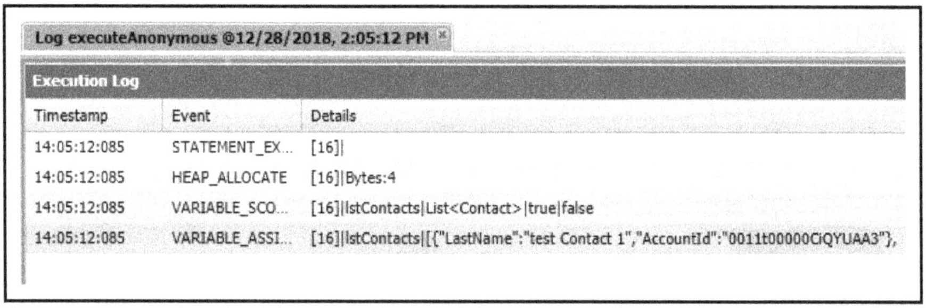

If you create a query to select the account with the ID that you find in the debug logs, you will not find the account:

That's the power of transaction control in Apex. The account was successfully created, but due to the rollback in the `catch` block and the savepoint before the creation of the account, we could roll back the database before the creation of the account. If we add a `LastName` to the last contact (`c4`), the account will be created, including the four contacts linked to that account.

Try it out for yourself! Just change the line for `c4` by adding a `LastName` assignment, and run it again:

```
Contact c4 = new Contact(LastName = 'test Contact 4', AccountId = a.Id);
```

Updating records

The user can update records when he/she has the profile access **Edit** on the respective object to update. When you need to update records with a DML statement, there is always one item required: the `recordId`. You cannot update a record without the 15-or-18 character-long identifier of that record.

The use of the DML statements to update is more or less the same as the statements for inserting records. Instead of the `insert` statement (to insert records), we now use the `update` or `Database.update(Object)` statement. Let's update some records:

1. First of all, we need to select some records to update. Let's select some `Cast` records and update the rating of how well the role is played by the actor.
2. Then, we will create a new custom field on the `Cast__c` object, with the following parameters (you should know how, and where, to do this by now):

   - **Field Type**: **Picklist**
   - **Field Name**: **Rating**
   - **Options**: The numbers from 1 to 5:

Cast
New Custom Field

Step 2. Enter the details

Field Label	Rating ⓘ
Values	○ Use global picklist value set
	⦿ Enter values, with each value separated by a new line

```
1
2
3
4
5
```

☐ Display values alphabetically, not in the order entered
☐ Use first value as default value ⓘ
☑ Restrict picklist to the values defined in the value set ⓘ

Field Name	Rating ⓘ
Description	
Help Text	ⓘ
Required	☐ Always require a value in this field in order to save a record
Default Value	Show Formula Editor

ⓘ Use formula syntax: Enclose text and picklist value API names in double quotes : ("the_text"), include numbers without quotes : (25), show percentages as decimals: (0.10), and express date calculations in the standard format: (Today() + 7)

3. Now, let's select all of the Cast records and update the ratings of these records with a default of 3:

```
// Select the cast records with the Id
List<Cast__c> lstCasts = new List<Cast__c>([SELECT Id FROM
Cast__c]);
For (Cast__c theCast : lstCasts){
 theCast.Rating__c = '3'; // while this is a picklist field, we
need to provide a String to this field even though it looks like a
number
}

// We use the short version of the DML statement here
try {
 Update lstCasts;
} catch (DMLException ex) {
 System.debug(ex.getMessage());
}
```

4. Copy this code into your Developer Console (executeAnonymous) and see what happens.
5. Filter your debug log with the word DML. In the first line, you can see how many records are updated (the number of rows is the number of records that are in the list to update; you can also see the same number on the last line, which means they all successfully updated):

Execution Log		
Timestamp	Event	Details
15:23:48:022	DML_BEGIN	[9]|Op:Update|Type:Cast__c|Rows:22
15:23:48:087	DML_END	[9]|
15:23:48:000	LIMIT_USAGE_...	Number of DML statements: 1 out of 150
15:23:48:000	LIMIT_USAGE_...	Number of DML rows: 22 out of 10000

If you select the records in the Developer Console with a query (select the **Name** and the **Rating__c** field), you will see that every record is updated with the rating of **3**:

```
SELECT Name, Rating__c FROM Cast__c
```

Query Results - Total Rows: 22	
Name	Rating__c
Andy Dufresne	3
Ellis Boyd 'Red' Redding	3
Warden Norton	3
Don Vito Corleone	3
Kay Adams	3
Sonny Corleone	3
Tom Hagen	3
Jim Gordon	3
Rachel	3
Alfred	3
Lucius Fox	3
Joker	3
Bruce Wayne / Batman	3
Ducard	3
Bruce Wayne	3
Lucius Fox	3
Alfred	3

Isn't that easy?

Of course, we can do the same with the database statement. For an exercise, you can write the code to update the records with the `Database.update` statement and `catch` the failed records (you'll find the solution in the *Appendix* of this book).

Upserting records

Upserting records is the combination of inserting and updating records. The user needs to have access to **Create** and **Edit** on the object that we need to upsert. But when should you use this functionality? This functionality is very useful when writing code for integration with other systems.

A table with data in a different database system will probably have another unique key. A company can have a database with the contacts of a company, and their key is the email address (because it should be a unique reference). Based on this unique reference, Salesforce can decide whether a record already exists.

Based on that decision, Salesforce will insert your record if the email address does not exist in the table with contacts, or it will update the record if the record with that email address already exists. You can upsert records based on each unique and external reference in Salesforce. This is a custom text field that is configured as a unique identifier and as an external identifier (checkboxes, when creating fields in Salesforce). If so, the external data can be synchronized with Salesforce, and vice versa.

The following table explains the external data:

Id	Last Name	First Name
001	L. Jackson	Samuel
002	Hanks	Tom
003	Willis	Bruce

This is the corresponding table of the `Person` object in Salesforce. The external ID is the `Id` from the preceding table. Through this `Id`, we know that the record in the preceding table (the external system) and the record in the Salesforce table are the same people, but with a Salesforce ID:

ID	External ID	Last Name	First Name
18-character string of Salesforce, the record ID	001	L. Jackson	Samuel
18-character string of Salesforce, the record ID	002	Hanks	Tom
18-character string of Salesforce, the record ID	003	Willis	Bruce

If you upsert a record with the external ID 003, Salesforce will update the third record in the table (the record with the external ID 003; in this table, `Bruce Willis`). If you upsert a record with the external ID 004, Salesforce will insert a new record, because this external ID doesn't yet exist in Salesforce.

In the `upsert` statement, you can define which field is used to verify the existing record. In our table, we use the `External_Id__c` field, which is configured as a unique field and as an external identifier. The `upsert` statement should look as follows:

- **The short method**: Upsert `listRecords External_Id__c`
- **The database method**: `List<Database.UpsertResult>`
  `Database.upsert(listRecords, External_Id__c, AllorNone)`

The statement now has three parts, instead of two:

- Upsert (your DML statement).
- `listRecords`: The list with records you want to insert or update.
- `External_Id__c`: This is the field you need to verify whether the record exists. If this field is not defined, the Salesforce ID is used as an identifier.

Exercise

To complete the following exercise, you create a new custom field on the object `Person`:

- **Type Field**: **Text**
- **Properties**:
  - **Label**: **External Id**
  - **Length**: **20**
  - **Unique**: **true, Treat "ABC" and "abc" as duplicate values (case insensitive)**
  - **External Id**: **true**

Don't fill the field in with information yet; we will do that later, during the exercise.

The exercise will use everything you have learned up until now, and it contains the following requirements.

- Update all the existing person records with a unique external ID (from one until the end of your `Person` table).
- Write the logic to update the external ID with the unique reference (a counter from one until the end of your table; convert this integer to a string).
- Upsert the following list into your database:
  - Prepare the records (you need to create the birth dates with an initiation of the `Date` class; also, see the primitive data types).
  - Write the first part of the code with the short version of the `upsert` statement and `upsert` the first six records of the following table.
  - Write the same logic with the `Database.upsert` statement with the other part of the records (an external ID from `117` until `120`).

The results are stored in `Database.UpsertResult class.`

The field that you need to compare to in your database statement is from the `Schema.SObjectField` class. We note that field as `ObjectName.fields.FieldName` (for example, `Account.fields.Name` or `Movie__c.fields.Director__c`). We will discuss this later in this book.

Let's take a look at the following table:

External ID	Name	Birth Date
8	Morgan Freeman	1/06/1937
3	James Caan	26/03/1940
25	Shannen Doherty	12/04/1971
26	Jennie Garth	03/04/1972
27	Jason Priestly	28/08/1969
28	Luke Perry	11/10/1966
117	Kaley Cuoco	30/11/1985
118	Jim Parsons	24/03/1973
119	Melissa Rauch	23/06/1980
120	Aarti Mann	03/03/1978

I recommend that you try to write this code in your Developer Console, and execute the code. I'll give you a part of the complete solution. Please read the comments, where you need to write some extra code:

```
// Define a counter to compile the external id
Integer iCounter = 1;

// Select the person records and add the data to a list of the object
// Person__c. Name the variable of your list 'lstPersons'. Add your
// code below this line


// loop through the person records and update the External ID with the
// string value of the counter
For (Person__c thePerson : lstPersons){
  // assign the string of the counter to the property External_Id__c of
// the object person.Add your code below this line
  // increment the counter with 1 (to give the next record a new External
Id). Add your code below this line
}

Try {
```

```
  // update the list of persons with the short notation of the DML
Statements.Add your code below this line
} catch (DMLException ex){
  // all records should pass. If an error, adapt the data in the
// corresponding failed records
  // if not, write here a debug statement with the error message. Add
// your code below this line
}


// prepare the records to upsert via the short notation
Person__c actor1 = new Person__c(Name = 'Morgan Freeman', Birthdate__c =
Date.newInstance(1936,6,1), External_Id__c = '8');
// prepare all other records you need for this exercise. Add your code
below this line. Yes you need to write them out (see table above for the
values)


// Add the actors to a list to upsert into the database. Add your code
below this line



try {
  // upsert the list with persons. Use the external reference to find out
if the record already exist or not. Add your code below this line
  // add a debug statement to check if all actors are upserted. Add your
code below this line
} catch (DMLException ex){
  // Something can go wrong ! Write a debug statement with the error
message. Add your code below this line
}


// Prepare the records
// Create your records from the table. Add your code below the first actor
Person__c actor1 = new Person__c(Name = 'Kaley Cuoco', Birthdate__c =
Date.newInstance(1985,11,30), External_Id__c = '117');

// put the actors in a list. Add your code below this line


// Get the field to compare the person records
Schema.SObjectField fieldToCompare = Person__c.fields.External_Id__c;

// execute the DML statement. The referrer if an actor already exists is
the field External_Id__c. The DML result for an upsert call is a
Database.UpsertResult object. Name the variable of your results
```

```
'lstUpsertedPersons. Add your code below this line


// loop through the results and check if the records is upserted
For (Database.UpsertResult savedPerson : lstUpsertedPersons){
  // Check if the savedPerson is upserted or not. Create 2 debug statements
(success and failed). If failed, add the error message into th debug
logs.Add your code below this line.


}
```

If you have written a working solution, you can verify your code in the *Appendix* of this book.

Deleting and undeleting records

When a user needs to delete records, the user needs to access **Delete** on the object that needs to be deleted. Records can be deleted using the `delete` operation, and you only need to pass it one parameter, the *record ID*. A deleted record is not permanently deleted. It stays in what is called the recycle bin for 15 days. This way, you can restore it if a mistake was made. Also, you need to be aware that the `delete` action supports cascading delete. This means that when you delete a parent record in a master-detail relationship, it will also delete its children.

If at least one of the children has failed to delete, the `delete` operation for the parent record will fail, as well. The `undelete` operation recovers the deleted records from the recycle bin. This operation also supports the recovery of the children of the deleted parent. This means that if you undelete the parent record, all the related deleted children will be recovered, as well. You can also recover the records that are deleted during a `merge` statement (combining at least two records into one record).

When you want to recover records from your database, you need to add the section `ALL ROWS` at the end of your query. For example, if you want to recover all the actors without a biography, your query should be like this:

```
SELECT Id FROM Person__c WHERE Biography__c == null ALL ROWS
```

To delete or undelete records from the database, you can use the same principles as for the `insert`, `update`, and `upsert` operations.

Let's look at how to delete and undelete records. In the following code, we will remove all the accounts that have not been updated in the last year. I have given two notations in one piece of code, divided by a comment. The result of the `Database.delete` operation is a `Database.DeleteResult` class.

The code to remove the accounts through the short notation is as follows:

```
Date dueDate = Date.today().addYears(-1); // today minus 1 year
List<Account> lstAccounts = new List<Account>([SELECT Id FROM Account WHERE
LastModifiedDate < :dueDate]);

// we perform only the operation if there are records in the list
if (lstAccounts.size() > 0){
   // the short notation of the DML statement
   try {
     delete lstAccounts;
     System.debug(String.valueOf(lstAccounts.size()) +  'accounts
deleted');
   } catch (DMLException ex){
     System.debug(ex.getMessage());
   }
}
```

This is the code to use if you need to delete the accounts through the database operations:

```
Date dueDate = Date.today().addYears(-1); // today minus 1 year
List<Account> lstAccounts = new List<Account>([SELECT Id FROM Account WHERE
LastModifiedDate < :dueDate]);

// we perform only the operation if there are records in the list
if (lstAccounts.size() > 0){
   List<Database.DeleteResult> deletedAccounts =
Database.delete(lstAccounts, false);
   for (Database.DeleteResult removedAccount : deletedAccounts){
     if (removedAccount.isSuccess()){
       System.debug('Account Deleted');
     } else {
       System.debug(removedAccount.getErrors()[0].getMessage());
     }
   }
}
```

You can use the undelete operation in the same way, but keep the following differences in mind:

- Select your data with the `ALL ROWS` notation at the end of the query.
- The result of `Database.undelete(ListWithRecords, AllOrNone)` is a `Database.UndeleteResult` class.

Merging records

In Apex, you can combine a maximum of three records and retrieve one record that you want to keep with the information of all the three records. This is a very useful functionality when you want to deduplicate data and merge all of the related children into one parent record.

For example, a company might have a database with its accounts and linked contacts and opportunities. When the Salesforce administrator verifies duplicates in the accounts, he finds three accounts with more or less the same name. The sales manager of that company says, *"Yes, it's the same account, but I want to keep one account (this is the most complete account) and the related contacts and opportunities of the three accounts."* That works for the powerful `merge` functionality of Salesforce.

You can only merge records of the following objects:

- `Account`
- `Contact`
- `Lead`

The `merge` functionality doesn't support bulk operations. You can't merge `20` records in one operation. When you want to merge records in Apex, you need the following items:

- One master record: If you want some field values from another *duplicate* record, you need to first update the master record with this information (the record that you want to keep).
- At least one supplementary record, and a maximum of two supplementary records (the duplicate records that you want to be thrown away).

The following is an example of merging records in Apex, with the explanation in the comments:

```
// Let's insert some records to merge
List<Account> lstAccounts = new List<Account>{
 new Account(Name = 'Acme'),
 new Account(Name = 'Acme Inc.'),
 new Account(Name = 'Acme NV')
};

// we need to insert 2 object types, linked to each other. If the second
operation fails, I don't need the accounts.
Savepoint currentStatus = Database.setSavepoint();
try{
 // insert the accounts to be sure you have these accounts in your database
 insert lstAccounts;

 // define now 2 variables for the master account and the duplicate account
 Account aMaster = lstAccounts[0];
 List<Account> lstDuplicateAccounts = new
List<Account>{lstAccounts[1],lstAccounts[2]};

 // insert now a contact on each of the accounts. We do this in the same
try catch module
 List<Contact> lstContacts = new List<Contact>{
 new Contact(LastName = 'Acme', FirstName = 'Contact', AccountId =
aMaster.Id),
 new Contact(LastName = 'Acme Inc.', FirstName = 'Contact', AccountId =
lstAccounts[1].Id),
 new Contact(LastName = 'Acme NV', FirstName = 'Contact', AccountId =
lstAccounts[2].Id)
 };

 insert lstContacts;
 System.debug('Accounts and contacts inserted');

 // the merge operation
 merge aMaster lstDuplicateAccounts;
 System.debug('Accounts merged');

} catch (DMLException ex){
 Database.rollback(currentStatus);
 System.debug(ex.getMessage());
}
```

Copy the preceding code into your Developer Console (executeAnonymous) and investigate the code. Execute it, and verify the debug logs. After the execution of the code, verify that the accounts and contacts that you have inserted in your database are present. You should have one account (your master account with the name **Acme**, with three contacts (of the three accounts we have merged together)):

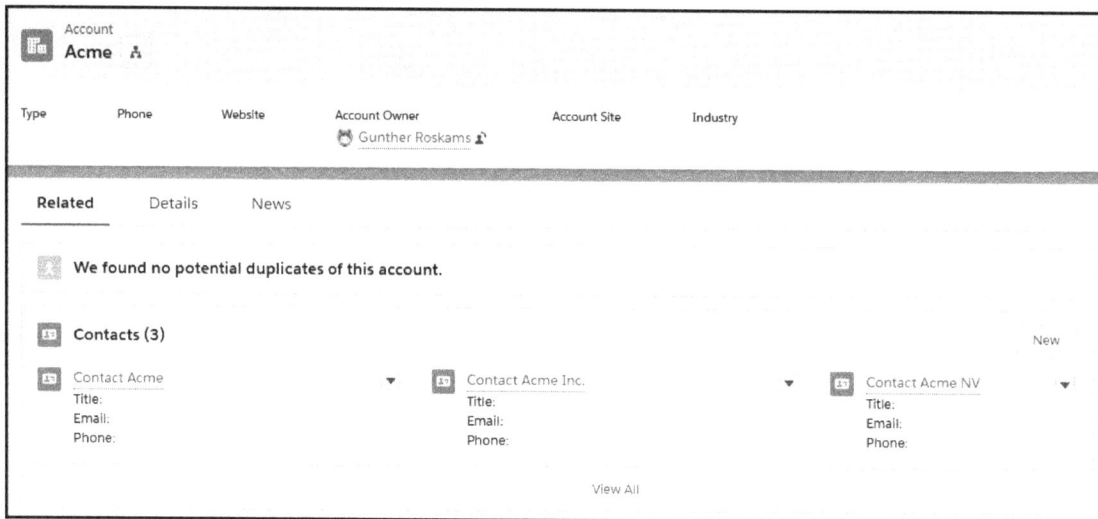

If you don't have this result, debug your code to see what happened.

Summary

In this chapter, you learned about the basics of Apex—its development and usage—along with using the Developer Console. You also learned about the application of variables, constants, expressions, different types of conditional statements, and access modifiers. You found out how to work with data using SOQL and SOSL.

In the next chapter, we will take one step further and go beyond the basics of Apex.

Quiz

Let's see whether you are on the right track to become a certified Salesforce developer. You'll find all the answers to these questions at the end of this book. Try to answer the questions without looking at the answers. You'll find the answers the *Appendix*:

1. What is the capability of the Developer Console?
    a. Execute Anonymous Apex code, create/edit code, view debug logs.
    b. Execute Anonymous Apex code, run the REST API, create/edit code
    c. Execute Anonymous Apex code, create/edit code, deploy code changes.
    d. Execute Anonymous Apex code, run the REST API, deploy code changes.

2. Suppose that a developer needs to provide a web service class for an external application. Which access modifier does the developer use to ensure the external application can consume this service?
    a. Private
    b. Public
    c. Protected
    d. Global

3. Suppose that a developer needs to develop a page with the weather conditions. In the summer, you have more sun, while in the winter, the chance of snow is higher than during the spring. In which type will the developer define the seasons in a variable, knowing that the seasons are always the same? (choose two options):
    a. Four final variables (`'Spring'`, `'Summer'`, `'Autumn'`, `'Winter'`)
    b. Four string variables (`'Spring'`, `'Summer'`, `'Autumn'`, `'Winter'`)
    c. Enum variable (`'Season'`)
    d. List with string variables (all seasons in a list from the `String` type)

4. What is the value of x after the following code segment executes?

```
String x = 'A';
Integer i = 10;
if ( i < 15 ) {
    i = 15;
    x = 'B';
} else if ( i < 20 ) {
    x = 'C';
} else {
    x = 'D';
}
```

    a. 'D'

    b. 'A'

    c. 'B'

    d. 'C'

5. Suppose that a developer has the following query:

```
Contact c = [SELECT id, firstname, lastname, email FROM Contact
WHERE lastname = 'Smith'];
```

What does the query return if there is no contact with the last name 'Smith'?
    a. A contact initialized to null
    b. An error that no rows were found
    c. An empty list of contacts
    d. A contact with empty values

6. Suppose that a developer writes an SOQL query to find the child records for a specific parent. How many levels can be returned in a single query?
    a. 1
    b. 7
    c. 5
    d. 3

7. What is the minimum log level needed to see user-generated debug statements?
    a. DEBUG
    b. FINE
    c. INFO
    d. WARN

8. Suppose that a developer needs to create records for the object `Property__c`. The developer creates the following code block:

```
List<Property__c> propertiesToCreate =
helperClass.createProperties();
try {
    // line 3
} catch (Exception exp ) {
    //exception handling
}
```

Which line of code would the developer insert at `line 3` to ensure that at least some records were created, even if a few records had errors and failed to be created?

    a. `Database.insert(propertiesToCreate, false);`

    b. `insert propertiesToCreate;`

    c. `Database.insert(propertiesToCreate, System.ALLOW_PARTIAL);`

    d. `Database.insert(propertiesToCreate);`

9. Which data type, or collection of data types, can SOQL statements populate or evaluate to? (choose three):

    a. A single sObject

    b. An integer

    c. A string

    d. A list of sObjects

    e. A Boolean

10. What is the result of the following code block?

```
Integer x = 1;
Integer Y = 0;
While(x < 10){
Y++;
}
```

    a. An error occurs

    b. `Y = 9`

    c. `Y = 10`

    d. `X = 0`

5
Apex - Beyond the Basics

You have already learned a bit about basic Salesforce Apex coding, such as the different types of variables, operators, `if...else` structures, and different types of loops. Now it's time to dig deeper into the more object-oriented stuff and learn how to define a good programming structure with classes.

In this chapter, we will be covering the following topics:

- Apex classes and interfaces
- Apex triggers
- The order of execution in Salesforce

Apex classes and interfaces

A class is a blueprint of an object, and you've learned in `Chapter 4`, *Apex Basics* that a class contains properties (member variables) and implementations of behavior (the methods in your class). The class also contains a constructor; this is the only method that does not contain a return value (including `void`) and has the same name as the class. The members of a class (variables or methods) can have different access modifiers and can be defined as static or non-static.

If you are familiar with programming Java, you will see some similarities, but also some differences. Let's look at an overview of the major differences between Java and Apex:

- Inner classes and interfaces can be only declared one level deep in a parent class.
- Static variables and methods can be declared in a parent class, not in an inner class.
- An inner class acts like a `static` class (`Database.SaveResult.SaveResult` is an inner class in the `Database` class).
- Private is the standard access modifier for class members. If you don't define an access modifier, your member is only accessible in the same class.
- Interface methods don't have access modifiers; they are always global.

Now, let's go one step further. As you can link objects to each other, you can link classes, extend classes, or reuse classes to minimize the number of lines of code and create the possibility to reuse existing functionality.

Later in this book, when we handle Visualforce controllers and exceptions, you will see the benefit of reusing existing functionality. Let's take a look at how Salesforce handles some functionality to reuse code and how we can extend an existing class.

Interfaces

An interface can actually be seen as a class without any functionality, which in fact is just a blueprint of an object. It's used to make sure that classes implementing this interface provide all the methods declared in the interface. These are the first type of classes. The interface only provides the methods that are needed. The class that implements this interface needs all of these methods. Let's look at an example to clarify how an interface works.

During a connection to an API, we always need an endpoint, a username, and password. But what if you need to authenticate with a username and password to different APIs? Well, then you can use an interface. The structure of the authentication details is always the same, but the data will differ.

The interface contains the structure of the authentication details. Remember that you can only define functions in an interface, and these functions don't need an access modifier. Since an interface should be implemented in another class (and you need to call the interface from another class), the access modifier for the interface is always global. The methods can be defined with or without parameters. If you define parameters, you need to define the parameters in your class later on, as well.

Let's go back to our movies. When you create a movie, you can use a template to create that movie. Let's look at an example to create different types of movies (action movies, thrillers, or comedy):

```
public interface MovieInterface {
    String getMovieType();
}
```

Great! You've built your first interface. As you can see, there are only methods without logic. But now what?

We create two different types of movies. Let's build the classes. Please note that if you implement the interface, you need to implement all the methods of that interface:

```
public class ActionMovie implements MovieInterface {
    public String getMovieType(){
        return 'Action movie';
    }
}

public class ComedyMovie implements MovieInterface{
    public String getMovieType(){
        return 'Comedy';
    }
}
```

As you can see, we used for both classes a kind of template that a developer needs to follow to receive the complete configuration of a movie type. The first class is intended for an action movie; the second class for a comedy movie.

Another example of an interface is the `Batchable` interface from Salesforce. Let's take a look at it:

```
Public class Database {
    Public interface Batchable {
    Database.QueryLocator start(Database.BatchableContext bc);
    void execute(Database.BatchableContext bc, List<SObject> sObjects);
    void finish(Database.BatchableContext bc);
    }
}
```

The following code shows the `MyBatchClass` class that implements the interface:

```
public class MyBatchClass implements Database.Batchable<SObject> {

    public Database.QueryLocator start(Database.BatchableContext bc){
        // logic to select your data
```

```
    }
    public void execute(Database.BatchableContext bc, List<SObject> scope){
        // logic to execute with the scope of records
    }
    public void finish(Database.BatchableContext bc){
        // logic to execute when all records are processed
    }
}
```

Each batch class that you will develop in the future will need to implement this interface.

Salesforce has a lot of interesting standard interfaces that you can use:

- **Schedulable**: Creates logic that you need to execute on a certain timestamp.
- **Comparable**: Sorts records in an order that you want.
- **Iterator and iterable**: These are interfaces used for batch implementations. They are used to walk through each item in a collection.
- **Queueable**: Puts logic execution in a queue; used for callouts in triggers or DML operations with a huge amount of records.

Virtual and abstract classes

The second type of classes is abstract and virtual classes. Let's start with the abstract classes.

Abstract classes

You can compare the definition of an abstract class with an interface. It's a class with abstract methods and no functionality into the methods. The abstract class cannot be constructed (like any other class) and can only be used in a class that extends the abstract class.

The big difference with an interface is that you can add member variables and methods with logic in the class, and call the logic from the child class. Before going back to our movies, we will create an abstract class with the movie object and the child classes will earn the functionality from the main movie class.

This following code includes the abstract class, where we create a model for the movie (including the functionality). We define this class with the optional modifier, `abstract`. Following this class, you will find a line-by-line explanation:

```
public abstract class Movie {

    private Id movieId = null;
    public String movieType = '';

    public Movie(Id idMovieId){
        this.movieId = idMovieId;
    }

    public Movie__c selectMovie(){
        if (this.movieId != null){
        List<Movie__c> lstMovies = [SELECT Id, Name, (SELECT Id,
    Person__r.Name FROM Cast__r) FROM Movie__c WHERE Id = :this.movieId];
            if (lstMovies.size() == 1){
            // check if there is a record
            return lstMovies[0];
            }
        }

        return new Movie__c();
    }

    public abstract void insertMovie();
}
```

What does this code do? As you can see, this code is partially executable (all non-abstract methods) and partially not. All the abstract methods are defined as you saw with the interface, with only the method name with the return and an optional parameter. These methods need to be implemented in the class that extends this abstract class.

Now, I'll explain the preceding code line by line:

```
public abstract class Movie
```

This line of code is the initiation of your class. For an abstract class, we use the `abstract` keyword. This keyword means that you cannot call this class, like any other public class, with the `new` keyword; you can only use the class with an extension. You will see an example later in this chapter. Like any other class, we give the class a name:

```
private String movieType = '';
```

In this class, we define some member variables. If you remember, with the structure of an interface, you don't have the possibility to define some member properties. However, in abstract classes, this is possible. In this class, I defined only a string to demonstrate the usability of the abstract class:

```
public Movie(String sMovieType){
    this.movieType = sMovieType;
}
```

This is the constructor of the abstract class. Like any other class, the abstract class can have a constructor as well. The constructor does not contain a return value and always has the name of the class. In this class, only an initiation with a parameter of the object type String is allowed.

Maybe this is a bit confusing to you, because I said you cannot call an abstract class, and now, I'm showing you that you can initiate this class in another class. Later, in the example of the child class, I'll show you how we do the initiation of an abstract class and where we need to do that initiation (in this case, with a string).

The lines in the constructor will set the Id member variable, which is dependent on the value in the parameter (the ID of the movie):

```
protected List<Movie__c> selectMovies(){
    List<Movie__c> lstMovies = [SELECT Id, Name, (SELECT Id, Person__r.Name
FROM Cast__r) FROM Movie__c WHERE Genre__c = :this.movieType];

    return lstMovies[0];
}
```

When we create an abstract class, we can execute some logic in a method. This method can be called (if the access modifier is protected or public) from a child class that extends the abstract class. In this example, I used the protected keyword to illustrate that this method cannot be accessed from outside the class, except for child classes.

This logic selects the movies from the database, including the cast, where the movie genre is the type we defined in the parameter of the class. For each type of movie, we use the same logic to select these movies:

```
public abstract void insertMovie(String sType);
```

This is an abstract method. For each class that uses (or extends) this abstract class, you are required to define this method. In the abstract method, you don't implement the logic (just as for the interfaces); the logic is implemented in the child class. In this case, we will implement logic to insert a movie, which for each type should be different.

When we define a child class, we need to **override** this method in our child class (more on that later in the child class example).

Inheritance from abstract classes

When we define a class and want to use the functionality of the abstract class, we extend the class with our abstract class. This class will be a child class and we take over the complete functionality, written in the abstract class. The only thing we need to do is to implement the abstract methods of the abstract class into the child class and implement the logic for these methods. This is what we call **inheritance**. The child class uses the same functionality as the parent class (it inherits the logic from the abstract class) and can overwrite some additional functionality (the abstract methods).

In the following code, I wrote two classes that use the functionality of our Movie abstract class, the ActionMovie class, and the Comedy class—the latter of which are both movie types:

```
public class ActionMovie extends Movie{

    public ActionMovie(){
        super('Action');
    }

    public override void insertMovie(){
        Movie__c newActionMovie = new Movie__c(Name = 'Action Movie',
Genre__c = 'Action');
        try {
            insert newActionMovie;
        } catch (DMLException ex){
            System.debug(ex.getMessage());
        }
    }

    public List<Movie__c> getActionMovies(){
        return this.selectMovies();
    }
}


public class Comedy extends Movie{

    public Comedy(){
        super('Comedy');
    }
```

```
    public override void insertMovie(){
        Movie__c newComedy = new Movie__c(Name = 'Comedy', Genre__c =
'Comedy');
        try {
            insert newComedy;
        } catch (DMLException ex){
            System.debug(ex.getMessage());
        }
    }

    public List<Movie__c> getComedyMovies(){
        return this.selectMovies();
    }
}
```

Did you see the advantages of the abstract class? If not, don't worry, as I'll explain both classes, line by line:

```
Public class ActionMovie extends Movie
Public class Comedy extends Movie
```

The preceding code statement leads to the creation of the respective classes. We create these classes as child classes of the `Movie` class. Both child classes inherit the logic of this class:

```
public ActionMovie(){
 super('Action');
}

public Comedy(){
 super('Comedy');
}
```

Do you remember that I said: *You cannot call an abstract class, but you can initiate the abstract class in your child class*? Well, this is it. The `super` keyword means the initiation of the abstract class in your child class. When we call the `ActionMovie` class (with `ActionMovie theActionMovie = new ActionMovie();`), the class immediately has the `Action` value assigned to the `movieType` member variable. This member variable is not present in the `ActionMovie` class, but only in the `Movie` class. Remember, the child inherits all the variables and methods from the abstract class.

In the second class, we defined the `Comedy` class, where the `Comedy` value is assigned to the `movieType` variable. Be careful, as this initiation needs to be the same as in your constructor of the abstract class. If you don't provide any parameters in the constructor of your abstract class, you cannot define a parameter in the initiation (somewhat similar as in a non-abstract class, when you create an instance of the class). In this case, the constructor of our abstract class was `public Movie(String)`, so the initiations for both child classes need to be `super(String)`:

```
public override void insertMovie(){
  Movie__c newActionMovie = new Movie__c(Name = 'Action Movie', Genre__c =
'Action');
  try {
  insert newActionMovie;
  } catch (DMLException ex){
  System.debug(ex.getMessage());
  }
}

public override void insertMovie(){
  Movie__c newComedy = new Movie__c(Name = 'Comedy', Genre__c = 'Comedy');
  try {
  insert newComedy;
  } catch (DMLException ex){
  System.debug(ex.getMessage());
  }
}
```

This is the method we are required to implement. The modifier of this method in the abstract class was `abstract`, which means we need to implement this method in our child class. During this implementation, we must use the `override` keyword to mention this is a method that comes from the abstract class and this logic can be different for other child classes. This is similar to driving a car—you need a driver's license to drive a car, but if you drive a small car, you have another driver's license, and then you drive with a bus (which is another type of vehicle).

We implement the logic into this `override` method and when we call this class, we can execute this method (if the method is defined as `public`):

```
public List<Movie__c> getActionMovies(){
    return this.selectMovies();
}

public List<Movie__c> getComedyMovies(){
    return this.selectMovies();
}
```

The last part of our child classes is a method to select the movies for the respective type. Did you remember the inheritance of the functionality of the abstract class by the child classes? This example illustrates perfectly how this happens. I created a method in my child class that calls the `selectMovies()` function of my abstract class. Due to the initiation of the abstract class with a type, the logic in the abstract class knows which movies need to be selected. This method returns in both classes other results:

- In the `ActionMovie` class, a list of action movies
- In the `Comedy` class, a list of movies of the comedy genre

We placed the logic to select the movies in our abstract class, due to the same functionality for both classes—`ActionMovie` and `Comedy` (and all other child classes), so we don't need to retype the same query in every class, execute this query, and return the list. This is already done in our abstract class, and due to the inheritance of this logic by the child class, we can reuse this logic.

But why did I create these methods? Do you remember the access modifier of the `selectMovies()` method in the abstract class? Right—it is protected. This means the functionality is only available to the class itself (the abstract class) or its child classes. So if I call the `Comedy` class and call the `selectMovies()` method, which is the logic from the abstract class, in another class or in a developer console code execution, you will receive an error:

```
Comedy theMask = new Comedy();
System.debug(theMask.selectMovies());
```

The preceding code shows how the method is not visible. If we call the same class and call the `getComedyMovies()` function, we'll receive all the comedies, because we call the `selectMovies()` method in our child class, and not outside the class and child class:

```
Comedy theMask = new Comedy();
System.debug(theMask.getComedyMovies());
```

This will result in a list of all the comedies from the database.

Virtual classes

The third type of reusable functionality of Apex classes is virtual classes. This methodology is the most used in the programming world. This type has more flexibility and more internal functionality than an abstract class.

The virtual classes have more or less the same functionality, but there are some big differences to the abstract classes:

Abstract classes	Virtual classes
Uses the `abstract` keyword in class modifier and methods.	Uses the `virtual` keyword in class modifier and methods.
All abstract methods in the abstract class must be implemented in the child class.	Not all virtual methods need to be implemented in the child class. If you have five virtual methods, you can decide to implement three of them, instead of five.
The abstract methods don't have logic in the body.	The virtual methods need to implement (basic) logic, but you can override the methods with other logic. If you don't override the method in your child class, the method in the virtual class can be called from the child class (if the access modifier is `protected` or `public`) and executes the logic from the virtual class. If you override the method in a child class, the logic in the child class will be executed.
You cannot initiate an abstract class with the `new` keyword and you cannot construct the class. The only way to use it is to create a class and extend the class with the abstract class.	You can initiate the class into another class with the `new` keyword. You have the possibility to construct the class.

The usability of a virtual class is the same as an abstract class, except for the preceding differences. An example of a virtual class is shown here:

```
public virtual class MovieVirtual {

private String movieType = '';

public MovieVirtual(String sMovieType){
this.movieType = sMovieType;
}

protected List<Movie__c> selectMovies(){
List<Movie__c> lstMovies = [SELECT Id, Name, (SELECT Id, Person__r.Name
FROM Cast__r) FROM Movie__c WHERE Genre__c = :this.movieType];
return lstMovies;
}
```

```
public virtual void insertMovie(){
// We implement a basic logic in the virtual method. If you don't override
this method in the child class, you can call this method from the child
class and executes this logic
System.debug('insertMovie from MovieVirtual');
}

public virtual void updateMovie(){
System.debug('updateMovie from MovieVirtual');
}
}
```

A child class from this virtual class can be as follows:

```
public class FamilyMovie extends MovieVirtual{

public FamilyMovie(){
// the same initiation of the parent class as for the abstract class
super('Family');
}

public override void insertMovie(){
// I override the initial functionality and implement new logic for this
specific child
System.debug('insertMovie From FamilyMovie');
}

// I didn't implement the second virtual method, is not necessary

// reuse of the implemented logic in the virtual class
public List<Movie__c> getFamilyMovies(){
return this.selectMovies();
}
}
```

If I initiate the FamilyMovie class and call the insertMovie() method, I will receive some text reading insertMovie From FamiliyMovie in the debug logs. If I call the updateMovie() method, which is not present in the FamilyMovie class, but is present in the MovieVirtual virtual class, I will receive text reading updateMovie from MovieVirtual. This is just to illustrate how a virtual class delivers the functionality to the child class that uses (that is, extends) the virtual class.

You can construct a virtual class, which isn't possible with the abstract class. And that's a huge advantage for the virtual class:

```
MovieVirtual theVirtualMovie = new MovieVirtual('Science Fiction');
```

You don't need to create a child class to use the functionality of a virtual class. In the preceding example, I created a new instance of the `MovieVirtual` class, and you see that I can use the functionality as any other normal class.

Annotations

Like Java, you have the possibility to add a kind of syntactic metadata, called an **annotation**. These annotations can be used in classes, methods, and properties.

For instance, if you don't need a method anymore in a new version of your class, you can give this method the `@deprecated` annotation to warn another developer that this method was used in a previous version of the software, but the method is not used anymore.

The following list is an overview of the annotations used in Apex. If you are familiar with Java, you will recognize some of them. Other annotations are unique to Apex and Salesforce:

- `@AuraEnabled`: This annotation is used to enable access to a method from a Lightning component. If a component needs support from the server, you are able to create an Apex controller and give the `AuraEnabled` annotation.
- `@Deprecated`: This annotation is used to visualize that you cannot reference the class, method, or property anymore. It is frequently used in the development of managed packages.
- `@future`: A method with `@future` annotation will be executed asynchronously. This is used in asynchronous web service calls or really complex calculations that require lots of resources.
- `@InvocableMethod`: A method with this annotation identifies that you can run this method as an invocable action. These methods are called via the REST API. If you want to execute Apex in a Process Builder flow, you need to give this annotation to your method.
- `@InvocableVariable`: A variable with this annotation is used in a class with a method that has the `@InvocableMethod` annotation. This is an input or output variable for the invocable method.
- `@IsTest`: A class or method with this annotation is used in a test context. Like Java, each functional class, method, and property needs to be covered in a unit test (you will learn about this later in this book). To use your classes and methods as a unit test, give this annotation to your class or method.

- `@ReadOnly`: A method with this annotation allows you to perform unrestricted queries (in normal behavior, the number of results is limited to 1,000 in the Visualforce context). While this annotation does not have restrictions on the number of query results anymore, it restricts several other operations, such as calls to asynchronous methods, `System.schedule` methods, and DML operations.

- `@RemoteAction`: This annotation provides support for Apex methods to call the methods by JavaScript. This process is also called JavaScript remoting (it calls Apex methods via JavaScript in a Visualforce page).

- `@SuppressWarnings`: This annotation is used to provide information to third-party tools.

- `@TestSetup`: This annotation is used to create test data during unit tests. In each test class, you can create your test data in one method. The data will not be added to the database with this annotation. This annotation can only be used in a test context.

- `@TestVisible`: This annotation enables a more permissive access level for private and protected methods or classes during tests. The access of the variable or the method does not change for non-test classes, only in a test context.

Besides these annotations, you also have annotations used especially to create a REST web service in Apex. More detailed information can be found in the documentation, available at: `https://trailhead.salesforce.com/en/content/learn/modules/apex_integration_services/apex_integration_webservices`. This covers an advanced level of Apex development/integration, which is not in the scope of this book. But feel free to read the preceding article:

- `@RestResource(urlMapping='/yourUrl')`: This annotation is added to a class to define this class as a REST service. You can call this class from an external application, after authentication with user credentials or connected applications.

- `@HttpDelete`: This annotation is used during the development of a REST web service in Apex. When an application performs an HTTP DELETE request to this service, you'll use this annotation. Most of the time, this is used to delete data from your database.

- `@HttpGet`: This annotation is used during the development of a REST web service in Apex. When an application sends an HTTP GET request to this service, you'll use this annotation. This type of request is used to return data from your database, based on parameters or specific resources.

- @HttpPatch: This annotation is used during the development of a REST web service in Apex. When an application sends an HTTP PATCH request to this service, you'll use this annotation. This type of request is used to update data in your database.
- @HttpPost: This annotation is used during the development of a REST web service in Apex. When an application sends an HTTP POST request to this service, you'll use this annotation. This type of request is used to create a new resource (via the insertion of data).
- @HttpPut: This annotation is used during the development of a REST web service in Apex. When an application sends an HTTP POST request to this service, you'll use this annotation. This type of request is used to create or update a set of data.

> To use these annotations, your Apex class and methods need to have the, Global access modifier. The methods have to be defined as a static method.

Object schema

You have now learned a lot about classes and objects. But what about every single object type in Salesforce? Every object you see in Salesforce (including standard objects, such as account, contact, an Apex class, and an Apex trigger, or custom objects you defined yourself) has properties (fields), methods (which define field values), relationships (master-detail or lookup relations with other objects), and so on. This is what we call the object schema.

If we need some information about the object (such as which fields are visible for a specific user), we can call the object schema via some methods to retrieve this information.

getGlobalDescribe()

This method is used to retrieve the information of every single object that is available in your org. This method returns a map with the (API) name of your object as the index and an object token as the value. This token is an instance of the Schema.SObjectType class.

If you copy and paste the following code in your developer console and execute this code, you will retrieve the map with all the objects:

```
Map<String, Schema.SObjectType> mapObjects = Schema.getGlobalDescribe();
System.debug(mapObjects);

{acceptedeventrelation=AcceptedEventRelation, account=Account,
accountchangeevent=AccountChangeEvent, accountcleaninfo=AccountCleanInfo,
accountcontactrole=AccountContactRole,
accountcontactrolechangeevent=AccountContactRoleChangeEvent,
accountfeed=AccountFeed, accounthistory=AccountHistory,
accountpartner=AccountPartner, accountshare=AccountShare, ...}
```

Hmm, was this more objects than you expected? Yes, for sure. There are more objects than you see in tabs or that are really visible in your screens, such as the `AccountShare` object, which is an object that defines if a user has access to an account or not. This is dependent on the role of the user, or whether or not sharing rules have user access to an account. If the user has access, an `AccountShare` record is created with the account and the user.

Object description

Each object has a description. No, not a description like *this object is used for...*, but a description of the fields that are available in the object, the field sets, and the prefix of the object (the first three characters of the ID describes the type of your object). For standard objects, a global prefix defined, but not for custom objects. You can find this prefix via this schema. Along with the label in the language of the user, plural labels, and information about the record types if the user is able to create a record of this object.

If you use this object description, the result is dependent on which user executes the following code:

```
Map<String, Schema.SObjectType> mapObjects = Schema.getGlobalDescribe();
DescribeSObjectResult accountDescription =
mapObjects.get('account').getDescribe();
System.debug(accountDescription);
```

This is the result of the execution:

```
Schema.DescribeSObjectResult[getHasSubtypes=false;getIsSubtype=false;getKey
Prefix=001;getLabel=Account;getLabelPlural=Accounts;getName=Account;getReco
rdTypeInfosByDeveloperName={Master=Schema.RecordTypeInfo[getDeveloperName=M
aster;getName=Master;getRecordTypeId=012000000000000AAA;isActive=true;isAva
ilable=true;isDefaultRecordTypeMapping=true;isMaster=true;]};isAccessible=t
rue;isCreateable=true;isCustom=false;isCustomSetting=false;isDeletable=true
;isDeprecatedAndHidden=false;isFeedEnabled=true;isMergeable=true;isMruEnabl
```

```
ed=true;isQueryable=true;isSearchable=true;isUndeletable=true;isUpdateable=
true;]
```

You can see in this result that this user can see an account record (he/she has read access to the object account via a profile or permission set) via the isAccessible property and can also create an Account record via the isCreatable property. You can also see which record types are available for this object and which types can be initiated by the user.

There aren't any fields, right? If you analyze the full result of your object description, you'll miss some crucial things. One of them are the fields in the object. That's correct. You don't find these in the basic object description, but in the fields property of the object description. We can go further with our account object:

```
Map<String, Schema.SObjectType> mapObjects = Schema.getGlobalDescribe();
Map<String, Schema.SObjectField> accountFields =
mapObjects.get('account').getDescribe().fields.getMap();
System.debug(accountFields);
```

You can compare the result with the global schema of the objects. Just the name of the field and a token. The token is now an instance of the Schema.SObjectField class. This is the result of the execution of the preceding code:

```
{accountnumber=AccountNumber, accountsource=AccountSource,
active__c=Active__c, annualrevenue=AnnualRevenue,
billingaddress=BillingAddress, billingcity=BillingCity,
billingcountry=BillingCountry,
billinggeocodeaccuracy=BillingGeocodeAccuracy,
billinglatitude=BillingLatitude, billinglongitude=BillingLongitude, ...}
```

As you can see, each field is in this map, including standard fields and custom fields. Now, we can verify if a user has access (read, edit, or both) to this field. This is defined for each user via profile or permission set and can be found in the field description of the respective field you want to verify.

Field description

In the field description, you will find all the information on the field requested:

- Which type is the field (lookup, number, text)?
- What kind of access does the user have to this field?
- What are the labels of the field? (if translated, the user will have the label in his/her language?)

To retrieve the information of the field, you call the `getDescribe` method of the field. The following is an example:

```
Map<String, Schema.SObjectType> mapObjects = Schema.getGlobalDescribe();
Map<String, Schema.SObjectField> accountFields =
mapObjects.get('account').getDescribe().fields.getMap();
Schema.DescribeFieldResult yourField =
accountFields.get('Name').getDescribe();
System.debug(yourField);
```

The preceding code returns the following result:

```
Schema.DescribeFieldResult[getByteLength=765;getCalculatedFormula=null;getC
ompoundFieldName=Name;getController=null;getDefaultValue=null;getDefaultVal
ueFormula=null;getDigits=0;getFilteredLookupInfo=null;getInlineHelpText=nul
l;getLabel=Account
Name;getLength=255;getLocalName=Name;getMask=null;getMaskType=null;getName=
Name;getPrecision=0;getReferenceTargetField=null;getRelationshipName=null;g
etRelationshipOrder=null;getScale=0;getSoapType=STRING;getSobjectField=Name
;getType=STRING;isAccessible=true;isAggregatable=true;isAiPredictionField=f
alse;isAutoNumber=false;isCalculated=false;isCascadeDelete=false;isCaseSens
itive=false;isCreateable=true;isCustom=false;isDefaultedOnCreate=false;isDe
pendentPicklist=false;isDeprecatedAndHidden=false;isDisplayLocationInDecima
l=false;isEncrypted=false;isExternalId=false;isFilterable=true;isFormulaTre
atNullNumberAsZero=false;isGroupable=true;isHighScaleNumber=false;isHtmlFor
matted=false;isIdLookup=false;isNameField=true;isNamePointing=false;isNilla
ble=false;isPermissionable=false;isQueryByDistance=false;isRestrictedDelete
=false;isSearchPrefilterable=false;isSortable=true;isUnique=false;isUpdatea
ble=true;isWriteRequiresMasterRead=false;]
```

From the previous code, you will find the type of the field (in this case, a string), whether the user may update the information of this field in your record, (`isUpdatable`), the label of the field (in the language of the user), the API name of the field, and so on.

A lot of functions are available to get the necessary information about the objects or fields. Unfortunately, there are too many to include in an overview of this book, but you can find all the functions and methods for the object and field information on these pages:

- For the object information, see the documentation available at: `https://developer.salesforce.com/docs/atlas.en-us.apexcode.meta/apexcode/apex_methods_system_sobject_describe.htm?search_text=DescribeSObjectResult`

- For the fields information, see the documentation available at: `https://developer.salesforce.com/docs/atlas.en-us.apexcode.meta/apexcode/apex_methods_system_fields_describe.htm?search_text=DescribeFieldResult`

Apex triggers

Next, to the Apex class. We use the Apex language also to create complex logic during an event. Imagine a user creates a new actor and wants to verify the actor details with an external database. You can translate this user action as the following event—after inserting an actor, make a callout to a database and add the details of the actor (such as their birthday, male/female, the color of their eyes, and so on). This means that you need to perform an action after the insertion of a record. That's what we call a **trigger**.

A Salesforce trigger is only executed before or after a DML operation. Yes, it can be *before* and *after*. You will learn that in *The order of execution of a DML statement* section. When a user inserts a new record, Salesforce will verify whether the record is compliant to all your required fields, validation rules, Apex triggers, workflow rules, Process Builder flows, and so on, before it is definitely saved to the database.

You can execute trigger logic before a DML statement is executed (for instance, before a record is inserted) and after a record is inserted. Please think about which scenario you want to perform some complex trigger logic, because your requirements can possibly fit with one of the declarative solutions in Salesforce.

Triggers are executed during a transaction for all the records that are in that operation. If you perform a DML operation with a list of records, the logic of the trigger will be executed by each of the records in the list. This means if you execute data loads (say, in batches of 200 records), the trigger logic will run for these 200 records.

A trigger logic needs to be **bulkified**. The logic needs are written so that you perform your trigger logic for your list of records, and not for each record in the list.

But when you need to use triggers, what are possible other solutions to do the same logic? Probably, you have another solution, such as workflow rules, Process Builders, auto-launched flows, validation rules, duplicate rules, and so on, to avoid the use of complex triggers. But in some circumstances, you don't have any other choice and you need to use a trigger.

The following is a short overview of cases you where don't have another solution:

- Complex validations between more than one object (such as when you create a contact, but need to verify on the account if you may create a contact for that account)—in this case, we will use a before trigger, because the validation needs to be done before the creation of the record.
- When creating a parent record before the creation of a child record—in this case, we use a before trigger that will insert another record (the same or another linked object) before the insert of the record that we inserted via the user interface.

- For every action that you need to perform *before* the new values are inserted or updated in the database, you need to use a trigger. All declarative solutions (such as workflow rules and Process Builders) will only be executed after the DML operation.

In some circumstances, you also need a trigger after the DML operation, for instance, when you need to perform a web service call to update some account details when you compared your account with a trusted database, such as Dun and Bradstreet. Callouts in trigger logic aren't allowed, but you can implement a workaround via an asynchronous method or a `Queueable` class. We will learn more on this topic later (in this chapter, in the *Web service callouts* section).

You can implement a trigger during the following DML operations:

- **Insert**
- **Update**
- **Delete**
- **Undelete**

Dependent on the DML statement, you can decide to execute your logic before or after the DML operation, but not all the possibilities are supported, which make sense. Before an undelete operation, you cannot do anything, as you don't have any information about the records that are deleted.

The following combinations are supported:

Before	Insert	The logic in the trigger will be executed before the insert of 1 or more records (validation, add some extra field info from other linked object)
After		The logic in the trigger will be executed after the insert of 1 or more records (perform callouts after insert of records)
Before	Update	The logic in the trigger will be executed before an update of 1 or more records
After		The logic in the trigger will be executed after an update of 1 or more records
Before	Delete	The logic in the trigger will executed before a record is deleted (perform a check if a record may be deleted or not)
After		The logic in the trigger will be executed after a record is deleted (probable delete of the parent object if all of the children are deleted)
After	Undelete	The logic in the trigger will be executed after the recovering of a record

Now, let's look at the trigger syntax.

Trigger syntax

An Apex trigger is created on a Salesforce object where triggers are allowed. Yes, not every object allows triggers. You learned about the object schema in the previous section. You can find that information in the object schema of your object:

```
Map<String, Schema.SObjectType> gd = Schema.getGlobalDescribe();
Schema.DescribeSObjectResult theObject = gd.get('Account').getDescribe();

String sobjStruct = JSON.serialize(theObject);
DescribeSobjectResultJSON sobjProps = (DescribeSobjectResultJSON)
JSON.deserialize(sobjStruct, DescribeSobjectResultJSON.class);
System.debug(sobjProps);

// Wrapper with the JSON result
public class DescribeSobjectResultJSON {
 public String name {get;set;}
 public Boolean triggerable {get;set;}
}
```

Now, check in the debug log for the `triggerable` variable and the value after the variable—you will see that you are able to define a trigger for the `Account` object, but not for the standard object, `PricebookEntry`; for example:

```
DescribeSobjectResultJSON:[name=Account, triggerable=true]
DescribeSobjectResultJSON:[name=PricebookEntry, triggerable=false]
```

You can define a trigger on each custom object. An Apex trigger is defined a little bit differently than an Apex class. The following is a basic template for an Apex trigger:

```
Trigger YourTriggerName on ObjectAPIName (all your trigger events){
 // your trigger logic
}
```

These are the different definitions of your trigger parts:

- `YourTriggerName`: The name of your trigger; as follows the same principles as a class. Give your trigger a name so you can recognize what this trigger stands for. In a later stage (*Best practices* section for trigger development), you will see that we define only one trigger per object.
- `ObjectAPIName`: The API name of the object where you need the trigger; for instance, `Account`, `CustomObject__c`.

- All your trigger events—these are the events that we saw earlier in this section. You have the choice of when to implement a trigger:
  - Before insert
  - After insert
  - Before update
  - After update
  - Before delete
  - After delete
  - Before undelete
- Your trigger logic: The logic you want to execute during the DML operation of your object.

Let's look at a small example:

```
Trigger ShowHelloWorld on Account (before insert, before update){
  System.debug('Hello World');
}
```

This trigger will be activated when a user inserts or updates an account record. The trigger will display Hello World in the debug log. Let's see how we do this, as follows:

1. Open your developer console and create a new trigger.
2. Click the **Setup** gear in your Salesforce org and click **Developer Console**.
3. Click **File | New** and click **Apex Trigger**:

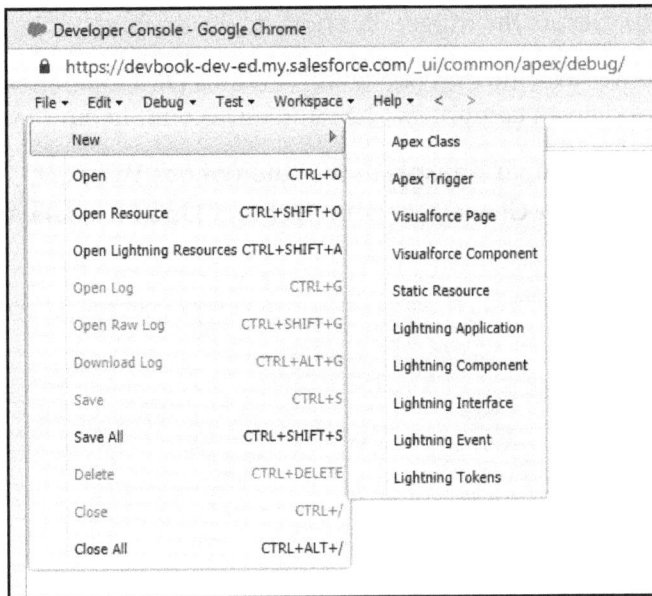

4. Give your trigger a name, then select the **Account** object and click on **Submit**:

5. Copy and paste the example code into your code window and save your code:

Now, we are going to execute the trigger. But how do we do that?

Remember, a trigger will execute the code when you do a DML operation; in this case, before we insert or update an account. So, let's add an account in our developer console:

1. Open your **Developer Console** in the **Anonymous Window**.

2. In your **Developer Console**, click on **Debug | Open Execute Anonymous Window**:

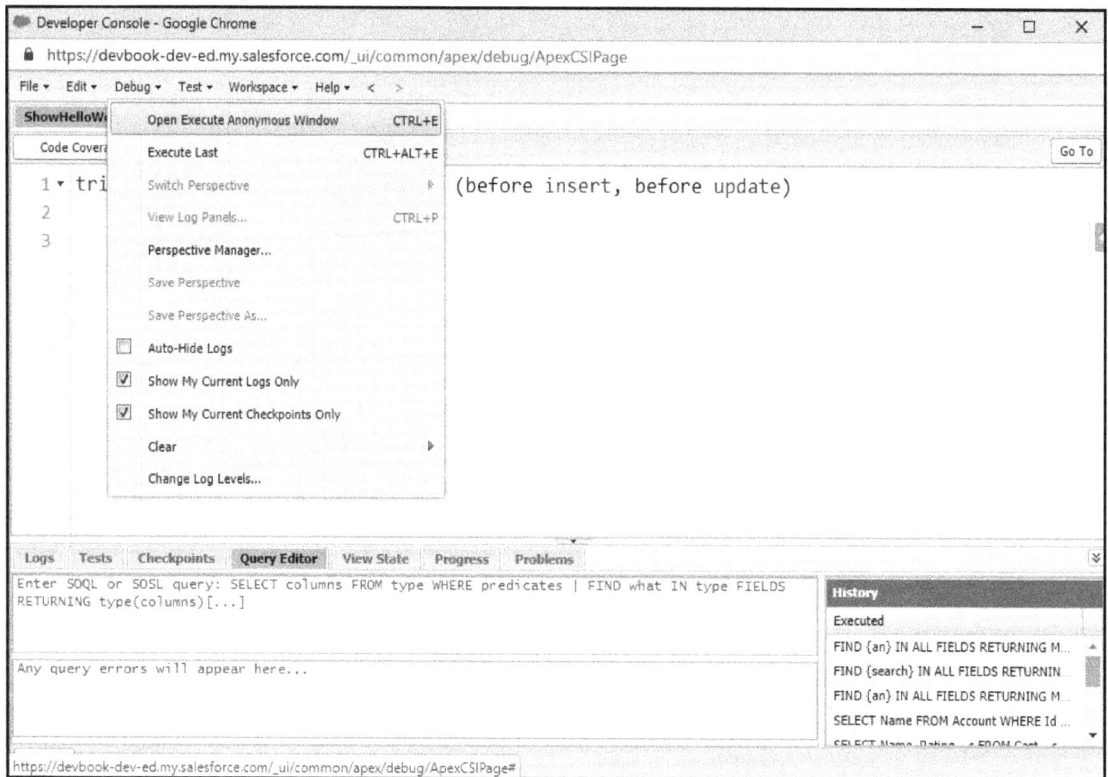

3. Copy and paste the following code into your window.

```
Account a = new Account(Name = 'TestAccount');
insert a;
```

4. Mark the **Open Log** checkbox, if this is not already marked.

5. Inspect the debug logs. Did you find the line with the
   USER_DEBUG [2]|DEBUG|Hello World? as seen in the following screenshot:

Execution Log		
Timestamp	Event	Details
16:30:50:003	HEAP_ALLOCATE	[2]|Bytes:8
16:30:50:003	1 DML_BEGIN	[2]|Op:Insert|Type:Account|Rows:1
16:30:50:003	HEAP_ALLOCATE	[EXTERNAL]|Bytes:8
16:30:50:056	2 CODE_UNIT_STARTED	[EXTERNAL]|01q1t000000Fidi|ShowHelloWorld on Account trigger event BeforeInsert|__sfdc_trigger/ShowHelloWorld
16:30:50:056	HEAP_ALLOCATE	[EXTERNAL]|Bytes:8
16:30:50:056	HEAP_ALLOCATE	[EXTERNAL]|Bytes:1
16:30:50:056	HEAP_ALLOCATE	[EXTERNAL]|Bytes:4
16:30:50:056	VARIABLE_SCOPE_BEGIN	[1]|this|ShowHelloWorld|true|false
16:30:50:056	VARIABLE_ASSIGNMENT	[1]|this|{}|0x2559c17d
16:30:50:057	HEAP_ALLOCATE	[EXTERNAL]|Bytes:4
16:30:50:057	VARIABLE_SCOPE_BEGIN	[1]|this|ShowHelloWorld|true|false
16:30:50:057	VARIABLE_ASSIGNMENT	[1]|this|{}|0x2559c17d
16:30:50:057	STATEMENT_EXECUTE	[1]|
16:30:50:057	STATEMENT_EXECUTE	[2]|
16:30:50:057	HEAP_ALLOCATE	[2]|Bytes:11
16:30:50:057	3 USER_DEBUG	[2]|DEBUG|Hello World
16:30:50:057	CUMULATIVE_LIMIT_USAGE	
16:30:50:057	LIMIT_USAGE_FOR_NS	(default)|
16:30:50:000	LIMIT_USAGE_FOR_NS	Number of SOQL queries: 0 out of 100
16:30:50:000	LIMIT_USAGE_FOR_NS	Number of query rows: 0 out of 50000
16:30:50:000	LIMIT_USAGE_FOR_NS	Number of SOSL queries: 0 out of 20
16:30:50:000	LIMIT_USAGE_FOR_NS	Number of DML statements: 1 out of 150
16:30:50:000	LIMIT_USAGE_FOR_NS	Number of DML rows: 1 out of 10000
16:30:50:000	LIMIT_USAGE_FOR_NS	Maximum CPU time: 0 out of 10000
16:30:50:000	LIMIT_USAGE_FOR_NS	Maximum heap size: 0 out of 6000000
16:30:50:000	LIMIT_USAGE_FOR_NS	Number of callouts: 0 out of 100
16:30:50:000	LIMIT_USAGE_FOR_NS	Number of Email Invocations: 0 out of 10
16:30:50:000	LIMIT_USAGE_FOR_NS	Number of future calls: 0 out of 50
16:30:50:000	LIMIT_USAGE_FOR_NS	Number of queueable jobs added to the queue: 0 out of 50
16:30:50:000	LIMIT_USAGE_FOR_NS	Number of Mobile Apex push calls: 0 out of 10
16:30:50:000	LIMIT_USAGE_FOR_NS	
16:30:50:057	CUMULATIVE_LIMIT_USAGE_E...	
16:30:50:058	4 CODE_UNIT_FINISHED	ShowHelloWorld on Account trigger event BeforeInsert|__sfdc_trigger/ShowHelloWorld

Let's look at the explanation:

1. A trigger executes when a DML operation occurs. In this case, we insert an account. You find the DML statement begins in point 1, as highlighted in the preceding screenshot. This is the start of the transaction where we insert the account.

2. During this DML statement, a trigger is executed. You will find the trigger that you wrote in the previous paragraph in point 2. Next to point 2, you can see that the trigger logic starts to execute the logic in your trigger. You'll see also when the trigger executes, before or after the DML operation (in this case before the insert), and you'll find the name of the trigger. This is handy when something goes wrong during the execution of logic in different triggers, as you know where you need to look into.

3. The full execution of the trigger logic is between point 2 (`CODE_UNIT_STARTED`) and point 4 (`CODE_UNIT_FINISHED`). Between these two points, we can analyze the logic. In our example, we only displayed `Hello World` in the debug logs. This line you'll find next to point 3.

4. Before each trigger logic is finished, you will find the number of some limits during the execution of your trigger logic. This is really handy, as if you hit one of these limits, you'll get an error. You can immediately find out which limit is hit, and in which trigger logic, so you can start to analyze why the limit was hit.

One of the most hit limits is the limit of the SOQL queries in one transaction. You may run only 100 SOQL queries in one transaction, and perform a DML operation for 200 records in one transaction. We will discuss this later in the paragraph about *Trigger design patterns* section. Next, in point 4, the execution of the code of our trigger is finished successfully.

Trigger variables

During the execution of a trigger, you have some variables that are useful for determining which records are involved during the execution of your logic, and in which circumstances the logic is executed. We call them **trigger context variables**. The following is an overview of the variables, and the utility and result of each variable. Each of these variables is called with the `System.Trigger` class (or, for short, `Trigger`).

Trigger.isExecuting

This returns true if the code is called in the trigger context. If you write an Apex class with several methods, the same methods can be executed by a Visualforce page, anonymous Apex, a web service, or a trigger. Only if a trigger calls this method, you will receive a true for the variable.

Trigger.isInsert

This returns `true` if the trigger has fired due to an `insert` DML operation:

```
if (Trigger.isInsert){
 // perform logic when a record will be inserted
}
```

Trigger.isUpdate

This returns true if the trigger has fired due to an `update` DML operation:

```
if (Trigger.isUpdate){
 // perform logic when a record will be updated
}
```

Trigger.isDelete

This returns true if the trigger has fired due to a `delete` DML operation:

```
if (Trigger.isDelete){
 // perform logic when a record will be deleted
}
```

Trigger.isUndelete

This returns true if the trigger has fired due to an `undelete` DML operation:

```
if (Trigger.isUndelete){
 // perform logic when a record will be undeleted
}
```

Trigger.isBefore

This returns true if the trigger has fired before the record was saved to the database:

```
if (Trigger.isBefore){
 // perform logic before the record is saved to the database
}
```

Trigger.isAfter

This returns true if the trigger has fired after the record was saved to the database:

```
if (Trigger.isAfter){
  // perform logic after the record is saved to the database
}
```

Trigger.new

This returns a list with the new version of the records. This variable returns a list of sObjects, so if you want to use properties of the specific object type (such as `Account`), you need to cast your list to a list from the specific object. This variable is only available in the following contexts:

- Before and after insert
- Before and after an update
- After an undelete operation:

```
List<Account> lstAccounts = (List<Account>) Trigger.new; // the
list
// 'SObject' is casted to a list with 'Account' records
```

You can modify the records in this list only in a *before* context, not in an *after* context.

Trigger.newMap

This returns a map with the new version of the records. The index of the map is the ID of the record that is impacted by the trigger. This variable returns `map<Id, SObject>`, so if you want to use the properties of your specific object type, you need to cast your map into the specific map. This variable is available in the following circumstances:

- After insert
- Before and after an update
- After an undelete operation:

```
Map<Id, Account> mapAccounts = (Map<Id, Account>) Trigger.newMap;
```

Trigger.old

This returns a list with the old version of the records. This variable returns a list of sObjects, so if you want to use properties of a specific object type (such as `Account`), you need to cast your list to a list from the specific object. This variable is only available in the following contexts:

- Before and after an update
- Before and `after delete`:

```
List<Account> lstAccounts = (List<Account>) Trigger.old; // the
list 'SObject' is casted to a list with 'Account' records
```

Trigger.oldMap

This returns a map with the old version of the records. The index of the map is the ID of the record that is impacted by the trigger. This variable returns `map<Id, SObject>`, so if you want to use the properties of your specific object type, you need to cast your map into the specific map. This variable is available in the following circumstances:

- Before and after an update
- Before and after a delete operation:

```
Map<Id, Account> mapAccounts = (Map<Id, Account>) Trigger.oldMap;
```

Trigger.size

This returns the size of the list or map with the number of records that are involved in the trigger:

```
Integer iNumberRecords = Trigger.size;
```

Governor limits

In your journey as a Salesforce developer, you will definitely hit one of the governor limits of Apex. Salesforce has to implement a lot of limits due to the fact that Apex runs in a multi-tenant architecture. If you hit one of these limits, you receive a runtime exception that your transaction cannot be handled and the code will not be executed anymore.

The full overview of the limits can be found in the documentation, at: `https://developer.salesforce.com/docs/atlas.en-us.apexcode.meta/apexcode/apex_gov_limits.htm`.

You can have a look at the limits in several categories:

- Per-transaction Apex limits
- Per-transaction managed package limits
- Lightning Platform limits
- Static Apex limits
- Size-specific limits
- Miscellaneous Apex limits

Per-transaction limits

These are limits for one transaction. If you update one record in one time or 200 records in one time (update the list with records). This is calculated as one transaction. The limits are different for synchronous and asynchronous calls. If you run an update in a batch, you are able, for instance, to perform more SOQL queries that if you run the update in a synchronous context.

A small overview of the per-transaction limits that you definitely will hit is given in the following table:

	Synchronous	Asynchronous
Number of SOQL queries	100	200
Number of records received by a SOQL query	50,000	NA
Number of SOSL queries	20	NA
Number of records received by a SOSL query	2,000	NA
Number of DML statements	150	NA
Number of records processed in a DML result	10,000	NA
Number of callouts	100	NA

You can also find specific limits with the `Limits` class, together with the specific method or property. More info about this class can be found at `https://developer.salesforce.com/docs/atlas.en-us.apexcode.meta/apexcode/apex_methods_system_limits.htm`.

With this class and methods, you can call your processed records and the limit of your records. And in the debug logs, you will also find a section with the most important limits that you can hit during the execution of your code:

```
11:59:17:000    LIMIT_USAGE_...    Number of SOQL queries: 0 out of 100
11:59:17:000    LIMIT_USAGE_...    Number of query rows: 0 out of 50000
11:59:17:000    LIMIT_USAGE_...    Number of SOSL queries: 0 out of 20
11:59:17:000    LIMIT_USAGE_...    Number of DML statements: 1 out of 150
11:59:17:000    LIMIT_USAGE_...    Number of DML rows: 10 out of 10000
11:59:17:000    LIMIT_USAGE_...    Maximum CPU time: 0 out of 10000
11:59:17:000    LIMIT_USAGE_...    Maximum heap size: 0 out of 6000000
11:59:17:000    LIMIT_USAGE_...    Number of callouts: 0 out of 100
11:59:17:000    LIMIT_USAGE_...    Number of Email Invocations: 0 out of 10
11:59:17:000    LIMIT_USAGE_...    Number of future calls: 0 out of 50
11:59:17:000    LIMIT_USAGE_...    Number of queueable jobs added to the queue: 0 out of 50
11:59:17:000    LIMIT_USAGE_...    Number of Mobile Apex push calls: 0 out of 10
```

Per-transaction managed package limits

Managed packages need to pass a security review for the AppExchange have their own set of limits for most per-transaction limits. A package developed by a Salesforce ISV (Independent software vendor) has always a unique namespace. The common limits count for each separate namespace. For instance, you install a managed package with a namespace from Vendor X. the limits in this namespace for DML statements are 150 statements per transaction. A second package has a separate set of limits, so another 150 DML statements in that namespace.

Lightning Platform limits

These limits are enforced by the Lightning Platform and are not transaction related. These are the most important limits:

Description	Limit
Maximum of asynchronous Apex method executions (batch Apex, future methods, queueable Apex, and scheduled Apex) per a 24-hour period	Maximum 250,000 executions or the number of user licenses in your org multiplied by 200, if greater
Maximum Apex jobs in the Apex flex queue that are in the status **Holding**	100

More of these limits , you will find it on the page `https://developer.salesforce.com/docs/atlas.en-us.apexcode.meta/apexcode/apex_gov_limits.htm`.

Static Apex Limits

These are limits to protect the Lightning framework:

Description	Limit
Default timeout of callouts in one single transaction	10 seconds
Maximum size of callout request or response	6 MB for synchronous Apex 12 MB for asynchronous Apex
Maximum query run time before cancelling transaction by Salesforce	120 seconds
Maximum number of classes and triggers in an APEX deployment	5,000
Batch size in a `for` loop list	200
Maximum number of records returned for the method`Database.QueryLocator`	50 million

Size-specific limits

Limits to define maximum sizes:

Description	Limit
Maximum characters for one class	One million
Maximum characters for one trigger	One million

Miscellaneous Apex limits

Lots of other limits to guarantee the optimal performance on the Lightning Platform. Lots of limits are described on the page `https://developer.salesforce.com/docs/atlas.en-us.apexcode.meta/apexcode/apex_gov_limits.htm`.

When you start with Apex development, you definitely hit one of these limits during trigger development. the following paragraph will assist you to avoid hitting these limits. Let's take a look how we develop a trigger with good performance.

An Apex trigger pattern for efficient data processing

All right, you've learned how an Apex trigger needs to be built, and you've learned about the specific trigger variables and the limits. Now it is time to learn how to process data via triggers, and how we implement the logic for data processing. You will learn about some best practices and I will give you some advice that you need to take into account. Besides that, I will also give you some advice about design patterns to create trigger logic.

Best practices

You need to know that a trigger executes logic for each of the records in the list with records that you want to update or insert, even if you don't want it to trigger the logic. If you created a trigger for an account that executes logic after the creation of the account, the logic will trigger after each insert operation of an account. This probably isn't necessary, and you can avoid executing some logic when it is not necessary:

- **Define criteria**: If you define the circumstances for when a trigger needs to execute logic, the performance of the execution of your DML operation will significantly improve. Let me explain that with an example. If you need to execute business logic only when a specific field has changed, you can specify that as a criterion. The trigger variables allow you to determine if the value of a specific field is changed. The following is an example code where we use the trigger variables to determine if the name of an account has changed. Only when the criteria are met will the logic be executed:

    ```
    Map<Id, Account> mapOldAccounts = (Map<Id, Account>)
    Trigger.oldMap;
    For (Account tAccount : (List<Account>) Trigger.new) {
     // loop through the accounts in the list from the trigger
     Account oldVersion = mapOldAccounts.get(tAccount.Id);
     If (oldVersion.Name != tAccount.Name){
     // execute the logic only if the name is changed
     }
    }
    ```

    And if the field is not changed, the logic will not execute.

    This is a strictly recommended best practice; otherwise, your trigger can cause a loop during the execution of your DML statement.

If you update a record in the execution logic of your trigger, you will update your record again and again without doing anything. And, yes, you can update a record after another update. With a little trick, you are able to update the same record again, just after you have updated it. But that's for the advanced level.

- **Bulkify your triggers**: This is one of the hardest parts when writing triggers. Know that your logic will be executed for each record in your list. Take into account for each trigger logic that you can perform a data load in batches of 200 records. You may not hit the limits when you perform DML operations with this amount of records. But how you will do that? That's the principle of performing bulk actions.

One of the most common mistakes created by novice Salesforce developers is to execute a SOQL or perform a DML operation in the trigger loop. In our previous example, you saw the construction to loop through to the records in the trigger. This pattern is used due to the need to execute the logic for each record in the list coming from your operation. This can be one record, or even 200 records (when you perform a data load):

```
For (Account tAccount : (List<Account>) Trigger.new){
  // loop through the accounts in the list from the trigger
  List<Contact> lstContact = [SELECT Lastname, FirstName FROM
Contact WHERE AccountId = :tAccount.Id];
  }
```

Look at the preceding example. What do you do to select contacts from each account? Is it looking good? What do you think that is wrong with this code? Or is there something wrong with this code at all?

The answer is, there is nothing wrong with the code, but this code cannot be used in a bulkified context. If I use this code for a single DML operation (that is, a DML with one record), everything runs fine. But if I use this code to update 200 records, I hit one of the crucial Apex limits (the number of SOQL queries in one transaction). If I update 200 records, I perform one transaction. In the preceding code example, I will run 200 SOQL queries in the same operation, and will receive a limit exception at record `101`.

But how can you solve this issue? In this case, we make full use of our trigger variables. We use the list or map variables with the current values of the records. In our case, we need to select the contacts of our accounts that are part of our trigger.

The IDs of the accounts are in the map with the new version of the records, and we can perform only one query to select every contact from the full account list:

```
Map<Id, Account> mapAccounts = (Map<Id, Account>) Trigger.newMap;
List<Contact> lstContacts = [SELECT Firstname, LastName FROM
Contact WHERE AccountId IN : mapAccounts.keySet();
```

We ran only one query and we can select the contacts of one account or even 200 or more accounts (if you don't have more than 50,000 contacts on the accounts).

- **One object = one trigger**: Create only one trigger for one object to create an overview of the different logic for the object. Nothing is so confusing than to have 10 separate trigger functionalities in different circumstances and for different (or the same) DML operations.

Again, here are our trigger context variables, which form a crucial instrument to differentiate logic in different circumstances. You can create one trigger that fires when a record is updated, inserted, or deleted. The following is an example:

```
trigger Account_Trigger on Account (before update, after update,
after insert, after delete) {
 If (Trigger.isDelete){
 // perform logic when your record(s) has been deleted
 } else if (Trigger.isUpdate){
 // perform logic when your records are updated
 If (Trigger.isBefore){
 // execute the logic before the update of the record(s)
 } else if (Trigger.isAfter){
 // execute the logic after the update of the record(s)
 }
 } else if (Trigger.isInsert){
 // perform logic before a record is inserted
 }
}
```

In the following *Trigger design patterns* section, you will learn more about this pattern and how we can call logic in these types of triggers.

- **Large datasets**: If you need to query a large dataset (more than 50,000 records), a single SOQL is not optimized and can hit the limit of the heap limit or the maximum CPU time limit:

```
List<Account> lstAccounts = [SELECT Id FROM Account]; // more than
// 50k records runs into a limit
```

A more efficient way to select and execute logic with selected records is the following code snippet:

```
List<Account> lstAccounts = new List<Account>();

For (Account selectedAccount : [SELECT Id, Name FROM Account]){
  // if account meets some criteria, add the account to the list
  }
```

Trigger design patterns

In this section, you will learn how you can call logic from a class into a trigger. Imagine that you need to do complex calculations for opportunities and the related products; you will write these calculations only once and want to reuse this logic in several circumstances (for a Visualforce page, a Lightning component, and a trigger). We will call this logic from a class and execute this logic during the execution of a DML operation (before or after an insert or update of a record).

One best practice of trigger design is to have one trigger for one object and one or more classes, where you call the logic in the different types of DML operations (before or after insert, update, delete or undelete). When implementing logic by static methods, you don't need to initiate the class itself, as you are able to call several methods and properties in a trigger. And you can definitely use the trigger context variable, `Trigger.isExecuting`, to determine if your logic is called in the trigger context or not.

Let's take a look in the following example:

```
public with sharing class Account_TriggerHelper {

  public static void beforeUpdate(List<Account> lstAccountsInTrigger){
  // perform before update logic
  }

  public static void beforeInsert(List<Account> lstAccountsInTrigger){
  // perform before insert logic
  }
}
```

The following trigger has been created:

```
trigger Account_Trigger on Account (before update, before insert) {
    if (Trigger.isBefore){
        if (Trigger.isInsert){
            Account_TriggerHelper.beforeInsert((List<Account>)
Trigger.new);
```

```
        } else if (Trigger.isUpdate){
            Account_TriggerHelper.beforeUpdate((List<Account>)
Trigger.new);
        }
    }
}
```

You see, now it is pretty easy to extend your logic for each object. When you become a more advanced developer, you will work with a trigger framework with an interface and subclasses to separate the different logics.

Web service calls in triggers

Imagine the following use case: when you create an account with a company registration number, you need to get the company details from a trusted database, such as Data.com or D&B. You need to do a web service call after the insertion of your account. I can hear you think: *I'll create a trigger and write some separate logic to do the callout*. That's right!

You need to know that in a trigger context, your code always executes synchronously and you may not perform a web service callout during the execution of synchronous trigger logic. So, we need to do the callout asynchronously.

At an advanced level, you will learn about the details of asynchronous actions. For now, I'll outline the possibilities for running code asynchronously for your callout.

@future

You saw this earlier during the chapter about the annotations. The `@future` annotation means that the code in the method will run asynchronously (when Salesforce resources are available). So, it can be 10 seconds later, but also for 2 minutes. This functionality will typically be used during callouts to external web services (`@future(callout=true)`).

The `@future` functionality has the following limits:

- It is always a `public` and `static` method.
- It returns only a `void` type.
- If you want to provide extra parameters to the method, the parameters need to be primitive data types or collections of primitive data types. This means you cannot provide a list with accounts to the `@future` method.
- You cannot call another `@future` method in your future method class.

A common pattern for processing a list of accounts with a @future method provides a set or list with IDs and selects the records based on this set of IDs:

```
public class SomeClass {
 @future
 public static void someFutureMethod(List<Id> recordIds) {
 List<Account> accounts = [Select Id, Name from Account Where Id IN
:recordIds];
 // process your accounts
 }
}
```

In your trigger, you will call the class in the same way as you did in Chapter 4, *Apex Basics*:

```
trigger Account_Trigger on Account (before update, before insert) {
 if (Trigger.isUpdate){
 Map<Id, Account> mapAccounts = (Map<Id, Account>) Trigger.newMap;

 // This is the asynchronous method from the class
 SomeClass.someFutureMethod(mapAccounts.keySet());
 }
}
```

Queueable interface

Salesforce has defined some interfaces that you can use during your development. One of them is the Queueable interface. You launch a job and place this job in a queue.

In this class, you can perform your callout in the main execute method of the class (don't forget, an interface has methods where you need to implement all of them), and you call the Queueable class from the trigger.

The benefits of a Queueable class are the support for things that the @future method doesn't have:

- It's a separate class; you can implement what you want, how you want.
- The class needs to implement the execute(QueueableContext) method. In this method, you perform the logic you need to execute.
- You can provide every type of object as a parameter—not only a primitive data type or a set of primitive data types, but you can also provide one or more sObjects or Apex objects.
- You have the possibility to chain jobs. Once the first job is finished, you can start a second queueable job.

An example of a trigger logic Queueable interface pattern is shown here:

```
public with sharing class YourCallout_Logic implements Queueable,
Database.AllowsCallouts{

 public List<Account> listAccounts {get; private set;}

 public Account_TriggerHelper(List<Account> lstAccounts){
 this.listAccounts = lstAccounts;
 }

 public void execute(QueueableContext qc){
 // implement your (callout) logic to execute here

 }
}
```

If you need to do callouts in your logic, you need to implement the
Database.AllowsCallouts interface as well. The trigger looks like this:

```
trigger Account_Trigger on Account (after insert) {
 if (Trigger.isAfter && Trigger.isInsert){
 Account_TriggerHelper queueJob = new Account_TriggerHelper((List<Account>)
 Trigger.new);
 Id jobId = System.enqueueJob(queueJob);
 // implement logic to monitor your job
 }
}
```

So, you have now learned a lot about the triggers and how to build them in a safe and structured way. Let's go on to explain when these triggers are executed. Look out; this is one of the most important sections of this book, and in Salesforce development more broadly. What happens if you perform a DML operation and when will it happen?

The order of execution

The order in which Salesforce executes certain actions is one of the most important concepts that every admin and developer should know by heart.

As developers, we need to grasp how the platform will process and validate the data that we are inserting, updating, deleting, and even undeleting in the Salesforce database. Like any system, the rules in Salesforce follow a very specific pattern, known as the **order of execution**. Over time, your org will get more and more customized with validation rules, workflow rules, processes, assignment rules, escalation rules, entitlements, and most probably, lots of programmatic logic and automation.

As a developer or admin, we need to understand exactly how the system works. So, we'll explain all the steps Salesforce performs on each and every DML statement, no matter if it originated through the user interface, through the API with Data Loader or other data tools, or through Apex code.

Salesforce performs **20 specific steps** in the following order:

1. **Salesforce simulates the insertion or update of the new record**:
    - **During the insert of a new record**: The record will be initiated for an upsert statement.
    - **During an update:** Salesforce loads the initial record values from the database.

2. **During the update statement, Salesforce loads the new record field values** from the request and overwrites the old field values. Depending on the source of the request, Salesforce performs some basic record validations:
    - If the request is coming from the standard user interface, Salesforce runs the following system validations on the record:
        - Compliance with layout-specific rules.
        - Check the required values on the page and field-definition level.
        - Validation on the field types (you cannot enter a text in a `Date` field).
        - Maximum field lengths (the name of a record can have a maximum of 80 characters).

- If the request comes from other sources, such as Apex code or an API call, the following validations are performed:
  - Usage of foreign keys (use of the correct and existing records in the lookup of the master-detail relationship).
  - Check whether the foreign keys refer to the record itself (hierarchy constraints).
  - In certain circumstances, Salesforce runs validations (defined by the user) when multiline items were created (such as quote line items on the `Quote` object and opportunity line items on the `Opportunity` object).

3. **Executes all triggers** with the execution type **before** (`before update`, `before insert`).
4. After the changes in the before triggers, the system runs most **system validation** steps again, such as verifying the value of the required fields and runs all the user-defined validation rules for that object. The layout-specific rules don't run a second time when the request is coming from the Salesforce standard user interface.
5. Executes the **duplicate rules**. If a record is identified as a duplicate by a duplicate rule and the rule uses the block action, the record will not be saved and breaks up the transaction. No further steps, such as process flows, Process Builders, or workflow rules are taken.
6. **The system saves the record to the database** but doesn't commit yet. A new record gets now a temporary Salesforce ID.
7. **Executes all triggers** with the execution type `after` (`after update`, `after insert`, `after delete`).
8. Executes the **assignment rules** for that object.
9. Executes the **auto-response rules** for that object.
10. Evaluates all the **workflow rules for the object** and execute the workflow actions for the workflow rules for which the criteria are met.
11. If the workflow rules executed field updates, the record will update again.

12. In this case, `before update` **triggers, and** `after update` **triggers** run one more time (and only one more time), in addition to the standard validations. User-defined validation rules, duplicate rules, and escalation rules will not run again.

13. Executes **Process Builder flows** and **Visual Flows** (launched via processes and flow trigger workflow actions). When a process or flow executes a DML statement, the affected record goes through the save procedure (these 20 steps will be repeated again for this record).

14. Executes the **escalation rules**.

15. Executes the **entitlement rules**.

16. If the record has a **roll-up summary field** or the record is a part of a **cross-object workflow,** the system performs all the calculations and **updates** the roll-up summary field in **the parent record**. **The parent record will trigger an update and goes through the update procedure** (these 20 steps will be repeated for the parent record, and will be saved before the initial record).

17. If the **parent record** is **updated (due to an update of the initial record)** and a **grandparent** record **has a roll-up summary field** or is a part of a **cross-object workflow**, the system will perform all the calculations and **updates** the roll-up summary field in the **grandparent record**. Then, the **grandparent record goes through the save procedure** (again, the same 20 steps will be executed for the grandparent record).

18. Executes **sharing evaluation**. The system evaluates which user has access to this record and which does not. The system performs these changes in the sharing tables of the record.

19. **Commits** all the DML statements **to the database**.

20. Executes **post-commit logic**, such as sending an email or executing postponed logic, including batches or future logic.

The following diagram is a visual representation of this execution context:

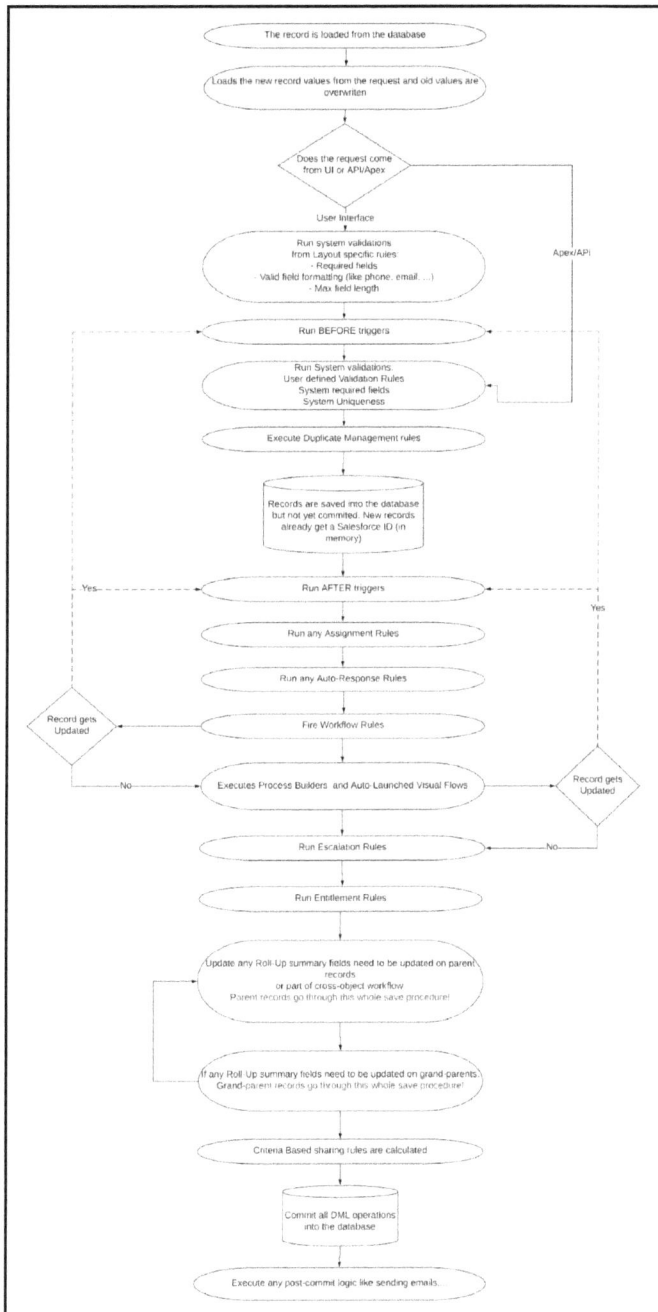

Let's check how to handle the exception.

Exception handling

What happens if you update a record and the update fails because you entered the wrong data? Yes, correct—you get an error message. But behind the scenes, this is what we developers call *an exception*.

In Salesforce, you have two big types of exceptions:

- Standard exceptions
- Custom exceptions

Standard exceptions are predefined in Salesforce. If you update a record and the update fails, you'll receive a DML exception. If a callout to a web service fails, you will receive a callout exception. You can find all types of standard exceptions in an overview at `https://developer.salesforce.com/docs/atlas.en-us.apexcode.meta/apexcode/apex_classes_exception_methods.htm`.

But how do we use the standard exceptions? Do you remember, in one of the first lessons of this book, the `try...catch` structure?

Yes, we `try` to execute some logic, and if the execution fails, we `catch` the error message.

For instance, imagine that we update our records, but one of the updates fails, and we get a DML exception. This exception is a predefined error that can be caused by validation rules, a Salesforce limit, or something else that doesn't allow the execution of our order to the database. Look at the following example:

```
try {
 Update lstAccounts;
} catch (DMLException ex){
 // execute this logic when you hit this type of exception
}
```

The DML exception in this example will predefine an error, and you cannot change this error or provide another error message that is more user-friendly.

The second type of standard exceptions are the errors during the execution of trigger logic. In this case, you can add an error to your sObject. If you update a list of records and one record fails, you can add an error on that record and display the error in an error list. (When you perform a data load, you don't need a `try...catch` module. `SObject.addError` is usable for each sObject, standard or custom.)

Let's take a look at an example:

```
List<Database.SaveResult> lstSavedRecords = Database.update(lstAccounts,
false);
Integer iCounter = 0;

for (Database.SaveResult savedAccount : lstSavedRecords){
 if (! savedAccount.isSuccess()){
 // self made error with a custom label
 lstAccounts[iCounter].addError(Label.Please_enter_your_Error_here);

 // the exception thrown
 lstAccounts[iCounter].addError(savedAccount.getErrors()[0].getMessage());
 }

 iCounter++;
}
```

In the preceding example, we simulate an update of records, done by the database statements, so we can filter out the erroneous records. If two records in a batch fail, then for these two records, we can provide a self-made error (defined in a custom label), or we can take the error provided by the system—`savedAccount.getErrors[0].getMessage()`.

Custom exceptions

A custom exception is an exception written by a developer. This is an Apex class that extends the `Exception` class. We'll consider some more information about this class in a minute.

You cannot create an exception with the `new` keyword (such as `throw new Exception()`), but you need to extend this class and provide the error message you want via this extension. The following is an example of a custom exception. The name of this class needs to have a name that ends with `Exception`:

```
public with sharing class MyCustomException extends Exception {
    public MyCustomException(String sErrorCode, String sErrorMessage){
        String theErrorMessage = sErrorCode + ': ' + sErrorMessage;
        this.setMessage(theErrorMessage);
    }
}
```

Because this class is an extension of the parent class, `Exception`, you can use the parent functionality of the `Exception` class, but the constructor of `Exception` is not usable.

Instead of the parent constructor, you need to use the child constructor (`MyCustomException`) to initiate your exception. But with this child constructor, you can provide only a message or a code and a respective message as parameters. With the two parameters, you call your constructor and the constructor will construct your error message, such as `'ERRCODE, this is an error message'`:

```
try {
  update lstAccounts;
} catch (Exception ex){
  //throw new MyCustomException('ERRCODE', 'this is an error message');
  //throw new MyCustomException('this is a custom error');
  System.debug(ex.getMessage());
}
```

Exception class

You just learned how to build a custom `Exceptions` class to extend the Apex `Exception` class. But what's the `Exception` class?

In each exception, you can get the error message, the location of the error, and the path of the error. For instance, you have a method in class A, called by a method in class B, and you caught the exceptions in class B. You don't need to look in class B, but in class A. The exception will tell you where you need to start your troubleshooting. Even the line number, the type of exception (callout error, `Nullpointer`, `QueryException`, and `DMLException`) are present in the `Exception` class.

The following are the methods of the `Exception` class that you can use in your error handling:

- `getCause()`: Returns the cause of the exception
- `getLineNumber()`: Returns the line number in your code where the exception was thrown
- `getMessage()`: Returns the error message of the exception
- `getStacktraceString()`: Returns a stack trace of the exception
- `getTypeName()`: Returns the type of the exception
- `initCause(Exception)`: Sets a cause; this is an exception
- `setMessage(String)`: Sets a custom message

And you can use these methods to get some error information to be logged in the debug logs or in a logging system:

```
try {
  insert lstAccounts;
} catch (Exception ex){
  System.debug(ex.getCause());
  System.debug(ex.getMessage());
  System.debug(ex.getLineNumber());
  System.debug(ex.getStackTraceString());
  System.debug(ex.getTypeName());
}
```

The `DMLException` and the `EmailException` classes have some more methods that are able to show you more information about the executed DML statements.

You can find more information about these methods at `https://developer.salesforce.com/docs/atlas.en-us.apexcode.meta/apexcode/apex_classes_exception_methods.htm`

Security in Apex

One of the most important things in programming and executing DML operations is security. You don't want to provide user access to delete records via Apex while the user is not allowed to do that operation in the regular user interface.

In the chapters about data modeling, you learned about the different ways to provide access to an object, a field, or a record. Be aware that Apex, in certain circumstances, runs in system mode, and the execution of the code doesn't take into account the user's access rights (with the result that the user can do things that are not available in the regular interface). Let's take a look at what we need to perform to protect our data in Apex.

DML security

Via Apex, you have the possibility to grant access to users to insert, update, or delete records when the user's profile does not grant that access. If you don't want to grant that access (via a Visualforce page or Lightning component), you need to verify whether the user has the access to do that.

You learned in the `Schema` class about the possibilities to get a lot of information about the object. In this class and subclasses, you will also find the information about whether a user can access and/or modify the object. Each object has some properties in the `DescribeSObjectResult` class that reflect the access rights of the user.

You can find the full information about an object with only one line of code. The following is the code to get the object description of an account and a custom object:

```
Schema.DescribeSObjectResult accountDescription =
Account.SObjectType.getDescribe();
Schema.DescribeSObjectResult custObjectDescription =
CustomObject__c.SObjectType.getDescribe();
```

The following is an overview of these properties and the user's access:

Profile-access	DescribeSObjectResult **property**
Read access	isAccessible
Create access	isCreatable
Edit access	isUpdateable
Delete access	isDeletable

The outcome of these variables is in line with the user's access. If a user has a read-only profile on the account (so only read access), you will receive in `DescribeObjectResult` the following properties for the account:

- `isAccessible = true`
- `isCreatable = false`
- `isUpdateable = false`
- `isDeletable = false`

The check to determine if a user has access to delete some records can be done with the following code. This is a shorter way than getting the full schema, then the object, and at least the description of that object:

```
if (Account.SObjectType.getDescribe().isDeletable()){
 // perform logic to delete the account
}
```

Field-level security

Selecting fields in a query and Apex running in system mode will provide user access to a field that probably contains sensitive information, and you don't want to share this information with all your users. So, we should verify if a user has access to the respective fields. Sometimes, you want this (if a value that the user doesn't see needs to be compared with a specific value), but sometimes not.

With the `Schema` class and the `DescribeFieldResult` class, you can access the information about whether the user has access to the respective field of the respective object. With the following code, we receive the full field description of a field in an object:

```
Account.Industry.getDescribe();
```

The most important properties to get access for a specific field are as follows:

- The user can access the field (via profile or permission set)
- The user can edit the value of the field

You can define that in the field-level security of your field. To determine the access via Apex, we call the field description functionality, as we did earlier, and return the following properties:

Field-level access	`DescribeFieldResult` **property**
Read	`isAccessible`
Edit	`isUpdateable`

To determine if the current user has access to the industry field of the account, you can use the following code. Also, in the case of the field description, you have a shorter way to determine if a user has access to a specific field:

```
if (Account.Industry.getDescribe().isUpdateable()){
 // perform logic to update the field Industry on Account
 }
```

SOQL injection

You've learned a lot about SOQL and the possibilities with Salesforce queries. But if you want to select some records based on a user's input, you need to be aware that the user can input everything into your database, or select everything that they want.

Salesforce has already implemented some security for SOQL queries to limit the risk of SQL injection:

- Wildcards for field selection (`Select * FROM Account`) are not supported
- You can only select data from the database with SOQL; you cannot do DML operations with SOQL
- Use of `JOIN` in a query is not supported in SOQL

If a user adds (a better word, in this case, is `injects`) some malicious code into your form (such as JavaScript in a text area), your page can be hacked and the content of your page can be changed by something other than your page. You don't want that, so we need to protect ourselves to ensure that a user's content in your form is verified and cannot execute JavaScript or select some data that is not allowed for that user.

In this section, you will learn how to protect your Apex code against SOQL injection.

Let's look at a simple example to start with. Your page will search an account, dependent on the name that the user gives in a text field on a form. Your SOQL query can be written like this:

```
String sParameter =
ApexPages.currentPage().getParameters().get('YourTextfieldParam');
String sQuery = 'SELECT Id, Name FROM Account WHERE Name LIKE \'%' +
sParameter + '%\'';
Account a = (Account) Database.query(sQuery);
```

Looks clear, does it not? I get my parameter from my text field, put it in a query, and execute the query that returns the results. Fine. If I put `Myname` in the form, the database will execute this query:

```
SELECT Id, Name FROM Account WHERE Name LIKE '%Myname%'
```

Nothing is wrong with this query; I will receive the results from it. But what happens if I enter the value `% %`?

This is one of the most used strings to test whether your form is protected against a SOQL injection. The database will execute something like the following:

```
SELECT Id, Name FROM Account WHERE Name LIKE '% %'
```

If you analyze this query, the user has entered two wildcard signs with a space in between in the text field, so their query selects every single record of the accounts table. With this string, the user I'll select all the names in the customer base of the company. Hmm, are there any possible new leads?

Let's learn how we can protect our queries against SOQL injection.

Use bind variables

One of the most recommended methods to mitigate SOQL injections is bind variables. You have already learned in the chapter about the SOQL statements that you can use dynamic variables in your queries.

This is what we call a bind variable. By setting the user input as a variable, you ensure that the user's input is treated as a variable and not as an executable element of the query:

```
Set<String> setWithStrings = new Set<String>{'test','account'};
List<Account> lstAccounts = [SELECT Id, Name FROM Account WHERE Name IN
:setWithStrings];
```

From our previous example, we will rewrite our code as follows:

```
String sParameter = '%' +
ApexPages.currentPage().getParameters().get('YourTextfieldParam') + '%';
List<Account> lstAccounts = [SELECT Id, Name FROM Account WHERE Name LIKE
:sParameter];
```

The `sParameter` is now a bind variable, and will be executed just like a variable.

Escape SingleQuotes

Another, and equally highly recommended, option to mitigate SOQL injection is to escape single quotes. This prevents a user's input from being treated as code by constraining them to the boundary of the string.

We use the `String.escapeSingleQuotes()` function to add a backslash before every single quote in the parameters.

If you execute the following code in your developer console, you will see the difference in your query:

```
String sString = 'This is a \'Single Quote\' test';
String sEscapedString = String.escapeSingleQuotes(sString);
System.debug(sString); // this returns the string "This is a 'Single Quote'
test"
System.debug(sEscapedString); // this returns the string "This is a
\'Single Quote\' test"
```

Replacing characters

Next, to the escape of single quotes and the bind variables, we need to check that the user didn't apply some tags or characters that are useful to take over the control of our query. Something like + or = (`equalsTo character`) can be used to execute the following query:

```
String sQuery = 'SELECT Id FROM User WHERE isActive = ' + myVariable;
```

If I enter the `true AND Name Like '%%'` value, the whole database is selected again.

I will remove the `AND` and `Like` words (and there are more than only these characters) in the query, in combination with `escapeSingleQuotes`, I receive a complete string, such as `'true Name \'%%\'`, which delivers no result (it will result in an exception).

Whitelisting

Check the input of the value to what a user may input to your form. You can probably solve that issue with the replacement of a text field into a picklist, or validate what a user may input in your text field.

In the following example, I check if the parameter contains the `OR` or `AND` operators. If so, the code will not execute the query but will define an error on my page:

```
String sInput = Apexpages.currentPage().getParameters().get('textInput');
if (sInput.containsIgnoreCase(' AND ') || (sInput.containsIgnoreCase(' OR
'))){
  // return an error
} else {
  // execute query
}
```

You can do the same action with the +- sign or the =- sign. Put all your **forbidden** words and characters in a set and check if the characters are present. In combination with the replacement of characters, you can remove these characters or words completely from your query.

Record security – with and without sharing

You have learned a lot about sharing, which is one of the most important (and powerful) security layers of Salesforce. You can decide which user has access to which record. Even if your database has tons of records, the system can decide very quickly if the user has access to the record or not.

In Apex, you need to verify if the user has access to the record or not by sharing. For each object that has a sharing model other than `public Read/Write`, you have a `Share` object as well (such as `AccountShare`). This share object is a junction object between your record and the user. If you execute the query, you can find out if a user has access to the account mentioned:

```
SELECT UserOrGroupId, AccountId, AccountAccessLevel FROM AccountShare WHERE
UserOrGroupId = :userId AND AccountId = :idAccount
```

By default, in Apex, every user has access to every record. And a developer can enforce or avoid sharing by the keywords `with sharing` or `without sharing`. As the default for each class (and if you don't define your sharing level), the class is defined `without sharing`.

If you force sharing by creating the `with sharing` class, all the sharing calculations will be done by the application. If you create a query and select `Accounts`, to which the user doesn't have any access via sharing, the result will be empty. If the class is not created with the `with sharing` keyword, the user will see the accounts that they don't have access to.

The same issue applies when a user wants to edit an account. If the sharing on a class is enabled, the user will not be able to modify that account due to the sharing definition in the class:

```
// in this class, we enforce the sharing and the access on the records for
the user
Public with sharing class MySharingClass {

}

// in this class, we avoid the sharing and the access on the records. The
user has always access to the records
Public without sharing class MyWithoutSharingClass {

}
```

So, if you need to verify if a user may only update or see records where he/she has access to them, you need to use `with sharing`.

Web service callouts

The last part of our Apex journey is a callout to a web service. You know that Twitter and Facebook, and even Salesforce, have a web service that you can connect with and grab the information you need. Some APIs are free to use, but for some information, you need to pay if you want to use or store that information.

For each secure web service, you need to authenticate to the service. This can be done in different ways and is dependent on the web service itself. Some easy APIs use only an API key, while other services use OAuth2.0 to authenticate.

The type of authentication should be found in the documentation of the API. Most of the time, you can find this documentation online, or contact the API vendor to receive this information.

In this book, we will use an API to get information about movies. There is an API called *The Movie DB* (`https://www.themoviedb.org/`), where we can easily find movie information by providing the movie title. The API processes the title and returns the movie data.

I talked about authentication; this API uses a simple API key, but you need to register to get an API key. Don't worry, it's free of charge. So, let's sign up for the API key at `https://www.themoviedb.org/account/signup`.

After your sign-up, you need to log in to your account and get the API key by filling the form in the **Account Settings | API** section, as follows:

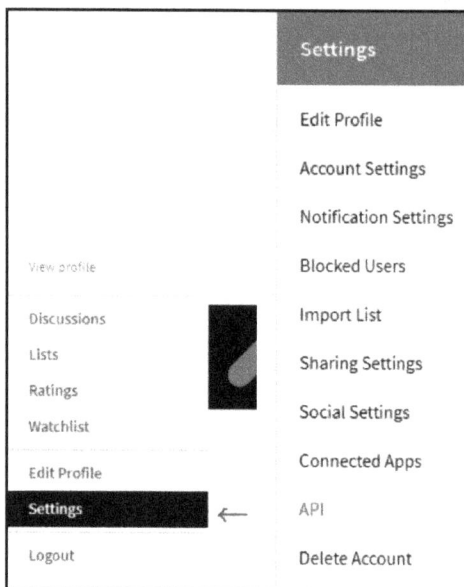

When you receive your API key, you are able to create your first API request.

In the documentation on the API (you can find this at `https://developers.themoviedb.org/3/getting-started/introduction`), you will find the endpoints of the different services. In the following service, we will search for the details of the movie, *Lethal Weapon*.

Copy and paste your API key in the following URL. Replace the full string as: `<YOUR_API_KEY>` with your API key:
`https://api.themoviedb.org/3/search/movie?api_key=&query=Lethal%20Weapon`.

Now copy this full URL, paste it in your preferred browser, and take a look at what you see.

You will see some text in a structured way. This is called a JSON string. This kind of export is frequently used in JavaScript and can be used to display the information from the result.

The result depends on the service that you connect with. It could be JSON or XML, and you can find out which in the documentation of the web service.

In this service, we always receive a JSON string so we can transform this answer into an Apex object. We create a connection with an API via an HTTP request object (`HttpRequest`) and we receive an HTTP response object (`HttpResponse`). These two classes are the most important to perform an outbound service call to a web service. You have also another way to connect to a web service (the SOAP service), but these are advanced development skills, which are not needed to achieve the certificate.

Let's create a connection with this service; be aware you already have an API key to this service.

The endpoint

First of all, we need to configure the endpoint with our named credentials. Why do we do that? With a named credential, you can simplify the authentication to a web service by configuring your web service endpoint and your type of authentication. Named credentials support basic authentication through OAuth.

Let's configure our API endpoint:

1. Go to your Salesforce **Setup** screen and type in `Named` (of **Named Credentials**):

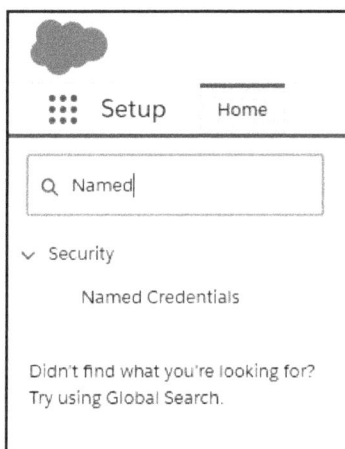

2. Click on **Named Credentials** and add a new **Named Credential**:

3. Fill in the following information:
   - **Label**: Put what ever you want for this field. Choose a name that fits with the endpoint of the API. We choose `The Movie DB`.
   - **Name**: This will automatically be filled in if you given a **Label**.
   - **URL**: This is the basic endpoint URL of the API. You can find it in the documentation. In our API, the endpoint is `https://api.themoviedb.org/3/`.

- **Identity Type**: Due to the API key that we need in the URL, no other authentication is needed to connect with the API, so in this case it is **Anonymous**.
- **Authentication Protocol**: **No Authentication**. We only need to apply the API key into the URL. We do that later in our class and method.
- Check the box next to **Generate Authorization Header**.

Save the credential. You can see the label and the name of the credential. Copy this name and paste it into your favorite text editor. We need these details for our class that we will create in a few moments.

The HTTP request

After configuring the endpoint, we will create the class to connect to our API. Let's start to identify the basics for our HTTP request.

What we need to create an HTTP request is our endpoint URL. We only configured the basic URL, but we didn't add the available resource.

If we want to use different resources, we need to define different endpoints. In the documentation of our API, you can find different resources (TV, search, movies). Each of these resources has its own definition. In one resource, you probably have some sub-resources, such as in the **Search** resource, you will find some sub-resources (for example, **Search Companies** or **Search People)**. Each of these resources and sub-resources has a different endpoint URL.

In our example, we will implement the **Search Movies** and **Search People** resources:

```
SEARCH

GET    Search Companies

GET    Search Collections

GET    Search Keywords

GET    Search Movies

GET    Multi Search

GET    Search People

GET    Search TV Shows
```

And you can see immediately the second important parameter—the type of the request.

The type of the request to be used is (again) dependent on that specified in the documentation of the service. Both resources that we will implement are GET resources, so we will receive some information from a database. Other commonly used types of requests are as follows:

- POST: Sends information to a resource, such as uploading a file
- PUT: Edits information of a resource, such as editing/updating an actor or a movie
- HEAD: The same as GET, but transfers a header section only
- DELETE: Removes resource information, such as removing an actor

The third part of our request is the timeout. It is not required to configure this (the default timeout from Salesforce is 20,000 ms). This is only needed when you want to deviate from the standard.

Let's write some code. Open your developer console and create a class, WebserviceCallout. This class will perform the callout and store our response in an object.

I will provide you with the code, step by step. Look out; this code is written so that you can understand this as a novice developer.

Let's start with our basic parameters:

```
public with sharing class WebserviceCallout {

    private final static String authToken = '<YOUR API KEY HERE>';
    private final static String sEndpoint = 'callout:The_movie_DB';
    private final static Integer iTimeout = 20000;

}
```

I'll quickly go over these variables. These are the variables for the token, the endpoint, and the timeout, respectively. You need to fill in your API key in the authToken variable. The best practice is to configure this token in a protected custom setting or custom metadata type, but just as an example and to keep things simple, we will configure it in the code. But what's that with the endpoint?

Yes, due to the configuration of our named credential, Salesforce performs the callout via the named credential. The basic endpoint is configured in the named credential and Salesforce will grab the URL from the credentials that you provided (in this case, the credential with the API name of The_movie_DB.

Finally, we configure a custom timeout value:

```
private static String searchCallout(String sParameter, String sResource){
  String theEndpoint = sEndpoint + '/search/' + sResource + '?api_key=' +
authToken;

  HttpRequest theRequest = new HttpRequest();
  theRequest.setMethod('GET');
  theRequest.setEndpoint(theEndpoint + '&query=' +
EncodingUtil.urlEncode(sParameter, 'UTF-8'));
  theRequest.setTimeout(iTimeout);

  // perform the callout
  Http oHttp = new Http();
  HttpResponse theResponse = new HttpResponse();

  theResponse = oHttp.send(theRequest);
  return theResponse.getBody();
}
```

The preceding code is the code to perform an API call. In this case, we have our resource and the parameters to search for a movie or a person.

First of all, during the construction of the HTTP request object, we construct the final endpoint based on the resource and the parameters. As you can see, we also provide our API token in the URL. `EncodingUtil` will convert your parameters into URL-readable characters (for example, space is converted as `%20`). Following the endpoint URL, we define the request method and the custom timeout in the HTTP request object.

After the construction of the request, we send the request to the API. We define an HTTP response object and return the body of the response. You can access the body of the response of the HTTP request via the `HttpResponse.getBody()` method. Look out, this can return an error or a valid response. This is what we call callout error handling. This error handling is not defined in this class, but I wanted to warn you to foresee this in your code in actual real-life environments. If a resource cannot be found, you will receive a status code 200 (meaning a successful response), but there could be another kind of response (such as an error code or an error message.)

If we create this method as a `public` method, you can call this method with the **Developer Console Anonymous Window**, with the following code:

```
System.debug(WebserviceCallout.searchCallout('Lethal Weapon','movie'));
```

You will see the full response of the movie, which we will model in the following class:

```
USER_DEBUG
[1]|DEBUG|{"page":1,"total_results":4,"total_pages":1,"results":[{"vote_cou
nt":2149,"id":941,"video":false,"vote_average":7.1,"title":"Lethal
Weapon","popularity":14.626,"poster_path":"\/drp80fBSWhz0vAmzUibXDyn0Pjo.jp
g","original_language":"en","original_title":"Lethal
Weapon","genre_ids":[12,28,35,53,80],"backdrop_path":"\/xQpCA4QIEKcfsLf7CSe
SM0tHCY7.jpg","adult":false,"overview":"Veteran buttoned-down LAPD
detective Roger Murtaugh is partnered with unhinged cop Martin Riggs, who -
- distraught after his wife's death -- has a death wish and takes
unnecessary risks with criminals at every turn. The odd couple embark on
their first homicide investigation as partners, involving a young woman
known to Murtaugh with ties to a drug and prostitution
ring.","release_date":"1987-03-06"},{"vote_count":1200,"id":944,"video":fal
se,"vote_average":6.5,"title":"Lethal Weapon
4","popularity":10.21,"poster_path":"\/kpC9Y0jhwTqtRlcetxbgn3crnlU.jpg","or
iginal_language":"en","original_title":"Lethal Weapon
4","genre_ids":[28,12,35,80,53],"backdrop_path":"\/jssTFAf5MCBbZPA02vRSYSeV
tHh.jpg","adult":false,"overview":"In the combustible action franchise's
final installment, maverick detectives Martin Riggs and Roger Murtaugh
square off against Asian mobster Wah Sing Ku, who's up to his neck in slave
trading and counterfeit currency. With help from gumshoe Leo Getz and
smart-aleck rookie cop Lee Butters, Riggs and Murtaugh aim to take down Ku
and his
gang.","release_date":"1998-07-10"},{"vote_count":1282,"id":943,"video":fal
se,"vote_average":6.6,"title":"Lethal Weapon
3","popularity":9.99,"poster_path":"\/pr5RcT2TdJ09PkETdhRiwixf8PW.jpg","ori
ginal_language":"en","original_title":"Lethal Weapon
3","genre_ids":[12,28,35,53,80],"backdrop_path":"\/rnMLbWNSWX70eWFxWOpkfngX
twD.jpg","adult":false,"overview":"Archetypal buddy cops Riggs and Murtaugh
are back for another round of high-stakes action, this time setting their
collective sights on bringing down a former Los Angeles police lieutenant
turned black market weapons dealer. Lorna Cole joins as the beautiful yet
hardnosed internal affairs sergeant who catches Riggs's
eye.","release_date":"1992-05-15"},{"vote_count":1619,"id":942,"video":fals
e,"vote_average":6.9,"title":"Lethal Weapon
2","popularity":9.715,"poster_path":"\/7XAusKpFNv8x9sHpFLAS21WCT81.jpg","or
iginal_language":"en","original_title":"Lethal Weapon
2","genre_ids":[28,12,35,80,53],"backdrop_path":"\/7AwySjHxakk3yCItwtjQbYhW
AOg.jpg","adult":false,"overview":"In the opening chase, Martin Riggs and
Roger Murtaugh stumble across a trunk full of Krugerrands. They follow the
trail to a South African diplomat who's using his immunity to conceal a
smuggling operation. When he plants a bomb under Murtaugh's toilet, the
action explodes!","release_date":"1989-07-07"}]}
```

We will use this JSON response to generate an Apex object so we can visualize this information, in Chapter 6, *The Salesforce User Interface*.

Let's model the response object. We only model the results of the different movies; the bold section of the preceding JSON response.

If you analyze the model of the JSON, you will see the different properties of the movie, such as the title, a poster image file path, and the release date. We will model this movie in a class with inner classes.

The movie model will look like this:

```
public class MovieResponse {
 public Integer vote_count {get; set;}
 public Integer id {get; set;}
 public Boolean video {get; set;}
 public Decimal vote_average {get; set;}
 public String title {get; set;}
 public Decimal popularity {get; set;}
 // to get the picture of the movie: https://image.tmdb.org/t/p/original +
 the string retrieved from the poster_path
 public String poster_path {get; set;}
 public String original_language {get; set;}
 public String original_title {get; set;}
 public List<Integer> genre_ids {get; set;}
 public String backdrop_path {get; set;}
 public Boolean adult {get; set;}
 public String overview {get; set;}
 public String release_date {get; set;}
 }
```

But why do we need to write so much code? This is what we call an Apex object. Salesforce has very good JSON support; by using the JSON parser, we can easily convert a full JSON object (which you find between the curly brackets). All the properties between these brackets are part of the object. Dependent on the type of value, you need to define a string, a decimal, or a Boolean:

```
"Vote_count":2149, ⇒ Integer

"Id":941, ⇒ Integer

"Video":false, ⇒ Boolean

"Vote_average":7.1, ⇒ Decimal

"title":"Lethal Weapon", ⇒ String

"Popularity":14.626, ⇒ Decimal

"poster_path":"\/drp80fBSWhz0vAmzUibXDyn0Pjo.jpg", ⇒ a String
```

```
"Original_language":"en", ⇒ a String

"original_title":"Lethal Weapon", ⇒ a String

"Genre_ids":[12,28,35,53,80], ⇒ a list with integers

"backdrop_path":"\/xQpCA4QIEKcfsLf7CSeSM0tHCY7.jpg", ⇒ a string

"Adult":false, ⇒ a Boolean

"overview":"Veteran buttoned-down LAPD detective Roger Murtaugh is
partnered with unhinged cop Martin Riggs, who -- distraught after his
wife's death -- has a death wish and takes unnecessary risks with criminals
at every turn. The odd couple embark on their first homicide investigation
as partners, involving a young woman known to Murtaugh with ties to a drug
and prostitution ring.", ⇒ a String

"Release_date":"1987-03-06" ⇒ a String (that we will convert later to a
date by a function)
```

Exercise

Now, execute the same command for a person record. We use the `Person resource` and search for `travolta`. With this response, you need to create the same type of model for the `Person` object. Look out: maybe you can reuse the preceding object. You can find the solution to this exercise in the appendix of this book.

Now, we will convert our JSON response into the object records:

```
private static List<MovieResponse> constructMovies(String sResponse){
 List<MovieResponse> lstMovies = new List<MovieResponse>();
 if (sResponse != null){
 JSONParser theParser = JSON.createParser(sResponse);
 while (theParser.nextToken() != null){
 if (theParser.getCurrentToken() == JSONToken.FIELD_NAME &&
theParser.getText() == 'results'){
 theParser.nextToken();
 theParser.nextToken();
 lstMovies.add((MovieResponse) theParser.readValueAs(MovieResponse.class));
 }
 }
 }

 return lstMovies;
}
```

We use the JSONParser class to convert the JSON response to our movieResponse model. Because of the fact that we only need the movies and not the number of results, we need to start at JSONToken with the results label . We will proceed with two further tokens (we need to proceed from results token and the token where an array starts). Now we are at the start of the beginning of a movie object.

The code is as follows:

```
theParser.readValueAs(MovieResponse.class)
```

The preceding code will convert the full JSON objects in the array in our defined model, in the MovieResponse inner class. So, we will receive a list of movies, constructed in our model.

And, at least, we will code a public method to search our movies, based on the parameter:

```
public static List<MovieResponse> searchMovies(String sParameter){
  List<MovieResponse> lstMovies = new List<MovieResponse>();
  try {
  String sMoviesFromCallout = searchCallout(sParameter, 'movie');
  lstMovies = constructMovies(sMoviesFromCallout);
  } catch (Exception ex){
  System.debug(ex.getMessage());
  }

  return lstMovies;
}
```

We define an empty list with movies, where we add the movies that can be found by our parameter. Fine, now we have a connection with our API and we are able to find one or more movies with the given parameter.

Now, it is your turn. You have already created the Person object, but you can't yet find an actor/actress with some movies in which they play a role. Create the construction of the Person records (such as with the constructMovies method) and foresee a public method that we can use in a Visualforce or Lightning component. For sure, we will use it later on in the visualization of our Person and Movies object.

You can find the solution to the creation of records at the end of the book, in the *Appendix*. But, don't look directly at the solution. Try to build the solution with the examples. Good luck!

Summary

Apex is a language with a lot of possibilities, but it is too extensive to explain everything in one book. We would copy the whole Apex developer guide for Salesforce!

As I said at the beginning of this book, Salesforce works with the MVC pattern. We've looked at the model (the database), and the controller (our Apex code), so now it is time to learn about the view: Visualforce.

After Visualforce, you will also get an introduction in Lightning components. But first of all, what did you learn during this chapter? Let's take the following quiz to test our new knowledge.

Quiz

Let's see if you are on the right track to becoming a certified Salesforce developer. You'll find all the answers to this chapter summary quiz at the end of this book. Try to answer the questions without looking at the answers.

1. Which trigger event allows a developer to update fields in the `Trigger.new` list without using an additional DML statement? (Choose two answers.)
    a. Before insert
    b. Before update
    c. After update
    d. After insert

2. How can a developer determine, from `DescribeSObjectResult`, if a given user will be able to create records for an object in Apex?
    a. By using the `isInsertable()` method
    b. By using the `isCreatable()` method
    c. By using the `hasAccess()` method
    d. By using the `canCreate()` method

3. What is the order in which Salesforce events are executed on saving a record?
   a. Before triggers; validation rules; after triggers; workflow rules; assignment rules; commit
   b. Before triggers; validation rules; after triggers; assignment rules; workflow rules; commit
   c. Validation rules; before triggers; after triggers; workflow rules; assignment rules; commit
   d. Validation rules; before triggers; after triggers; assignment rules; workflow rules; commit

4. A Salesforce developer with 100 contacts executes the following code using the developer console:

```
Contact myContact = new Contact(Name = 'MyContact');
insert myContact;

For (Integer x = 0; x < 150; x++) {
    Contact newContact = new Contact (Name='MyContact' + x);
    try {
        Insert newContact;
    } catch (Exception ex) {
        System.debug (ex) ;
    }
}
insert new Contact (Name='myContact');
```

How many contacts are in the org after this code is run?
   a. 101
   b. 100
   c. 102
   d. 252

5. A developer needs to display the available record types for the
   `Opportunity` object. The developer also needs to display the picklist values for
   the `Opportunity.StageName` field. Which action does the developer need to
   take to get both—the record types and picklist values—in the controller? (Choose
   two)

   a. Using `Schema.PicklistEntry`, returned by
      `Opportunity.StageName.getDescribe().getPicklistValues()`

   b. Using `Schema.RecordTypeInfo`, returned by
      `Opportunity.sObjectType.getDescribe().getRecordTypeInfo
      s()`

   c. Using SOQL to query `Case` records in the org to get all the
      `RecordType` values available for `Case`

   d. Using SOQL to query case records in the org to get all values for the
      `Status` picklist field

6. A developer has the following code:

```
try {
    List<String> nameList;
    Account a;
    String s = a.Name;
    nameList.add(s);
} catch (ListException le ) {
    System.debug(' List Exception ');
} catch (NullPointerException npe) {
    System.debug(' NullPointer Exception ');
} catch (Exception e) {
    System.debug(' Generic Exception ');
}
```

   What message will be logged?

   a. A list exception

   b. A `NullPointer` exception

   c. A generic exception

   d. No message is logged

7. What is good practice for a developer to follow when writing a trigger? (Choose
   two.)

   a. Using `@future` methods to perform DML operations

   b. Using the `Map` data structure to hold query results by ID

   c. Using the `Set` data structure to ensure distinct records.

   d. Using synchronous callouts to call external systems

8. Which statement should a developer avoid using inside procedural loops? (Choose two.)

    a. `System.debug('Amount of CPU time (in ms) used so far: ' + Limits.getCpuTime())`

    b. `List contacts = [SELECT Id, Salutation, FirstName, LastName, Email FROM Contact WHERE AccountId = :a.Id];`

    c. `If(o.accountId == a.id)`

    d. `Update contactList;`

9. A developer created an Apex helper class to handle complex trigger logic. Which of the following options in the helper class can warn users when the trigger exceeds DML governor limits?

    a. Using `PageReference.setRedirect()` to redirect the user to a custom Visualforce page before the number of DML statements is exceeded

    b. Using `Messaging.sendEmail()` to continue the transaction and send an alert to the user after the number of DML statements is exceeded

    c. Using `ApexMessage.Messages()` to display an error message after the number of DML statements is exceeded

    d. Using `Limits.getDMLRows()` and then displaying an error message before the number of DML statements is exceeded

10. Which action can a developer perform in a `before update` trigger? (Choose two.)

    a. Display a custom error message in the application interface

    b. Change field values using the `Trigger.new` context variable

    c. Delete the original object using a `delete` DML operation

    d. Update the original object using an `update` DML operation

6
The Salesforce User Interface

In this chapter, you'll learn everything you need to know about programmatic visualization. You'll learn about the different ways of visualizing your data, how to create user interfaces, and how you can use the pages and components that are available in existing pages.

After completing this chapter, you will be able to do the following:

- Create a Visualforce page and visualize your data, based on a standard controller, standard set controller, an extension on a standard controller, or a full custom controller.
- Define the advantages of the Lightning framework.
- Create and use a Lightning component in your Lightning pages.

Introduction

In the previous chapters, we learned about the model (how to create your data structure) and about the controller (Apex classes, controllers to process data, and so on), so now it is time to create a view for this data, which is the last part of our **Model-View-Controller** (**MVC**) pattern.

In Salesforce, you have two different view types of user interfaces, with their own components to display data:

- **Salesforce Classic**: This is the classic view of Salesforce and has become outdated over the years. All of the features that are developed in new releases are mainly created for Lightning Experience, the new interface. Nowadays, if you enable a new org, you will be activated in Lightning Experience.
- **Lightning Experience**: This is the new view (UI) of Salesforce. Since August 2015, Salesforce has been constantly improving Lightning Experience to provide you with a better interface with more point and click possibilities, just like the previous view of Salesforce (Classic).

The following table gives you an overview of the two view types and their components:

Salesforce Classic	Lightning Experience
Visualforce pages (builds what you want in one page)	Lightning pages (different types of pages)
Visualforce components	Lightning components (first generation of components that can be added to new or existing pages) Lightning web components (second generation of Lightning components)

Now, we will go over how to create Visualforce pages and how to interact with our model and controllers.

Displaying Salesforce data using Visualforce

Visualforce is a framework of components that allows you to build custom **user interfaces (UIs)** for mobile and desktop apps that are hosted on the Lightning Platform. With Visualforce, you can extend existing (built-in) Salesforce functionality, but you can also build your application from scratch. You can also combine the *old* Visualforce technology with the Lightning Experience styling so that the user won't see the difference between your Visualforce page and a Lightning component. Be careful, though: not every standard Visualforce component is supported in the Lightning styling.

Each Visualforce page has its own URL. The URL always starts with your default organization URL (or the URL of an installed app). After the base URL, you will find /apex and, after this path, you will find the name of your page. So, if the name of the page is YourVisualforcePage, you will find a URL similar to the URL in the picture, as shown in the following diagram:

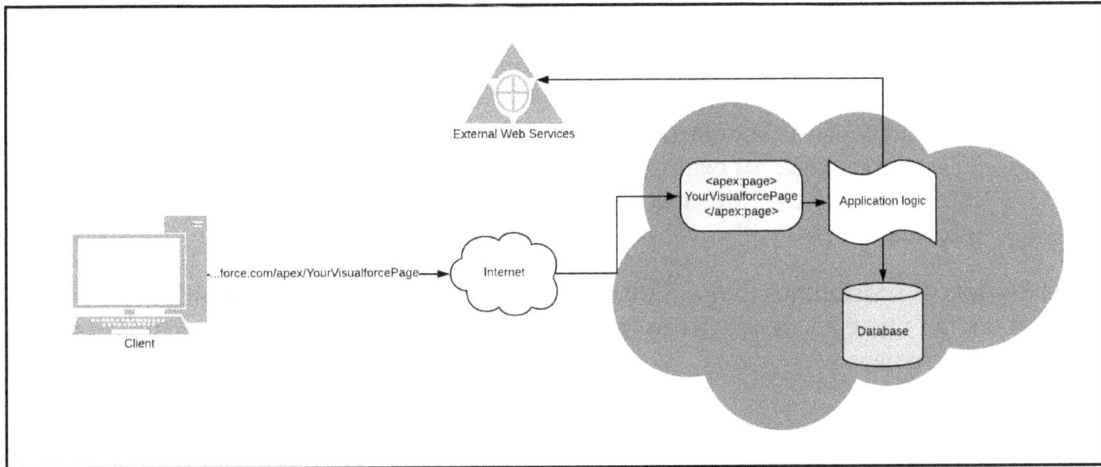

As you learned previously, Salesforce uses the MVC framework. The preceding diagram shows you how a Visualforce page will display your database records via application logic. We've already seen a lot of application logic in the chapters regarding the Apex classes in Chapter 4, *Apex Basics* and Chapter 5, *Apex - Beyond the Basics*, but we need something more to connect our Visualforce page with our application and/or business logic—in other words, we need a controller.

Where is this used?

Visualforce pages can be used in several circumstances and can meet a lot of business requirements. Let's say I push a button on a Movie record page. The functionality needs to open a popup with all the information about that movie (the title, director, which actors are in the movie, and so on) all in one view. As you already know from Chapter 2, *Understanding Data Modeling and Management*, you've built the data model into several objects, but in a Visualforce page, we can display everything.

The following is an overview of where you can use a Visualforce page:

- Open a Visualforce page from the App Launcher: You can create an app for the App Launcher and open a Visualforce page for this app. For example, a recruitment app doesn't need the basic layout for the accounts; in this case, you build an app with the necessary objects, logic, and pages. Afterward, you decide which page is shown in your app.
- Open a Visualforce page from the navigation bar: You can link a tab to a Visualforce page and add the tab to an application or as a standalone tab.

- Add a Visualforce page in a standard page layout in a separate section.
- Create a quick action and open a Visualforce page via this quick action. Like a form, you do this to create a new, related record.
- You can override standard actions (like **New**, **View**, **Edit**, and so on) with a Visualforce page, for example, when you want to create a movie via a custom interface (only the title) and call the web service to enrich more movie information (we will cover this example in an exercise).

You have lots of possibilities to use a Visualforce page during the customization of your application. Let's take a look at how to create a Visualforce page and the most important components of a page.

Visualforce language

First, let's talk a little bit about the Visualforce language itself. The Visualforce programming language isn't a difficult language. Visualforce uses a tag-based markup language that is similar to HTML. Each tag corresponds to a user interface component, such as a section of a page, a button, or an individual field. Visualforce has nearly 150 built-in components, and you can even create your own. Visualforce markup can be freely mixed with HTML markup, CSS styles, and JavaScript libraries.

Explaining each standard, Visualforce component will bring us too far into detail—we would need to update this book every release since each release will bring us new standard components.

> Don't hesitate to explore the full component base at `https://developer.salesforce.com/docs/atlas.en-us.218.0.pages.meta/pages/pages_compref.htm`. Here, you will find the full base of the standard components, along with their properties, such as what they will display (like a button or a panel and where they can be used).

Creating Visualforce pages

Let's create a new page to display something where each developer starts with `HelloWorld`. You can create Visualforce pages in your developer console as well. Let's create our `HelloWorld` page:

1. Open your **Developer Console** and click **New** in the navigation menu.
2. Click the **Visualforce** page, choose a name, and click **OK**:

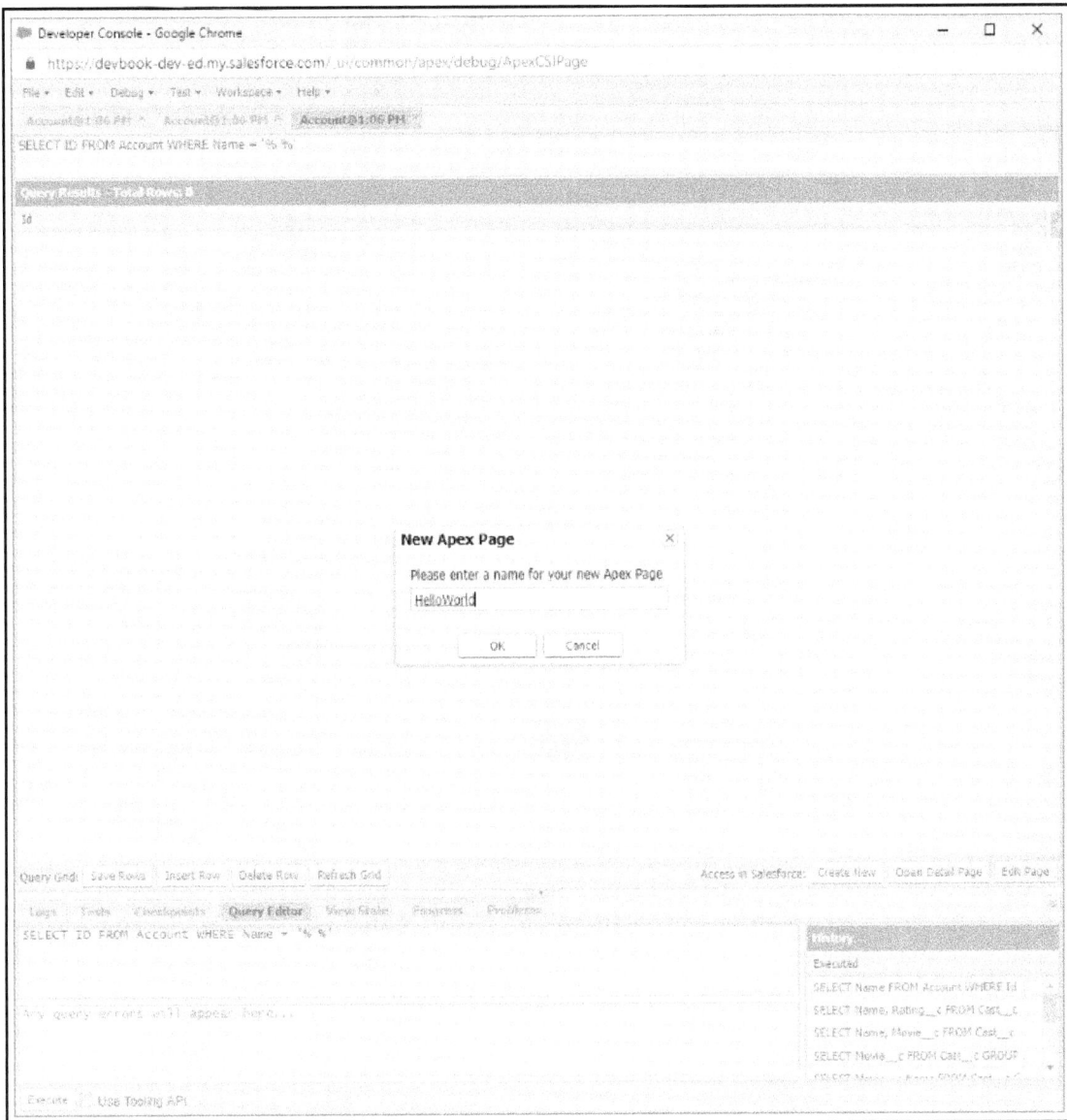

3. Congratulations! You've created your first Visualforce page. The start tag and end tag are already in place, so now you can proceed with your page.
4. Add some tags and attributes to the page, combined with HTML and CSS.

5. Copy and paste the following code into the frame in your page and save the code:

```
<apex:page sideBar="false" tabStyle="Movie__c">
    <style type="text/css">
        .container{
            width: 1080px;
            margin: 20px auto;
        }
    </style>
    <apex:outputPanel layout="block" styleClass="container">
        <apex:pageBlock title="This is my first Visualforce page">
            <apex:pageBlockSection title="Hello">
                Hello World
            </apex:pageBlockSection>
        </apex:pageBlock>
    </apex:outputPanel>
</apex:page>
```

6. Open the page in your favorite browser and view the result. You should have something like this:

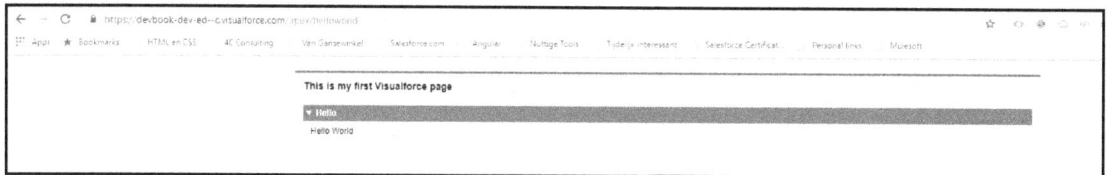

Nice and neat for that little bit of code, isn't it? Let's explain this piece of code, where you just show a panel with a title and some text in the body of the panel. These panels are the same as the standard page layouts in Salesforce Classic. With one extra attribute in the `apex:page` element (`lightningStylesheets="true"`), you can transform your complete page into the Lightning Experience styling:

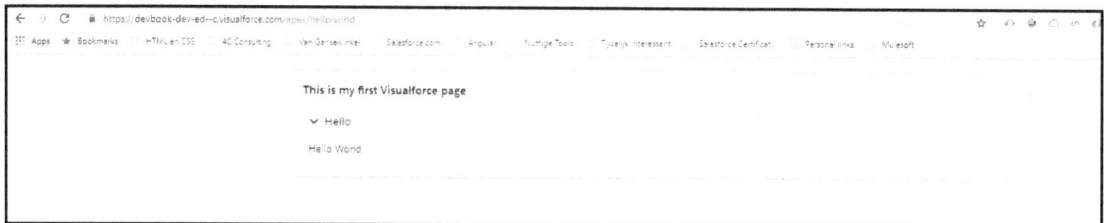

Not bad! You probably know by now that the `apex:page` tag has everything to do with the complete page. In this tag, I placed an extra attribute to avoid having to display the sidebar. If I build my own application, I don't want a Salesforce sidebar on the left-hand side. In this tag, you can also decide which tab styling will be used to open your page. I made the choice to give the page the color from our `Movie` object tab. If you configured your tab in the Classic setup, you will see the respective color for your tab. If you don't add this tab style, you will get a black color instead.

There are some other interesting attributes regarding the `page` tag:

- **action**: You can perform actions when the page is loaded, such as rendering actions before the page is displayed. If you want to create a dispatcher page that redirects to a certain page in certain circumstances, you can use this attribute.
- **applyBodyTag - applyHtmlTag**: When you create a Visualforce page and display this page, you automatically earn the HTML, `head`, and `body` tags. In certain circumstances, you want to build some applications where you need to define some namespaces in your HTML tag. With this attribute, you avoid the fact that Salesforce adds the HTML or `body` tag in your page, but you need to define it by yourself.
- **cache**: This can be used if you want the page to be cached by the browser. A cached page loads faster (because the page is loaded from your computer and not from the internet). By default, the page is not cached and reloads every time a user requests the page from the server.
- **Content-Type**: This is a very handy attribute that you can use to create a Visualforce page and transform this page into another MIME type of file. If you want to create a Visualforce page and want to render this as an Excel file, you'll add an attribute such as `Content-Type="application/vnd.ms-excel"`.
- **doctype**: If you want to generate an HTML 5 document, you can add this attribute to your `page` tag.
- **Language**: The language of your page. You can add the language of the user on your page.
- **lightningStylesheets**: When you add this attribute, your page will be in the Lightning style guide.
- **readOnly**: This attribute can be interesting if you need to display thousands of records. In normal circumstances, you can only iterate over 1,000 items in a list, but with this read-only attribute, you have the possibility to iterate over 10,000 items. The limit of query results will relax from 50,000 rows to 1,000,000 rows. However, you can't execute a DML operation in your page (it isn't read-only anymore).

- **renderAs**: This tag is used when you want to render your Visualforce page as a PDF document.

- **standardStylesheets**: If you want to define your own stylesheet (for a custom application, you don't want the Salesforce default styling), you can disable the standard stylesheets by adding this attribute with the value `'false'`.

- **tabStyle**: Next to the default stylesheets, you can decide which colors will be used on your page. Based on an object tab (the tab of an object), you can create a page with components in the colored style of your `object` tab.

- **title**: The title of your page. If you don't mention a title, the title of the page will be the URL of the page.

- **standardController**: Together with the attribute controller, this is one of the most used attributes in the `page` tag. With this attribute, you will link the functionality of a standard object to your page. If you want to save a record with a standard controller, you don't need to write extra code to do so:

```
<apex:page id="ExampleSTD" standardController="Movie__c">
    <apex:form>
        <apex:inputField value="{!Movie__c.Name}" /><br/>
        <apex:commandButton action="{!Save}" value="Save" />
    </apex:form>
</apex:page>
```

No Apex code is required anymore.

- **Controller**: This is one of the most used attributes. This is how we link the page with custom logic. We'll learn about the differences between a standard controller and a custom controller in the next paragraph of this book.

- **Extensions**: This attribute is used when you've built an extension on a standard controller. You've built a page where you use a lot of the standard functionality of an object (like save, delete, and so on), but you need some extra functionality besides the standard logic. You'll build an Apex extension (nothing more than a class with a special constructor; more on that later) and you *extend* your standard controller with one or more extensions.

This is only the explanation of the `page` tag. During the Visualforce section of this book, we will use more standard components. We have already used the `apex:pageblock`, `apex:pageblockSection`, and `apex:form` tags, but there are many more tags and attributes that you can use during the development of your pages.

> You can find all the available tags at `https://developer.salesforce.com/docs/atlas.en-us.pages.meta/pages/pages_compref.htm`.

Let's take a look at how we can link standard and custom logic to our page, starting with standard controllers.

Standard controllers

A standard controller is also called a **Visualforce controller** because you only use these controllers in a Visualforce context. If you need to create a button on an object to display a Visualforce page, you'll need to use a standard controller.

Standard controllers already contain some standard logic, like save a record, delete a record, and so on, so you can use this functionality without any extra classes or writing extra functionality. This functionality results in the same behavior as the functionality in the standard page layouts of Salesforce. The save functionality of your standard controller, `Account`, is the same functionality that you will use to save an account in the standard Salesforce pages.

We saw already how to assign these types of controllers to our Visualforce page via our `apex:page` tag:

```
<apex:page standardController="Movie__c">
</apex:page>
```

You just assigned the standard logic of the `Movie` object to your page. Let's take a look at what this means for the rest of your page.

Exercise

Let's have a look at the following steps. We will build a little form and save the movie that we added in our form.

1. Go to your Developer Console and create a new page with the name `AddNewMovie`. Assign the standard controller `Movie__c` and add the Lightning stylesheets to your page.

2. If you want to see the Lightning stylesheet, you need to enable your view in Lightning Experience, not in Salesforce Classic.

3. Next, you will add some additional tags to your form (use the `apex:form` tag to create a form).

4. First of all, we want to display error messages or confirm messages. You use the `apex:pageMessages` tag for that.

5. Second, you will add some fields to your form. To add a field, you can group the fields in `apex:pageblock`, `apex:pageblockSection`, and `apex:pageblockSectionItem`. The label of your field is `apex:outputLabel` and the value is available in the object schema, which you can call directly in Visualforce with (`$ObjectType.YourObject__c.fields.YourFieldName__c.Label`). For the input of the values, you need the `apex:inputField` tag. The fields you need to add are as follows:
   - `Name`
   - `Release_Date__c`
   - `Genre__c`
   - `Runtime__c`
   - `Description__c`

6. At the end of the form, add a new section with a button to save the record. This button is a command button.

7. You will find the solution to this at the end of this book, but try this on your own first. It's good practice to make yourself familiar with the most used Visualforce tags.

8. If you've completed the form, you should have something like this:

This is a great form, isn't it? It was only built with the visuals of a standard controller. No extra server (Apex) code was used. Let's try this form out. Fill in some details in your form and save the details you entered. What happens? The record will be saved and returns the Salesforce page with the saved record:

Isn't that great? Well, I'll show you more. What if you configure a validation rule where the genre is required and you don't fill in the kind of movie? You'll expect that the form says, *No, I cannot do that, because...*, and yes, your form will say that, again without any other Apex logic:

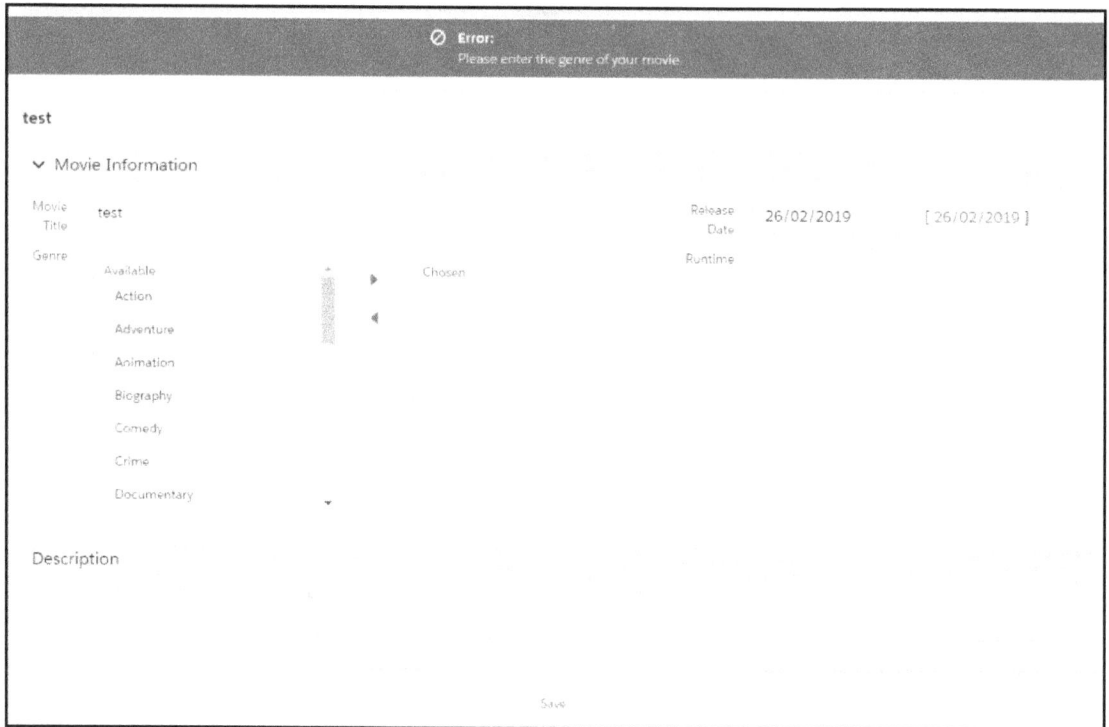

Now, that's the power of a standard controller. You don't need to build extra logic and you are able to define the layout that is required. Let's get to another type of standard controller, where we can handle a list or set of records: these are standard list controllers.

Standard list controllers

Standard list controllers are controllers that handle records in bulk. They are based on the standard object controller, but can also display records from your list.

Let's take a look at the following example:

```
<apex:page standardController="Movie__c" recordSetVar="movies"
tabStyle="Movie__c" lightningStylesheets="true">
    <apex:pageBlock>
```

```
        <apex:pageBlockTable value="{!movies}" var="aMovie">
            <apex:column value="{!aMovie.Name}" />
            <apex:column value="{!aMovie.Genre__c}" />
            <apex:column value="{!aMovie.Runtime__c}" />
        </apex:pageBlockTable>
    </apex:pageBlock>
</apex:page>
```

With this page, I'll display an overview of all the available movies in my database with the genre and the running time. The page will look something like this:

MOVIE TITLE	GENRE	RUNTIME
Grease	Family; Romance	
The Godfather	Crime; Drama	175
The Shawshank Redemption	Drama	142
The Dark Knight	Action; Crime; Drama	152
Schindler's List	Biography; Drama; History	195
Pulp Fiction	Crime; Drama	154
Bumblebee	Action; Adventure; Sci-Fi	113
Batman Begins	Action; Adventure; Thriller	140

You can imagine the possibilities of these standard (list) controllers, but sometimes, a standard controller cannot meet a specific requirement. For that, we can extend our standard controller (and in some cases, we are required to extend the standard controller) with extra logic. That's what we call a controller extension.

Controller extensions

The name says it all. This is an Apex class that extends the functionality of your standard controller. You can insert a new actor into a movie with the standard controller in a Visualforce page, but you need to verify whether this person already exists in our database or not. If the person already exists, you link this existing person to the movie; if not, you need to create them. Maybe you just want to select and display some more information about the related objects. There are many scenarios where you can use an extension on a standard controller:

- Show a Visualforce page when you click on a button. You need to define the standard object controller in your page in the way your button was configured.
- If you want to override standard actions like new, edit, and delete, you need to define the standard object controller regarding the object you want to override the standard action.

- Show a Visualforce page when you want to execute a custom action. You can define a custom action on an object. If you want to show a Visualforce page with this custom action, you need to define the standard object controller of the object where the custom action is configured.
- To add Visualforce pages into a Lightning record page, you have to define the standard object controller of the object where you define the Lightning page.

Working of a controller extension

Let's create a page of a movie with the complete cast on one page. Based on the movie, we will select the cast of the movie and display this cast. We will start with the extension of the controller. We need a class that transfers the details of our movie to a class via the standard controller.

Open your Developer Console and create a new class with the following code:

```
public with sharing class MovieExtension {

    private final Id movieId;
    public Movie__c theMovie {
    get{
    if (this.movieId != null){
    // select the movie and the cast from the Id.
    // We select records always with a list, even if you know it should be
a record.
    // if someone removes the record while you want to select it, you will
receive an exception
        try {
            Movie__c selectedMovie = [SELECT Description__c, Name,
Genre__c,Runtime__c,Release_Date__c,Cover_Url__c,Director__r.Name, (SELECT
Id, Name, Person__r.Name, Rating__c FROM Cast__r) FROM Movie__c WHERE Id =
:this.movieId];
            return selectedMovie;
        } catch (Exception ex){
            ApexPages.addMessage(new
ApexPages.Message(ApexPages.Severity.FATAL, 'Are you sure this movie exists
?'));
        }
    }

    return new Movie__c();
    }
    }

    public MovieExtension(Apexpages.StandardController stdMovie){
```

```
            this.movieId = stdMovie.getId();
    }
}
```

Do you notice anything special about the constructor? Yes, that's correct. Here, we extend our `Movie__c` standard controller. Via the parameter in the constructor, we receive the `Id` of the movie and all the functionality from the `Movie__c` object.

Please analyze the code a little bit with me:

- `private final Id movieId`: I put the received `Id` in a variable so that we can use this `Id` in several methods. This is a `final` variable because it will be set only once, in the constructor.
- `public Movie__c theMovie {get{}}`: This is a special variable. This is what we call a getter. You call the `get` function in the Visualforce page when you display the data (we will look at this later) or if you call the variable. When you want to set a value in the variable, you call the `set` function. In this case, we didn't define the `set` function, because we don't need to set a movie or a parameter at this stage. You can also define this variable in two separate methods: `getTheMovie()` (which requires that you always return an object) and `setTheMovie(value)`.
- **The constructor**: The parameter of the constructor is the record of the movie that calls this page. If you run your Visualforce page on a Lightning page from a movie record, you will receive that movie record in your standard controller parameter. We set this in our `Id` constructor in the constant (the `final` variable) and we call the method to select our movie details with the cast.

Now, create a Visualforce page with the Developer Console and paste in the following code:

```
<apex:page standardController="Movie__c" extensions="MovieExtension"
lightningStylesheets="true">
 <style type="text/css">
 .box-picture {
 box-shadow: 6px 6px rgba(20,20,20,.2);
 border: 1px solid #fff;
 -webkit-border-radius: 10px;
 -moz-border-radius: 10px;
 border-radius: 10px;
 }
 </style>
 <apex:pageBlock>
 <apex:pageBlockSection title="Details movie {!theMovie.Name}"
collapsible="false" columns="2">
```

```
<apex:outputField value="{!theMovie.Genre__c}" />
<apex:outputField value="{!theMovie.Runtime__c}" />
<apex:outputField value="{!theMovie.Director__c}" />
<apex:outputField value="{!theMovie.Release_Date__c}" />
</apex:pageBlockSection>
<apex:pageBlockSection title="The Cast" columns="2">
<apex:pageBlockTable value="{!theMovie.Cast__r}" var="actor">
<apex:column value="{!actor.Name}" />
<apex:column value="{!actor.Person__r.Name}" />
<apex:column value="{!actor.Rating__c}" />
</apex:pageBlockTable>
<apex:outputPanel layout="block" style="text-align: center;">
<apex:image styleClass="box-picture" value="{!theMovie.Cover_Url__c}"
height="400" />
</apex:outputPanel>
</apex:pageBlockSection>
</apex:pageBlock>
</apex:page>
```

Feel free to go into detail regarding this code as well.

I'll explain one important thing in this *extension* context. In any Visualforce page with an extension, you always have a standard controller, as we've seen in this class. This kind of standard controller is mentioned in the Visualforce page. Besides the standard controller, we also defined the extension in the `extension` attribute. `extensions` is the name of the class. You can use more than one extension via a comma-separated list.

Custom controller

Next, after the standard controller and the extensions, you are able to build a full custom controller. You don't need to use the logic from a standard controller or build a complex application with logic over different objects, so you can build custom logic and a full custom user interface to display this data and interact with this data in the MVC framework.

In this example, we will build a controller where the user will fill in the name of a movie, and we will do a callout to the movie DB API to search for movies with this title. In the end, the user can decide which movie he/she wants to insert.

I'll provide you the controller and the Visualforce page in the solutions section (at the end) of this book. The most important things I need to say regarding this custom controller are as follows:

- If you choose to work with a custom controller, you cannot use a standard controller. When you want to use a standard controller, you need to build an extension instead of a custom controller.
- You call the controller in your Visualforce page via the `'controller=''theNameOfYourClass'''` attribute. The class of your custom controller is a class like any other class, with properties (which can contain your data) and methods (the interaction with your user).
- Be aware of security. Custom controllers run in system mode. You need to secure your code, like you learned in the paragraphs about the Apex Security.
- If you link your page to a custom controller, you need a constructor in your controller without any parameter.

Now, let's have a look at the various controller methods.

Controller methods

During the development of your Visualforce page and the custom controller, you are able to use different types of methods. We call these controller methods. These methods are usable in full custom controllers or controller extensions.

You have three types of controller methods:

- Action methods
- Getter methods
- Setter methods

Action methods

Action methods execute logic when an event on the page occurs, such as when a user clicks on a button in the page. Action methods can be called by using the `{!}` notation in the `action` attribute in one of the following tags:

- `<apex:commandButton />`: The user clicks on a button
- `<apex:commandLink />`: The user clicks on a link
- `<apex:actionPoller />`: Calling an action in a certain period

- `<apex:actionSupport />`: Calling an action during an event, like a click, over hovering over an element
- `<apex:actionFunction />`: Define a JavaScript function that calls an action
- `<apex:page />`: Call an action when the page loads

In the following example, you can see the binding between a Visualforce command button and an action method in your controller:

```
public with sharing class MovieExtension{
    /**
     * When the user clicks on the button Submit Movie on the page
     */
    public PageReference submitMovie(){
        try {
            upsert theMovie;
        } catch (DmlException ex){
            ApexPages.addMessage(new
ApexPages.Message(Apexpages.Severity.FATAL, ex.getDmlMessage(0)));
        }
        return null;
    }
}
```

If you create a button in the Visualforce page and the button needs to execute the preceding action, the following code will create that button with the respective action:

```
<apex:commandButton value="Save" action="{!submitMovie}" />
```

Let's have a look at the second variant of the controller action.

Getter actions

The second type of controller actions are getters. You've already learned about the principal of the getter variable in this chapter. When you use a getter, you are able to define a method as well, and get the value of that variable so that you can call the variable of your getter method in your page. The name of this method needs to start with the word `get` and the name of the variable.

The following piece of code will help us get the value of a movie in the `Movie` variable:

```
public Movie__c getTheMovie() {
    if (this.movieId != null){
        // select the movie and the cast from the Id.
        // We always select records with a list, even if you know it should
    be a record.
```

```
        // if someone removes the record while you want to select it, you
will receive an exception
        try {
            Movie__c selectedMovie = [SELECT Description__c, Name,
Genre__c,Runtime__c,Release_Date__c,Cover_Url__c,Director__r.Name, (SELECT
Id, Name, Person__r.Name, Rating__c FROM Cast__r) FROM Movie__c WHERE Id =
:THIS.movieId];
            return selectedMovie;
        } catch (Exception ex){
            ApexPages.addMessage(new
ApexPages.Message(ApexPages.Severity.FATAL, 'Are you sure this movie exists
?'));
        }
    }
    return new Movie__c();
}
```

When you call the variable in your page, you define it like this:

```
<apex:outputField value="{!TheMovie.Name}" />
```

Apart from getter methods, you also have the ability to set any variables with the setter methods.

Setter methods

Setter methods pass values from the page to a controller, for example, the values of an input field. Any setter method in a controller is automatically executed before any action methods. The setter method has the same naming convention as the getter method, except `set` (to set a value in your property) is used instead of `get` (to return the data from your property). The name of the method should start with `set` and the name of the variable.

In the following code, we will set a search value:

```
private String searchString;
public void setSearchString(String sMovie){
    this.searchString = sMovie;
}
```

To set the variable in the page, we define an input field with the value of the `searchMovie` variable:

```
<apex:inputText id={!search}" value="{!searchString}" />
```

I need to mention that you need to be careful with these kinds of methods since there is no guarantee in which order the Apex methods and variables are processed by the extension or controller. It's good practice to call controller methods directly, so that you get the correct information. This applies specifically to setting variables and accessing data from the database.

Validation rules and custom controllers

When a user enters data in your Visualforce page because your form is built with the `apex:inputField` tag and the data will be incorrect due to custom validation rules, you can display your (error) messages in your page using the `apex:(page)messages` tag. In the following example, we only define the field name and a **Save** button. If you don't enter a name, the validation will fail and you'll receive an error on your page.

The following code is for the custom controller:

```
public class MyCustomController {
    private Movie__c movie;

    public PageReference save() {
        try{
            update movie;
        } catch(DmlException ex){
            ApexPages.addMessages(ex);
        }
        return null;
    }

    public String getName() {
        return 'MyController';
    }

    public Movie__c getMovie() {
        if(this.movie == null){
            this.movie = [SELECT Id,Genre__c, Name FROM Movie__c WHERE Id =
    :ApexPages.currentPage().getParameters().get('id')];
        }
        return this.movie;
    }
}
```

The code for the Visualforce page is as follows:

```
<apex:page controller="MyCustomController" tabStyle="Movie__c">
    <apex:pagemessages/>
    <apex:form>
        <apex:pageBlock title="Hello {!$User.FirstName}!">
            This is your new page for the {!name} controller. <br/>
            Change Movie Details: <p></p>
            <apex:inputField value="{!movie.name}"/> <br />
            <apex:inputField value="{!movie.Genre__c}" /><p></p>
            <apex:commandButton action="{!save}" value="Save New Movie
Title"/>
        </apex:pageBlock>
    </apex:form>
</apex:page>
```

Go to the page and add the following parameter to `url:id=` + `an account Id`. The
complete URL should be something like
this: `https://...salesforce.com/apex/YOURPAGENAME?id=A_Movie_Id` (for
example,
`https://devbook-dev-ed--c.visualforce.com/apex/MycustomPage?id=a001t000`
`002cT7nAAE`).

Remove the genres from this and try and save it. What do you see? Indeed, an error
message. You should see something like this:

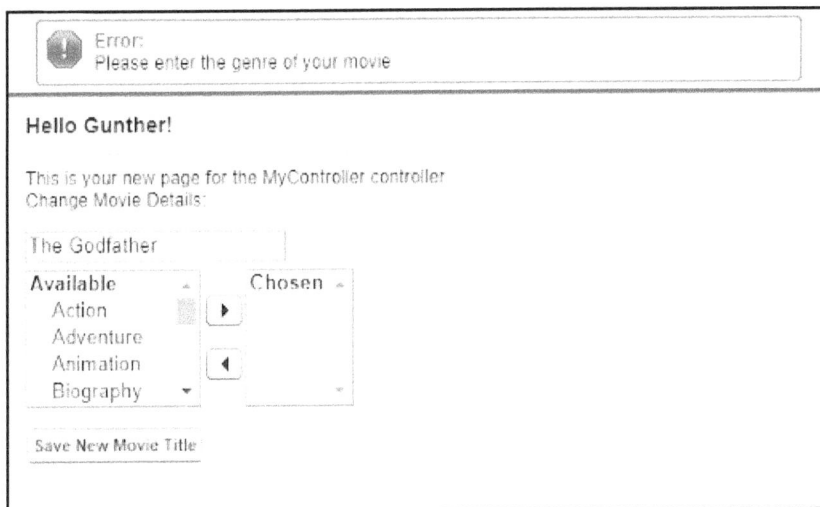

The difference between the `apex:messages` tag and `apex:pageMessages` is in the styling. In the `apex:messages` tag, you need to add some custom styling, whereas in `apex:pagemessages`, the styling is already there.

Web content in Visualforce

Visualforce pages use a lot of tags, which render their own HTML. Sometimes, you need an HTML tag that you cannot find in the standard Visualforce components. In your Visualforce pages, you are able to use all the HTML tags and attributes when you're displaying your data or building interactions with the users of your application.

You can also use JavaScript (frameworks) or standard and custom CSS styles in your pages. You are even able to combine the Visualforce tags and HTML tags to give your user interface or your data just a little touch-up.

Static resources

It's good practice to use custom CSS and JavaScript frameworks or images when you're using static resources. These resources can be a zipped folder where you collected your images, or different JavaScript and/or stylesheet in one file. You can use this file in your Visualforce page with the global variable `$Resource`. Let's do this now:

1. Add a static resource in Salesforce via the **Setup** menu in the **Static Resources** section.
2. Give the resource a valid name (we will use this name in our Visualforce page) and upload your (ZIP) file:

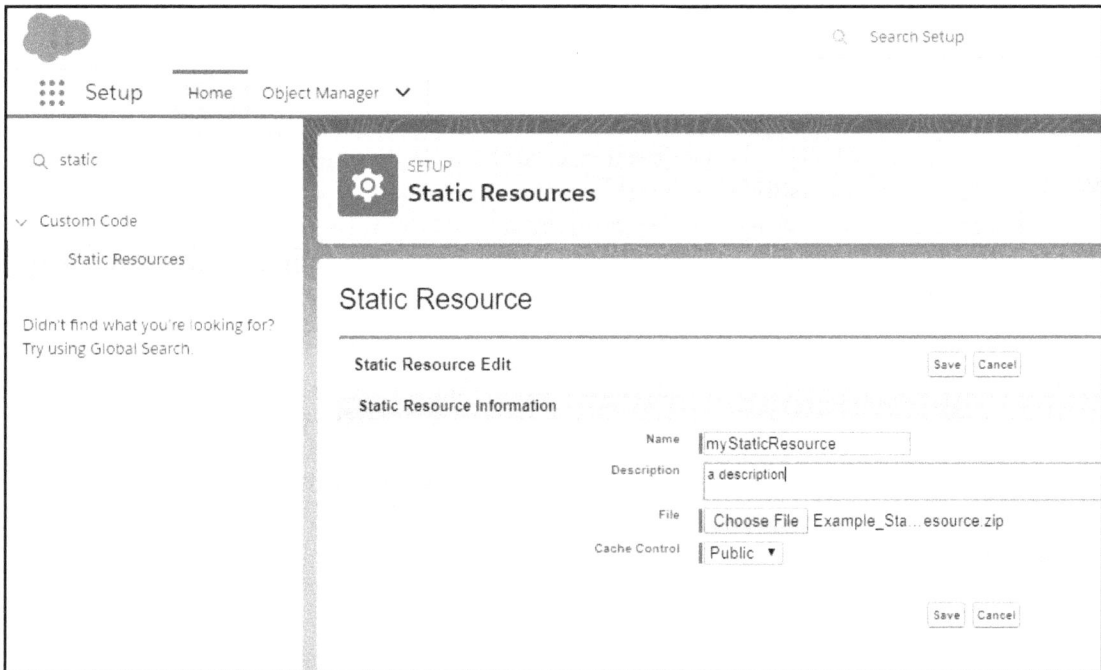

In the following code example, we use this static resource. The complete resource is a ZIP file with a folder called `js` and a folder called `css`. In the `css` folder, we added a file with the name `customCSS.css`.

3. Now, add our static resource via the `<apex:includeScript />` (for JavaScript) or `<apex:stylesheet />` tag for a supplementary stylesheet. Remember, if you only want to use this stylesheet, don't forget to disable the standard stylesheet in your `apex:page-tag`:

```
<apex:page standardStylesheets="false">
 <apex:includeScript value="{!URLFOR($Resource.myStaticResource,
'/js/customJavascript.js')}" />
 <apex:stylesheet value="{!URLFOR($Resource.myStaticResource,
'/css/customCSS.css')}" />
</apex:page>
```

We will now have a look at how we can incorporate a Visualforce page into Force.com.

Incorporating Visualforce pages into Force.com

Now that we are able to create a Visualforce page, we are ready to create a full Force.com (https://www.salesforce.com/products/platform/products/force/?d=70130000000f27V internal=true) site. This site can be used as a public website or in a custom community. You are able to use an existing domain (like salesforce-developer-1-certification.com) and register this domain in Salesforce. The registration of a custom domain (like for a branded website) is a small and technical procedure. You can find more information about this topic here: https://help.salesforce.com/articleView?id=sites_creating_subdomain.htmtype=5.

When you register your domain in Salesforce and define a custom site, you have the ability to develop several Visualforce pages and drop them in a site with your own domain.

> **Watch out**: This functionality is not available in developer organizations.

Force.com sites

With Force.com (https://www.salesforce.com/products/platform/products/force/?d=70130000000f27Vinternal=true) sites, you are able to configure and build a full website. You'll also have the ability to use standard templates. Of course, you are able to use your own stylesheet and colors to build a nice and neat website:

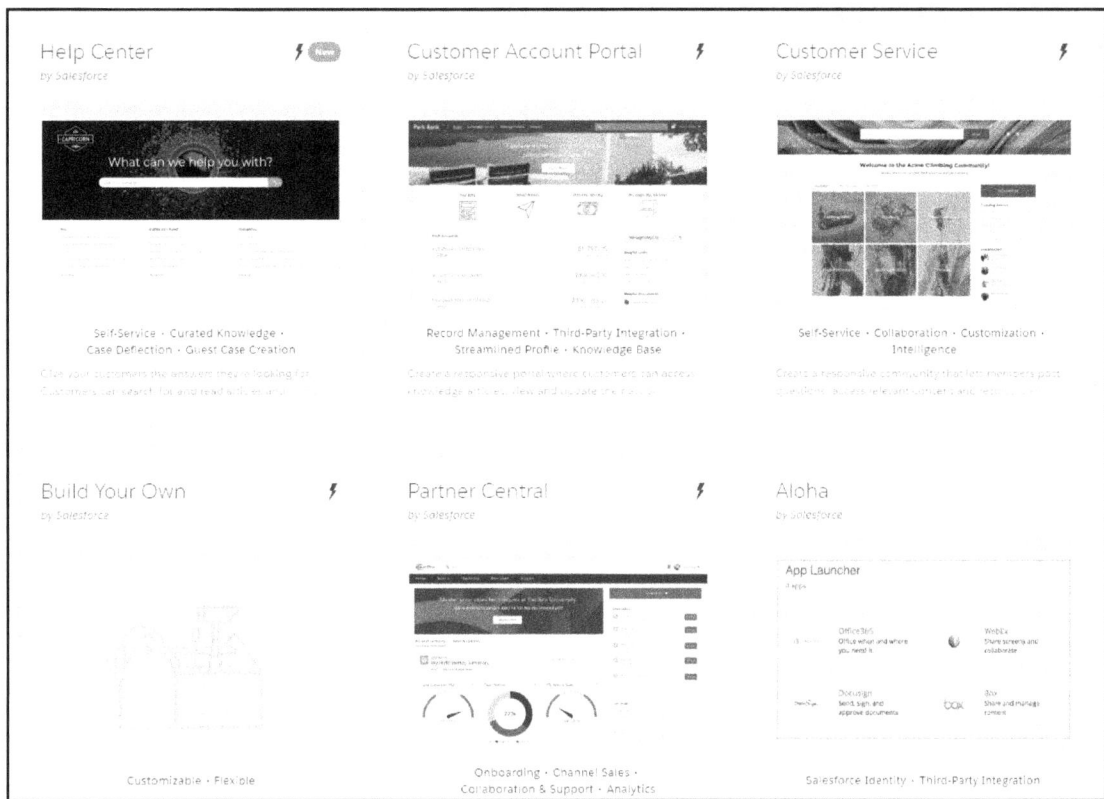

Configuration of a site

Force.com sites will be used to define your own corporate website, with several Visualforce pages, Lightning pages, Visualforce components, and Lightning components. But what about your data? What if a user on your website cannot access your data without logging in to Salesforce?

With Force.com sites, you can configure the following things:

- What a user can see when he/she isn't logged in
- Which type of data or which records can be accessed

Each Force.com site has a kind of guest user with guest access, and this guest access has access to the objects and records you configure.

I will not go into depth about the Force.com sites. All you need to know is that this exists and how to set up a basic configuration. The basic configuration includes the public access settings, such as guest access:

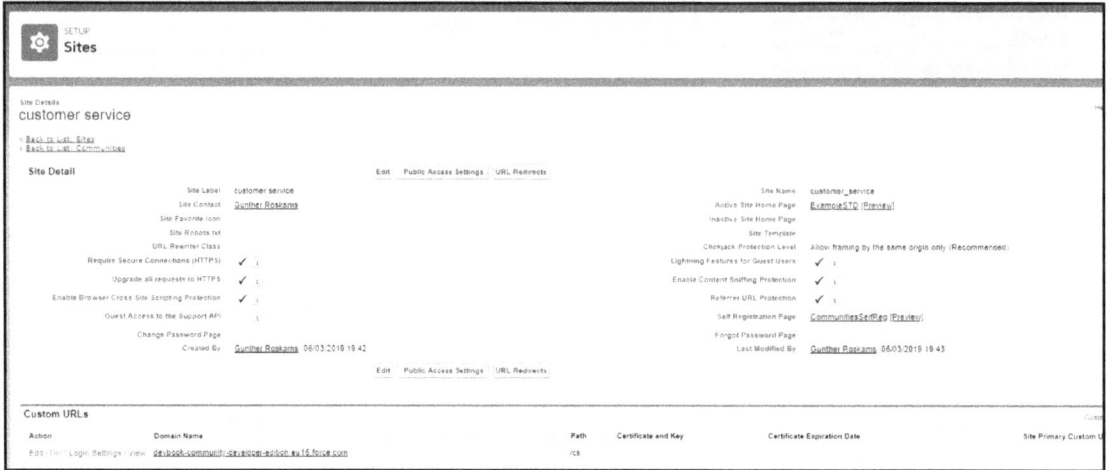

You can configure the public access settings, just like a profile or permission set. The access settings are more or less the same as a permission set, except for some access for the standard objects, such as accounts, contacts, and opportunities:

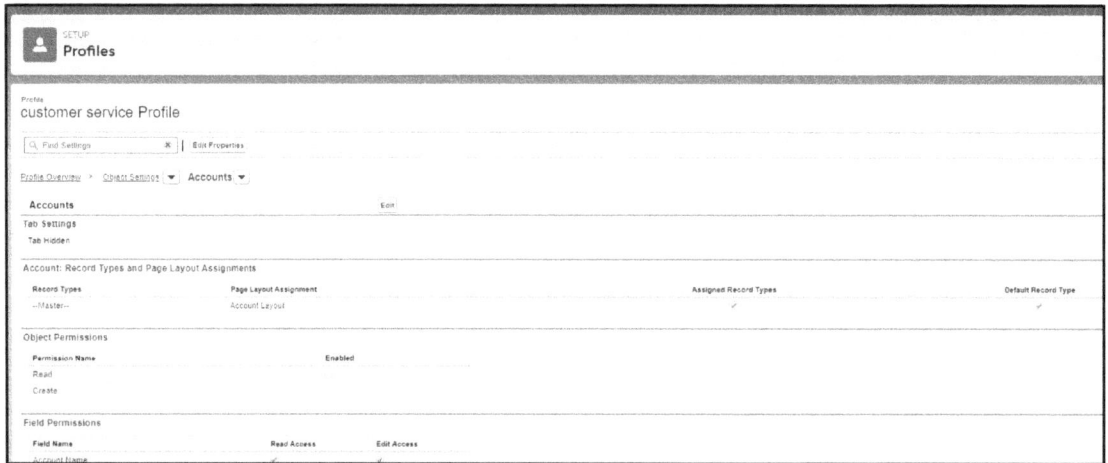

As we mentioned previously, a Force.com site is built with Visualforce pages or Lightning components. You can define the content of your site in the guest access (the visuals that are accessible without having to log in) or behind a login screen.

In the public access configuration, you define the pages that are accessible in the guest mode:

In the site configuration, you define all your pages:

Site Visualforce Pages

Visualforce Page Name

BandwidthExceeded

CommunitiesLanding

CommunitiesLogin

CommunitiesSelfReg

CommunitiesSelfRegConfirm

CommunitiesTemplate

ExampleSTD

Exception

FileNotFound

ForgotPassword

ForgotPasswordConfirm

InMaintenance

SiteLogin

SiteRegister

SiteRegisterConfirm

UnderConstruction

Now, I'll now show you another kind of visualization of your data—the Lightning components.

Lightning Component framework

The Lightning Component framework is a framework that's used for developing single-page web applications for mobile and desktop devices. Lightning components can be built by using two programming models:

- **Lightning web components**: These are custom HTML elements that are built using HTML and modern JavaScript.
- **Aura components**: These use JavaScript and predefined components, combined with HTML tags. You can use both components next to each other on one Lightning page.

In this book, I will not go too much into detail about this subject, because discussing the Lightning Component framework would take a book on its own. Instead, I will teach you the high-level basics of the Lightning Component framework and the most important things you need to know about regarding a Lightning component.

My Domain

First things first: if you want to start developing Lightning components, you are required to activate **My Domain** on your org. You probably saw in several screenshots in this book that the URL is `https://devbook-dev-ed.lightning.force.com`. The domain of this organization is **devbook-dev-ed** (the **dev-ed** suffix is only for developer editions), and we activated this domain for our users.

You can activate your organization domain in the **My Domain** section of the setup console:

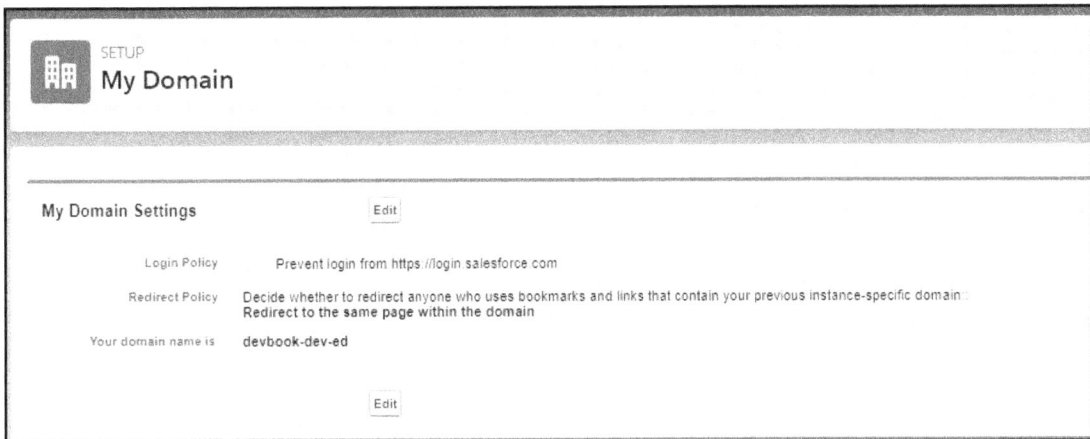

Now, we will look at the benefits of the Lightning Component framework.

Benefits of the Lightning Component framework

We've just seen how we can visualize our data in a Visualforce page or a Visualforce component. You must be thinking about why you should use a Lightning component while you can develop a Visualforce page. There are many benefits to using Lightning components.

The following is a small overview of some of these benefits:

- **Out of the box components**: The Lightning Component framework comes with pre-built, out of the box components. You don't need to spend time creating a little framework to display a calendar when a user needs to fill in a date in a form because it's already there.
- **Components ecosystem**: You are able to build full apps and share these with other users or customers, or you can build small components and reuse these components on different pages.
- **Cross-browser compatibility**: Lightning components can be used in any modern browser that supports HTML 5, CSS 3, and touch events. The apps or components you build have a responsive design with the styles of the Lightning design system. We will create a Lightning component in the upcoming sections, but first, we will discuss the different resources that are available in a Lightning component.
- **Events**: The Lightning Component framework uses event-driven programming, which means that you develop handlers that respond to interface events when they occur. You have two types of events:
  - **Component events**: Events are handled by the component itself or a component that initiates or contains the component from the event.
  - **Application events**: Events are handled by each component that is listening to the event.

Event handlers are written in JavaScript, in the controller of your Lightning component.

Resources in a Lightning component

You are able to build a Lightning component in your favorite Salesforce IDE, but you can use the Developer Console as well. As usual, I will explain how to use the Developer Console to create these kinds of resources, but don't hesitate to use your own (and favorite) IDE.

To start the development for a Lightning component, open the **Developer Console** and click **File | New | Lightning Component**:

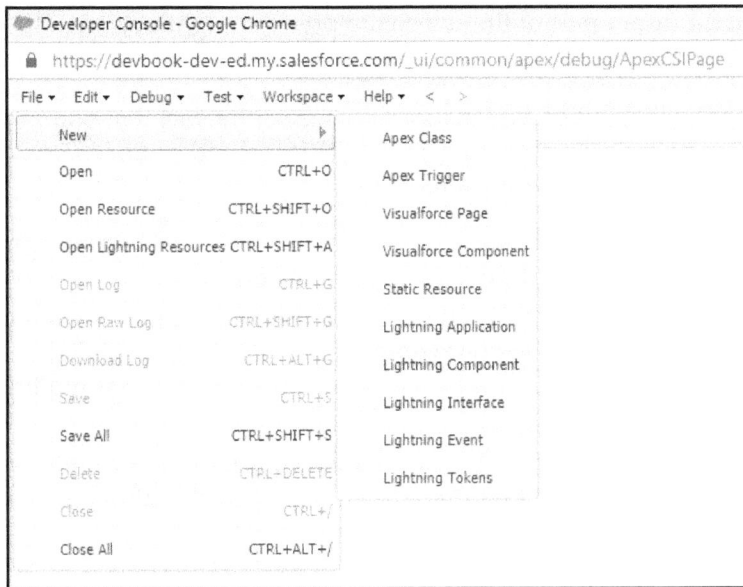

You will see a little screen with the name **New Lightning Bundle**. Yes—a Lightning component is a bundle of some files. We will go in-depth on each type of file in each component soon, but first, we will start by explaining this little screen:

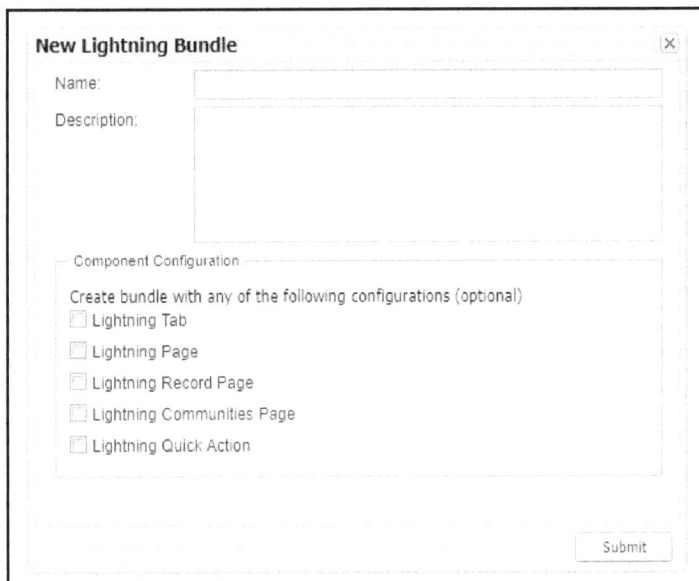

The two fields in the upper part of the screen are pretty straightforward—these are for the name of your component and a little description.

The next part needs a little bit of explanation. Because of the fact that you can use a Lightning component in different circumstances, you can add some optional configurations to your component, which adds some interfaces:

- **Lightning Tab**: Your component can be used in the tabbed navigation and adds the `appHostable` interface to your component.
- **Lightning Page**: Your component can be used in a Lightning home page. The interface that is added to your component is `flexipage:availableForAllPageTypes`, and the access modifier for the component is set to `global`.
- **Lightning Record Page**: Your component can be used in a Lightning page for a record (like an account Lightning page, or a contact Lightning page). The interfaces that are added to your component are `flexipage:availableForRecordHome` and `force:hasRecordId`. This last interface is a very nice interface, and it makes life easy when you want to retrieve the record ID of the record in your Lightning page. The access modifier of the component is set to global.
- **Lightning Communities Page**: Your component can be used in a Lightning page that is used in a community. The interface that's added to your component is `forceCommunity:availableForAllPageTypes`. The access modifier of your component is set to `global`.
- **Lightning Quick Action**: Your component can be used as a custom Lightning quick action. When you push on the button of a custom quick action, you are able to launch a Lightning component. The interface that's added is `force:lightningQuickAction`.

Fill in the name `MovieComponent` and a little description, activate the **Lightning Record Page** and **Lightning Quick Action**, and click **Submit**.

Great! You've just created your first Lightning component. Now, we will add some content to the component. Let's have a look at what we've just created:

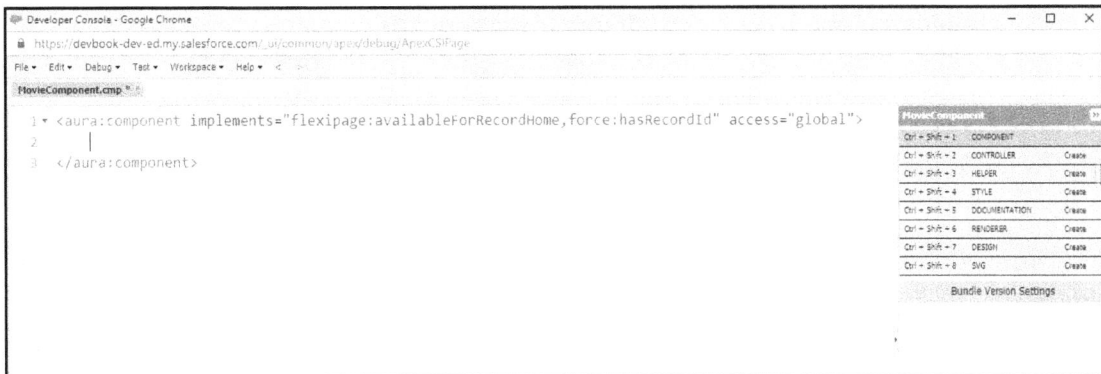

Right, an empty component. But if you did everything fine, you'll see the subcomponents of your Lightning component on the right-hand side of the screen. Let's discuss the different parts:

- **Component**: This is your master component. This part is required for each Lightning component. Here, you will put the component markup, like references to other components, HTML, Lightning component tags from the Lightning Component framework library, and so on. This part of the component has the suffix `.cmp`.

- **Controller**: This is the JavaScript client-side controller of your component. Here, you will define client-side actions based on events or the initialization of your component. In this part, you will only write JavaScript and the suffix will be `.js`.

- **Helper**: The same way you develop classes with methods is the same way you will develop helper methods. These methods support your main classes with some supplementary small common logic chunks of executable code, such as selecting some data, performing a callout, and so on. During the development of Lightning components, we will be using a JavaScript helper method to support our JavaScript controller. As we've seen in the controller, you can only write JavaScript in this part of your Lightning component.

- **Style**: Of course, you can use the default styling of Lightning components, which is the Lightning design system. However, you may want to build customer branded Lightning applications or components. That's why the component has a styling part. Within this part, you can give your component its own styling. Like the styling of an HTML page, we use the suffix `.css` in the Lightning component.

- **Documentation**: This is the most boring part of the component, but necessary. You can define a description or an example of the use of the component. The suffix for this part of the component is `.auradoc`.

- **Renderer**: You have the possibility to override the default rendering of your component. Because of the fact that this is a client-side custom renderer, you only write JavaScript in this part of your component. The suffix for this part of your component is `.js`.
- **Design**: This is a required part when you use your component in a Lightning page, in the Lightning App Builder, Community Builder, or Flow Builder. In this design file, you can define some configuration of your component and which object is supported for your component. If you want to use your component in an `Account` object, you can define this in the design part of your component. The suffix for this part of your component is `.design`.
- **Svg**: The last part of your component is `svg`. This file is the custom icon of your component. If you don't define an icon, the default icon of Lightning Experience is shown in the list, along with its available components. The suffix of this part of the component is `.svg`.

Now that we know all the parts of a Lightning component, we'll build a small component that shows you the big difference between Visualforce components (which are small Visualforce pages) and these Lightning components.

Component attributes

The variables of your Lightning component are called **attributes**. A Visualforce component also has attributes, but the main difference is that the attributes of a Lightning component can be filled in at the runtime of your component (when a user enters some information in a form), or when the user is calling an action by pressing a button.

Let's take a look at the following component with the name `HelloWorld.cmp`:

```
<aura:component
implements="flexipage:availableForRecordHome,force:hasRecordId"
access="global">            <aura:attribute name="message" type="String"
default="World" />
    <p>Hello {!v.message}</p>
</aura:component>
```

In this example, the output in your component will be `Hello World`. We've defined an attribute in our component and displayed the value of that attribute in the body of the component. If we use this component in another component, we can define the attribute of the component in the attributes, like so:

```
<aura:component
implements="flexipage:availableForRecordHome,force:hasRecordId"
```

```
    access="global">
        <c:MovieComponent message="TestMessage" />
    </aura:component>
```

I extended the `MovieComponent` that you created earlier with the first code block (see the preceding code block) and created a second component with the name `MovieDependent` with the second code block (see the preceding code block). Now, you'll be able to drag the second component onto the movie Lightning page and save it. You will see `Hello TestMessage` as a message in your component. So, depending on the content of your attribute, the content of your attribute will be displayed on your component:

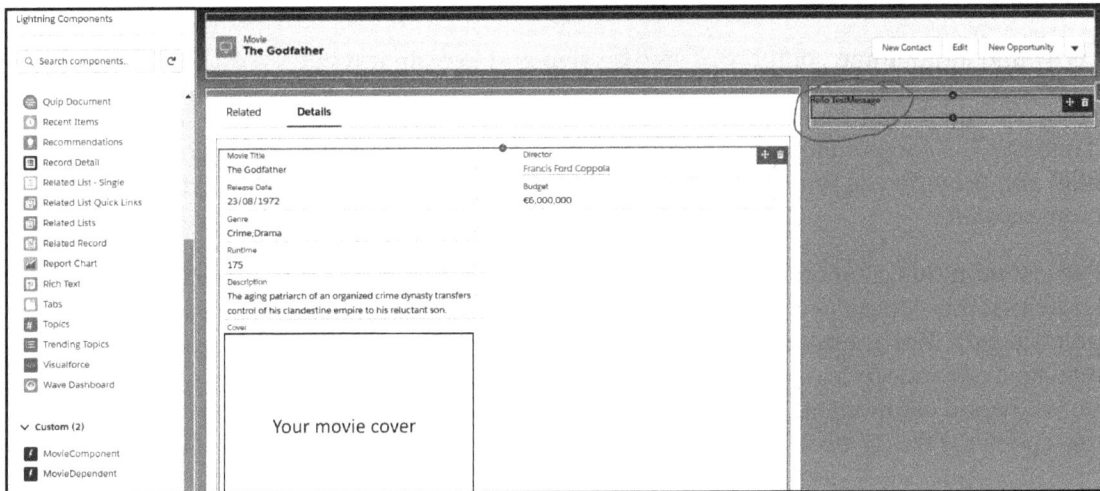

Here, you have learned how to use (and reuse) your existing Lightning components. Let's dig a bit deeper into the different tags of a component body and discover how we can use all these types of tags.

Expressions

To visualize our attribute in the component, we used an expression. The `message` attribute is displayed as an expression, like `{!v.message}`. It's just a formula or calculation that's displayed in a textbox, a panel, or a layer.

The expressions are not only used for display purposes but also when you want to execute a method from your JavaScript controller. For example, `{!c.handleMyEvent}` in the `onclick` attribute of a button will handle the method with the name `handleMyEvent` in your component controller.

Value providers

You've just seen the different prefixes to call a method or display some variables. We call these prefixes value providers. Let's have a look at the different value providers:

- **v**: The *v* (like `{!v.message}`) stands for view. You will display the data after the provider. In this case, this is the value of the attribute `message`.
- **c**: The c (like `{!c.handleMyEvent}`) stands for controller. You will call a function from the JavaScript controller in your component, or from an outside Apex class into your JavaScript controller or helper. You can call a custom event from this value provider with `c:myEvent`.

Let's build a Lightning component step by step and explain it while we do so.

We will build a Lightning component that will call service and add a movie into your database. The component will give you the possibility to search for a movie (based on its title) and provide you with several options. The user has the choice of importing one or more movies.

I've just built this component to let you discover the basics of a Lightning component. I know that this component can be improved by a lot of functionalities. You can already practice with this, and please feel free to improve your component with duplicate management, design features, a spinner during loading, and by processing your data. We saved the full component, controller, and files in a code repository. You can download all this code (it is free to use) via `https://github.com/PacktPublishing/Salesforce-Platform-Developer-I-Certification-Guide`.

The component

During the development of this component, we will override the standard action `New` in the `Movie` object, so we need to build some kind of a modal. (It looks like an alert window, but it's a little bit fancier.) Due to the restrictions that the modal is not shown while you override a standard action with a Lightning component, we need to build a *modal* like a page with some components.

We need to build two components: our modal and an SVG component. We will start with the SVG component, which will display an icon of the Lightning design system (`https://www.lightningdesignsystem.com/icons/`). The icon can be displayed on a button, or, in our case, it is the closing icon of our modal window.

Let's build this little component:

1. First of all, we need to define a static resource of the icons that are used in the Lightning design system. Due to the modal window close button, we need to display the icon to close the modal. (Actually, we navigate to the home page of the object.)
2. Browse to the repository and download the ZIP file in the static resource folder.
3. Create a static resource. (You can name it whatever you want, but the name needs to correspond with the name in your component.) We've named it `slds_283`. (At the time of writing, the Lightning design system version was 2.8.3.)
4. Now, to build the first component, open your developer console and create a new Lightning component. Name it `svgIcon`. In this component, copy and paste the following code (I will explain this later):

```
<aura:component description="svgIcon">
    <aura:attribute name="svgPath" default="" type="String"
description="the icon path in the static resource, used in the SVG
use tag" />
    <aura:attribute name="name" default="" type="String"
description="Name of the  icon symbol" />
    <aura:attribute name="class" default="" type="String"
description="the style class of the SVG tag" />
    <aura:attribute name="containerClass" default="" type="String"
description="Container class name for span container of icon" />
    <aura:attribute name="category" default="" type="String"
description="Category of icon- action, standard, utility etc." />
    <aura:attribute name="size" default="" type="String"
description="Size of icon-- small, medium, large" />
    <aura:attribute name="assistiveText" default="" type="String"
description="Description name of icon" />
    <span aura:id="container" class="{!v.containerClass}">
        <span aura:id="assistiveText" class="slds-assistive-
text">{!v.assistiveText}</span>
    </span>
</aura:component>
```

We've defined some attributes to configure our component:

- `svgPath`: The path of the icon in your static resource.
- `name`: The symbol name of your icon. Each icon is built with a directory (category) and a name. We will use the *close* icon of the `utility-sprite` folder.

- `class`: A special style class for your icon (for instance, if you want to display your icon in the color red).
- `containerClass`: A style class for your icon container.
- `category`: The category of your icon (standard, utility, action).
- `size`: The size of your icon (small, medium, large).
- `assistiveText`: The text when you hover over the icon; most of the time, this is a small description of (the functionality of) the icon.

It's good practice to give your attributes a description so that you can document your component. This way, any developer knows which attributes are there for which reason.

5. After all of these definitions, we define the content (the body) of our component. The component is just a container and the text of the icon. We render the icon in a renderer. I'll show you how to do this now.

6. Save your code and click on the right-hand side panel of your developer console on **Renderer**:

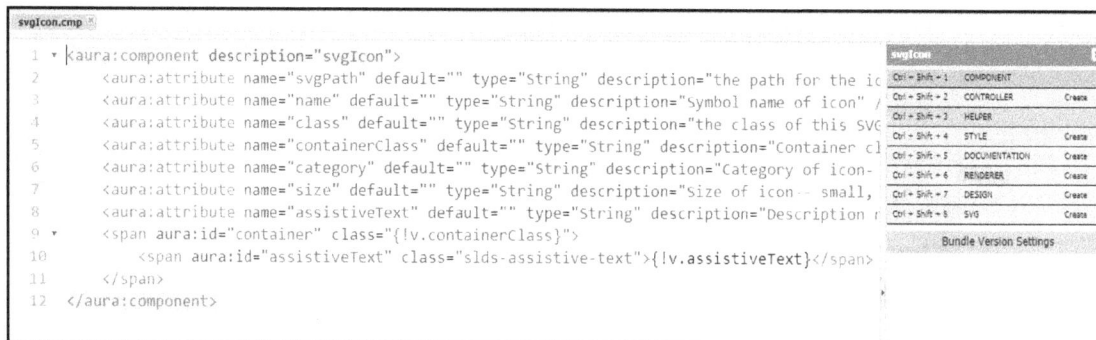

We receive a second screen with the start of our renderer code, which is just some curly brackets. We will copy and paste some code soon, but what is the functionality of this renderer part?

The renderer

The renderer of our component will render the icon that we configured in our parent component. In this part of the component, only a few methods are supported.

This is due to the renderer life cycle of your component:

- **Render**: Execute JavaScript logic during the rendering of the component.
- **afterRender**: Execute JavaScript logic after the rendering of your component is completed.
- **reRender**: Execute JavaScript logic after a Lightning event occurs. The components in your component that contain modified data will be re-rendered.

In the renderer part of your component, copy and paste the following code between the curly brackets and save it:

```
render: function(component, helper) {
    // By default, after the component finished loading data/handling
events,
    // it will call this render function this.superRender() will call the
    // render function in the parent component.
    var ret = this.superRender();

    // Calls the helper function to append the SVG icon
    helper.renderIcon(component);
    return ret;
}
```

In these few lines of code, we've created a method to render an icon in the component. A helper (in the second line) will help us to create this icon in the component rendering.

This is also one of the best practices during Lightning components development. A helper method is a method in JavaScript that you can reuse in each part of your component. With the `helper` attribute in your controller or renderer method, you will call the helper part of your component. Of course, helper methods are reusable in other helper methods, too.

At this stage, we don't have any helpers, but we will write one soon.

The Helper

Click in the left navigation and click on **Helper**. This is the same screen that was shown in the renderer part. Copy and paste the following code into this helper part of your component (again, between the curly brackets):

```
renderIcon: function(component) {
    var prefix = "slds-";
    var svgns = "http://www.w3.org/2000/svg";
    var xlinkns = "http://www.w3.org/1999/xlink";
    var size = component.get("v.size");
    var name = component.get("v.name");
```

```
    var classname = component.get("v.class");
    var containerclass = component.get("v.containerClass");
    var category = component.get("v.category");

    var containerClassName = [
        prefix+"icon_container",
        prefix+"icon-"+category+"-"+name,
        containerclass
        ].join(' ');
    component.set("v.containerClass", containerClassName);

    var svgroot = document.createElementNS(svgns, "svg");
    var iconClassName = prefix+"icon "+prefix+"icon--" + size+"
"+classname;
    svgroot.setAttribute("aria-hidden", "true");
    svgroot.setAttribute("class", iconClassName);
    svgroot.setAttribute("name", name);

    // Add an "href" attribute (using the "xlink" namespace)
    var shape = document.createElementNS(svgns, "use");
    shape.setAttributeNS(xlinkns, "href", component.get("v.svgPath"));
    svgroot.appendChild(shape);

    var container = component.find("container").getElement();
    container.insertBefore(svgroot, container.firstChild);
}
```

Save this code in the Developer Console.

Now, you have a reusable component so that you can display an icon in a screen, a button, and you can embed this component in several other components that you will build later on. We will reuse this component to display the close button on our New Movie modal. Let's build the second component.

We'll use the component that you created at the beginning of this chapter regarding Lightning components, that is, the MovieComponent component. In the Developer Console, click on **File (1)**| **Open Lightning Resource (2)**, click on the arrow next to the **c:MovieComponent** directory (3), and click on the **COMPONENT** part. Click on **Open Selected**-button (4) to open the component:

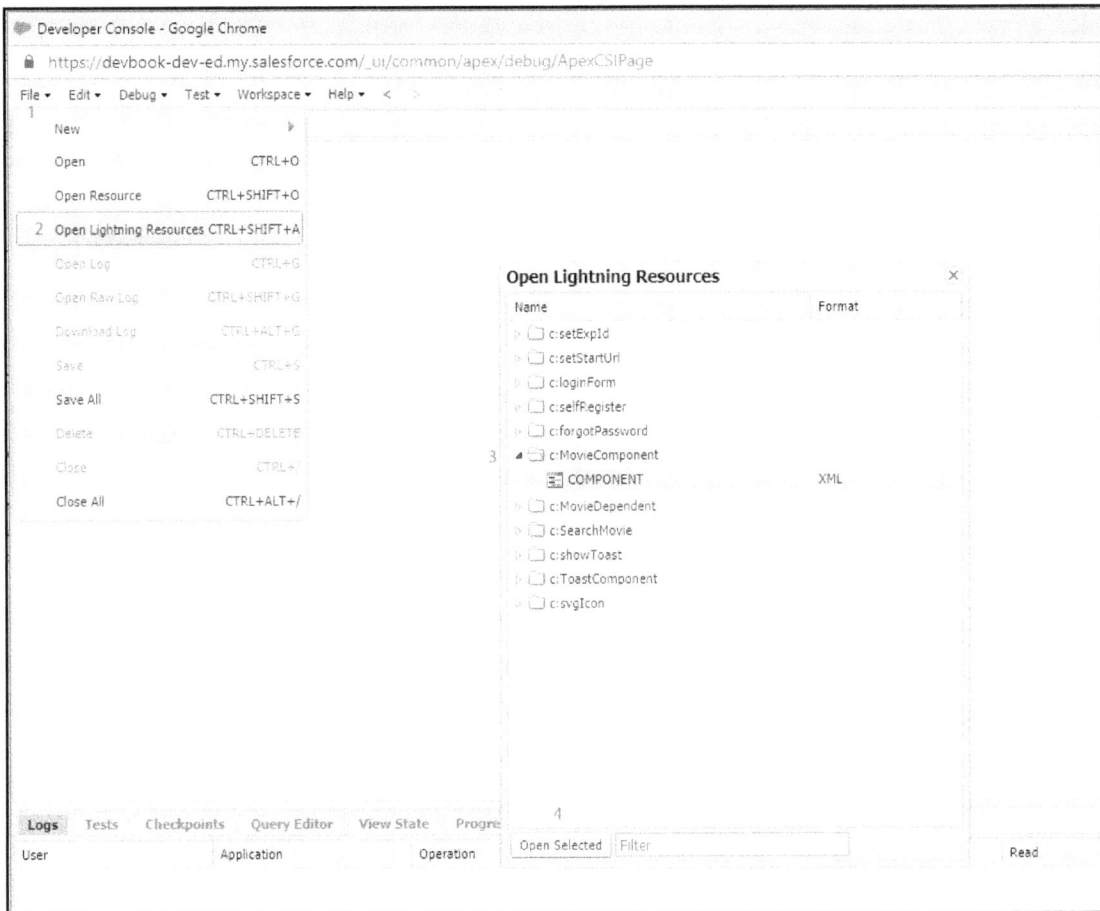

A screen will open with the component you've created.

Let's create the attributes for our movie insert. I hope you can do this by yourself by now. So, let's complete this exercise and create the following attributes in your component:

Name	Type	Default value
SearchCriteria	String	Empty string
lstMovies	List	NA
lstSelectedMovies	List	NA
search	Boolean	False
numberOfMovies	Integer	0

Don't forget to add a small description (at the end of this book, you'll find the solution with the description). After the creation of the attributes, we will create the design of our modal. Copy and paste the following code after your attributes:

```
<div aura:id="editDialog" role="dialog" tabindex="-1" aria-
labelledby="header43" class="slds-modal slds-fade-in-open">
        <div class="slds-modal__container">
            <div class="slds-modal__header">
                <button class="slds-button slds-button_icon slds-
modal__close slds-button_icon-inverse" title="Close"
onclick="{!c.closeModal}">
                    <c:svgIcon svgPath="/resource/slds_283/utility-
sprite/svg/symbols.svg#close" category="utility" size="small" name="close"
class="slds-button__icon slds-button__icon_large" />
                    <span class="slds-assistive-text">Close</span>
                </button>
                <h2 id="modal-heading-01" class="slds-text-heading_medium
slds-hyphenate">Insert new movie</h2>
            </div>
            <div class="slds-modal__content slds-p-around--medium slds-grid
slds-wrap">
            </div>
            <div class="slds-modal__footer">
            </div>
        </div>
    </div>
<div aura:id="overlay" class="slds-backdrop slds-backdrop--open"></div>
```

I think this full code needs some explanation. During the creation of this code, I used a lot of default functionalities of the Lightning framework to give you an idea of what's possible in this framework out of the box. Now, let's take a look at the code:

```
<div aura:id="editDialog" role="dialog" tabindex="-1" aria-
labelledby="header43" class="slds-modal slds-fade-in-open">
```

If you are familiar with HTML, you definitely know the `div` tag. As we saw at the very beginning of the Lightning components section, the body of your component can be a mix of `aura` tags and standard HTML tags. In the preceding code, I've used the `div` tags in combination with an `aura` ID. With this `Id`, you can reference the element with the respective aura `Id` in your component via the JavaScript command `component.find('yourAuraId')`:

```
var myDiv = component.find('editDialog');
```

The second remark in this code is the usage of the `slds` classes. When you develop a Lightning component, the Lightning design system is automatically added as a stylesheet so we can use these Lightning stylesheets and classes. In this case, I've used the `css` classes to display a modal window:

```
<button class="slds-button slds-button_icon slds-modal__close slds-
button_icon-inverse" title="Close" onclick="{!c.closeModal}">
 <c:svgIcon svgPath="/resource/slds_283/utility-
sprite/svg/symbols.svg#close" category="utility" size="small" name="close"
class="slds-button__icon slds-button__icon_large" />
 <span class="slds-assistive-text">Close</span>
</button>
```

In this code, I've displayed a button to close our modal screen. In our case, we just navigate to the home page of the `Movie__c` object when we click on it, which is basically the tab page. I'll come back later to how we can navigate a Lightning component with an event.

The component that we built earlier is embedded in our `MovieComponent`. We've embedded the component via the `<c:` tag and the name of our component. Besides that, we've configured the component with the `svgPath` attributes (the path of our static resource and directory in the resource). Here, you can see the name of our static resource (`slds_283`). However, if you've named your static resource another way, you need to adopt the name in this link.

The very special thing in this piece of code is the `onclick` handler of the button. When a user clicks this button, some functionality needs to run. This is always defined in the JavaScript controller of your component. The controller can call a helper if needed.

In this case, we need to build a method with the name `closeModal`, the controller of our component. We will do that later when we create the controller of our component.

The rest of the code is more `div` tags (which is a kind of a layer in HTML), where we'll put some extra code later. As you can see, every `div` tag in the component is provided with a SLDS style class. Each SLDS style class is coming from the Lightning Experience styling sheet (the Lightning design system) and will style every little piece in your component.

More information about the different CSS styles in the Lightning design system can be found via `https://www.lightningdesignsystem.com/`.

The client-side controller

Let's build the client-side JavaScript controller for our component. We've just seen the call to the functionality to close the modal in the component, so let's write this code in our controller:

1. In the Developer Console, in the navigation of the component (on the right-hand side of the screen), click on the **Controller** link to write this part of our controller.
2. Again, we need to write our JavaScript methods between the two curly brackets.
3. Copy and paste the following code between the brackets:

```
closeModal: function(component, event, helper){
    var navToMovieTab = $A.get("e.force:navigateToObjectHome");
    navToMovieTab.setParams({
        "scope": "Movie__c"
    });
    navToMovieTab.fire();
}
```

In this small method, we call a standard event. You have a lot of standard events, like show a message (in Lightning, we call this *displaying a toast message*), navigate to a record, and navigate to a page. You can find every single standard event within the documentation in the Lightning component library's events section: `https://developer.salesforce.com/docs/component-library/overview/events`. The standard events are triggered by the application most of the time, and you can identify it via the `$A.get(event)` prefix instead of with `component.get(event)`. Custom component events can be called via the component.

Okay – now that we have a modal component without any content, let's add the content.

Server-side controller

Before we enrich the component with the code of the search movies functionality, we need to define some server-side actions. Due to several limits in regards to making callouts from the JavaScript in Lightning components, Salesforce recommends that we perform the callouts on an external system in an Apex class and call this class and method from a JavaScript controller/helper.

We wrote our search callout in Chapter 5, *Apex - Beyond The Basics*, and we want to reuse this logic. (We don't want to rewrite the same logic for the Lightning component.) We will call this function in a new Apex controller, which can be called by the Lightning Component framework. But why another controller?

The Lightning Component framework can only call methods that have the annotation `@AuraEnabled`. The methods need to be public and need to be defined as `static` methods. Let's build the callout functionality that can be called from the Lightning component:

1. In the Developer Console, create a new Apex class with the name `SearchMovie` and copy-paste the following code:

```
@AuraEnabled
public static List<WebserviceCallout.MovieResponse>
searchMovies(String searchTerm){
 return WebserviceCallout.searchMovies(searchTerm);
}
```

Here, we call the callout method for the search functionality and return the list with results to the Lightning component. Before we write the client-side controller, we need to define the properties of our `MovieResponse` object. They will all need the `@AuraEnabled` annotation.

2. Open the `WebserviceCallout` class that you built in the previous chapters and add the annotations before each property:

```
public class MovieResponse {
        @AuraEnabled
        public Integer vote_count {get; set;}
        @AuraEnabled
        public Integer id {get; set;}
        @AuraEnabled
        public Boolean video {get; set;}
        @AuraEnabled
        public Decimal vote_average {get; set;}
        @AuraEnabled
        public String title {get; set;}
        @AuraEnabled
        public Decimal popularity {get; set;}
        @AuraEnabled
        public String poster_path {get; set;}
        @AuraEnabled
        public String original_language {get; set;}
        @AuraEnabled
        public String original_title {get; set;}
        @AuraEnabled
        public List<Integer> genre_ids {get; set;}
        @AuraEnabled
        public List<String> genres {get; set;}
        @AuraEnabled
        public String backdrop_path {get; set;}
        @AuraEnabled
```

```
                    public Boolean adult {get; set;}
                    @AuraEnabled
                    public String overview {get; set;}
                    @AuraEnabled
                    public String release_date {get; set;}
        }
```

3. Save your class.

> **TIP**
>
> If you don't do this step, you will not see the results in the Lightning component. Each property that is not accompanied by this annotation isn't accessible by the Lightning component.

Let's go back to the Lightning component and build a connection with this Apex method:

1. First of all, we need to let the component know which server-side controller is used. This is simply defined in the `component` tag with the `controller` attribute in the main `component` tag. The name of the controller is the name of the Apex class that contains the methods to call in the JavaScript controller:

```
<aura:component controller='NameApexClass">
```

2. So, we add the `controller="SearchMovie"` attribute to our `component` tag:

```
<aura:component controller="SearchMovie"
implements="flexipage:availableForRecordHome,force:hasRecordId,forc
e:lightningQuickActionWithoutHeader,lightning:actionOverride">
```

3. Now that we've done that, we can add an input field to give the user the opportunity to fill in search criteria to find some movies.

4. Open your component and add the following lines of code between the `div` tag for the modal body, (`div class="slds-modal__content"`):

```
<lightning:input name="searchField" label=""
value="{!v.SearchCriteria}" class="slds-size_1-of-1"/>
<div class="slds-size--1-of-1 slds-text-align_center slds-m-
top_small">
    <lightning:button label="Search" variant="brand"
onclick="{!c.searchMovie}" />
</div>
```

5. In this code, we'll bind the attribute with the name `SearchCriteria` to the input field. As you can see, I've used a standard component to display this field, the same way we did for the button. I provided some attributes in the standard button component, which is already built-in. Something that's fairly important is the event of the button. In this case, as the user clicks this button, the JavaScript `controller` method `searchMovie` needs to run (which we will build right now).

6. Open the JavaScript controller of your `MovieComponent` in the Developer Console. First, we'll write the controller; after that, we'll update the component.

7. Copy and paste the following code into your controller. Separate your two JavaScript methods by a comma:

```
searchMovie: function(component, event, helper) {
        var searchCriteria = component.get('v.SearchCriteria');
        helper.calloutSearch(component, helper,  searchCriteria);
}
```

The full controller should now look something like this:

```
({
closeModal: function(component, event, helper){
        var navToMovieTab = $A.get("e.force:navigateToObjectHome");
        navToMovieTab.setParams({
            "scope": "Movie__c"
        });
        navToMovieTab.fire();
},
searchMovie: function(component, event, helper) {
        var searchCriteria = component.get('v.SearchCriteria');
        helper.calloutSearch(component, helper,  searchCriteria);
}
})
```

This `searchMovie` method is the action of the search button. Did you remember the action in the click event? Right—`c:searchMovie`. This action is now defined in the controller of our component.

We define a variable, named `searchCriteria`, which holds the input from the user. Due to the bind variable in the component (`inputfield` is linked with the `SearchCriteria` attribute), we are able to get the value of this attribute via the `component.get(theAttribute)` method.

The second important thing (and best practice) is the reference to the JavaScript helper in the component. The connection with the Apex controller will be done in the helper. (We need this code in another part of the component.) We will provide a function in the helper part of the component with the name `calloutSearch` and provide the component, helper, and search criteria as a parameter.

Now, let's create the helper of our component. For that, click in the right-hand side panel of your Developer Console on the helper link and copy-paste the following code (between the curly brackets):

```
calloutSearch: function(component, helper, searchCriteria){
        var action = component.get('c.searchMovies');
        action.setParams({
            searchTerm: searchCriteria
        });
        action.setCallback(this, function (result) {
            if (result.getState() === 'SUCCESS'){
                component.set('v.lstMovies', result.getReturnValue());
                component.set('v.search', true);
                component.set('v.numberOfMovies',
result.getReturnValue().length);
            }
        });

        $A.enqueueAction(action);
}
```

In this helper, some interesting things are to be discovered:

- The `action` variable in the JavaScript method is the link between the component and the server-side controller. In the component, we have the definition of the class, which is the server-side controller. In this server-side controller, you are able to define the methods that can be called by a Lightning component. In the controller that we defined earlier, we defined the `searchMovies(String)` method, which is an `AuraEnabled` method (the annotation to enable a method for a Lightning component).
- We've also set the parameters of this method. To pass the variable in the Apex method, we need to define parameters in the action call to the method. The line `action.setParams({})` transfers the data from the Lightning component client-side controller to the server-side Apex controller. The name of the parameters needs to be the same name as in the Apex controller, while the values of the parameters need to be of the same data type that was defined in the Apex method in the Apex controller.

- With the callback function, we can handle the response of the controller method. In our case, the method returns the results of our search functionality. So, we can display what we've received from the server-side controller. And that's exactly what we will do with these results.
- In the `result` parameter of the callback, you will find the status of the result (did you get an error or not ?) with the method `getState()` and the return value (if there are) with the `getReturnValue()` method.
- Dependent on the result, you can define some extra actions, like setting some attributes to store your result or showing an error message.
- The most important part is enqueuing the action. This sends your request to the server. This method adds your call to a queue of asynchronous server calls. That queue is an optimization feature of the Lightning Platform.

Now that we have the movies that match our search criteria, we'll display our results. For this, open the component part and the following code after the code for the input field:

```
<aura:if isTrue="{!and(v.search, v.numberOfMovies == 0)}">
 <div class="noMovies">No movies found</div>
</aura:if>
<aura:if isTrue="{!and(v.search, v.numberOfMovies != 0)}">
 <div class="movieSelection">
 <aura:iteration items="{!v.lstMovies}" var="movie">
 <div class="slds-grid slds-m-vertical_small">
 <div class="slds-col slds-size--2-of-12 slds-text-align_center">
 <img src="{!'https://image.tmdb.org/t/p/original' + movie.poster_path}"
class="movieImage" />
 </div>
 <div class="slds-col slds-size--10-of-12">
 <h1>{!movie.original_title}</h1>
 <p>{!movie.overview}</p>
 </div>
 </div>
 </aura:iteration>
 </div>
</aura:if>
```

Let's dig into the details:

- The first tag in this code block is an `aura` tag. The `aura:if` tag is a tag that's used to display content in case the criteria in the `isTrue` attribute is true. You can define a formula in this attribute as I did in this `aura:if` tag.
- We have two code blocks with an `if` statement. The first block is shown when you don't have any records and the user clicked the button to search some movies (the classic message: No movies found), while the second block of code will display the movies that were found via the service.
- The second part I want to discuss is `aura:iteration`. Did you remember the Visualforce tag `apex:repeat` in one of our pages? This `aura-tag` has exactly the same functionality, but for a Lightning component. The `items` attribute contains a list of items that need to be handled (in this case, displayed). With the `var` attribute, you create a variable to define a single record from your list. In this case, we've defined the `movie` variable to display the movie title, the movie description, and a thumbnail of the cover of the movie.

As in the previous code for the component, we've used some Lightning design system style classes to decorate our component. From now on, you have a variety of possibilities to extend this component. These are the basics of the Lightning components, but there are many more standard `component` tags and attributes to explore.

In the Git repository, we added the possibility to select a checkbox in front of the movie to add the movie into our database and show a toast message when something goes wrong during the callout. Feel free to explore the whole component, client-side controller, and server-side controller.

At the end of this exercise, we will override the *new* action on the `movie__c` object with this Lightning component. We do that with the following steps:

1. Go to the object manager in the setup screen and find the `Movie__c` object.
2. Click in the left-hand side navigation of this object on **Buttons, Links, and Actions**:

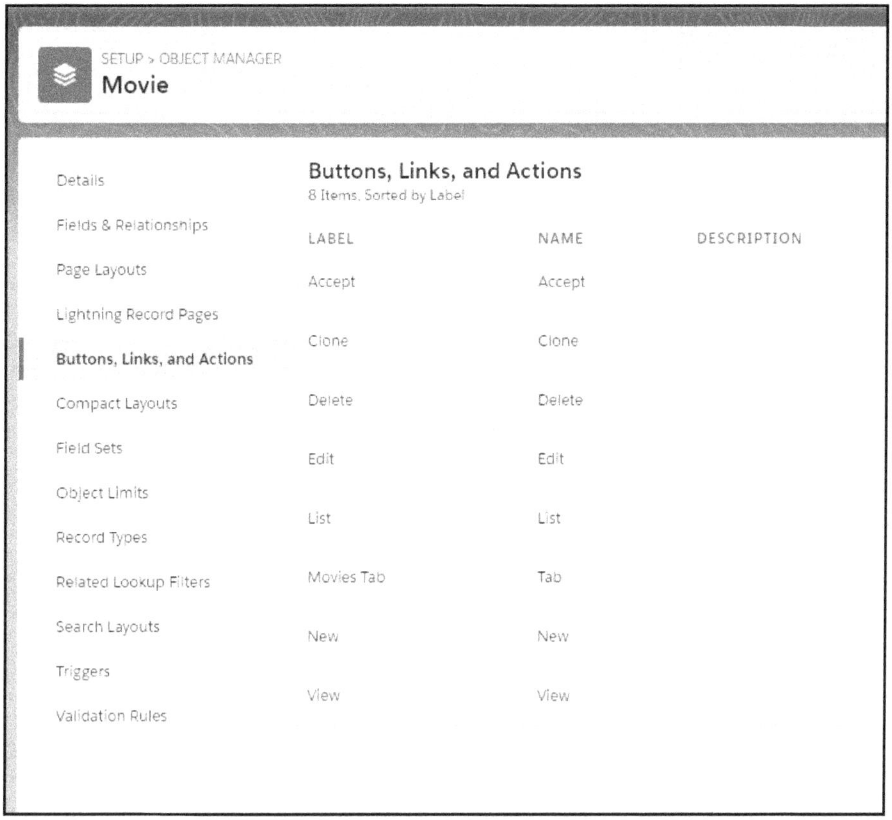

SETUP > OBJECT MANAGER
Movie

Buttons, Links, and Actions
8 Items, Sorted by Label

LABEL	NAME	DESCRIPTION
Accept	Accept	
Clone	Clone	
Delete	Delete	
Edit	Edit	
List	List	
Movies Tab	Tab	
New	New	
View	View	

Details
Fields & Relationships
Page Layouts
Lightning Record Pages
Buttons, Links, and Actions
Compact Layouts
Field Sets
Object Limits
Record Types
Related Lookup Filters
Search Layouts
Triggers
Validation Rules

3. At the end of the line with the **New** action, click on the arrow and click **Edit**. In the **Lightning Experience Override** section, check the check box next to **Lightning component** and find the **movieComponent** in the picklist.

4. Click **Save** to register the Lightning component as an override for the **New** action:

Override Standard Button or Link
New

Overriding a standard button or link changes what happens when a user clicks on it. For example, instead of having a standard Salesforce page appear when a user
instead.

Overrides also apply to programmatic customizations of the same actions. For example, firing the View record event uses the same setting, and performs the same a

You can set different override behavior for Salesforce Classic, Lightning Experience, and mobile

Override Properties   Save   Cancel

Label	New
Name	New
Default	Standard page
Salesforce Classic Override	◉ No override (use default) ⓘ
	○ Visualforce page --None-- ▼
Lightning Experience Override	◉ Lightning component c:MovieComponent ▼
	○ Use the Salesforce Classic override
Mobile Override	○ Lightning component --None-- ▼
	◉ Use the Salesforce Classic override
Comment	

Save   Cancel

5. If you followed along, you should have a screen like this when you click the **New** button:

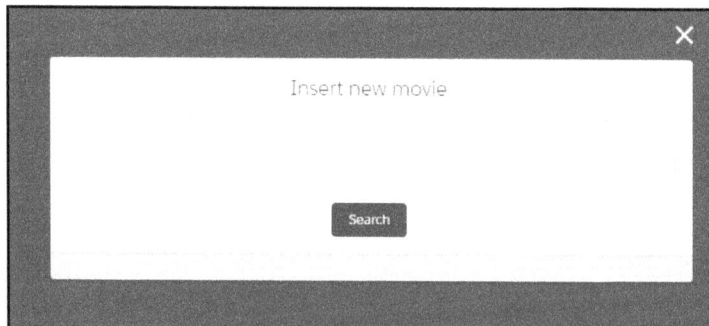

Insert new movie

Search

6. Fill in a part of the title of a movie and click search. What happened? If you've done everything right, you should see something like this:

Select one or more results and hit **insert movie**. The selected movies should have been created and filled with details coming from the external API website.

Summary

In this chapter, you've learned a lot about the two biggest kinds of visualizations: Visualforce pages (usually used in Salesforce Classic) and Lightning components (can only be used in Lightning Experience). 10% of your exam questions will be about Visualforce, Lightning components, and when you need to use the standard visualizations (like standard page layouts) or when you need to use customization.

In the next chapter, you will learn everything about testing, and believe me, testing is not just—*Hey dude, can you test this item for me?* But before we dig into the testing part of the development, let's take the quiz to see what you have remembered about the visualization of your data.

Quiz

1. What is the benefit of the Lightning Component framework?
   - a. Better integration with Force.com sites
   - b. Better performance for custom Salesforce1 mobile apps
   - c. More centralized control via server-side logic
   - d. More pre-built components to replicate the Salesforce look and feel

2. What is an accurate constructor for a custom controller named `MyController`?
   - a.
     ```
     public MyController () {
         account = new Account () ;
     }
     ```
   - b.
     ```
     public MyController (sObject obj) {
         account = (Account) obj;
     }
     ```
   - c.
     ```
     public MyController (List objects) {
         accounts = (List ) objects;
     }
     ```
   - d.
     ```
     public MyController (ApexPages.StandardController
     stdController) {
         account = (Account) stdController.getRecord();
     }
     ```

3. Which file types can be included in a Lightning component bundle?
   - a. Documentation
   - b. Adobe Flash
   - c. JavaScript
   - d. Apex class

4. A developer needs to create a Visualforce page that will override the standard account edit button. The page will be used to validate the account's address using a SOQL query. The page will also allow the user to make edits to the address. Where would the developer write the account address verification logic?
   - a. In a standard extension
   - b. In a standard controller
   - c. In a custom controller
   - d. In a controller extension

5. Which of the following statements about the Lightning Component framework is true?

    a. The component framework can be used for building single-page applications.

    b. The Lightning Component framework is a UI framework for developing web applications for mobile devices.

    c. The framework uses JavaScript on the client side and Apex on the server side.

    d. All of the above.

6. A Visualforce page has a standard controller for an object that has a lookup relationship to a parent object. How can a developer display data from the parent record on the page?

    a. By adding a second standard controller to the page for the parent record

    b. By using a roll-up formula field on the child record to include data from the parent record

    c. By using SOQL on the Visualforce page to query for data from the parent record

    d. By using merge field syntax to retrieve data from the parent record

7. When can a developer use a custom Visualforce page in a Force.com application? (Choose two)

    a. To generate a PDF document with application data

    b. To create components for dashboards and layouts

    c. To deploy components between two organizations

    d. To modify the page layout settings for a custom object

8. A developer creates a custom controller and custom Visualforce page by using the following code block:

```
public class myController {
    public String myString;
    public String getMyString() {
        return 'getmyString';
    }
    public String getStringMethodA() {
        return myString;
    }
    public String getStringMethodB() {
        if (myString == null)myString = 'MethodA';
        return myString;
```

```
```

```
{!myString}, {!StringMethodA}, {!StringMethodB}, {!myString}
```

What does the user see when accessing the custom page?

    a. `getMyString, MethodB, getMystring`

    b. `MethodB, getMyString`

    c. `MethodB`

    d. `getMyString`

9. What is the capability of `StandardSetController`? (Choose two)
    a. It allows pages to perform mass updates of records.
    b. It allows pages to perform pagination with large record sets.
    c. It enforces field-level security when reading large record sets.
    d. It extends the functionality of a standard or custom controller.

10. What is a valid way of loading external JavaScript files into a Visualforce page? (Choose two)
    a. Using an `<apex:includeScript />` tag
    b. Using an `<apex:define />` tag
    c. Using a `<link />` tag
    d. Using a `<script />` tag

Section 3: Testing, Debugging, and Exercise

3

In this last section, we will learn how we can make sure that our automated processes and custom logic perform just as we want them to perform. We need to make sure that we create tests so that we can be sure we will receive all the expected outcomes before we are able to deploy our custom solutions to a production environment. We will also cover the different ways that we can move our customizations into another environment, be it another sandbox or a production environment.

We will wrap up this section with a mock exam to check whether you have understood all the concepts we covered in the book and to prepare you for the actual Salesforce Platform Developer I Certification Exam.

The following chapters are included in this section:

- Chapter 7, *Testing in Salesforce*
- Chapter 8, *Debugging and Deployment Tools*
- Chapter 9, *Mock Tests*

Testing in Salesforce

7

To start and stop anonymous block execution when you're executing anonymous Apex code, testing your code and non-code is very important! This chapter will handle all the principles in regard to testing your code and the impact on testing when you modify a small thing on an object (such as adding a required field or a validation rule).

This chapter will help you describe the benefits of Apex testing, define a test class with test methods, and execute unit tests and analyze the test results.

By completing this chapter, you will be able to do the following:

- Describe the benefits of an Apex trial
- Define a test class with test methods
- Execute unit tests and analyze the test results

Testing deployment requirements and the testing framework

Salesforce Apex delivers a testing framework that allows you to write and run tests, check the test results, and determine your test coverage. Before you can deploy your code to a production environment, you need to cover at least 75% of your code, and all the written tests need to pass. I recommend that you use test-driven development, which means that you do your test development at the same time as your code development. Let's see why testing is so important during development.

The importance of testing

Why should you write extra code to test whether everything works like a charm? Well, testing is crucial in your development process and is the key to successful long-term development. It is very important to know whether the previous logic still works after a small change that can have an impact on the whole organization. For instance, you add a classic validation rule on an object to avoid having the user being unable to add some erroneous data. If you wrote a test class and created some data that isn't compliant with this rule, your test will fail.

Apex tests are needed for the following reasons:

- To make sure that there are no errors in your code and logic.
- To make sure you get the expected outcomes, as per the requirements you have received.
- To deploy your programmatic development to production organizations! Salesforce has some specific requirements that need to be fulfilled before you're able to deploy your development because you are working in a multi-tenant environment.

Testing your development is always done in the following two ways, and, most of the time, by different people:

- The first part of your testing is always done by the developer. As a developer, you need to know whether each possible scenario (a good or a bad scenario) is covered by your code. You perform these tests by writing unit test classes and test methods, and you perform these tests with test data.
- The second part of testing is functional testing. All of these tests will be performed (most of the time) by the end user. In this type of testing, the user asks the following questions:
  - Does the implementation meet the requirements of the customer?
  - Does it work as it should?
  - Does the code give you a reasonable and clear error when it should?

All these test methods will be executed when you deploy your code to a production environment. In this chapter, we will focus on this kind of testing.

Let's discuss development testing and take a look at how we write a test class with test methods, and how we will execute these tests.

In order to deploy your code to production, you must meet the following requirements:

- At least 75% of all Apex code in the production environment must be covered by unit tests:
    - The `System.debug()` statements are not counted as part of the code coverage.
    - Test methods, test classes, and comments do not count as code that needs to be covered. These lines aren't counted into the coverage percentage (if you wrote 100 lines of code with 10 lines of comment and 3 `System.debug` statements, you'd need to cover 87 lines of code).
- All tests must pass.
- Each individual Apex trigger must be covered by unit tests for at least 75% coverage.
- All Apex classes must compile successfully.

The four principles of a good testing approach

In this chapter, we will discuss some good practices in regard to testing. Keep in mind that each unit test (a happy test and an unhappy test) always contains three big parts:

- The setup of your test data.
- The execution of your test scenario (between the `Test.startTest()` and `Test.stopTest()` commands).
- Checking the outcome of the test; did you expect this result?

Let's discuss this in detail.

Creating test data from scratch

While running your tests and testing their execution, you don't want real data being created or modified in your production organization. Everything that your code does, creates, or updates while testing will be rolled back after the test is finished. For this reason, tests are run in an empty, simulated organization. It's as if you would just have gotten a brand new database from Salesforce without any records in the database.

This means that while running tests, you can't just query for any account and do something with it. You need to create all the records that you need for testing first!

There are some exceptions where you don't need to create the data or you cannot create the data:

- All the data of the setup objects are available, such as users, profiles, roles, and permission sets. In the case of users, it is still good practice to create your users the way you want. You probably want to test the same functionality with different types of users, which results in another outcome. Keep in mind that you cannot create a user with a username that already exists in your database. If you want to perform tests with an existing user (such as an integration user), you can only select this user via a query.
- The custom metadata types of settings are used as metadata, such as the definition of an object. These data types are available in the database.

Let's look at an example—you created a trigger that updates the mailing addresses of all related contacts when the billing address of the account is changed by the user. If you create a test, you start with a totally empty organization. This means that in my test class, I would first need to create at least one `Account` record, and then at least two or three `Contact` records related to that `Account`.

There is a way to use real data from your organization, but you have to specifically tell your test to use the real data by annotating your test class with `SeeAllData=true`. Be aware that this is to be used in really exceptional cases, such as implementation around reports and dashboards and `getContent()` structures. I would advise against using it, but it's a viable option if that's the path you want to go down.

Performing your test scenario

After the creation of your test data, you will describe your test scenario with a unit test. A unit test is a regular piece of code that executes a scenario, such as inserting a record or a user that pushes a button. In the upcoming chapters, we will see lots of typical scenarios. In our example, we will update the billing address of the account.

This part of your test is always included between the test commands. The `Test.startTest()` method is the point where your test actually starts. You can only call this method once per unit test. Any code that executes between the `Test.startTest()` and `Test.stopTest()` methods is assigned to a new set of governor limits.

The `Test.stopTest()` method is the point where your test ends. You need to use this method in conjunction with the `startTest` method. All asynchronous methods (such as batch jobs, future jobs, scheduled interface calls, and more) that are made after the `startTest` method are collected by the system. When `stopTest` is executed, all asynchronous processes run synchronously in a test context. After the execution of all the logic, you are able to verify the results of the outcome of your tests. If you hit one of the governor limits between these two methods, your test fails.

Be assert-ive!

Just calling (invoking) your methods so that they run and covering your code is not testing! Let's be clear about that. By calling your methods, you will only get code coverage. You could get enough code coverage to be able to deploy, but you're not testing whether the outcome is the actual outcome that you expect!

By being "assert"-ive, I mean that you should test any expected results by using the `System.assert(Boolean)`, `System.assertEquals('expected value', 'actual value')`, and `System.assertNotEquals('expected value', 'actual value')` methods. These methods are used to compare the results of your logic against an expected value. The `System.assert(Boolean)` function always needs a true Boolean. With this function, you are able to compare a function to the `True` Boolean.

If the formula returns false (`System.assert(false)`), the test fails. Sometimes, developers use this to test an exception. Take a look at the following code. In this code, I am trying to insert an account without a name. This is what we call an unhappy scenario. Inserting an account without a name will fail, and so we need to `catch` that exception and return a clear error message instead of the thrown default exception. But how can we test these kinds of things?

```
Contact c = new Contact(LastName = null);
try {
    insert c;
    System.assert(false);
} catch (Exception ex){
    System.assert(ex.getMessage.containsIgnoreCase('Missing field'));
}
```

As you can see, if I can insert an account without a name, my test needs to fail. I force this failure with a false assertion.

When the code inserts my account, the test fails and needs to go to the `catch` block to run the assertion of my created error. Does the error throw my text? If the error contains my text (in this case, `Missing field`), the test passes; otherwise, the test fails.

Breaking things

Other than testing what the logic should do, also test what it should **not** do. Test negative scenarios, like we did in the previous subsection. Let's go back to our example with the billing address, where we change the account and update the mailing addresses of the related contacts. You could also create a test that checks that the mailing addresses of the contacts change if you modify the billing address on an account, which is not related to these contacts. Alternatively, when you modify another field on the account, the mailing address on the related contacts remain the same, even if they are different. You could have made a mistake in your code and instead of querying only the contacts of the account where a change was made, you could have queried all the contacts in the database (which would be really bad, right?).

Be bulkyfied!

Always assume that your logic could receive a list of up to 200 records at once. For example, while loading data through a Data Loader, your logic must be executed for each of those 200 records. Even if you think that your code will only get triggered by a user action through the UI, you never know if somebody will perform a mass update via a Data Loader and your code wasn't ready for it!

Other stuff

One of the best practices is to give your test class the same name as your class, plus the word `Test`. By doing this, you'll always find the correct tests with the correct functional class, and you'll also know what you're testing.

That's enough theory for now—let's add some practice into the mix.

Writing Apex unit tests

A test class is the only class in Apex that can have a `private` access modifier. It always runs when you want to deploy any Apex code to a production environment using the default tests, or when you create a managed package. Due to the fact that unit tests, in principle, are not called from outside the class, you can define your test class with the `private` access modifier.

A test class is always written with the `@IsTest` annotation. In this type of class, you are able to define regular methods and test methods. For instance, if you want to create your test data in one method and run this method in each unit test, you are able to create a regular method in your test class where you create your data. The unit tests (methods to test your implementation code) are written in test methods. You are able to define your test methods in two ways:

- The method has the `@IsTest` annotation as well (like the class).
- The method has the `testmethod` keyword.

Each test method has the following characteristics:

- The method can be `public` or `private`, depending on the access modifier of your class.
- The method needs to be defined as a `static` method.
- The method can only be in a test class (the class that has the `@IsTest` annotation).
- The method always returns the `void` type.
- The method does not accept any parameters.

The following is a full basic skeleton for a test class and a method. In this skeleton, you'll see the two types of notation:

```
@IsTest
private with sharing class MyTestClass {
 // with the test annotation
    @IsTest
    private static void myTestMethod1(){
    }
 // without the test annotation and 'testmethod' keyword
    private static testMethod myTestMethod2(){
    }
}
```

Previously, we wrote some classes and triggers. Let's write some tests for these classes and/or triggers.

Let's start by covering the following code. This code selects a movie and updates when a user makes a modification to it (I know this is standard behavior, but we're looking at how we need to test every part of this class):

```
public with sharing class MovieExtension {

    private final Id movieId;
    public Movie__c theMovie {
    get{
        if (this.movieId != null){
            // select the movie and the cast from the Id.
            // We select records always with a list, even if you know it
should be a record.
            // if someone removes the record while you want to select it,
you will receive an exception
            try {
                Movie__c selectedMovie = [SELECT Description__c,
Name,Genre__c,Runtime__c,Release_Date__c,Cover_Url__c,Director__r.Name,
(SELECT Id, Name, Person__r.Name, Rating__c FROM Cast__r) FROM Movie__c
WHERE Id = :THIS.movieId];

                return selectedMovie;
            } catch (Exception ex){
                ApexPages.addMessage(new
ApexPages.Message(ApexPages.Severity.FATAL, 'Are you sure this movie exists
?'));
            }
        }

        return new Movie__c();
    }
    }

    public MovieExtension(Apexpages.StandardController stdMovie){
        this.movieId = stdMovie.getId();
    }



    /**
    * When the user clicks on the button Submit Movie on the page
    */
    public PageReference submitMovie(){
        try {
            upsert theMovie;
```

```
    } catch (DmlException ex){
        ApexPages.addMessage(new
ApexPages.Message(Apexpages.Severity.FATAL, ex.getDmlMessage(0)));
    }
    return null;
  }

}
```

Like we learned in the section about *The four principles of a good testing approach*, we need to set up our test data first.

Setting up test data

When you declare a test class with test methods, you need to assume that you have an empty database. So, we need to create some test data to perform our tests.

You can create test data in different ways. If you are already an advanced developer, you'll work with a test data factory, where you will be able to create predefined objects and records (each account record needs a name, so in the factory, you can define a name when you create a test account). A good example of a test data factory can be found here: `https:/ /medium.com/@medben/apex-test-data-factory-8ed14c2ca050`.

In this section, I'll teach you the basics of creating Salesforce test data, but don't hesitate to use a factory.

Without a factory, you are able to define test data in different ways in your classes. You can define your test data in a separate class (if you need this data in several classes, you can define your test data in a new class that has the `@IsTest` annotation), in a separate regular method in the test class, or in a method that has the `@TestSetup` annotation.

@TestSetup

The `@TestSetup` annotation is a bit special. With this method, you are able to define your test data, which will be created for each of the test methods in the same class. Take a look at the following example:

```
@IsTest
private with sharing class MyTestClass {

 @TestSetup
 private static void createMyTestData(){
```

```
    }

    @IsTest
    private static void myTestMethod1(){
    // test data defined in the method createMyTestData is created before the
    execution of this unit test
    }

    @IsTest
    private static void myTestMethod2(){
    // test data defined in the method createMyTestData is created before the
    execution of this unit test
    }
}
```

The first method in this class (which has the @TestSetup annotation inside of it) will contain the creation of the test data. This method will be executed before the execution of each of your unit test methods in this class and will count against the governor limits.

Mixed Data Manipulation Language (DML) operations

When you need to create setup objects (such as a user, territory, or permission set), you can't create any other regular object in the same unit test. If you do, you will receive an exception: MIXED_DML_OPERATION, DML operation on setup object is not permitted after you have updated a non-setup object (or vice versa). This means that you mixed up the creation of a setup object with a non-setup object (such as an account, contact, or custom object).

You can avoid this exception by creating your setup object asynchronously. In the following example, we will create the user asynchronously and the account in a separate method:

```
    @IsTest
    private with sharing class MyTestClass {

    @future
    private static void createTheUser(){
    // We select a standard profile
    Profile theProfile = [SELECT Id FROM Profile WHERE Name='Standard User'];
    UserRole theRole = [SELECT Id FROM UserRole WHERE Name='COO'];
    User testUser = new User(
    firstname = 'test', lastname = 'MyUser',
                alias = 'tuser',
                email = 'testuser@weare4c.com',
                emailencodingkey = 'UTF-8',
```

```
languagelocalekey='en_US',
            localesidkey='en_GB',
 profileid = p.Id,
            timezonesidkey = 'Asia/Kuala_Lumpur',
            username = '
testuser@weare4c.com
',
 userroleid = r.Id
 );
 insert(testUser);
 }

 private static void createTestAccount(){
 Account a = new Account(Name = 'Test account');
 insert a;
 }

 @IsTest
 private static void myTestMethod1(){

 createTheUser();
 createTestAccount();
 }
}
```

A second way of doing this is to set up the users in your @TestSetup method and create regular data in your test methods. You can do this by calling a method in your @TestSetup method when you need this data several times.

As you can see, setting up test data is not very difficult; you only need to find a system that creates predefined data for you that will leverage your required fields or validation rules (otherwise, the creation of your test data will fail, and your test will also fail).

Let's create this setup data as an exercise. Create a test class, name it MovieExtensionTest (remember that it's good practice to name your test class the same as your class, plus the word test), and create the test data in this class. We need the data in each of our tests. The data that you need to create is for a movie with the following properties:

- **Name**: Independence Day
- **Description**: Independence Day is an American science fiction action film directed and co-written by Roland Emmerich
- **Cover URL**: https://image.tmdb.org/t/p/original/ bqLlWZJdhrS0knfEJRkquW7L8z2.jpg
- **Genre**: **Action; Adventure; Science Fiction**

You can check the solution to this at the end of this book. As usual, I recommend trying this first on your own, and then verifying your solution afterward.

Creating a unit test

After setting up our test data, we need to perform a test scenario. In our case, I will perform a test by selecting a movie and verifying whether the data was selected correctly.

Keep the following scenarios in mind:

- When the controller receives a correct standard controller
- When the controller doesn't receive a correct standard controller

Do you still know which parts we need in the unit test? Let's repeat our theory:

- The test data
- The test scenario with the start of the test and the end of the test
- We need to check whether the outcome of our test is correct

Let's practice the first scenario. You will do the second in the form of an exercise.

For the first scenario, we need a correct movie that's been added in a standard controller. This standard controller is the parameter of the constructor of the class. Remember, we created a movie in our `testSetup` method, and the data that you create in a `testSetup` method is created for each of the unit tests in this class. So, if we create a unit test, our movie is already created and placed in the database. We can easily select the movie from our database.

To define your test methods, you have to choose the notation for the unit test method declaration. I prefer writing the unit test methods like this:

```
@IsTest
private static void methodName(){

}
```

The reason for this is that if I define non-test methods in the same class (such as helper methods, which are used in different methods), I can immediately see which method is a unit test, and which isn't.

Don't hesitate to use the following notation if you find it easier:

```
private static testMethod void methodName(){

}
```

Let's write the content of the test. Open your Developer Console (if it's not open yet) and open the `MovieExtensionTest` class you created. In this class, the data should be already set up. If not, go to the solutions corner at the end of this book and copy the code into `Test class MovieExtension - Setup Test data`. This provides you with the test data for your unit tests.

The following subsection shows the method for the test data, where we define a new method for the initial test. Let's name the method `selectCorrectMovie()`.

The test data

First of all, we need to select our movie. This is basically a query that selects the movie that you created in the setup method. We select the movie based on its name. This is the only data that we need in our test scenario:

```
Movie__c theMovie = [SELECT Id FROM Movie__c WHERE Name = 'Independence
day'];
```

Add this code to the `test` method you just created.

The test scenario

The second part of our test method is the scenario. Based on the preceding movie, the movie standard controller is the parameter that we need to provide in our constructor. So, we need to create a standard controller (this is a part of the `ApexPages` class) of that movie and pass this to the constructor of our controller.

Watch out—this is our test scenario, so we start with the following line of code:

```
Test.startTest();
```

This line of code assigns a new set of limits to our unit test. We need to know whether we hit some Salesforce limitations during the test. This line of code is always necessary if you perform unit tests for the asynchronous Apex. Otherwise, the code for the asynchronous calls will not be executed.

The code for the construction of our standard controller, and then passing it to the constructor, should look like this:

```
ApexPages.StandardController stdCtrl = new
ApexPages.StandardController(theMovie);
MovieExtension ext = new MovieExtension(stdCtrl);
```

It's very important that you close your test with the following line:

```
Test.stopTest();
```

This line will define the number of limits that you hit during your test (how many queries you executed, or how many DML statements you executed). Once you hit a limit, your test will fail.

Another important thing to know about this line is the execution of the asynchronous code of your class. If you need to test a trigger with a callout (remember, this is always done via an asynchronous call) or with a batch or queued functionality, the asynchronous code will be executed synchronously, immediately after this line of code.

Add the preceding four lines of code to your test method and save it.

Now you've written a unit test with test data that was created by your code and not selected from the real database. The last part, and maybe the most important part, is verifying whether your test returns the result that you expect.

What's the result of the test?

Now, here comes the most important question in testing: *Is the result of my test what I expect?*

We can provide an answer to this question with the following functions. For each of these methods, you are able to define an error message during the tests. These methods are as follows:

- `System.assert(Boolean Condition, Message)`
- `System.assertEquals(expected result, actual result, message)`
- `System.assertNotEquals(expected result, actual result, message)`

In our test, we need to verify whether the `private` variable in our class is the same as `movieId` that we provided in our constructor. We should write a line of code like this:

```
System.assertEquals(theMovie.Id, ext.movieId);
```

Add the preceding line of code and save your class. You'll see that you can't save this line of code, and you'll see the `Variable is not visible: MovieExtension.movieId` exception. What does this mean?

As you may remember from when we started the Apex development (and classes in general), you cannot access `private` member variables from outside the class where the member is defined. But how we can verify the result of that variable if we can't access it?

I can hear you saying *If I adapt the access modifier from private to public, my problem is solved*. Yes, it is solved, but in most circumstances, you don't want the variable to be accessible from outside the class.

In the test context, you can leave your variable as `private` with the `@TestVisible` annotation. The member variable is only accessible via a test class (and test method) and not from any other logic or functionality, which is not defined as a test.

Let's adapt the `MovieId` variable in the `MovieExtension` class:

```
@TestVisible
private final Id movieId;
```

Save this class and go back to the test class. Try to save the class again. Does it save? Of course, it does!

Your `movieID` member variable is now accessible from a test class, so we can save and compile the class. We've written our first test method, so now it's time to execute the unit test.

Executing test classes

When we write unit tests, we need to find out whether they pass or not. We need to execute the unit test and evaluate the result of it. If the test passes, everything runs fine. If the test fails, you need to find out why the test fails. Did you create the correct data? Is the result not the expected result? Maybe there's a scenario you didn't take into account while you were developing your code?

Let's look at how we can execute our code.

You can execute unit tests via your favorite IDE (**VS Code**, which is short for **Visual Studio Code**; IntelliJ with Illuminated Cloud; and Welkin Suite have built-in testing tools so that you can execute your unit tests), but you can also use your Developer Console.

Let's look at how we can execute our test method in the Developer Console:

1. To start a unit test, open your Developer Console and click on **Test | New Run** in the top navigation bar. A new window will open, showing all the different test classes:

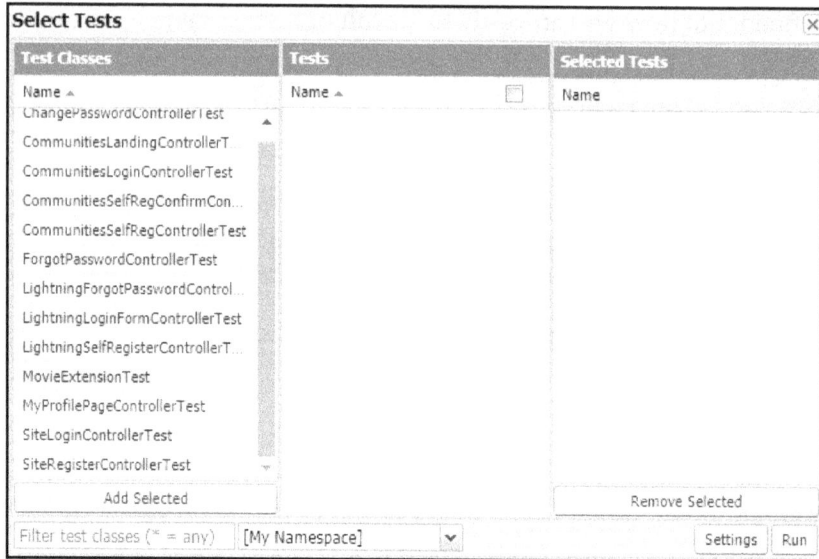

2. As you can see, one of the test classes is our `MovieExtensionTest` class. There are some more test classes here too, which are test classes from classes that you can implement without writing anything, especially for communities.

3. Let's click on the `MovieExtensionTest` class and see what happens. Our test method that we wrote a few paragraphs ago is displayed. If you wrote more test methods, you will see every test method here.

4. Check the box after the method and click on the **Run** button in the bottom-right of the screen:

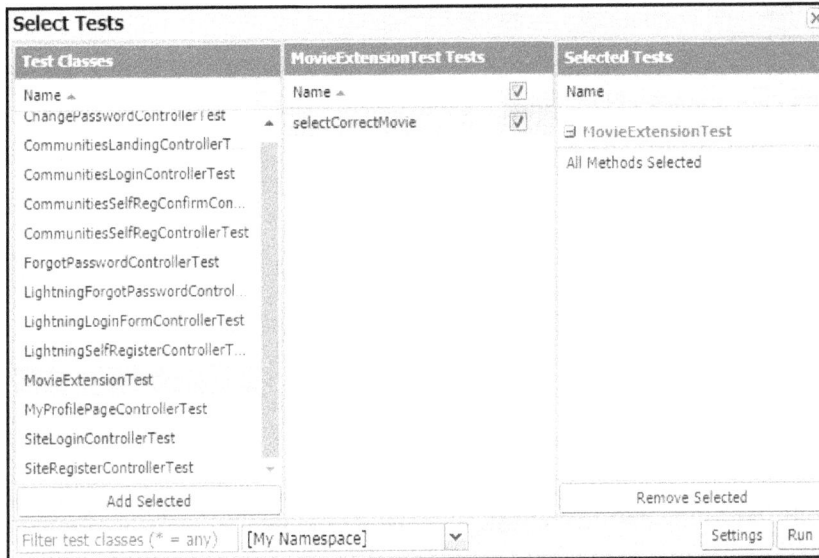

5. Let's see what happens. The test script is executing. Because this is a simple test, the script is running fast, but it is possible that this will take a while for more complex test methods.

6. The test should succeed. In the **Logs** panel, you'll see the result of your test with a status of **Success**:

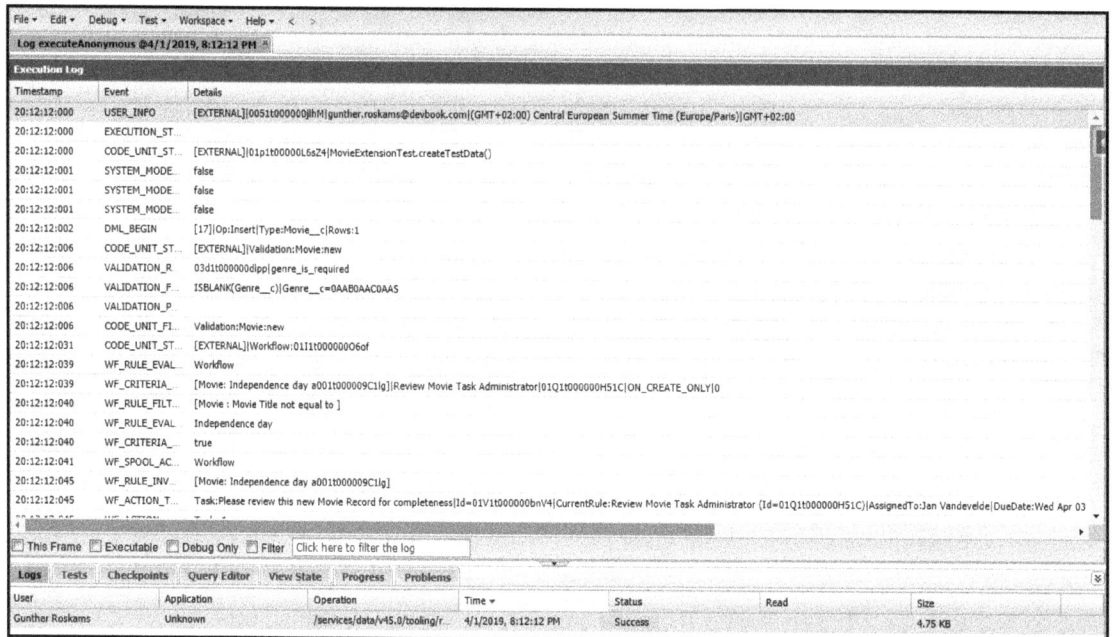

Let's take a look at the execution logs of our unit test. There are some interesting things here.

First of all, the unit test didn't fail, so that scenario is coded well. In the tests, you'll also see the Salesforce limits. In this case, we didn't use any DML or SOQL statements. You can see this in the **TESTING_LIMITS** section at the bottom of the logs:

20:12:12:000	LIMIT_USAGE_FOR_NS	
20:12:12:147	TESTING_LIMITS	
20:12:12:147	LIMIT_USAGE_FOR_NS	{default}|
20:12:12:000	LIMIT_USAGE_FOR_NS	Number of SOQL queries: 0 out of 100
20:12:12:000	LIMIT_USAGE_FOR_NS	Number of query rows: 0 out of 50000
20:12:12:000	LIMIT_USAGE_FOR_NS	Number of SOSL queries: 0 out of 20
20:12:12:000	LIMIT_USAGE_FOR_NS	Number of DML statements: 0 out of 150
20:12:12:000	LIMIT_USAGE_FOR_NS	Number of DML rows: 0 out of 10000
20:12:12:000	LIMIT_USAGE_FOR_NS	Maximum CPU time: 0 out of 10000
20:12:12:000	LIMIT_USAGE_FOR_NS	Maximum heap size: 0 out of 6000000
20:12:12:000	LIMIT_USAGE_FOR_NS	Number of callouts: 0 out of 100
20:12:12:000	LIMIT_USAGE_FOR_NS	Number of Email Invocations: 0 out of 10
20:12:12:000	LIMIT_USAGE_FOR_NS	Number of future calls: 0 out of 50
20:12:12:000	LIMIT_USAGE_FOR_NS	Number of queueable jobs added to the queue: 0 out of 50
20:12:12:000	LIMIT_USAGE_FOR_NS	Number of Mobile Apex push calls: 0 out of 10
20:12:12:000	LIMIT_USAGE_FOR_NS	
20:12:12:147	CUMULATIVE_LIMIT_USAGE_END	

You can filter these lines by the filter in your screen. Type TESTING in the filter window, click on the line, and remove the filter. You will see your test limits:

Execution Log

Timestamp	Event	Details
20:12:12:147	TESTING_LIMITS	

☐ This Frame ☐ Executable ☐ Debug Only ☑ Filter TESTING

This results in the following output:

20:12:12:147	TESTING_LIMITS	
20:12:12:147	LIMIT_USAGE_FOR_NS	(default)|
20:12:12:000	LIMIT_USAGE_FOR_NS	Number of SOQL queries: 0 out of 100
20:12:12:000	LIMIT_USAGE_FOR_NS	Number of query rows: 0 out of 50000
20:12:12:000	LIMIT_USAGE_FOR_NS	Number of SOSL queries: 0 out of 20
20:12:12:000	LIMIT_USAGE_FOR_NS	Number of DML statements: 0 out of 150
20:12:12:000	LIMIT_USAGE_FOR_NS	Number of DML rows: 0 out of 10000
20:12:12:000	LIMIT_USAGE_FOR_NS	Maximum CPU time: 0 out of 10000
20:12:12:000	LIMIT_USAGE_FOR_NS	Maximum heap size: 0 out of 6000000
20:12:12:000	LIMIT_USAGE_FOR_NS	Number of callouts: 0 out of 100
20:12:12:000	LIMIT_USAGE_FOR_NS	Number of Email Invocations: 0 out of 10
20:12:12:000	LIMIT_USAGE_FOR_NS	Number of future calls: 0 out of 50
20:12:12:000	LIMIT_USAGE_FOR_NS	Number of queueable jobs added to the queue: 0 out of 50
20:12:12:000	LIMIT_USAGE_FOR_NS	Number of Mobile Apex push calls: 0 out of 10
20:12:12:000	LIMIT_USAGE_FOR_NS	

Let's proceed:

1. You can find the start of your test scenario in the same way. Try and find your unit test method by typing the name of your test method in the filter:

Execution Log

Timestamp	Event	Details
20:12:12:128	CODE_UNIT_STARTED	[EXTERNAL]|01p1t00000L6sZ4|MovieExtensionTest.selectCorrectMovie()
20:12:12:147	CODE_UNIT_FINISHED	MovieExtensionTest.selectCorrectMovie()

☐ This Frame ☐ Executable ☐ Debug Only ☑ Filter selectCorrectMovie

2. Click on the line that says **CODE_UNIT_STARTED**—that's the start of your unit test. Remove the filter and analyze the code after that line. You should see the SOQL query that you executed:

20:12:12:128	CODE_UNIT_STARTED	[EXTERNAL]	01p1t00000L6sZ4	MovieExtensionTest.selectCorrectMovie()
20:12:12:129	SYSTEM_MODE_ENTER	false
20:12:12:129	SYSTEM_MODE_EXIT	false
20:12:12:129	SYSTEM_MODE_ENTER	false
20:12:12:129	SOQL_EXECUTE_BEGIN	[23]	Aggregations:0	SELECT Id FROM Movie__c WHERE Name = 'Independence day'
20:12:12:142	SOQL_EXECUTE_END	[23]	Rows:1
20:12:12:147	SYSTEM_MODE_EXIT	false
20:12:12:147	CUMULATIVE_LIMIT_USAGE	
20:12:12:147	LIMIT_USAGE_FOR_NS	(default)	

On line **23**, you can see the SOQL query that you executed in your test. By doing this, you can check whether your query returned any results or not:

```
20      @IsTest
21 ▾    private static void selectCorrectMovie(){
22          // select the movie, created in the setup method
23          Movie__c theMovie = [SELECT Id FROM Movie__c WHERE Name = 'Independence day'];
24          // start up your test scenario
25          Test.startTest();
26          ApexPages.StandardController stdCtrl = new ApexPages.StandardController(theMovie);
27          MovieExtension ext = new MovieExtension(stdCtrl);
28          Test.stopTest();
29          // verify if the Id of the movie is the same movieId in your controller
30          System.assertEquals(theMovie.Id, ext.movieId);
31      }
```

Great! You wrote a unit test and successfully executed your test scenario. Let's do some practice now.

It's time for an exercise. As you may remember, we need to write good test scenarios, but also bad test scenarios. Write a unit test for our second scenario. Provide no standard controller for the constructor of the extension and check whether the test passes. If not (if you copied and pasted the code that we looked at in this chapter, it won't), you need to find out what happened.

> You will receive a null pointer in the first line of the constructor because `standardcontroller` is not defined since the parameter of the constructor of the class is `null`:
> `MovieExtension ext = new MovieExtension(null);`

In this exercise, you will see the main goal of testing. In this case, it is not the test that went wrong (you did an *unhappy test*, but the code is not foreseen to capture a null as a parameter).

As usual, you can find the solution to this in the solutions section of this book.

Testing web service callouts

Do you remember our functionality in the Lightning component with the callout to the movie DB web service? As you know, every class needs a test class, and you also need to test the functionality of a callout.

In this section, I'll explain how to test these types of classes and methods.

Callout types

There are two different types of callouts:

- **Simple Object Access Protocol** (**SOAP**): This communication protocol uses XML to communicate between the two devices. You provide an XML-request (according to the WSDL structure of the service) to the SOAP service and receive an XML message as the answer.
- **REpresentational State Transfer** (**REST**): This communication protocol can use XML and JSON messages to communicate. Depending on the type of protocol (such as GET, POST, and DELETE), logic in the service will be executed with the data that's provided. The data can be in the body of your request, or in the URL. You've already seen that Salesforce URLs display data on your screen. This URL is always the same, but the parameter of recordId is different. Depending on the information that is requested (and which user performs the request), you will get the details of an account, contact, or movie.

WSDL2Apex

Beside the callout methods, you have the possibility to generate Apex classes and methods from a **Web Service Definition Language** (**WSDL**) with the WDSL2Apex function. This is the easiest way to perform a callout in Salesforce. In my experience, you can use this functionality for simple SOAP callouts when you need to get information from a SOA service to update an object. Let's get started:

1. In the setup section of **Apex Classes**, you'll find the **Generate from WSDL** button:

2. Simply load the WSDL definition (this should be an XML file) and click on the **Parse WSDL** button:

3. Salesforce will generate (if you loaded a valid WSDL) some classes. You only need to write test classes and methods. For the callout, you need to create a mock response.

4. This mock response class implements the `WebserviceMock` interface. The class with this interface needs to implement a method that generates a fake response for you:

```
@isTest
global class MockService implements WebServiceMock {
  global void doInvoke(Object stub, Object request, Map<String,
  Object> response, String endpoint, String soapAction, String
  requestName, String responseNS, String responseName, String
  responseType) {

  docSample.EchoStringResponse_element respElement = new
  docSample.EchoStringResponse_element();
  respElement.EchoStringResult = 'Mock response';
  response.put('response_x', respElement);
  }
}
```

5. This class needs at least the `public` access modifier because this class needs to be called from outside the class. In the test class, you will call the mock response class before you start with the test scenario (`Test.startTest()`):

```
Test.setMock(WebServiceMock.class, new MockService());
```

This is the first type of interface where you can write a mock service you are able to use. Let's go to the interface that's used most of the time and is easier to implement `HttpCalloutMock` is used for outbound REST or SOAP services that you write (like in our example with the movie DB service).

HttpCalloutMock

A second interface that can be used in Salesforce for testing web service callouts is the `HttpCalloutMock` interface. A class that implements this interface needs to implement the `HttpResponse` method (`HttpRequest`). Just like the access modifier, this must be a public class with the `public` method `respond`. You can use this interface for each other callout scenario between Salesforce and a web service (such as the SOAP and REST services):

```
global class MockResponse implements HttpCalloutMock {
    global HTTPResponse respond(HTTPRequest req) {
    // Create a fake response (HttpResponse class) with response values and
return this response
    }
}
```

When we use this type of mock interface, we need to call the class in our test method this. The same goes for what we said about the `WebserviceMock` interface previously. You need to call the `MockResponse` class before you start testing your scenario:

```
Test.setMock(HttpCalloutMock.class, new MockResponse());
```

So, that's all about the testing of an outbound callout via Apex. Watch out, as you'll receive some questions about this subject. Remember that you can't perform testing for the real web service. If you don't implement `MockService`, you will receive an error stating `Methods defined as TestMethod do not support web service callouts`.

Invoking Apex to execute anonymously versus unit tests

So far, you've learned the basics about testing your Apex code and how you need to test an external call to a web service. You also learned that testing must use test data (and not real data) and that the data in these test scenarios isn't really submitted to your real database. After the execution of your test scenario, the data that's created for your test will be removed from memory. But what if you want to test and add data to your database? You have the Execute Anonymous Window for this. Hopefully, you remember this functionality from when we started with Apex in `Chapter 4`, *Apex Basics*. We used this functionality to write our first piece of code.

With this functionality, we can invoke classes and methods that are declared as a `public` or global class. The same is possible in a unit test, but the data isn't stored in your database. Some more differences are given in the following table:

Anonymous Apex	Unit tests
Always enforces user permissions.	Always runs in system mode. If you run the test code as a user (`System.runAs(User)`), the permissions of that user are enforced.
Output in the debug logs.	The output is provided in the debug logs and calculates the coverage of your code.
The creation of records in your code is saved into the database.	The creation of records in your code isn't saved in your database. The data that's created in unit tests is removed after the execution of the tests.
Runs real callouts to a web service.	You need to implement a mock service to test a callout.

Uses the governor limits for the complete block of code.	You are able to set up a new set of limits during your test scenario (only for the scenario, and not for the creation of the data and test scenario).
You can only use the logged-in user (if you are logged in as another user, you use the permissions of that user).	You are able to use the `System.runAs()` functionality to pretend to be another user (probably a non-existing user).
Default sharing mode is always `with sharing`.	The default sharing mode is `without sharing`, but this depends on the running user and the definition of the class (`with` or `without sharing`; the default is `without sharing`).
You can perform any function in an anonymous Apex session that's allowed for your user.	Some functionalities are not allowed during unit tests, such as sending an email (you are able to test whether an email has been sent, but you cannot send an email in test context, executing multiple executes in batch context).

Now you know the difference between Apex testing and just executing Apex in the Developer Console. Let's go over some useful functions that you can use during unit testing.

Test functions

Some functions are only available in a testing context and are very useful. Here's an overview of some useful test functions:

Function	Comments
`Test.getStandardPricebookId()`	When you need to create product and prices data, you need to add your product prices to the default price book. Instead of querying the default price book (`Pricebook2.isStandard = true`), you are able to use this function to get the default price book ID. The return value of this method is the ID of the price book that you configured as the standard price book (only one is available).

`Test.isRunningTest()`	This function is useful in your real code. With this function, you're able to verify whether your code runs in a user or system context or in a test context. This method returns a Boolean value.
`Test.setCurrentPage(Page)`	With this function, you are able to perform a test with a Visualforce page. If the user posts some variables via a form, you are able to simulate the page with the form, the headers, and the content of the page.
`Test.setMock(interfaceType, mockResponse)`	You've seen this function already when you tested a callout. This function is used to set a mock response when you're testing callouts.
`Test.startTest()`	The start of your test scenario.
`Test.stopTest()`	The end of your test scenario.

It's good if you remember these because some of these functions are used in questions in the exam. Some of these functions are essential, while others are only used occasionally. You need these functions to avoid SOQL queries. If you want to learn about more of these functions, you can search the internet.

The next part of this book covers one of the most important parts of testing.

The impact on code during declarative changes

It is possible to break your good working functionality in just a few seconds. Imagine the following scenario: you developed a page so that you could create a new movie via a Lightning component with a callout to verify some data. You test everything and wrote your test code. Everything executed successfully.

Your customer wants to congratulate you on your nice work and is very happy with the new implementation, so they ask for a new field that's required in your movie object. They want to see the different genres of movies that are available, but these genres need to be requested (which is not always present in our movie DB service).

You think: "OK. I'll create a new field on the `Movie__c` object and make it required." Once you've done that, you run your unit tests again. The test fails. Now what? Everything ran fine, but after this change, the functionality doesn't work anymore. This is what we call the impact on code during declarative changes. In this case, your test fails during the creation of the test data. While we created a movie in our test without this new field, the test will fail because the value of this new field is empty. We need to provide a value for this new field in the test data and run the test again. Now, the test will pass.

Summary

In this chapter, you've learned every basic step of unit testing in Salesforce. These basics are necessary for any deployment process.

Salesforce recommends 75% overall coverage, but I recommend covering as much as possible. You can't test everything, such as throwing an exception during a network interruption, but most of the time, you are able to have test coverage for at least 85% for classes with more than 50 lines.

Remember, there are three important steps that you must take into account while you are creating your tests: create your own test data, perform your test scenario and execute it between the `Test.startTest()` and `Test.stopTest()` functions, and verify your retrieved result with assertions.

Happy testing!

It's time to check whether you remembered what we went through in this chapter by completing a quiz. As always, the solutions are at the end of the book.

In the next chapter, we will discuss how to monitor and access various types of debug logs. We also cover Developer Console options for viewing logs such as using logs perspective and filtering logs.

Quiz

1. Which statement would a developer use when creating test data for products and price books?
   a. `Id pricebookId = Test.getStandardPricebookId();`
   b. `Pricebook pb = new Pricebook();`
   c. `IsTest(SeeAllData = false);`
   d. `List objList = Test.loadData(Account.sObjectType, 'myResource');`

2. A developer creates an Apex class that includes private methods. What can the developer do to ensure that the private methods can be accessed by the test class?
   a. Add the `TestVisible` attribute to the Apex class.
   b. Add the `SeeAllData` attribute to the test methods.
   c. Add the `TestVisible` attribute to the Apex methods.
   d. Add the `SeeAllData` attribute to the test class.

3. What is the proper process for an Apex unit test?
   a. Query for test data using `SeeAllData = true`. Call the method being tested. Verify that the results are correct.
   b. Query for test data using `SeeAllData = true`. Execute `runAllTests()`. Verify that the results are correct.
   c. Create data for testing. Execute `runAllTests()`. Verify that the results are correct.
   d. Create data for testing. Call the method being tested. Verify that the results are correct.

4. A developer needs to confirm that an account trigger is working correctly without changing the organization's data. What would the developer do to test the account trigger?
   a. Use the **Test** menu on the Developer Console to run all test classes for the account trigger.
   b. Use the **New** button on the **Salesforce Accounts** tab to create a new `Account` record.
   c. Use the **Open Execute Anonymous** feature on the Developer Console to run an insert `Account` DML statement.
   d. Use **Deploy** from the Force.com IDE to deploy and insert an `Account` Apex class.

5. What's the benefit of using `Test.startTest( )` and `Test.stopTest( )`?

    a. To indicate test code so that it does not Impact Apex line count governor limits.

    b. To start and stop anonymous block execution when executing anonymous Apex code.

    c. To create an additional set of governor limits during the execution of a single test class.

    d. To avoid Apex code coverage requirements for the code between these lines.

6. A developer needs to create a new Visualforce page with an Apex extension and writes test classes that cover 95% of the code of the new Apex extension. The change set's deployment to production fails with the following test coverage warning: *Average test coverage across all Apex classes and triggers is 74%, at least 75% test coverage is required*. What does the developer need to do to successfully deploy the new Visualforce page and extension?

    a. Select **Fast Deployment** in order to bypass running all the tests.

    b. Select **Disable Parallel Apex Testing** to run all the tests.

    c. Create test classes to exercise the Visualforce page markup.

    d. Add test methods to existing test classes from previous deployments.

7. Which statement is accurate when you're creating unit tests in Apex?

    a. System assert statements that do not increase code coverage contribute important feedback in unit tests.

    b. Unit tests with multiple methods result in all methods failing every time one method fails.

    c. Triggers do not require any unit tests so that we can deploy them from sandbox to production.

    d. Increased test coverage requires large test classes with many lines of code in one method.

8. A developer has developed one single custom controller class that works with Visualforce pages (a wizard that contains different Visualforce pages) to support creating and editing multiple sObjects. The wizard accepts data from user inputs across multiple Visualforce pages (via forms) and from a parameter on the initial URL. Which statement is unnecessary inside the unit test for the custom controller? (Choose two answers)

    a. `Test.setCurrentPage(pageRef)`

    b. `public ExtendedController (ApexPages.StandardController cntrl) { }`

    c. `String nextPage = controller.save().getUrl();`

    d. `ApexPages.currentPage().getParameters().put('input', 'TestValue')`

9. What features are available when writing Apex test classes? (Choose two answers)

    a. The ability to select error types to ignore in the Developer Console.

    b. The ability to write assertions to test after a `@future` method.

    c. The ability to set and modify the **CreatedDate** field in Apex tests.

    d. The ability to select testing data using `.csv` files stored in the system.

10. A developer needs to know whether all the tests currently pass in the Salesforce environment. Which feature can the developer use? (Choose two answers)

    a. Developer Console

    b. ANT Migration Tool

    c. Salesforce UI Apex Test Execution

    d. Workbench Metadata Retrieval

11. Where is an Apex code unit tested? (Choose two answers)

    a. Anonymous test

    b. Production

    c. Sandbox

    d. Testing platform

8
Debugging and Deployment Tools

While developing applications, you might encounter errors you didn't expect. In this chapter, you will learn how to check your logic for bugs. Once your application is bug-free and working, you'll want to be able to push your customizations to a production or other type of environment.

The following topics will be covered in this chapter:

- Debugging your application
- Different development tools at your disposal
- Different types of Salesforce environments
- Different deployment methods

Monitoring and accessing debug logs

Sometimes, while developing, you will encounter an unexpected error, and you'll have to find out why the error happened and how to solve it. On the other hand, it might happen that you have already deployed some customizations into a production environment and only months later, an end user calls with an unexpected error. If only there were some tools or features to let you check which steps the user took to reproduce the error. That's exactly why Salesforce has a monitoring and debugging functionality.

What is a debug log?

A debug log is a file that contains a detailed log for all database operations, underlying system processes, and eventual errors occurring while executing transactions or unit tests. It helps you in debugging issues related to the following:

- Database changes
- HTTP callouts
- Apex errors
- Workflow rules
- Assignment rules
- Approval processes
- Validation rules

Debug logs can be consulted/viewed from **Setup** (within the Developer Console) and from any Salesforce compatible IDE, such as the Force.com IDE, VS Code, Welkin Suite, and Illuminated Cloud.

Debug logs can be customized to show more or less detailed information (called **DebugLevel**), because they have a size limit of 2 MB per log and an org-wide limit of 50 MB of debug logs, you can adapt the debug levels to be able to show the data you want. When you would exceed this limit, you would still be able to see the log file, but at the end it will be truncated.

To enable a debug log, navigate to **Setup** | **Environments** | **Logs - Debug Logs**, click on **New**, and enter the following information:

- **Traced Entity Type**: An automated process, Apex class, Apex trigger, or user you want to track.
- **Traced Entity Name**: Look up the user, process, class, or trigger from the org you want to track the logs of.
- **Start and Expiration Date**: Because there is a limit on debug logs, set the date and time from when you want to track the entity until the tracking expires.
- **Debug Level**: The level of detail you want in your **Debug Logs** (**NONE, ERROR, WARN, INFO, DEBUG, FINE, FINER,** or **FINEST**):

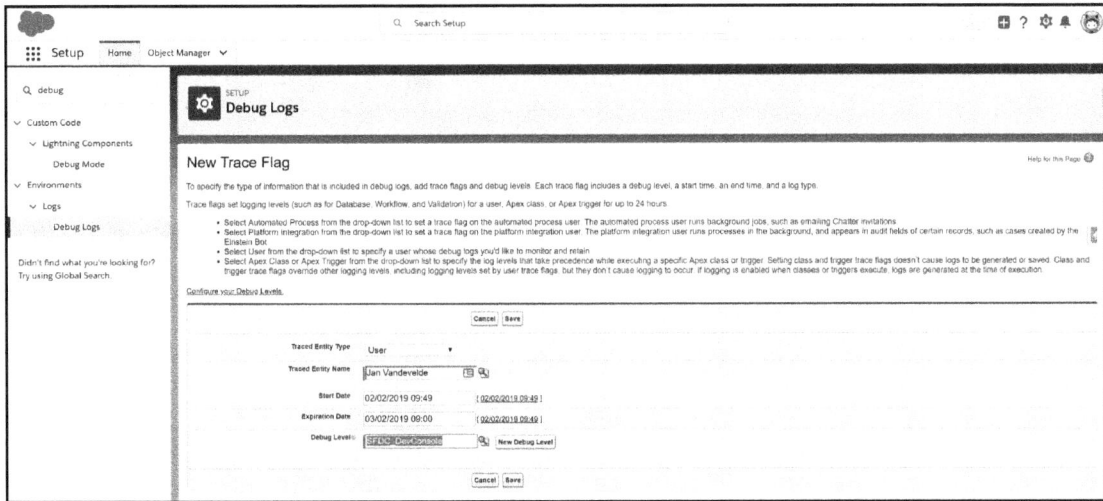

You can create your own **Debug Levels** (each debug level includes a **Log Level** (level of detail) per **Log Category** (categorization of actions on the platform)). The levels are listed from the lowest detail to the highest detail.

The log levels can show more or fewer details about a category, as follows:

- **NONE**
- **ERROR**
- **WARN**
- **INFO**
- **DEBUG**
- **FINE**
- **FINER**
- **FINEST**

The log categories are as follows:

Database	Provides you with information about database activities, like DML statements, SOQL, and/or SOSL queries.
Workflow	Provides information on declarative automation, like workflow rules, flows, and processes. It shows you the name of the process and which actions are taken.
Validation	Provides details on validation rules, such as the name and whether the rule evaluated to true or false.
Callout	Provides details on interactions (API calls) with web services. It shows what was requested of, and what the response was from, the external system.
Apex Code	Provides information on your Apex code execution. It can show error messages from DML statements, SOQL or SOSL queries, when triggers started and ended their execution, and the execution of any unit tests.
Apex Profiling	Provides information on limits, like the number of DML statements executed and how many are left, the number of SOQL queries and how many there are left before hitting the limit, the number of emails sent, and so on.
Visualforce	Provides information on events happening in your Visualforce pages, including the view state.
System	Provides information on all the `System` class methods called within your execution context, like calls to `System.debug()`.
Nba	Provides information on Einstein Next Best Action activity, like strategy execution details from Strategy Builder.
Wave	Provides information on Einstein Analytics (formerly known as Wave Analytics).

The following image shows a custom **DebugLevel** setup:

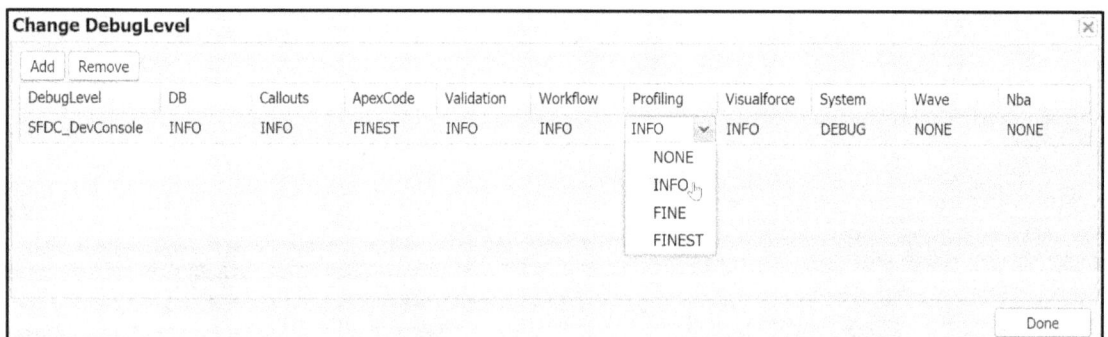

Working with the Developer Console, Workbench, and Force.com IDE platforms

The Developer Console, Workbench, and different IDEs are all tools that connect to your Salesforce environment through the Salesforce API, which means that the permission to use the API should be enabled to use one of these tools by the user.

Developer Console

The Developer Console is the out-of-the-box, cloud-based IDE that Salesforce provides you with. It is only connected to one org—the one from which you start up the Developer Console. It's not possible to open the Developer Console from your production org and connect it to one of your sandboxes or other environments!

The Developer Console can be used to:

- Create, edit, and delete Apex classes, triggers, Lightning components, Visualforce pages, and Visualforce components.
- Execute unit tests and analyze the test results.
- Write and execute SOQL and SOSL queries to visualize data from within your org.
- Execute code in an anonymous context directly on your database, including SOQL and DML statements.
- Debug your code by generating debug logs and analyzing them.
- Set breakpoints in your Apex code to identify and resolve errors.

Use the Developer Console if you don't have an IDE installed on your computer, or when you only need to connect to one org and you don't need version control of your code. In most cases, the Developer Console is there for emergencies only, or if you are a solo admin/developer on an org. When working with a team of developers, the best practice is to use a professional IDE with version control and link your code/configuration to a code repository! Working in the Developer Console is nice and all, when you are a solo admin/developer in an org, but when working in a team, you might overwrite code of your colleagues without having a history on changes.

Workbench

Workbench is a powerful, web-based toolset that was created for administrators as well as developers to connect to, interact with, and explore any Salesforce org through APIs.

Workbench was created by an employee at Salesforce for his own use and maintained as an open-source project, but it's not officially supported by Salesforce. Workbench can be accessed through `https://workbench.developerforce.com`, and you'll have to log in with your Salesforce username and password to connect to your org:

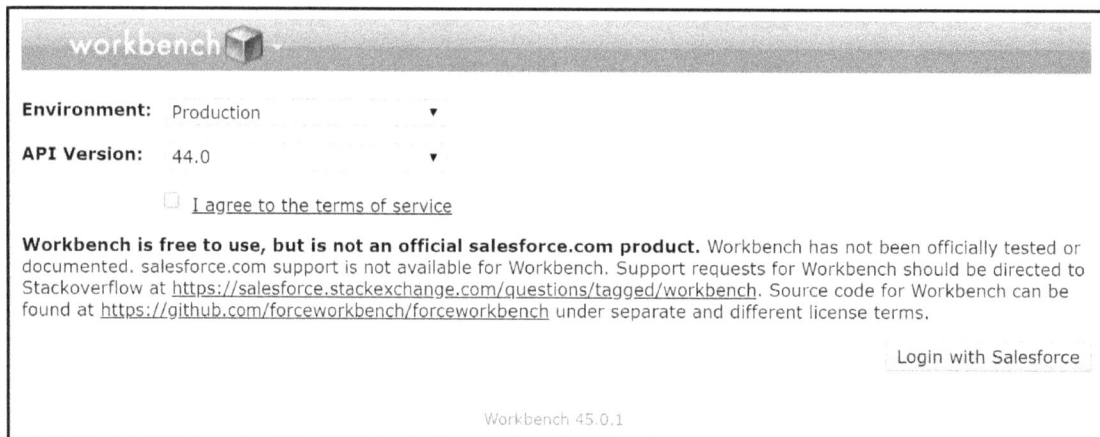

Workbench can be used for a variety of tasks and actions:

- To get information about the metadata in your org, such as objects, attributes, fields, record types, and relationship models.
- You can run SOQL and/or SOSL queries, much like you can from the Developer Console. You can view your data, and even export it to CSV files.
- You can manipulate data by using DML statements against one record that's specified or a list of records from a CSV or ZIP file.
- Retrieve and deploy metadata from and to your org.
- Use Execute Anonymous to execute code chunks directly.
- Run and test web service calls.

I use Workbench, for example, when I'm going to give an end user training as a new customer, to create users, and to give them all the same password before the training starts. This way, I can make it personalized, and I won't lose half an hour with users searching for their activation emails.

To do that, just create your users in the training environment, but uncheck the **Send the password and notify new user** checkbox. This way, your users will be created without receiving the activation email. Then, navigate to Workbench, and under **utilities**, select **Password Management**. For each user, enter their Salesforce ID and set a catchy password, for example, `TrainingWithJan1!`, and hit **Change Password**:

If you need more information on how to use Workbench and what you can do with it, check out the wiki at `https://github.com/forceworkbench/forceworkbench/wiki`.

The Force.com IDE

For years, the Force.com IDE has been the integrated development platform to develop Salesforce on, but it isn't supported anymore. You can still use it, but Salesforce no longer provides any support.

> It's a plugin built on top of the open source Eclipse platform and is available for download from: `https://developer.salesforce.com/docs/atlas.en-us.eclipse.meta/eclipse/ide_install.htm`.

The plugin lets you interact with the Salesforce.com platform. The Force.com IDE can connect to multiple orgs. By creating a project and downloading your orgs metadata, you can then start modifying, creating, and deleting the metadata. After you have made your changes, you can deploy the new version of the metadata to the org. All of this is done through the metadata API:

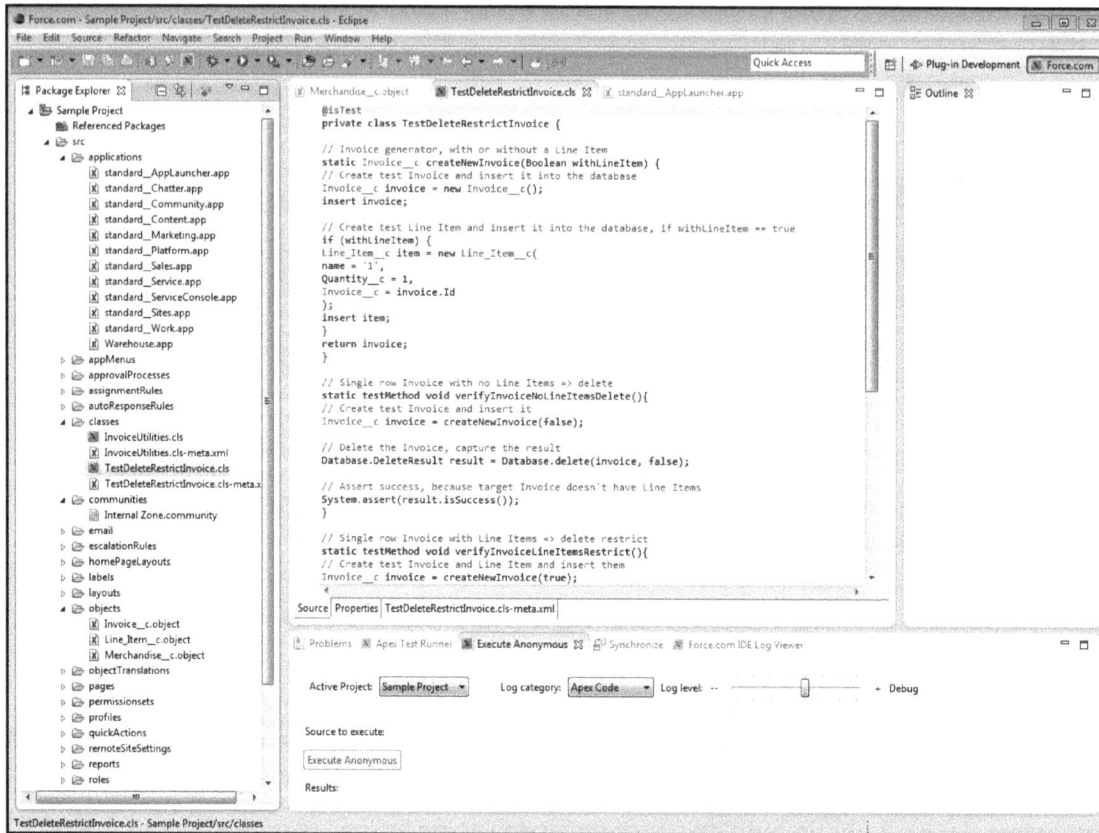

Development on the Salesforce Platform is now primarily done through Visual Studio Code. VS Code is a free IDE used to develop in multiple languages like Java, JavaScript. If you want to use it specifically for Salesforce development then it can be extended with Salesforce Extensions for VS Code. The **Salesforce Extensions for VS Code** can be found at: `https://forcedotcom.github.io/salesforcedx-vscode/articles/getting-started/install`.

From Spring 2019, this will be the only IDE supported by Salesforce:

Of course, there are other commercial IDEs specifically for development on the Salesforce Platform, as well, which are widely used, because Visual Studio Code and the Salesforce extensions are still quite new.

The most popular commercial IDE's are

www.welkinsuite.com and www.illuminatedcloud.com.

Salesforce environments

When we refer to environments, we are talking about an org or an instance. These three words can be used interchangeably.

It's *your* little space from the multi-tenant environment—*your* instance of the Salesforce Platform. When you sign up for an org, you get access through your unique username. As stipulated in Chapter 1, *Salesforce Fundamentals*, your username must be unique worldwide and org-wide. It's through the username that Salesforce knows to which instance it needs to grant you access. There are different types of environments, and we can categorize them as follows:

- **Production environments**: These are Salesforce environments that contain active and paying licenses. Most companies will only have one production environment, but they can have multiple environments if their business process and data processing laws demand the separation of data among legal entities, business units, or countries. They contain business-critical data and support day-to-day business processes.

- **Development environments**: These are environments created specifically to learn to extend, integrate, and develop on the platform without any risk of blowing up the production org. They are also used by Trailhead to do exercises to learn how to work with the platform. They contain most features (even paying add-ons) that production has, but only have two full Salesforce licenses to play with. It's kind of a limited edition of a production-worthy environment. They are free to use, but are deactivated after six months of inactivity. This is the kind of environment we have used throughout this entire book.

- **Test environments**: These are also known as sandboxes. Every production instance comes with one or more sandboxes linked to your production, and they come in different shapes. They are specifically used to configure or develop new functionality or processes; test these before deploying to production or releasing to your customers. When I say they come in different shapes, I mean there are four different types of sandboxes:
    - **Developer sandbox**: A maximum of 200 MB of data can be refreshed on a daily basis. This is an exact replica of your production's metadata, but it does not copy over any data. It's mostly used by developers to create a small piece of functionality.
    - **Developer Pro sandbox**: A maximum of 1 GB of data, and can be refreshed on a daily basis. This is an exact replica of your production's metadata, but does not copy over any data. Use it to create a new piece of functionality, but you need some more data to thoroughly test things, like stress testing.

- **Partial Copy sandbox**: A maximum of 5 GB of data can be refreshed on a weekly basis. It is an exact replica of your production's metadata and includes a subset of production records. You can define which objects it should copy with a standalone template. Mostly used for user acceptance testing or as a training environment before deploying to production. One Partial Copy sandbox is included in the Enterprise edition of Salesforce.
- **Full Copy sandbox**: This is an exact replica of your production environment, including all data. It can be refreshed once a month. It can be used for user acceptance testing and as a training environment, as well as for integration testing with other systems. It can also be used as a backup for all your production data, but it does not come cheap! One Full Copy sandbox is included in the Unlimited edition of Salesforce.

A Developer edition is ideal if the following applies:

- You are a partner or ISV who intends to build an app available for distribution through either the unmanaged package or managed package on the AppExchange (`http://www.appexchange.com/`).
- You are a customer with a Professional, Group, or Personal edition, and you do not have access to a sandbox. You can use a developer environment to create and test changes and deploy to your production instance through a package or IDE.
- You are a developer or Salesforce enthusiast looking to learn and explore the capabilities of the Salesforce Platform for *free*! Think Trailhead!

Note that, only Developer edition environments can create managed packages.

A sandbox is ideal if the following applies:

- You are a customer with the enterprise, unlimited, or Force.com edition, which includes a sandbox. The sandbox is related to your production, and you can use change sets to deploy easily.
- You are developing an application or extending a business process specifically for your production environment.
- You are not planning to distribute your configuration through packages.
- You have no intention of creating a commercial application meant for the AppExchange.

Deploying metadata to another org

Everything we have built throughout this book is considered metadata—the BIM DB application containing the movie, person, cast, review, and production company objects and their fields are; the records we created, like `The Godfather`, are considered data! You already saw how you we can export and import data in `Chapter 2`, *Understanding Data Modeling and Management*, in the *Importing and exporting data into development environments* section. Now, we are going to explore the different ways to move (deploy) our metadata (all our customizations) from one org to another.

To deploy metadata between Salesforce orgs, you can use change sets, the Force.com IDE, any other IDE (with Salesforce plugins), or the Force.com migration tool (ANT).

Before we start, I want you to know that this will be a more theoretical chapter. As we are developing on a developer org, I will not be able to give you lots of exercises. I will demonstrate some of the deployment methods using an example production environment with connected sandboxes, and will provide screenshots as we go.

The easiest and most declarative way is by using change sets, so let's start with that.

Deploying metadata with change sets

Using change sets is the most common and easiest way to deploy metadata from a sandbox to another sandbox or your production environment. It's important to note that the orgs need to be connected to each other; that's why I specifically say from a sandbox to another sandbox or production! You can't use change sets to deploy data from a developer org to another developer org, because those aren't and can't be connected to each other.

A change set is a little container, a package, containing the components you created or modified in your sandbox that you would like to deploy to your production after it has been carefully tested.

To use change sets, both orgs need an established deployment connection. This means that on the target org, you'll need to approve a specific sandbox as an inbound connection; similarly, on the source org, you'll need to approve an outbound connection with the target org.

To showcase this, I have a real production org on which I'll create a sandbox.

> You can't do the following on your Developer edition, but you'll need to know the functionality on the exam. So, just follow along.

To create a sandbox, navigate to **Setup** in a production instance and search for **Sandboxes**:

At the moment, we have no sandboxes set up, so let's create one by clicking on the **New Sandbox** button. Give your sandbox a very short name (because it will be used in usernames). In our example, we call it `Dev` and add a description. Click on the **Next** button in the column representing the type of sandbox you would like to create and which is still available. I'm choosing **Developer Pro**:

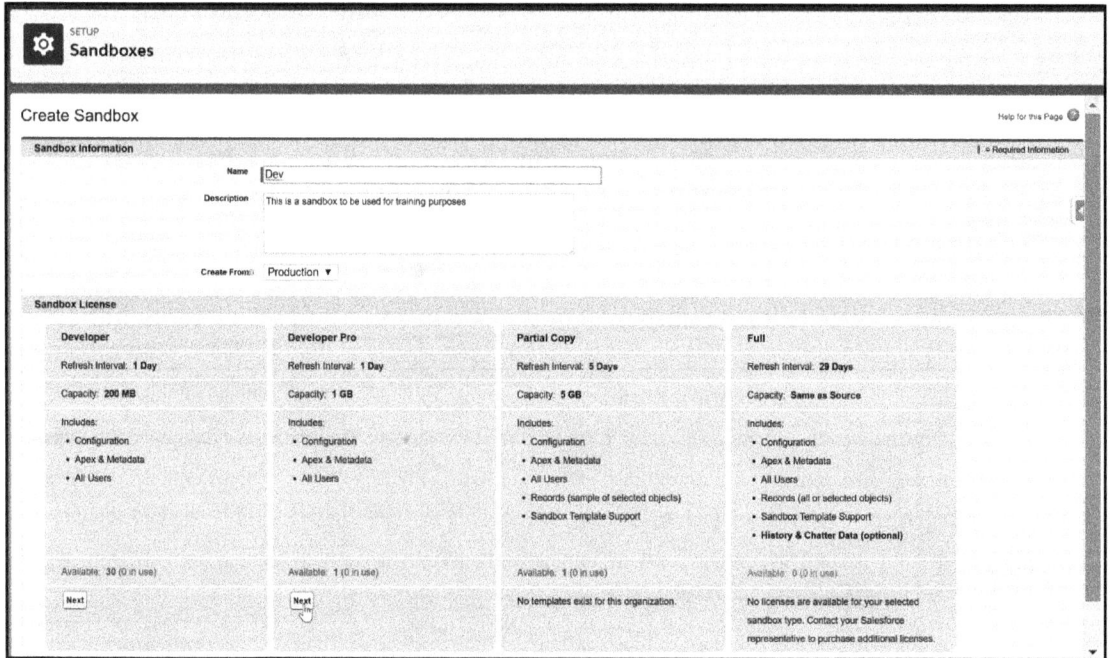

Where it asks for the **Apex Class**, just leave it blank. You could choose to run an Apex class that will be called automatically, once the sandbox is ready for use. This is useful for creating or populating your sandbox with some test data, or to perform some post-sandbox creation installation steps.

You'll see that the creation of your sandbox will be put into in a queue:

You can track the progress by refreshing the page a couple of times:

You will receive an email once the sandbox has been created and is ready for use.

Once it's ready, you should have a login link next to your sandbox record in production. You can click on it and log in to your sandbox:

Now, to show you how to deploy something from a sandbox to a production org using change sets, I'm going to create a custom object with two fields, a workflow rule with a field update, and I'm going to deploy that to the production environment.

First, we created a new object called `TestObject` with a **Picklist** field called `Segment` (values: `bronze`, `gold`, `silver`, or `platinum`) and a secondary number field called `Segment Score`:

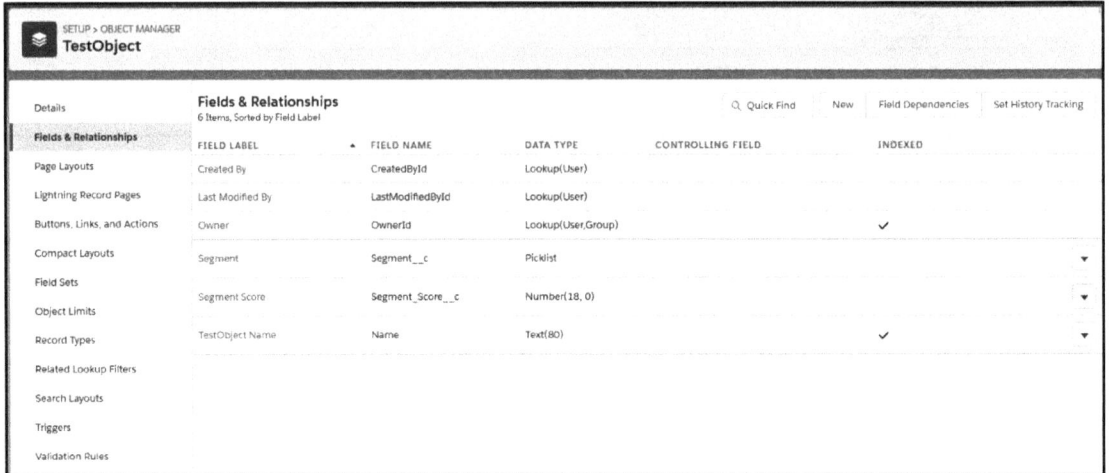

Next, we create a workflow rule that will update the segment score with a number, based upon the segment chosen. Let's have a look at the **Workflow Rules** page as follows:

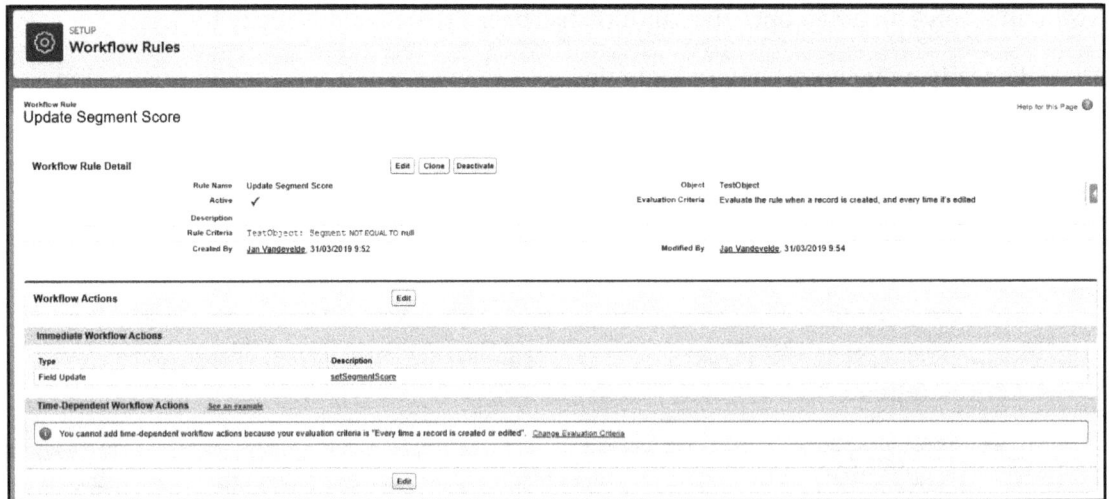

This is the field update:

Now, we'll show you a deployment of this custom object and fields, including the workflow rule and its field update.

The first thing to do is create an **Outbound Change Set** from the sandbox. An outbound change set is the container (package) in which you will put all the metadata components you would like to deploy to another related environment.

We navigate to **Setup** and we quickly, search for **Outbound Change Sets**:

To create a new change set, we click on **New**, giving our change set a name and a description. Depending on your release management strategy, a common naming convention is to name your change set with the name of a sprint or a build, which you are going to release. If you don't know what a sprint or build is, I refer you to the article at: `https://www.scrum.org/resources/what-is-a-sprint-in-scrum`, as it is beyond the scope of this book. But let's just say it's a piece of ready-to-deploy functionality.

I've called mine `Sprint 1`:

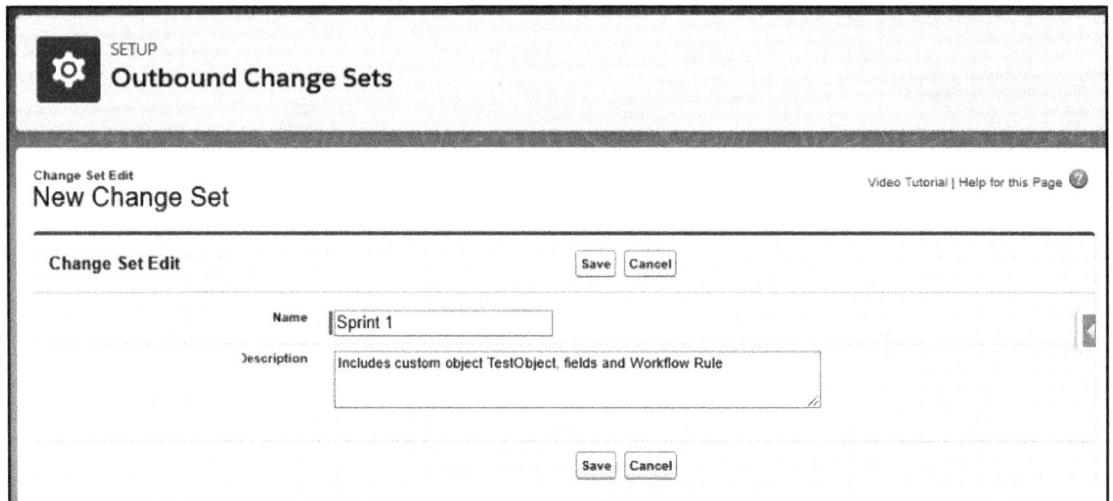

SETUP
Outbound Change Sets

Change Set Edit
New Change Set

Video Tutorial | Help for this Page

Change Set Edit   Save   Cancel

Name | Sprint 1

Description | Includes custom object TestObject, fields and Workflow Rule

Save   Cancel

The following screen is divided into two parts:

- **Change Set Components** (you will add the metadata components to deploy).
- **Profile Settings for Included Components** (includes profiles, access, and visibility for the corresponding metadata included in your change set):

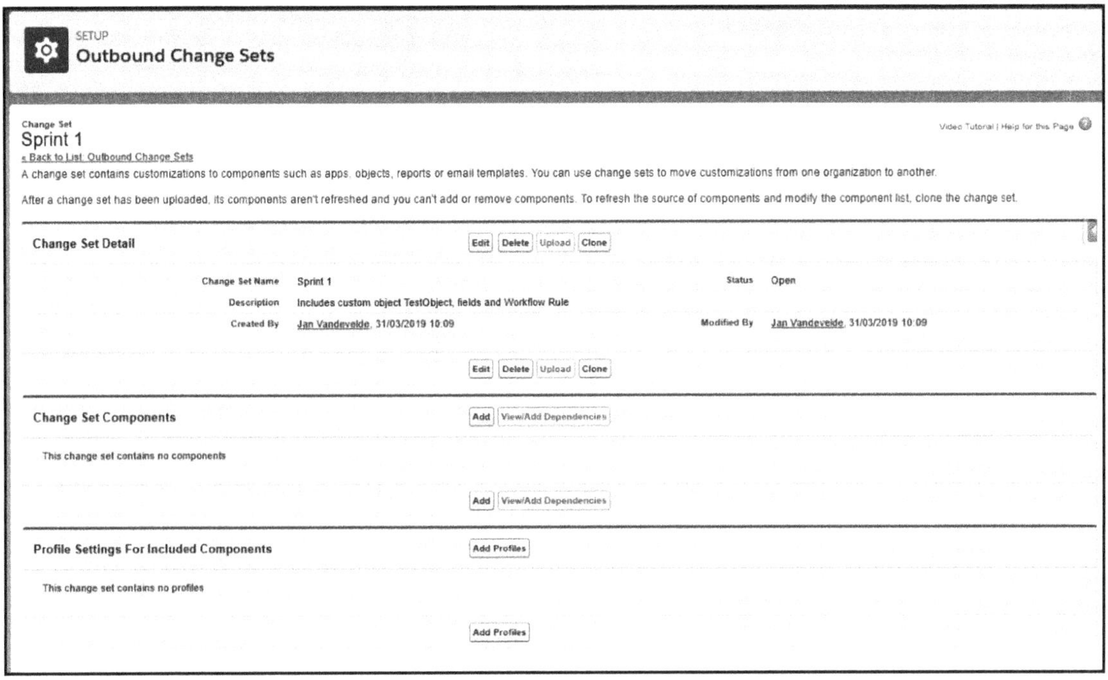

To add metadata components, we click on the **Add** button from the **Change Set Components** section, and we select which type of component we would like to add. First, we want to add a **Custom Object**:

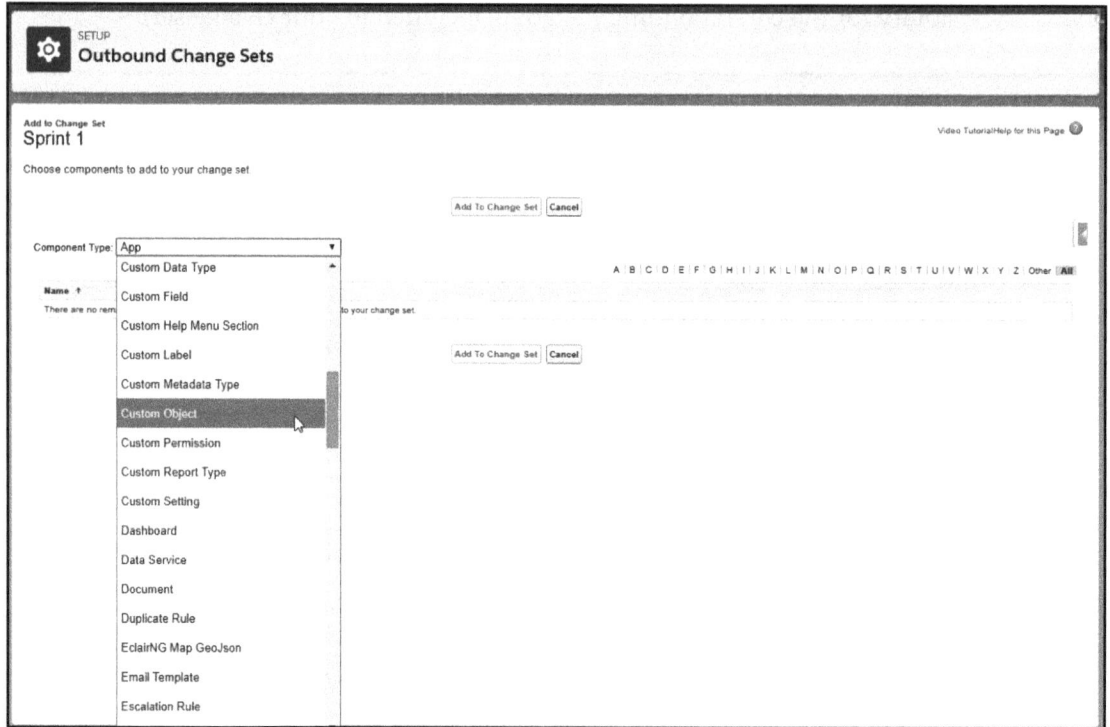

So, when we select **Custom Object**, we will be presented with a list of all custom objects in our environment:

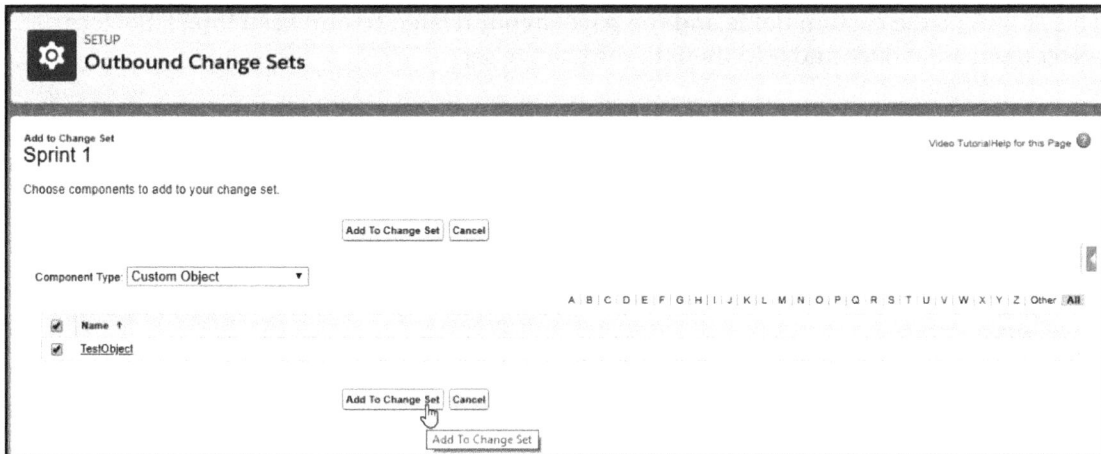

We only have one custom object, and that's my **TestObject**, so I'll select that and click on the **Add To Change Set** button.

When this is added, we are redirected to the change set overview, and we'll see that our **TestObject** is included. Now, we know that we created fields on our **TestObject**, and each object also automatically comes with a page layout (otherwise, we would never be able to add data). We could add each of those components individually, the same way we just did, but there is a special button (**View/Add Dependencies**) that shows any dependencies of metadata. Let's click on that:

This shows us the custom fields and the page layout related to our **TestObject**. So, let's select them all at once and add them to the change set:

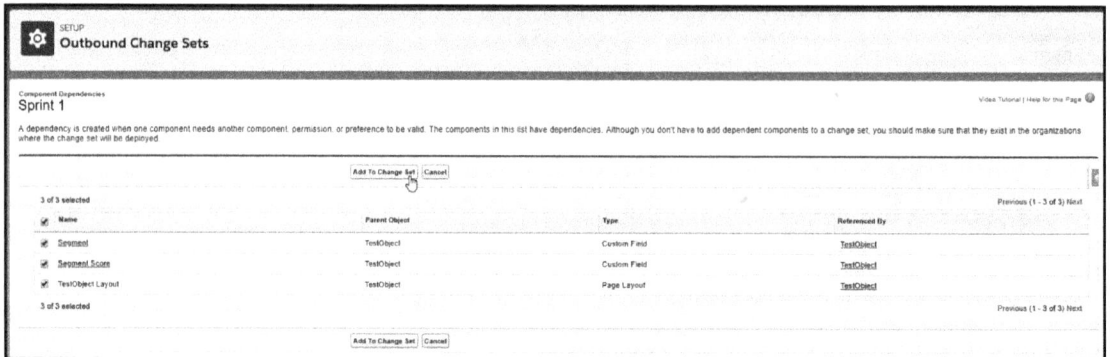

The next thing we want to include is our **Workflow Rule**. So, we click on **Add** again, select the **Workflow Rule** type, and add our **Update Segment Score** workflow rule:

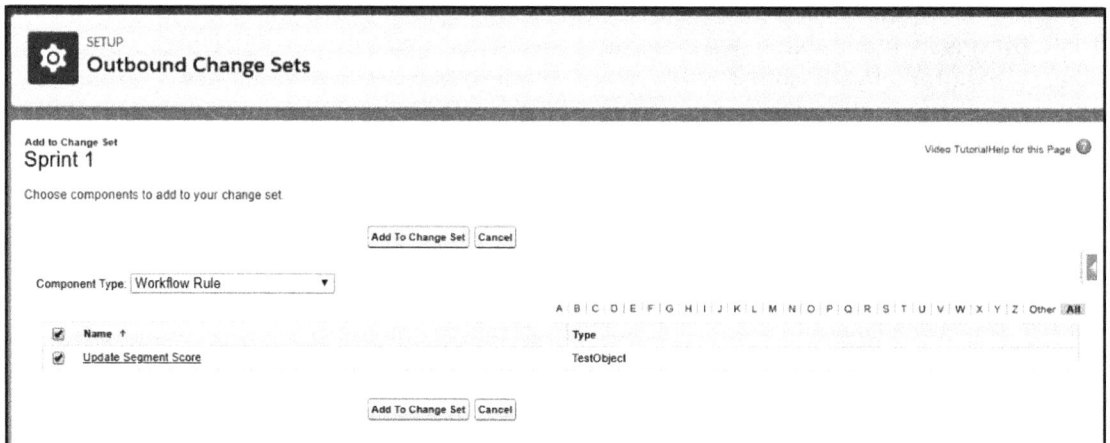

Once that's added, we can click on the **View/Add Dependencies** button again to show us if we haven't forgotten anything. This will also show us the field update action related to our workflow rule. So, we'll add that, too:

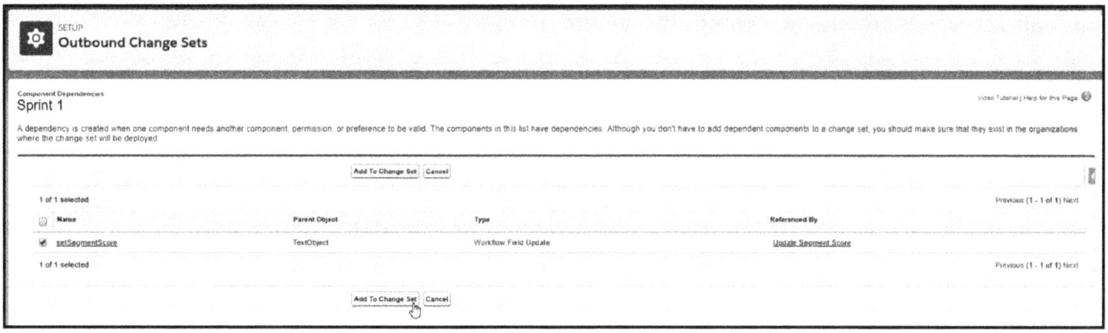

Now, everything is in our change set, so let's also add the **System Administrator** profile to the **Profile Settings For Included Components** section, so that after the deployment, we will have the same access rights in our production environment as we have here in our sandbox. Our complete change set now looks like this:

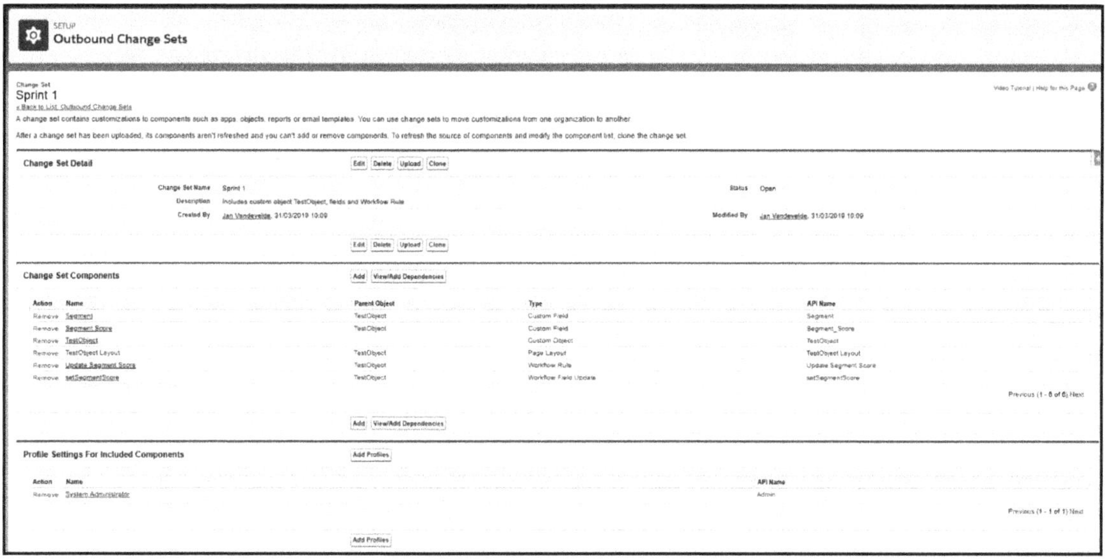

We are now ready to upload our change set to the target environment, which, in our case, is production. To be able to upload to another environment, we need to establish a **deployment connection**. When we click on **Upload** at this time, we will receive the following error message, because we haven't established a deployment connection between our sandbox and our production environments:

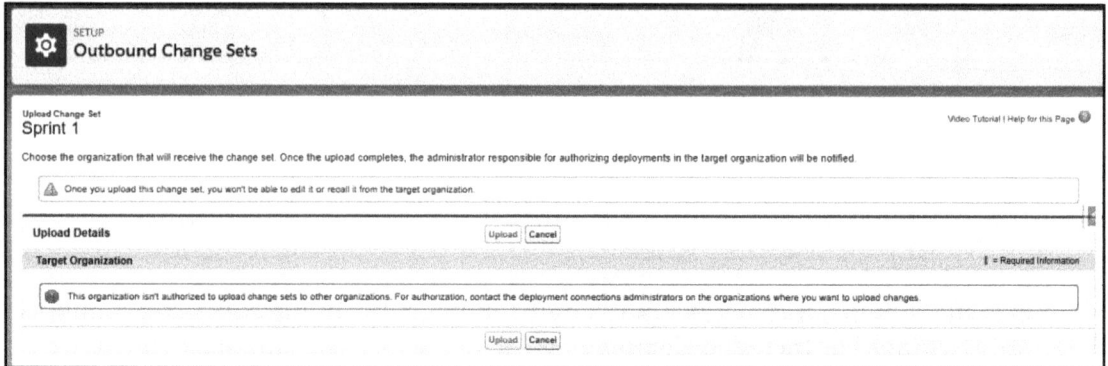

To establish a deployment connection, you must create this from the target environment as an incoming connection.

So, we log in to our production, navigate to **Setup**, and search for **Deployment Settings**, where we can see that we have a related sandbox called **Dev**, but with a broken connection symbol as shown in the following:

We need to edit this connection and check the checkbox **Allow Inbound Changes**, then hit **Save**:

Once this is done, we will have approved changes to be deployed coming from our **Dev** environment into our **Production** environment:

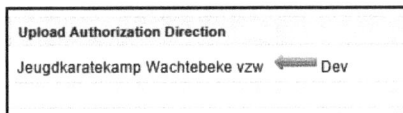

So, now that we have an active connection between the two, we head back to our sandbox and hit **Upload** again from our change set, and we should be able to select our **Production** environment to upload our change set to, like so:

Once the upload has finished successfully, you'll see that our change set has been **Closed**:

This means you can't make any modifications to this change set anymore. You can clone it and make changes and re-upload this cloned version of your change set, but this one isn't modifiable anymore.

Uploading a change set to another org (what we just did) doesn't mean it's deployed. In most cases, it's the customer's system administrator that will deploy this change set in the target org. Validating and deploying a change set needs to be done on the side of the target org. So, let's go back to our production environment and take a look at **Setup** at **Inbound Change Sets,** and we'll see our **Sprint 1** change set waiting for us to get it validated and/or deployed:

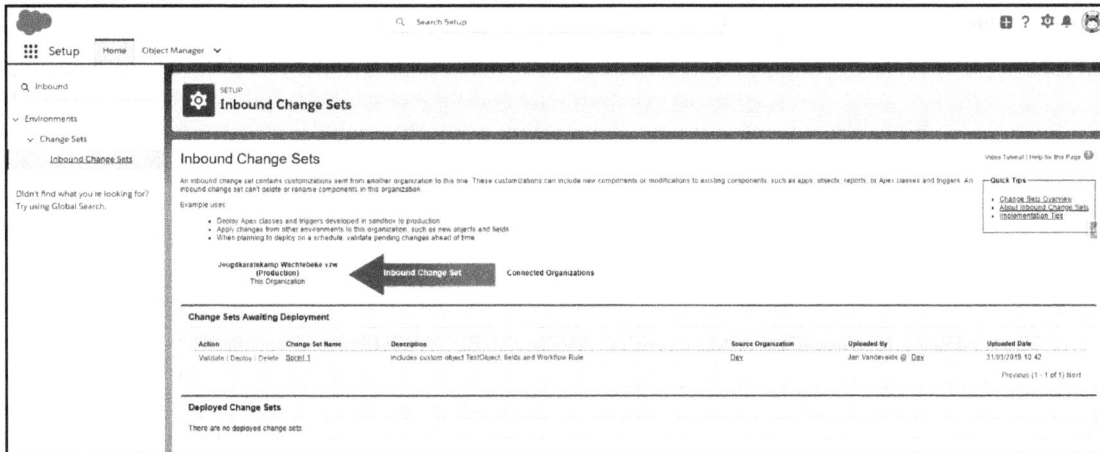

The best practice is to first validate your change set and, once it's validated, to deploy it. Validating a change set will run tests on the side of your target org to ensure the changes in metadata you are deploying won't break anything, or that you are not missing any dependencies. Also, when you have code in your org, the validation will run all test classes (depending on which test option you choose) and check whether you have enough code coverage and enough unit tests, and that all tests pass.

Remember that in `Chapter 7`, *Testing in Salesforce*, we learned that everything that you want to deploy to production, especially code, needs to adhere to certain rules, like having at least 75% of your code covered by tests, and so on. Well, this validation will check that. You might ask yourself—Why validate first; shouldn't we just hit **Deploy**? Hitting **Deploy** will automatically run the validation first; there is no way to circumvent the validation process! And you shouldn't want to.

When you click on **Validate,** you'll be presented with a choice of tests:

- **Default**: Keeps the following default behavior. In a sandbox, no tests are executed. In production, all local tests are executed if your change sets contain Apex classes or triggers. Local tests are all tests, except the ones that originate from managed packages. If your package doesn't contain Apex components, no tests are run.
- **Run Local Tests**: All tests in your org are run, except the ones that originate from installed managed packages. This test level is the default for production deployments that include Apex classes or triggers.

- **Run all Tests**: All tests in your org are run, including tests of managed packages.
- **Run Specified Tests**: Only the tests that you specify are run. Provide the names of test classes in a comma-separated list. Code coverage requirements differ from the default coverage requirements when using this level in production. The executed tests must cover the class or trigger in your change sets with a minimum of 75% code coverage. This coverage is computed for each class or trigger individually and is different from the overall coverage percentage.

Let's run the default, as this is the type of testing you should choose when deploying!

You'll get a **Deployment Status** screen, and in our case, the validation was successful:

This means our change set is actually ready to be deployed. So, let's hit **Deploy** on our inbound change set.

While the deployment is in progress, you'll see the status update:

If everything worked out fine, you should get a **Deployment Succeeded** message:

We successfully deployed some customizations that we did in a sandbox to our production environment via the use of **Change Sets**. This is the most common way to deploy and is completely declarative, without the need for any other tools.

Just like a system administrator can check through **Setup | View Setup Audit Trail** to see any changes made to the configuration in the org's setup, all components and changes made through a deployment can be traced in the audit trail, too. Here is an example of our **Sprint 1** deployment:

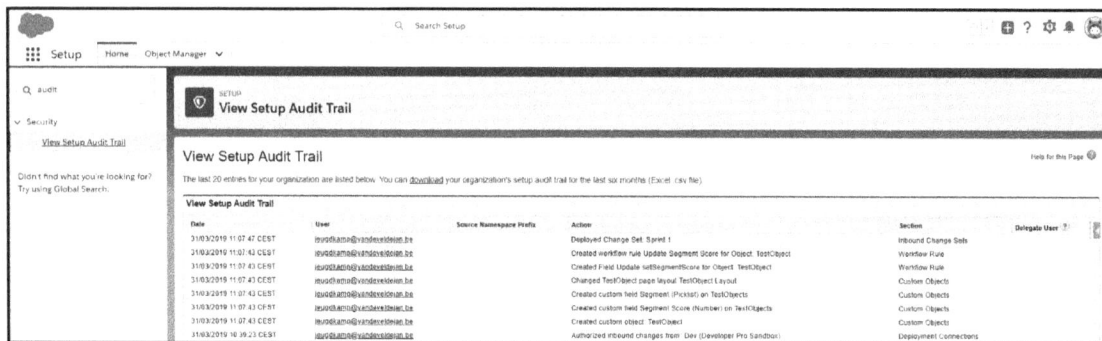

If you have multiple administrators or development teams deploying into an environment, you can use the **View Setup Audit Trail** to see who changed what, and when.

Some things to be aware of while deploying are as follows:

- To deactivate an Apex class or Apex trigger in a production environment, you can do it on a sandbox and then deploy it as inactive, through change sets.
- You cannot perform any destructive changes by deploying through change sets. This means that you can't use a change set to remove/delete metadata from your production environment. You can manually delete objects, page layouts, fields, and so on, but not Apex! To delete/remove Apex, you'll need to deploy using some tool that uses the metadata API, like an IDE, for example.

Deploying metadata through unmanaged packages

Another way to deploy customizations or code is through packages. Deploying through a package is much like installing an app from the AppExchange.

You will create an unmanaged package in your developer org that contains all the components that need to be deployed to a target org. Once your package is complete, an installation link will be generated. You, or somebody else, will then be able to install/deploy your package by clicking on that link and selecting on which org it needs to be deployed.

It's important to note that packages can only be created from developer orgs. Luckily for us, we did everything in a developer org. Also, deploying through the use of packages lets you deploy your components to any target org. So, they don't have to be related!

As an example and exercise, we are going to register for yet another brand new developer org and install/deploy some components from our BIM DB app into that org. We will not be deploying everything, as that would take too long to explain, but just a custom object and some fields, like in the previous example, that we will package up and then install in a totally unrelated org. So, let's do that:

1. Navigate to **Setup** | **Package Manager**:

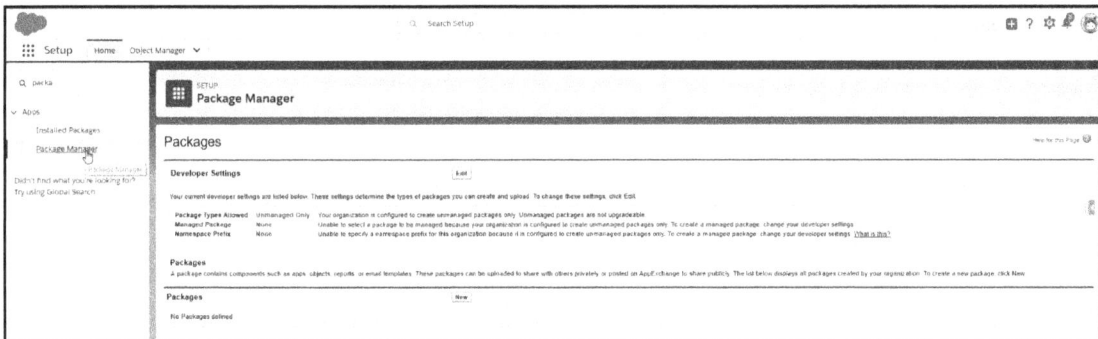

2. Click on the **New** button under the **Packages** section and give your package a name and description:

3. You'll find yourself on a similar screen to add components to your package, like we did when adding components to change sets:

4. So, click on the **Add** button, select **Custom Object** as the component type, select the **Company** object, and click **Add to Package**. You should see a screen like this:

5. You'll notice that the **Package Manager** automatically detects any dependencies and adds those to your package for you.

6. For this example, that's it. We will be installing/deploying this custom object into another developer org.

7. So, to generate your installation link, you need to upload this package. Click on the **Upload** button. The next screen will ask you to give it a **Version Name**:

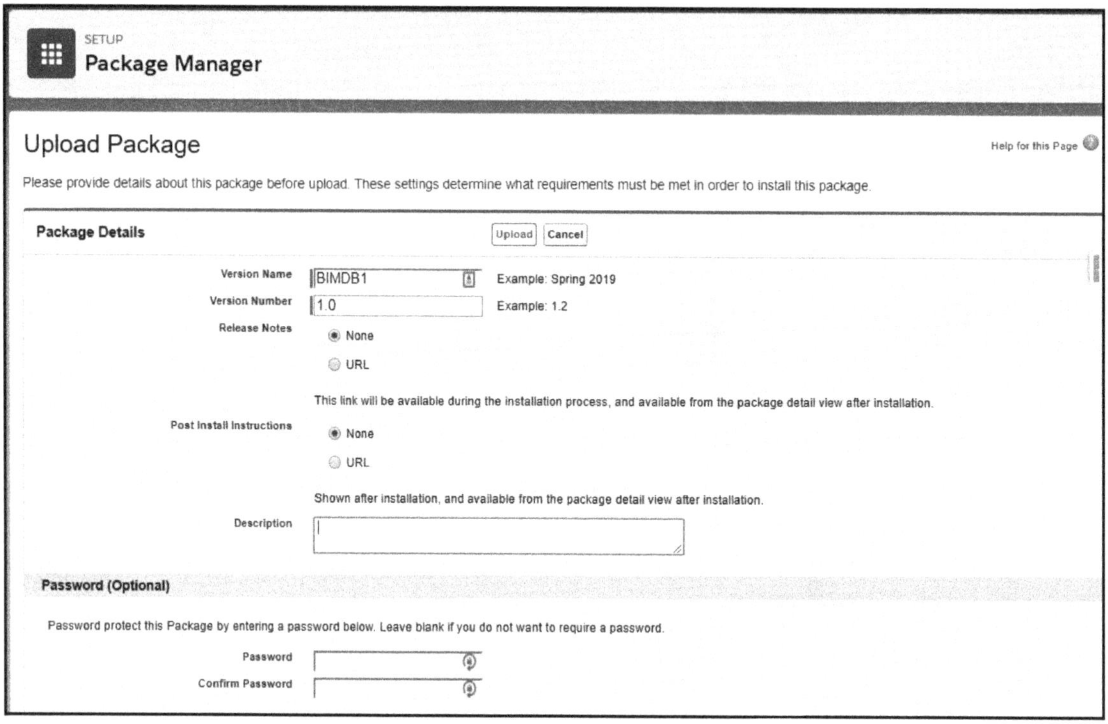

8. When creating a package, you can provide a URL to a page containing the release notes on that package version, and also a URL to post-install steps. If you want, you can also protect your package with a password, which would be asked for upon installation. This is because the link for an unmanaged package is public, and if somebody has that link, they can install the package. Protecting it with a password provides an extra security layer. For this example, we are not going to do that. So, leave everything as default, and just provide a version name.

9. In the package requirements section, you could mark the Salesforce features that need to be enabled in the target org because, some components in your package depend on the Salesforce features. For example, if you created some specific functionality for `Person Accounts`, then you would mark the enablement of `Person Accounts` as a prerequisite to installing your package; otherwise, it would fail to install.

10. We just have a custom object in our package, so no real dependencies. Leave all of the defaults and just click on the **Upload** button at the bottom of the page. Once the upload is complete, you'll see the following screen:

11. This provides you with an overview of all the included components, and, most importantly, your installation URL! You will also receive an email notification with your installation link in it:

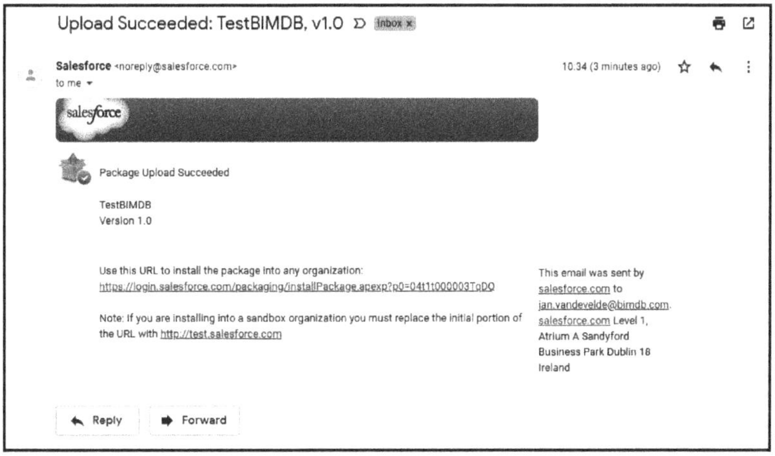

12. To test this out, we will need a new developer org. So, head over to `https://developer.salesforce.com/signup,` fill in the details, and log in to your new developer org. Now, while logged in to your brand new developer org, click on the installation link from your email.

13. You will see the installation screen, the same as you would see when installing apps from the AppExchange:

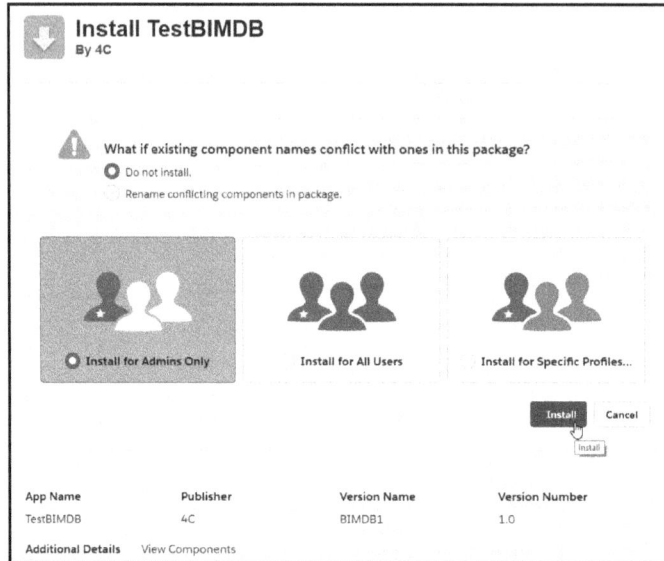

14. It asks you whether you want to provide access immediately, to only admins, to all users, or only for specific profiles. We'll leave this set to admins only! Just click on **Install**. You'll see that the installation will be in progress:

15. Once it's complete, you'll see the following screen:

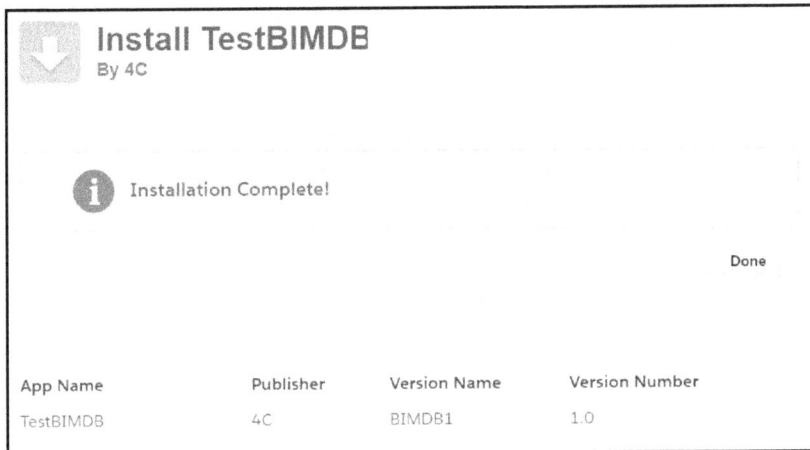

16. Now, click on the **Done** button. We are done. Let's check whether the installation worked for us. Navigate to **Setup | Object Manager**. You should find our custom object called `Company__c`:

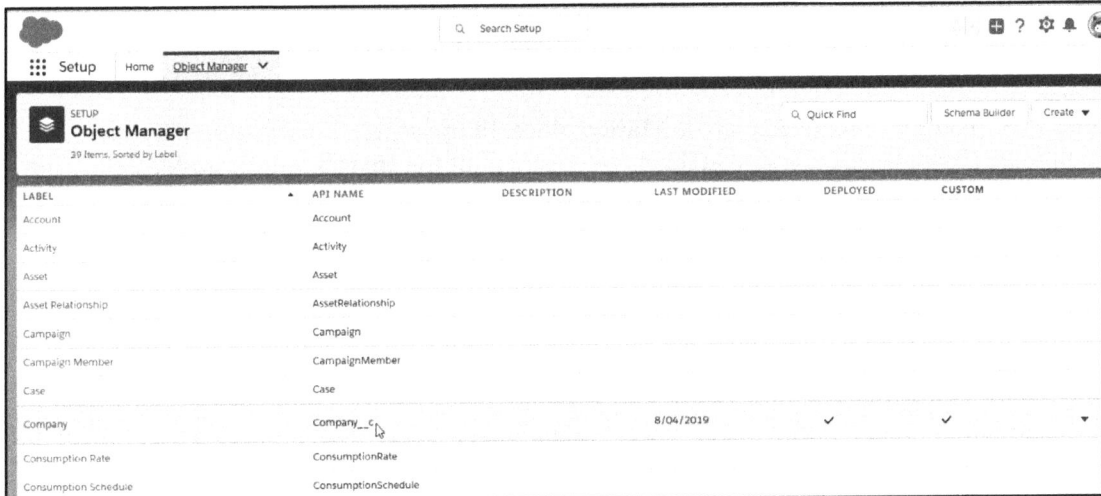

Congratulations; you have successfully created an unmanaged package and deployed it to another totally unrelated org! Easy, wasn't it?

Deploying metadata through an IDE

As we've mentioned a couple of times throughout this book, there are several tools available to use as an IDE, and I can't provide an example of all of them.

Which tool you use is more a matter of personal preference. I mostly use either Welkin Suite or Illuminated Cloud. I'll provide a very basic example of the use of Illuminated Cloud. Illuminated Cloud is a plugin that was created on top of IntelliJ Idea. You can download the free Community version of IntelliJ from: `https://www.jetbrains.com/idea/download/#section=windows`:

1. Just run the installer for your operating system; it's really straightforward. Once it's installed, you'll see the welcome screen.

2. Click on the **Configure** button at the bottom and select **Plugins**:

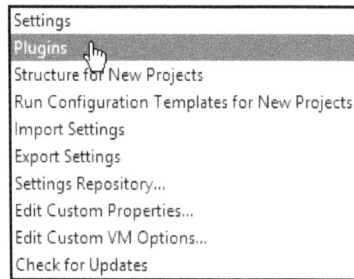

3. You'll be redirected to the **Marketplace**. In the search bar on top, search for `illuminated`, and you'll get two results; hit the **Install** button under **Illuminated Cloud 2**:

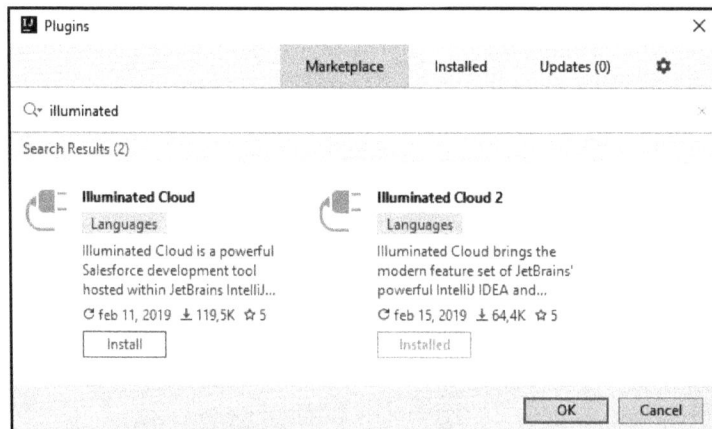

4. This will install the plugin (on my screen, you can see that it was already installed). Once that's done and you get back to the welcome screen, you can click on **Create New Project**. The first thing you need to select in the sidebar is the type of project you want to create. In our case, it's an **Illuminated Cloud** project, and we'll first want to create a connection to our BIM DB Dev 2 developer org (you know the second one we just deployed the unmanaged package in):

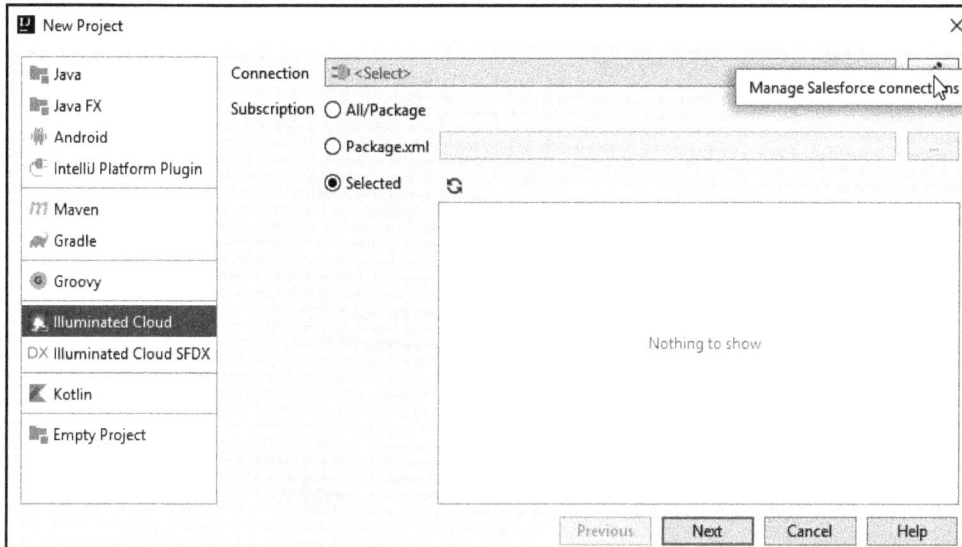

5. Now, remember that in Chapter 1, *Salesforce Fundamentals*, when we created our developer org, we also made some modifications, such as opening up the IP range on the system administrator profile so we wouldn't need to use any security tokens. Well, we didn't do those steps in the second developer org that we just created. It is a best practice to not open up your IP ranges, but this has the consequence that tools connecting through the API (like an IDE) will need a security token!

6. After creating your connection, you'll get the following error message when you click on the **Test** button to test your connection:

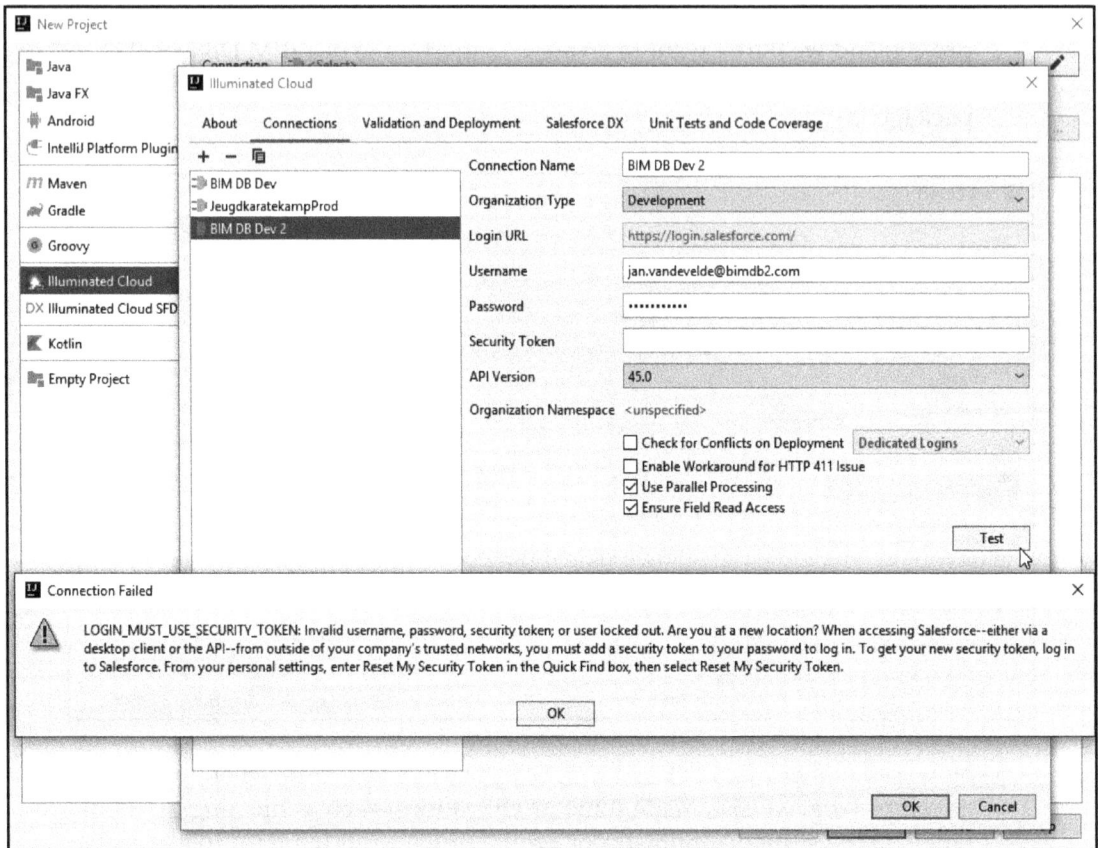

7. So, first, let's get our security token. Log in to your second developer org and click on your avatar (the little image on the top-right of the screen), then select **Settings**:

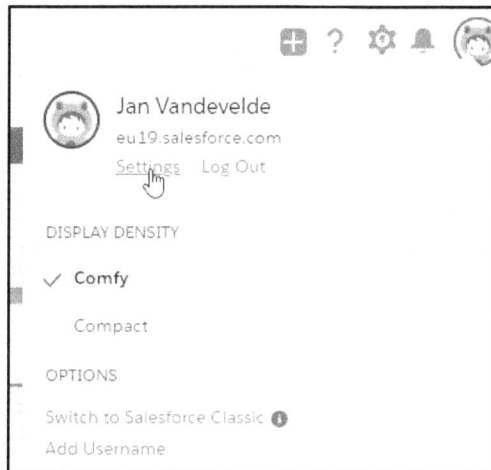

8. On the left sidebar, you'll find the **Reset My Security Token** menu:

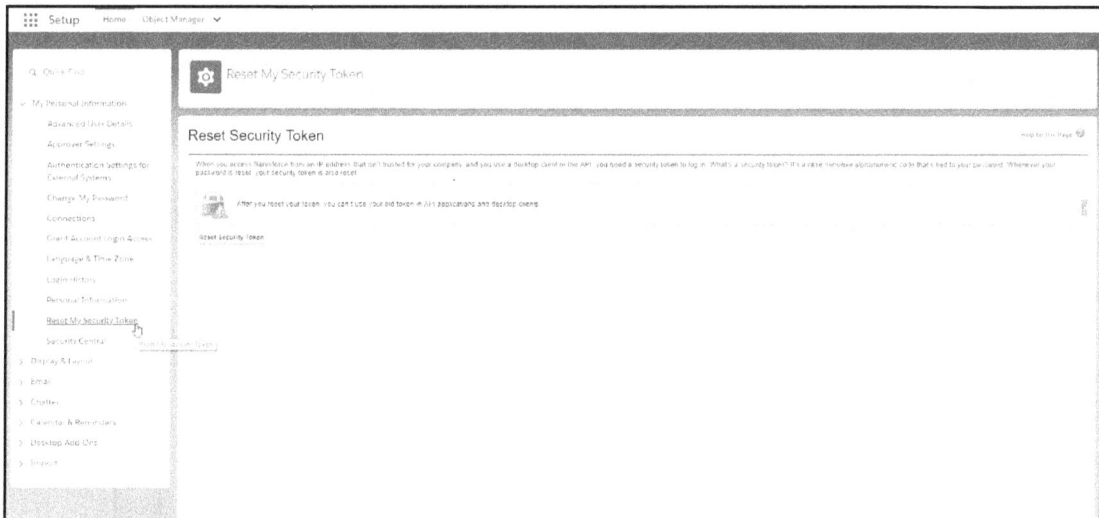

9. Click on the big button in the middle of the screen called **Reset Security Token,** and you'll receive a very long code by email:

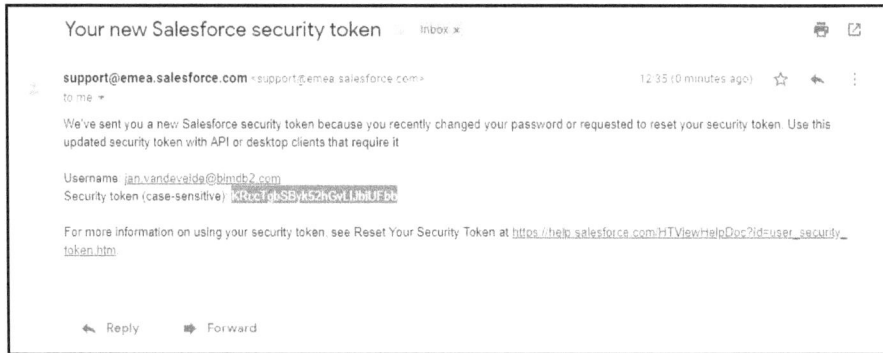

10. Copy and paste that code in to the **Security token** field in **Illuminated Cloud | Connections,** and click on the **Test** button again; you should now receive a **Connection Succeeded** message:

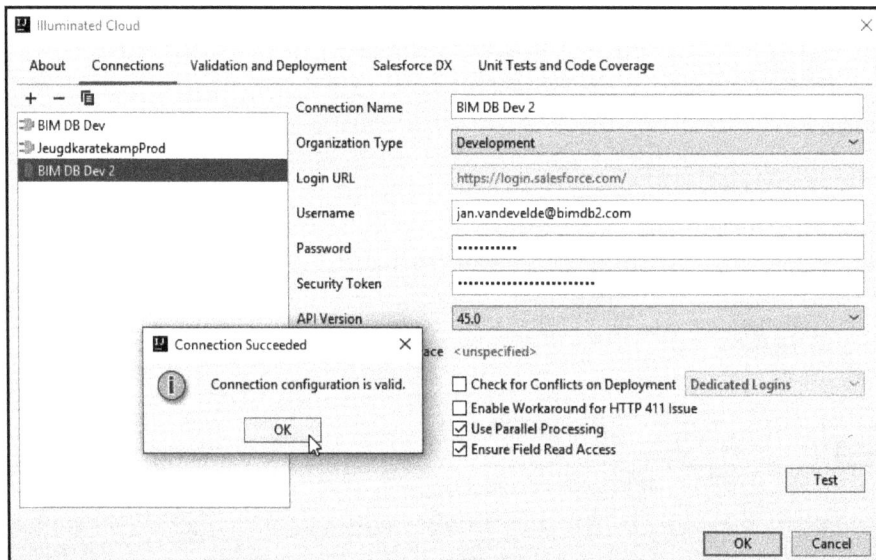

11. Click on **OK,** and then click on the **Next** button. **Illuminated Cloud** will start pulling all available metadata components from your org and present you with the following screen:

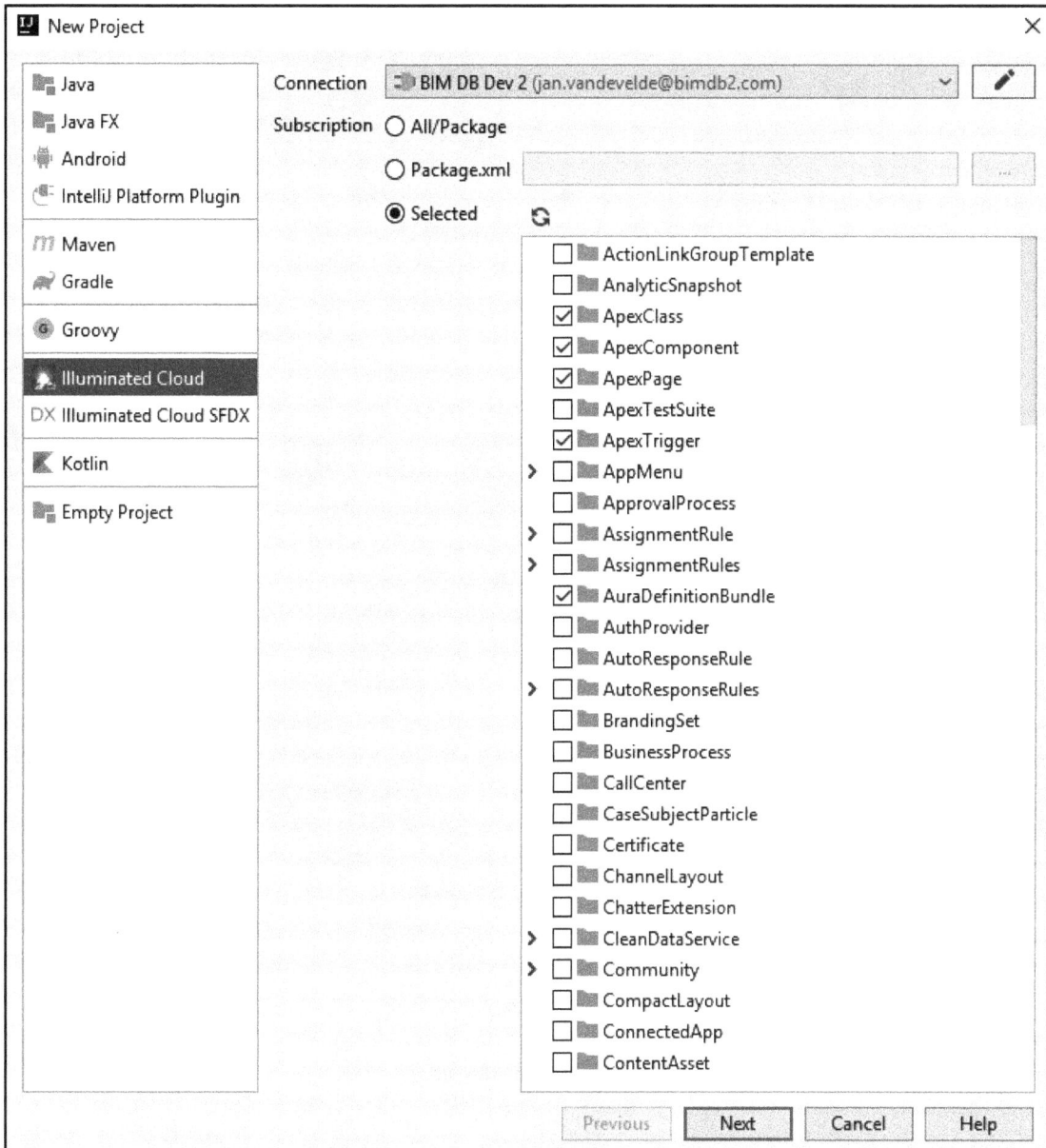

An IDE is mostly used purely for development, so the default selection of metadata is mostly like Apex classes, Apex triggers, Visualforce pages, Lightning components, and so on. However, you can select the metadata components you wish to download to your local machine to work on.

12. Just for fun, select every component you can select, and hit **Next**. The next screen will ask you where you want to save the project on your local drive. You can leave the defaults:

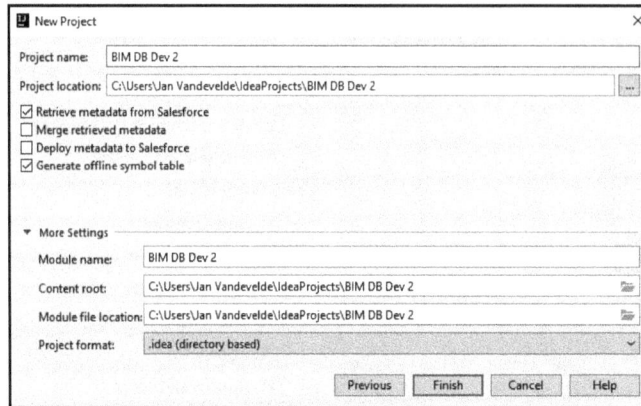

13. Click on **Finish**. It will start creating the project, and you'll see some warnings pop up. Don't worry about that too much; that's because **Illuminated Cloud** created an offline symbol table, and that will take a while. You'll get the following message, asking you to reload the project:

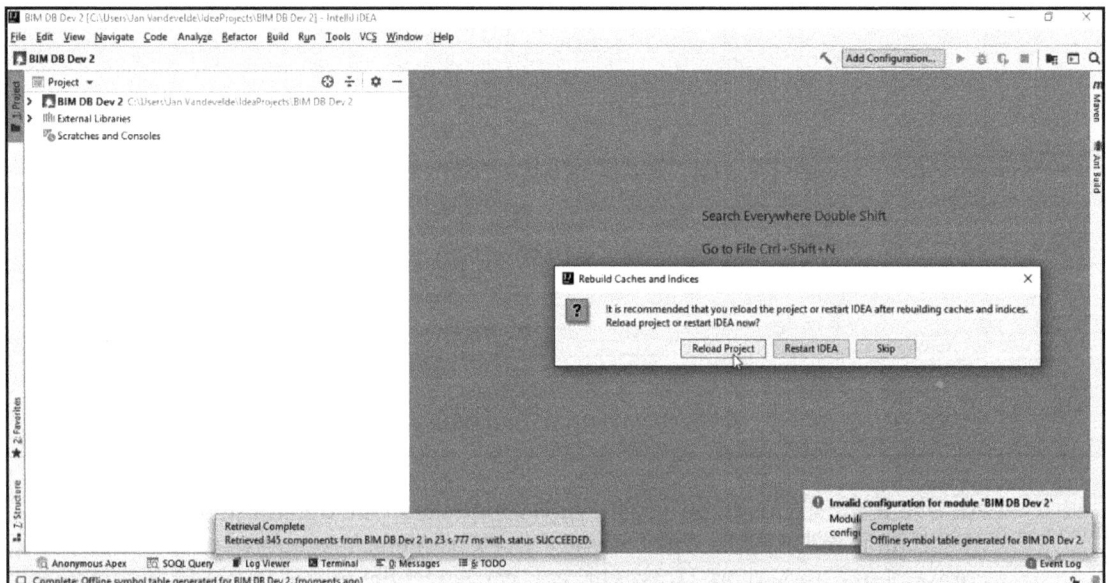

14. Click on **Reload**. Now, when you click in the left sidebar on our project name and expand it, you'll find all the metadata components that are in that org, including the custom object that we deployed earlier, called `Company__c`, in the `Objects` folder:

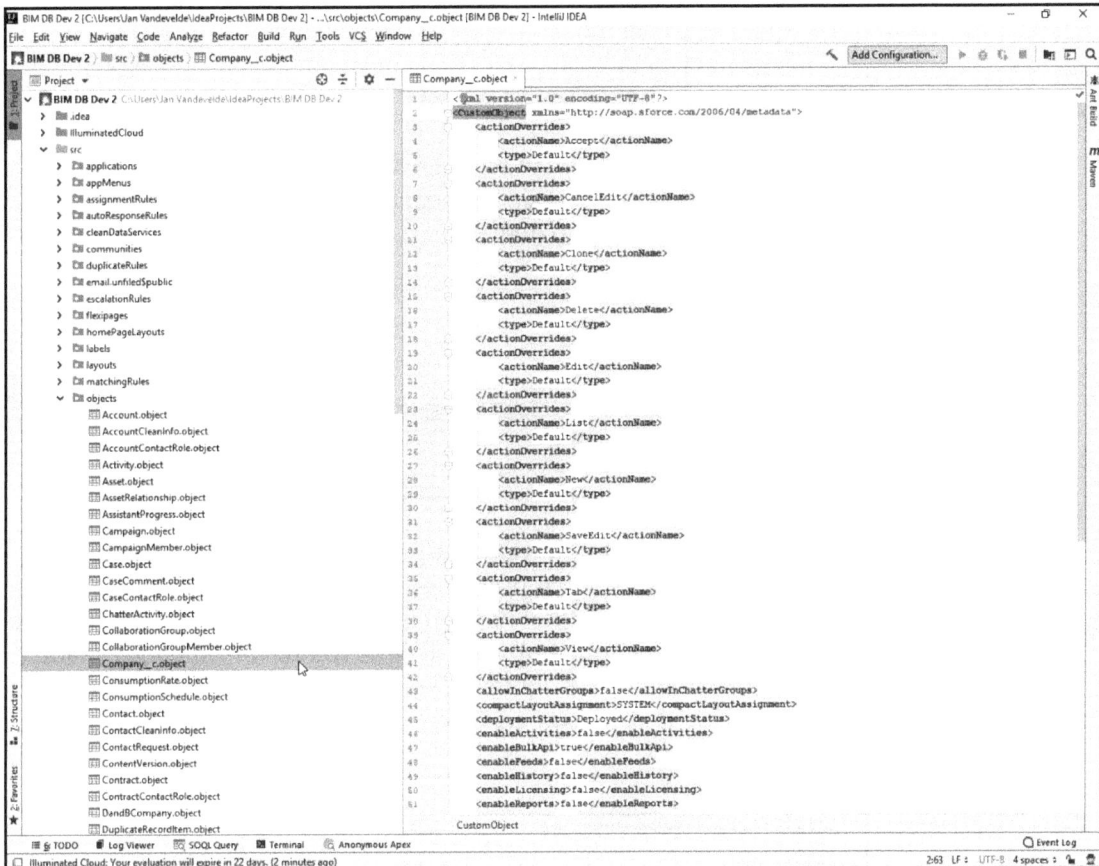

15. When double-clicking on a file, you'll see (and be able to modify) the contents of the XML file. However, we will not do that here, as it is beyond the scope of this book. What I would like you to do is right-click on our `Company__c.object` file and click **Delete**.

16. A popup will open, asking you if you want to check if there are references to the object and want them deleted. Click on **OK**:

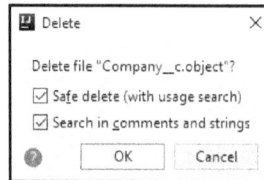

17. The next question asks if the object can be removed from your org, as well. This will actually make a destructive change by means of deployment. So, click **Yes**, because that's what we are trying to do here:

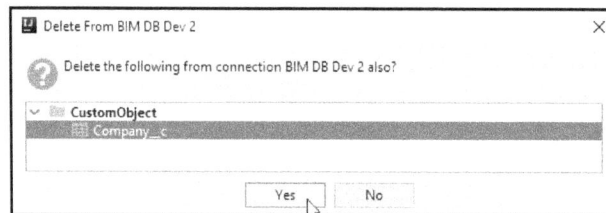

18. The last question will ask you if you want to update the metadata subscription. Say yes to this, as well. A metadata subscription means that your IDE is subscribed to receive any changes that happen in the org on that object. This is so that when you, as a developer, open up your IDE next time, if somebody made changes to code or metadata in the org itself, you'll be prompted to import those changes into your IDE so that you are in sync:

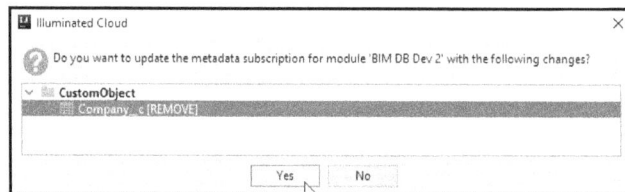

You should receive a message saying that the deletion was successful, as follows:

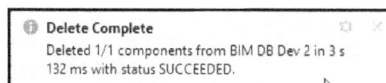

19. Let's check the **View Setup Audit Trail** in our developer org. Yes; we succeeded in deleting a whole object through a destructive deployment from an IDE:

Remember the following about deployments

While we have covered the different deployment methods, the next points will summarize some things to remember for the exam:

- Change sets can contain a maximum of 5,000 components and have a maximum size of 400 MB.
- You cannot delete or rename components through change sets!
- When deploying to a production environment using a change set, all the tests of Apex code will run and will have to pass, and you'll need enough code coverage on your target org. If you don't have enough code coverage (less than 75%), you will not be able to deploy! There is an exception to this, however; when you deploy a change set containing code and you select **Run Specified Tests** on deployment, it will deploy if the specified tests provide enough code coverage to the deployed components and pass. This ensures being able to make corrections to low code coverage when it's really urgent.
- Use the **Audit Trail** from **Setup** to see who deployed or modified any configurations, and when.
- Packages can be used to distribute your metadata configuration to any unrelated org.

Summary

Congratulations! You have made it to the end of the final chapter of this book. What a journey it has been. You should be ready to pass the Salesforce Platform Developer I certification exam. At least, I hope you are.

You have learned about the fundamentals of the Salesforce Lightning Platform and how to extend the out-of-the-box capabilities this powerful platform provides you with to support your business needs. In this book, you learned all about the different process automation tools at your disposal, like workflow rules, Process Builder, and flow. From creating your own custom objects, fields, and business logic, to working with data on the platform and importing, exporting, updating, and deleting data, one by one or in bulk.

You've seen how to extend the capabilities of the platform programmatically, through Apex, Visualforce, and Lightning components, and how to query data programmatically through the use of SOQL and SOSL. You learned about Apex classes and triggers, and how they can be leveraged.

We checked the limits you need to adhere to on the platform, testing your code following the best practices and test frameworks. You've seen how to use web service callouts to connect Salesforce with other data sources. You also saw how to extend, modify, and overwrite the user interface, and how to debug your code and deploy configuration and development from one environment to another.

Since we're done with the book now, I wish you lots of success in passing the exam and in your future career with the Salesforce Platform, but before you go, I've got one last assignment for you.

Quiz

You've learned a lot about debugging and deployment. Let's go through the summary quiz to see what you have remembered:

1. Which statement do you use to log something to the console?
    a. `System.log();`
    b. `Log();`
    c. `System.debug();`
    d. `Debug();`

2. To be able to use change sets, which of the following do you need to do? (Choose three)
   a. Establish a deployment connection between the source org and the target org.
   b. Install and use an IDE.
   c. Create an outbound change set.
   d. Validate and deploy an inbound change set.

3. Which of the following tools is able to delete components from a production environment? (Choose two.)
   a. An IDE
   b. A (un)managed package
   c. A change set
   d. Workbench

4. Which of the following actions can be done manually and directly on a production environment? (Choose two.)
   a. Creating a workflow rule
   b. Editing a Visualforce page
   c. Creating a trigger
   d. Deleting an Apex class

5. Packages (unmanaged and managed) can be created on which of the following?
   a. Sandboxes
   b. Production orgs
   c. Developer orgs
   d. Full Copy sandboxes only

6. Before Apex code can be deployed on production, what percentage of test coverage must be achieved?
   a. 25%
   b. 50%
   c. 75%
   d. 100%

7. Suppose that an issue was reported regarding an approval process. We have to analyze this issue by doing a review of the debug messages that are generated for a specific user. Select the feature of the platform that can be used for supporting this requirement.
   a. System logs
   b. Debug logs
   c. Audit trail
   d. Event monitoring

8. Suppose that while debugging an issue, you came to the conclusion that somebody changed the field type of a specific field. You need to find out who made this change and when the change was made. Where could you start this analysis?
   a. System logs
   b. Debug logs
   c. Audit trail
   d. Event monitoring

9. What is the capability of Sandbox templates? (Choose two)
   a. Choose how many records per object need to be copied over.
   b. Select from which objects data needs to be copied over.
   c. Select the data ranges to filter the data that needs to be copied over.
   d. Save the template for future use.

10. What happens if a deployment fails due to one specific component?
   a. All changes, except for the one failed component, get deployed.
   b. The entire deployment fails.
   c. The entire change set gets deployed.
   d. The deployment time will increase drastically.

Mock Tests

Mock exam

This is a mock exam. It is used to test your knowledge and give you a feeling of what the real exam is like. The exam contains 60 scored multiple choice questions, and you will need a score of at least 65% to pass the actual exam. This mock exam does not contain the real exam questions, but they will be very similar. If you feel you are ready, take this exam without looking at the solutions. If you get a score of 80% or above on this one, you can be sure you are ready to take the actual exam, and you will have a really good chance of passing.

So what are you waiting for? Go for it:

1. A developer would like to relate an external data object to the contact object in Salesforce to track every post on social media; the contact was made in an external system. How can a developer achieve this?

    a. Create a lookup relationship and update the record ID through integration.

    b. Create a master-detail relationship and update the record ID through integration.

    c. Create an external lookup relationship using a custom field with an external ID and unique attributes.

    d. Create an indirect lookup relationship using a custom field with an external ID and unique attributes.

2. A developer is creating an online learning application to track courses and the enrollment of candidates. Each candidate can enroll in multiple training courses at a time. How can a developer achieve this?

    a. Create a master-detail relationship between `Candidate` and `Training Course`.

    b. Create a junction object to relate many candidates to many training courses through master-detail relationships.

    c. Create a lookup relationship between `Candidate` and `Training Course`.

    d. Create a junction object to relate candidates to training courses and use lookup relationships to relate the junction object to candidates and training courses.

3. Which of the following are part of the Model in the MVC model? (Choose three.)

    a. Tabs

    b. Fields

    c. Relationships

    d. Objects

4. Which of the following best describes the Lightning Component framework? (Choose two.)

    a. It is device-aware and supports cross-browser compatibility.

    b. It has an event-driven architecture.

    c. It automatically upgrades all preexisting Visualforce pages and components.

    d. It uses ODS as its data format.

5. Which of the following statements about the `IF-ELSE` statement are true? (Choose two.)

    a. The `IF-ELSE` statement provides a secondary path of execution when an `IF` clause evaluates to true.

    b. An `IF` statement can be followed by a discretionary `ELSE` statement that executes when the Boolean expression is false.

    c. An `IF-ELSE` statement can have a number of possible execution paths.

    d. The `IF-ELSE` statement permits a choice to be made between two possible execution paths.

6. Developers have proposed a recruiting application that covers job vacancies and respective applications. The business wants to display the number of applications for every job vacancy, without inheriting the security of the parent record (the job vacancy itself). The developer should (choose two):
   a. Create a lookup relationship between the two objects.
   b. Create a master-detail relationship between the job vacancy and the job application.
   c. Create an Apex trigger that will count all job applications on each job vacancy and update a field on the parent object.
   d. Create a roll-up summary on the `Job Vacancy` object.

7. Which of the following is a best practice when writing test classes?
   a. Use the `System.assert()` methods to verify test results.
   b. Use `SeeAllData=true`.
   c. Use the `System.debug()` method to verify test results.
   d. Use the `@Future` annotation.

8. Given the following options, what are the valid ways to declare a collection variable? (Choose three.)
   a. `New Account(<name='Business Account'>)`
   b. `New Contact[]{<elements>}`
   c. `New Integer()`
   d. `New List<Account>()`
   e. `New map<Id, Account>()`

9. A new developer frequently experiences governor limit errors when running Apex triggers. As a more experienced developer, which of the following are best practices that you could advise? (Choose two.)
   a. Use a combination of collections (such as maps and lists) and streamline queries.
   b. Use SOQL queries only within `for` loops.
   c. Use an Apex handler class for multiple triggers.
   d. Use lists to perform DML operations on multiple records.

10. Which output component can be used to display a table of data in a Visualforce page?
    a. List components
    b. Iteration components
    c. Table components
    d. Set components

11. Which of the following are capabilities of an IDE specifically made for Salesforce development? (Choose three).

    a. Running Apex tests

    b. Executing SOQL queries

    c. Creating change sets

    d. Deploying metadata components from one org to another unrelated org

12. Which of the following statements are true about controller extensions? (Choose three.)

    a. A controller extension is an Apex class that extends the functionality of a standard or custom controller.

    b. Only one controller extension can be defined for a single page.

    c. The extension is associated with the page using the `extensions` attribute of the `<apex:page>` component.

    d. If an extension works in conjunction with a standard controller, the standard controller methods will also be available.

13. A developer is considering using a standard controller on a Visualforce page. Which of the following are valid considerations about standard controllers? (Choose three.)

    a. Every standard controller includes a getter method that returns the record specified by the `id` query string parameter in the page URL.

    b. The standard controller provides a set of standard actions, such as create, edit, save, and delete, that you can add to your pages using standard user interface elements such as buttons and links.

    c. To associate a standard controller with a Visualforce page, use the `standardController` attribute on the `<apex:page>` tag and assign it the name of any Salesforce object that can be queried using the Force.com API.

    d. A standard controller can retrieve a list of items to be displayed, make a callout to an external web service, and validate and insert data.

14. A developer has written a code block that does not include the `with/without sharing` keyword. Which of the following will use the sharing settings, field permissions, and OWD for the running user?

    a. Apex triggers

    b. Web service callouts

    c. Anonymous blocks

    d. Apex classes

15. Which of the following statements are true about creating unit tests in Apex? (Choose two.)

    a. Lines of code in test methods and test classes are not counted when calculating Apex code coverage.

    b. Since data created in tests does not commit, you will not need to delete any data.

    c. If the code uses conditional logic (including ternary operators), one scenario will automatically cover all conditions.

    d. Use the `System.assert()` method to test your application in different user contexts.

16. How can a developer get all picklist values of a specific field via Apex?

    a. Use the `describePicklist` method.

    b. Use the `globalPicklist` method.

    c. Use the `getPicklistValues` method.

    d. Use the `fieldPicklist` method.

17. The **Stage** field of all related `Opportunity` records should be updated to **Closed Lost** when the associated `Account` record becomes **Inactive**. What could be used for this?

    a. A workflow rule

    b. Flow

    c. The approval process

    d. Process Builder

18. Which of the following is required when defining an Apex class method?

    a. The return data type

    b. Access modifiers

    c. Input parameters

    d. Definition modifiers

19. What are some of the limitations of changing the data type of a custom field? (Choose three.)

    a. The file field type in Salesforce knowledge can be changed as long as it is not referenced in an Apex class.

    b. The option to change the data type of a custom field is not available for all data types.

    c. Developers cannot change the data type of a custom field that is referenced by a Visualforce page.

    d. Developers cannot change the data type of a custom field if it is referenced in Apex.

20. Which of the following statements is true about defining getter methods?
    a. Every value that is calculated by a controller and displayed in a page must have a corresponding getter method.
    b. It is suggested that getter methods include logic that increments a variable, writes log messages, or adds a new record to the database.
    c. Use the name of the getter method in an expression to display the results of a getter method in a page.
    d. The [get] method is used to pass data from the Visualforce page to the Apex controller.

21. What will be the result of running the following code snippet?

```
for(Integer x=0; x < 200; x++){
    Account newAccount = new Account(Name='MyAccount-' + x);
    try{
        Insert newAccount;
        System.debug(Limits.getDMLStatements());
    }
    catch(exception ex){
        System.Debug('Caught Exception');
        System.Debug(ex);
    }
}
insert new Account(Name='MyAccount-last');
```

    a. A limit exception will be caught and one account will be inserted.
    b. 201 accounts will be inserted.
    c. 150 accounts will be inserted.
    d. No accounts will be inserted.

22. A developer is required to override the standard new page when creating an account. How can this be done?
    a. This is not possible.
    b. Clone the standard page to be able to modify the look and feel of the page.
    c. Override the standard page by creating a Visualforce page.
    d. Create a new custom object with a custom page, because standard pages cannot be modified.

23. A developer notices that the following code returns only 20 account records, though he expected 60. Which of the following is true regarding SOSL query limits?

```
FIND{test} RETURNING Account(id), Contact, Opportunity LIMIT 60
```

    a. Limits cannot be set in SOSL queries.

    b. Results were evenly distributed among the objects returned.

    c. Limits have to be individually assigned per object.

    d. The SOSL syntax is incorrect.

24. A component bundle contains a component or an app and all its related resources. Which of the following resources are part of the standard component bundle? (Choose four)

    a. Helpers

    b. CSS styles

    c. Images and animations

    d. A renderer

    e. Documentation

25. A developer needs to access a list of data on a Visualforce page and represent the data as a table. However, the developer would also like to customize the look and feel, and not use the standard Salesforce styling. Which Visualforce components can the developer use? (Choose three.)

    a. `<apex:dataTable>`

    b. `<apex:table>`

    c. `<apex:dataList>`

    d. `<apex:repeat>`

    e. `<apex:listTable>`

26. Which of the following are true about cross-object formulas? (Choose four.)
    a. Cross-object formula fields can pull field values from objects that are up to 10 relationships away.
    b. Cross-object formula fields can pull field values from master-detail or lookup parent records.
    c. Cross-object formula fields can pull data from a record, even if the user does not have access to it.
    d. Cross-object formula fields can pull field values from their child records.
    e. For every object, cross-object formula fields can be used in three roll-up summaries.

27. What options are available to run unit tests in an org? (Choose three.)
    a. Run all methods in a specified class.
    b. Run all unit tests in an org.
    c. Run all methods in a specified class that does not contain test methods.
    d. Run a test suite.

28. Astro computing would like to be able to manage sales and support tasks differently, and display different fields for each department. How can this be achieved? (Choose two.)
    a. Record types
    b. Workflow rules
    c. Formula fields
    d. Page layouts

29. A managed package can be created in which of the following environments?
    a. The developer sandbox
    b. The partner developer edition
    c. The developer edition
    d. The full sandbox

30. How can SOQL injection be prevented?
    a. Use the `escapeSingleQuotes` method.
    b. Use the `preventInjection` method.
    c. Use the `preventDatabaseCommands` method.
    d. Use the `preventQuotes` method.

31. A developer needs to initialize a numerical value of `17`. What data type should the developer use?

    a. `String`

    b. `Blob`

    c. `Numeric`

    d. `Integer`

32. Which of the following ways can be used to throw a custom exception? (Choose three.)

    a. `throw new customExceptionName();`

    b. `throw new customExceptionName().addError('Error Message Here')`

    c. `throw new customExceptionName('Error Message Here');`

    d. `throw new customExceptionName(e);`

33. A custom object has a workflow rule that updates a field when a certain set of criteria is met. A before update Apex trigger has also been defined on the object. What will happen when a user updates a record so that it meets the criteria of the workflow rule?

    a. The Apex trigger will be fired first, voiding the workflow rule due to the order of execution.

    b. An exception will be thrown due to a conflict between the two.

    c. The Apex trigger will be fired twice.

    d. Both will be fired only once.

34. When test data cannot be created programmatically, how can pre-existing data be accessed?

    a. Annotate the test class or method with `[seeAllData=false]`.

    b. Annotate the test class or method with `[seeAllData=true]`.

    c. Annotate the test method with `[withSharing=true]`.

    d. Annotate the test method with `[withSharing=false]`.

35. A developer has written an Apex Trigger. He tested it, and the trigger is not functioning as expected. He now wants to debug the code. How can he accomplish this in the Developer Console?

    a. Go to the **Logs** tab in the **Developer Console**.

    b. Go to the **Anonymous Window** in the **Developer Console**.

    c. Go to the **Run Tests** window in the **Developer Console**.

    d. Go to the **Progress** tab in the **Developer Console**.

36. Which static methods are used when testing governor limits, executing test scenarios with a larger data set, or when creating an additional set of governor limits during the execution of a single test class?

    a. `Test.isTest()` and `Test.isnotTest()`

    b. `Test.runAs()` and `Test.getLimits()`

    c. `Test.startTest()` and `Test.stopTest()`

    d. `Test.setFixedSearchResults()`

37. A developer is required to create a trigger every time the **Type** field on the `Request` object is updated; the **Owner** field should be changed as well, either to a **User** or a **Queue**. Which trigger event should the developer use?

    a. Before update

    b. Before delete

    c. After update

    d. After merge

38. What are considerations for deciding between using Data Loader and the Data Import Wizard for loading data into a development environment? (Choose three.)

    a. The number of records to be loaded

    b. Whether or not triggers should run on import of the data

    c. Whether or not the data will need to be loaded multiple times

    d. Whether or not the object is supported by the Data Import Wizard

39. A developer needs to create a new contact record in his Apex trigger. Which DML statement should be used in the code?

    a. Merge

    b. Upsert

    c. Insert

    d. Create

40. Which of the following field types can a roll-up summary calculate?

    a. **Number**

    b. **Text**

    c. **Checkbox**

    d. **Picklist**

41. On which event (trigger context) should the following trigger be fired?

```
Trigger createCallingCard on Contact(EVENT){
    List<CallingCard__c> cardList = new List<CallingCard__c>();
    for(Contact con : Trigger.New){
        CallingCard__c newCard = new CallingCard__c();
        newCard.Name = con.Name;
        newCard.Phone = con.Phone;
        newCard.Address = con.Address;
        newCard.relatedContact__c = con.Id;
        cardList.add(newCard);
    }
    Insert cardList;
}
```

    a. After insert

    b. After update

    c. Before delete

    d. Before insert

42. Managers would like to be able to record the total amount of hours each team member works on projects. A team member can be related to multiple projects and each project can have multiple team members. How can the developer achieve this?

    a. Create a master-detail relationship on the `Project` object to the `Team Member` object.

    b. Create a lookup relationship on both objects to a junction object called `Project Team Member`.

    c. Create a master-detail relationship on the `Project` and `Team Member` objects to a `Project Team Member` junction object.

    d. Create master-detail relationships from a `Project Team Member` junction object: one to the `Project` object, and one to the `Team Member` object.

43. Which of the following statements about running Apex test classes in the Developer Console are true? (Choose three.)

    a. [Suite Manager] is used to abort the test selected in the **Tests** tab.

    b. An **Overall Code Coverage** readout is available that displays the percentage of code coverage for each class in the org.

    c. The **[Rerun Failed Tests]** option reruns only the failed tests from the test run that are highlighted in the **Tests** tab.

    d. The **Developer Console** runs tests asynchronously in the background, unless the test run includes only one class and **[Always Run Asynchronously]** in the **Tests** menu is not chosen.

44. Which of the following statements about defining an Apex class are true? (Choose three.)

    a. A definition modifier is required in the top-level class.

    b. An access modifier is required in the declaration of a top-level class.

    c. The [class] keyword, followed by the name of the class, is necessary.

    d. A developer may add optional extensions and/or implementations.

45. Astro Computing would like to generate invoices in Salesforce, allow customers to pay their invoices from their email, and process the payment. Which of the following should be used to meet this requirement?

    a. An AppExchange app

    b. Lightning Process Builder

    c. A custom Apex solution

    d. Workflow rule and formula fields

46. The following code snippet fails during bulk data load:

```
for(Contact con : Trigger.New){
    if(con.PostalCode != null){
        List<State__c> stateList = [Select id, Postal__c From
State__c Where Postal__c =:con.PostalCode];
        if(stateList.size() > 0){
            con.State__c = statelist[0].Id;
        }
    }
}
```

What would be the root cause?

    a. A SOQL query is located inside the `for` loop code block.

    b. The `con` variable is not declared.

    c. No update DML over list of contacts.

    d. The condition is invalid and will always be null.

47. Which of the following correctly describes how the platform features map to the MVC pattern?

    a. Model: JavaScript code; view: Visualforce pages; controller: custom Apex Code.

    b. Model: standard and custom objects; view CSS and images; controller: standard and custom controllers.

    c. Model: Apex classes; view: pages and components; controller: Apex triggers.

    d. Model: standard and custom objects; view: pages and components; controller: standard and custom controllers.

48. A developer requires a `numberOfStudents` variable with a constant value of `25` that is accessible only within the Apex class in which it is defined. Which of the following is the best variable declaration?

    a. `global static Integer numberOfStudents = 25;`

    b. `private static final Integer numberOfStudents = 25;`

    c. `public Integer numberOfStudents = 25;`

    d. `protected final Integer numberOfStudents = 25;`

49. A developer is trying to create a trigger that will set the record type of an `Invoice` record, prior to insertion, based on the value of the industry picklist that is selected. What trigger event (trigger context) should the developer use?

    a. After update

    b. Before delete

    c. Before insert

    d. After insert

50. Which of the following are capabilities of the schema builder? (Choose three.)

    a. Export the schema definition.

    b. Delete a custom object.

    c. Create lookup and master-detail relationships.

    d. Create a custom object.

51. Record types have been defined on the `Account` object. What does this mean? (Choose two.)
   a. Different users can be assigned to each record type.
   b. Different page layouts can be assigned for each record type.
   c. Different fields can be defined for each record type.
   d. Different picklist values can be defined for each record type.

52. Which of the following are valid considerations that a new developer should be aware of when developing in a multi-tenant environment? (Choose two.)
   a. Governor limits ensure that the amount of CPU time is monitored and limited per customer over a defined time period, to ensure that performance in one org is not impacted by another.
   b. The number of allowed API calls is unlimited.
   c. Many customers share the same instance, so queries need to ensure the correct organization `id` is referenced to return the correct organizational data.
   d. Restrictions are enforced on code that can be deployed into a production environment.

53. What is true in the following debug log line?

   ```
   20:43:52.588(7632137015) | LIMIT_USAGE | [137] | SOQL | 38 | 100
   ```

   a. `LIMIT_USAGE` is the name of the event that occurred.
   b. It denotes that 137 SOQL queries were executed out of a limit usage of 100.
   c. The preceding debug log line was triggered when the code reached the 38th line.
   d. The numbers `20:43:52.588(7632137015)` correspond to the timestamp of the log line.

54. Which standard objects in the following list are not supported by DML operations? (Choose two.)
   a. Profile
   b. User
   c. Opportunity line item
   d. Record type

55. Which attribute should the developer use to render a Visualforce page as a PDF file?

    a. `contentType="application/vnd.pdf"`

    b. `doctype="pdf-1.0-strict"`

    c. `renderAs="pdf"`

    d. `doctype="pdf-5.0"`

56. Which of the following is the correct syntax for a `try-catch-finally` block?

    a. `finally{*code here*} catch(Exception e){*code here*} try{*code here*}`

    b. `catch{*code here*} finally(Exception e){*code here*} try{*code here*}`

    c. `catch {*code here*} try(Exception e){*code here*} finally{*code here*}`

    d. `try{*code here*} catch(Exception e){*code here*} finally{*code here*}`

57. Which of the following components are not available to deploy using the Metadata API? (Choose two.)

    a. Currency exchange rates

    b. Fiscal year

    c. Global picklist

    d. Queues

58. A developer needs to create a trigger that will throw an error whenever the user tries to delete a contact that is not associated with an account. Which trigger event (trigger context) should the developer use?

    a. Before insert

    b. After delete

    c. Before delete

    d. After insert

59. Astro Computing has been using Service Cloud to manage cases, but is now considering using it to manage field service jobs. They would like to track field service activity and assignments to technicians. Which is the recommended solution to meet these requirements?

    a. Use real-time API integration to connect Salesforce with an external field service application.

    b. Install an AppExchange product that provides field service functionality.

    c. Extend the Service Cloud configuration to handle field service cases.

    d. Utilize the `Work Order` standard objects and `Work Order` line items.

60. Which of the following use cases are valid for declarative customization? (Choose three.)

    a. Calculating the sales tax applicable to a quote is a complex calculation based on various factors such as product, state, and quantity.

    b. Calculating the number of days until an opportunity closes and displaying it on a report.

    c. Determining a lead rating, based on checking the value of the 3 lead fields.

    d. Displaying the number of employees of the account related to an opportunity on the opportunity page layout.

Appendix

Chapter 1

1. a, c
2. a
3. c
4. c
5. b
6. d
7. a
8. d
9. c
10. d

Chapter 2

1. c
2. d
3. b
4. c
5. c
6. b
7. c
8. b
9. c
10. b

Chapter 3

1. a, c
2. a, c, d
3. b
4. a, d
5. c
6. b
7. c
8. a
9. b, d
10. b

Chapter 4

1. a
2. d
3. a, c
4. c
5. b
6. a
7. a
8. a
9. a, b, d
10. a

Chapter 5

1. a, b
2. b
3. d
4. b
5. a, b
6. b

7. b, c
8. b, d
9. d
10. a, b

Chapter 6

1. d
2. a
3. d
4. d
5. c, d
6. d
7. a, b
8. a
9. a, b
10. a, d

Chapter 7

1. a
2. c
3. d
4. a
5. d
6. c
7. d
8. a, d
9. c, d
10. a, c
11. b, c

Chapter 8

1. c
2. a, c, d
3. a, d
4. a, b
5. c
6. c
7. b
8. c
9. b, d
10. b

Chapter 9

1. d
2. b
3. b, c, d
4. a, b
5. b, d
6. a, c
7. a
8. b, d, e
9. a, d
10. b
11. a, b, d
12. a, c, d
13. a, b, c
14. c
15. a, b
16. c
17. d
18. a
19. b, c, d

20. a
21. d
22. c
23. b
24. a, b, d, e
25. a, c, d
26. a, b, c
27. a, b
28. a, d
29. b, c
30. a
31. d
32. c, d
33. c
34. b
35. a
36. c
37. a
38. a, c, d
39. c
40. a
41. a
42. d
43. b, c, d
44. b, c, d
45. a
46. a
47. d
48. b
49. c
50. b, c, d
51. b, d
52. a, d
53. a, d
54. a, d

55. c
56. d
57. a, b
58. c
59. d
60. b, c, d

Code solutions

This section will contain the solutions to the exercises.

Code solution – DML update statement with Database.update statement

The following code snippet is the solution to writing the code for updating records with the `Database.update` statement:

```
// Select the cast records with the Id
List<Cast__c> lstCasts = new List<Cast__c>([SELECT Id FROM Cast__c]);
For (Cast__c theCast : lstCasts){
 theCast.Rating__c = '3'; // while this is a picklist field, we need to
provide a String to this field
}

List<Database.SaveResult> lstSavedCasts = Database.update(lstCasts, false);
For (Database.SaveResult savedCast : lstSavedCasts){
 If (! savedCast.isSuccess()){
 System.debug(savedCast.getErrors()[0].getMessage());
 } else {
 System.debug('Record is successfully updated');
 }
}
```

The **Execution Log** is displayed as follows:

Execution Log		
Timestamp	Event	Details
15:42:20:008	DML_BEGIN	[7]|Op:Update|Type:Cast__c|Rows:22
15:42:20:055	DML_END	[7]|
15:42:20:000	LIMIT_USAGE_...	Number of DML statements: 1 out of 150
15:42:20:000	LIMIT_USAGE_...	Number of DML rows: 22 out of 10000

Further detailing of the **Execution Log** is shown as follows:

Execution Log		
Timestamp	Event	Details
15:42:20:057	USER_DEBUG	[12]|DEBUG|Record is successfully updated
15:42:20:057	USER_DEBUG	[12]|DEBUG|Record is successfully updated
15:42:20:057	USER_DEBUG	[12]|DEBUG|Record is successfully updated
15:42:20:057	USER_DEBUG	[12]|DEBUG|Record is successfully updated
15:42:20:057	USER_DEBUG	[12]|DEBUG|Record is successfully updated
15:42:20:057	USER_DEBUG	[12]|DEBUG|Record is successfully updated
15:42:20:057	USER_DEBUG	[12]|DEBUG|Record is successfully updated
15:42:20:057	USER_DEBUG	[12]|DEBUG|Record is successfully updated
15:42:20:057	USER_DEBUG	[12]|DEBUG|Record is successfully updated
15:42:20:057	USER_DEBUG	[12]|DEBUG|Record is successfully updated
15:42:20:057	USER_DEBUG	[12]|DEBUG|Record is successfully updated
15:42:20:057	USER_DEBUG	[12]|DEBUG|Record is successfully updated
15:42:20:057	USER_DEBUG	[12]|DEBUG|Record is successfully updated
15:42:20:057	USER_DEBUG	[12]|DEBUG|Record is successfully updated
15:42:20:058	USER_DEBUG	[12]|DEBUG|Record is successfully updated
15:42:20:058	USER_DEBUG	[12]|DEBUG|Record is successfully updated
15:42:20:058	USER_DEBUG	[12]|DEBUG|Record is successfully updated
15:42:20:058	USER_DEBUG	[12]|DEBUG|Record is successfully updated
15:42:20:058	USER_DEBUG	[12]|DEBUG|Record is successfully updated
15:42:20:058	USER_DEBUG	[12]|DEBUG|Record is successfully updated
15:42:20:058	USER_DEBUG	[7]|DEBUG|Record is successfully updated
15:42:20:058	USER_DEBUG	[12]|DEBUG|Record is successfully updated

Code solution for upserting records

First, we will write the code to update the existing records with an external ID:

```
// Define a counter to compile the external id
Integer iCounter = 1;

// Select the person records
List<Person__c> lstPersons = new List<Person__c>([SELECT ID FROM
Person__c]);
// loop through the person records and update the External ID with the
string value of the counter
For (Person__c thePerson : lstPersons){
 thePerson.External_Id__c = String.valueOf(iCounter);
 // add the counter with 1 (to give the next record a new External Id)
 iCounter++;
}

Try {
 Update lstPersons;
} catch (DMLException ex){
 // all records should pass. If an error, adapt the data in the
corresponding failed records
 System.debug(ex.getMessage());
}
```

Verify whether the external IDs are in your records as follows:

	PERSON NAME	∨	EXTERNAL ID ↑	∨	CREATED DATE	∨	LAST MODIFIED
1	Al Pacino		1		22/11/2018 10:02		29/12/2018 09:32
2	Christopher Nolan		10		22/11/2018 10:02		29/12/2018 09:32
3	Christian Bale		11		22/11/2018 10:02		29/12/2018 09:32
4	Heath Ledger		12		22/11/2018 10:02		29/12/2018 09:32
5	Maggie Gyllenhaal		13		22/11/2018 10:02		29/12/2018 09:32
6	Michael Caine		14		22/11/2018 10:02		29/12/2018 09:32
7	Katie Holmes		15		22/11/2018 10:02		29/12/2018 09:32
8	Liam Neeson		16		22/11/2018 10:02		29/12/2018 09:32
9	Gary Oldman		17		22/11/2018 10:02		29/12/2018 09:32
10	Francis Ford Coppola		18		22/11/2018 10:02		29/12/2018 09:32
11	Steven Spielberg		19		22/11/2018 10:02		29/12/2018 09:32

The code to upsert the first six records in the list with the short notation is as follows:

```
// prepare the records
Person__c actor1 = new Person__c(Name = 'Morgan Freeman', Birthdate__c =
Date.newInstance(1936,6,1), External_Id__c = '8');
Person__c actor2 = new Person__c(Name = 'James Caan', Birthdate__c =
Date.newInstance(1940,3,26), External_Id__c = '3');
Person__c actor3 = new Person__c(Name = 'Shannen Doherty', Birthdate__c =
Date.newInstance(1971,4,12), External_Id__c = '25');
Person__c actor4 = new Person__c(Name = 'Jennie Garth', Birthdate__c =
Date.newInstance(1972,4,3),External_Id__c = '26');
Person__c actor5 = new Person__c(Name = 'Jason Priestly', Birthdate__c =
Date.newInstance(1969,8,28), External_Id__c = '27');
Person__c actor6 = new Person__c(Name = 'Luke Perry', Birthdate__c =
Date.newInstance(1966,10,11), External_Id__c = '28');

List<Person__c> lstPersons = new
List<Person__c>{actor1,actor2,actor3,actor4,actor5,actor6};
// upsert the list with persons. Use the external reference to find out if
the record already exist or not
try {
 upsert lstPersons External_Id__c;
 System.debug('all actors uploaded');
} catch (DMLException ex){
 System.debug(ex.getMessage());
}
```

Verify the `debug` statement at the end of the `try` block. If you see this statement, every person is upserted. The first two records are updated; the other four records should be inserted.

Verify your records in the `Person` table. You should see that the records with external IDs **3** and **8** are updated. The records with external IDs from **25** to **28** are inserted:

The code to upsert the other four records with the database statement is as follows:

```
// Prepare the records
Person__c actor1 = new Person__c(Name = 'Kaley Cuoco', Birthdate__c =
Date.newInstance(1985,11,30), External_Id__c = '117');
Person__c actor2 = new Person__c(Name = 'Jim Parsons', Birthdate__c =
Date.newInstance(1973,3,24), External_Id__c = '118');
Person__c actor3 = new Person__c(Name = 'Melissa Rauch', Birthdate__c =
Date.newInstance(1980,6,23), External_Id__c = '119');
Person__c actor4 = new Person__c(Name = 'Aarti Mann', Birthdate__c =
Date.newInstance(1978,3,3), External_Id__c = '120');

List<Person__c> lstPersons = new
List<Person__c>{actor1,actor2,actor3,actor4};

// Get the field to compare the person records
Schema.SObjectField fieldToCompare = Person__c.fields.External_Id__c;

// execute the DML statement
List<Database.UpsertResult> lstUpsertedPersons =
Database.upsert(lstPersons, fieldToCompare, false);

// loop through the results and check if the records is upserted
For (Database.UpsertResult savedPerson : lstUpsertedPersons){
 If (savedPerson.isSuccess()){
 System.debug('Person upserted');
 } else {
 System.debug('Record not upserted: ' +
savedPerson.getErrors()[0].getMessage());
 }
}
```

Check the debug logs to see whether every record is upserted:

Execution Log		
Timestamp	Event	Details
10:11:23:040	USER_DEBUG	[18]|DEBUG|Person upserted
10:11:23:040	USER_DEBUG	[18]|DEBUG|Person upserted
10:11:23:040	USER_DEBUG	[18]|DEBUG|Person upserted
10:11:23:040	USER_DEBUG	[18]|DEBUG|Person upserted

Also, check the upserted records in your database:

Code solution – API connection to the Person object

In this section, you will find the code solution for the `Person` object. We will reuse the `MovieResponse` object because the service provides a list of different movies in which the person has acted.

This is the full class for the `Person` object:

```
public class Person {
 public Decimal popularity {get; set;}
 public Integer id {get; set;}
 public String profile_path {get; set;}
 public String name {get; set;}
 public List<MovieResponse> known_for {get; set;}
}
```

This is the method that converts the JSON response into the `Person` object:

```
private static List<Person> constructPersons(String sResponse){
 List<Person> lstPersons = new List<Person>();
 if (sResponse != null){
 JSONParser theParser = JSON.createParser(sResponse);
 while (theParser.nextToken() != null){
 if (theParser.getCurrentToken() == JSONToken.FIELD_NAME &&
theParser.getText() == 'results'){
 theParser.nextToken();
 theParser.nextToken();
 lstPersons.add((Person) theParser.readValueAs(Person.class));
 }
 }
 }
 return lstPersons;
}
```

This is the `public` method for using the search functionality in a Visualforce page:

```
public static List<Person> searchActors(String sParameter){
 List<Person> lstPersons = new List<Person>();
 try {
 String sMoviesFromCallout = searchCallout(sParameter, 'person');
 lstPersons = constructPersons(sMoviesFromCallout);
 } catch (Exception ex){ System.debug(ex.getMessage()); }
 return lstPersons;
}
```

Visualforce page – AddNewMovie

The following code snippet helps in building `AddNewMovie` Visualforce page:

```
<apex:page standardController="Movie__c" lightningStylesheets="true"
extensions="MovieExtension">
    <!-- some extra css to make it nice and neat -->
    <style type="text/css">
        .txaDescription {
            width: 100%;
            resize: none;
        }
        .pnlCenter{
            text-align: center;
        }
    </style>
    <apex:outputPanel>
        <apex:form>
            <apex:pageMessages />
            <apex:pageBlock title="{!Movie__c.Name}">
                <!-- you can separate your fields in 2 columns with the
attribute columns -->
                <apex:pageBlockSection title="Movie Information"
columns="2">
                    <apex:pageBlockSectionItem>
                        <apex:outputLabel
value="{!$ObjectType.Movie__c.fields.Name.Label}" />
                        <apex:inputField value="{!Movie__c.Name}" />
                    </apex:pageBlockSectionItem>
                    <apex:pageBlockSectionItem>
                        <apex:outputLabel
value="{!$ObjectType.Movie__c.fields.Release_Date__c.Label}" />
                        <apex:inputField value="{!Movie__c.Release_Date__c}"
/>
                    </apex:pageBlockSectionItem>
                    <apex:pageBlockSectionItem>
```

```
                            <apex:outputLabel
value="{!$ObjectType.Movie__c.fields.Genre__c.Label}" />
                                <apex:inputField value="{!Movie__c.Genre__c}" />
                        </apex:pageBlockSectionItem>
                        <apex:pageBlockSectionItem>
                            <apex:outputLabel
value="{!$ObjectType.Movie__c.fields.Runtime__c.Label}" />
                                <apex:inputField value="{!Movie__c.Runtime__c}" />
                        </apex:pageBlockSectionItem>
                </apex:pageBlockSection>
                <!-- this demonstrates you how you can add another pageblock
section with 1 column -->
                <apex:pageBlockSection columns="1"
title="{!$ObjectType.Movie__c.fields.Description__c.Label}"
collapsible="false">
                        <apex:pageBlockSectionItem>
                            <apex:inputField value="{!Movie__c.Description__c}"
styleClass="txaDescription" />
                        </apex:pageBlockSectionItem>
                </apex:pageBlockSection>
            </apex:pageBlock>
                <!-- an output panel that acts like a div-tag in your HTML. An
outputpanel without the layout attribute acts like the html span-tag -->
                <apex:outputPanel layout="block" styleClass="pnlCenter">
                    <!-- the save action is coming from the standard controller
-->
                    <apex:commandButton value="Save" action="{!submitMovie}" />
                </apex:outputPanel>
        </apex:form>
    </apex:outputPanel>
</apex:page>
```

The MovieExtension test class – setting up test data

Let's have a look at the following `MovieExtensionTest` class:

```
@IsTest
private with sharing class MovieExtensionTest {

 @TestSetup
 private static void createTestData(){
 Movie__c aTestMovie = new Movie__c(
 Name = 'Independence day',
 Description__c = 'Independence Day is an American science fiction action
film directed and co-written by Roland Emmerich',
```

```
Cover_Url__c =
'https://image.tmdb.org/t/p/original/bqLlWZJdhrS0knfEJRkquW7L8z2.jpg',
Genre__c = 'Action;Adventure;Science Fiction'
);

insert aTestMovie;
}
}
```

Executing unit tests – example of a bad scenario

This is the code for the unit test:

```
@IsTest
private static void selectIncorrectMovie(){

 // start up your test scenario
 Test.startTest();
 MovieExtension ext = new MovieExtension(null);
 Test.stopTest();

 // verify if the Id of the movie is the same movieId in your controller
 System.assertEquals(null, ext.movieId);
}
```

The updated code (which was changed, as per the logic) is as follows:

```
public MovieExtension(Apexpages.StandardController stdMovie){
 if (stdMovie != null) {
 this.movieId = stdMovie.getId();
 }
}
```

Other Books You May Enjoy

If you enjoyed this book, you may be interested in these other books by Packt:

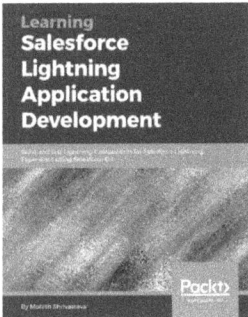

Learning Salesforce Lightning Application Development
Mohith Shrivastava

ISBN: 9781787124677

- Understand Lightning Components architecture
- Learn Locker security best practices
- Debug and Improve performance of your Lightning Components
- Use third-party libraries along with Lightning Component Framework
- Learn how to publish Lightning Components on AppExchange
- Use Lightning Out to take your Lightning Components outside the Salesforce platform

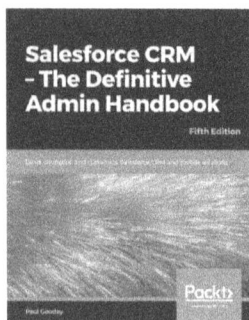

Salesforce CRM - The Definitive Admin Handbook - Fifth Edition
Paul Goodey

ISBN: 9781789619782

- Configure a variety of user interface features in Salesforce CRM
- Understand the capabilities of the Salesforce CRM sharing model
- Explore Einstein Analytics - Salesforce's new wave of advanced reporting
- Get to grips with the Lightning Process Builder workflow
- Set up user profiles, security, and login access mechanisms
- Find out how Apex and Visualforce coding can be used in Salesforce CRM
- Manage the transition from Salesforce Classic to Lightning Experience
- Implement data manipulation features to apply best practices in data management

Leave a review - let other readers know what you think

Please share your thoughts on this book with others by leaving a review on the site that you bought it from. If you purchased the book from Amazon, please leave us an honest review on this book's Amazon page. This is vital so that other potential readers can see and use your unbiased opinion to make purchasing decisions, we can understand what our customers think about our products, and our authors can see your feedback on the title that they have worked with Packt to create. It will only take a few minutes of your time, but is valuable to other potential customers, our authors, and Packt. Thank you!

Index